Picture

Librarianship

Picture
Librarianship

Edited by Helen P Harrison

ORYX PRESS
1981

The rare Arabian Oryx is believed to have inspired the myth of the unicorn. This desert antelope became virtually extinct in the early 1960s. At that time several groups of international conservationists arranged to have 9 animals sent to the Phoenix Zoo to be the nucleus of a captive breeding herd. Today the Oryx population is nearing 300 and herds have been returned to reserves in Israel, Jordan, and Oman.

Copyright © 1981 by Library Association Publishing Limited

Published by The Oryx Press
2214 North Central at Encanto
Phoenix, AZ 85004

Published simultaneously in Canada

Library of Congress Cataloging in Publication Data
Main entry under title:

Picture librarianship.

Bibliography: p.
1. Libraries and pictures.   2. Microforms.
I. Harrison, Helen P.
Z717.P52   025.17'7   81-11291
ISBN 0-89774-013-0   AACR2

My personal thanks go to immediate family and colleagues who have put up with the vagaries of the editorial process, but the handbook should be dedicated to all those who were prepared to further the craft of picture librarianship by contributing their experience and expertise for the benefit of all picture librarians; to those who were asked and contributed go grateful thanks; to those who were not asked, apologies must go. Further literature is needed and I hope that this book will stimulate others to contribute.

Helen P Harrison

Contents

PART 1   TECHNIQUES AND ORGANIZATION

v

vi

PART 2 CASE STUDIES AND SURVEYS OF PICTURE LIBRARIES

x

Part 1

TECHNIQUES AND ORGANIZATION

1

Introduction

Helen P Harrison

PICTURES AS INFORMATION

A picture is a source of visual information. It may be a photograph of a work of art or it may be a work of art in itself, but in library terms it is a piece of information to be used and evaluated as any other information available in the library. The information contained in a picture may be taken from life, of geographical features, scenery, street scenes, natural phenomena, animals, people, or activities, or a direct presentation of a work of art. Whatever the object of the photograph, it is a piece of information about that object whether it be a fireworks display, a film or drama set, an architectural feature, or a piece of scientific apparatus and it is this information which concerns the picture librarian.

PICTURE LIBRARIANSHIP

Libraries have traditionally been associated with books but into these libraries have come other materials and it is worth remembering that books have been illustrated or illuminated by pictures since they were first produced. Pictures are therefore no strangers in a library even if they have been concealed within the traditional covers of a book. Further to this, picture librarianship should not be considered as a branch of activity with all its own rules and practices; the very fact that the word 'librarianship' has been used suggests that this is not a passive collection of material and it exists to be used by a public, whether that public is a large general group or a small section of specialists. It is the information contained in the library which is of importance regardless of the medium on which the information is transmitted.

Information is the business of the librarian and if pictures or any other materials carry information the library will inevitably become involved with these other materials. Picture librarianship is only a convenient way of designating the application of the principles of librarianship to a particular group of materials and, as such, is an extension of librarianship rather than a separate branch. In recent years many other information carriers have been introduced into libraries in the form of maps, films, videotapes, sound recordings, and so on. The introduction of these materials has had a salutary effect on the profession and general principles of librarianship have been developed to encompass the materials rather than trying to thrust them out as a separate branch of librarianship.

Picture librarianship can be viewed in the light of 'traditional' librarianship and, in considering the particular materials involved, existing practices can be rethought. Common elements between books and pictures or other materials will emerge and many an existing procedure can be adapted to solve apparent problems. Many of the conventional skills of bibliographic control can easily be applied to pictures, but the different format, technical processes of production, storage, handling, and use need separate consideration. The librarian should not assume that the nature of the material precludes the successful use of traditional techniques. Throughout the handbook a flexible approach to picture librarianship will be demonstrated to try and indicate where existing practice can be modified or carried over into the handling of picture material.

Picture librarianship is often not practised in isolation. Organizing and exploiting a picture library can be done as part of the general work of a library, either by a subject specialist who is given charge of the art section containing the picture library, or by a form specialist who works with a picture collection in a general resources or audio-visual context. Those libraries which are devoted to pictures alone have often developed from different roots to the traditional library system and have been administered by people other than librarians. Indeed, in the UK there are very few commercial picture libraries administered by qualified librarians. With the introduction of pictures into traditional libraries or institutions supporting library services, the value of library principles has been demonstrated and there is the beginning of a movement of librarians into areas which have not been attempted before.

PICTURES

Pictorial representations of objects and ideas take many forms. A 'picture' may mean anything from a cave painting, fresco, or frieze through an original work of art on canvas or other base, to an engraving and further to a slide or other film frame of that work. Listing the forms which pictures can take presents problems as new formats appear or a picture is produced in a form which does not fit into any existing category. Paper formats vary from cigarette cards to bill posters, paintings from frescoes and cave paintings to watercolours and oils on a non-paper base. Film ranges from photographic negative to slide, film frame, or microform. Also many pictures can, and are, represented in more than one medium, whatever the original.

In the present context 'pictures' include all forms of pictorial illustration: monochrome and colour photographs, prints, slides, film strips, negatives, large colour transparencies, microfilm, and microfiche; illustrations in books and journals, book jackets, postcards, calendars, wallcharts, posters, as well as art originals, prints, and engravings. This in itself is a formidable list, but by the time the material finds its way into a picture library some of the more awkward aspects of 'pictures' may have been reduced to a paper format whether as a photograph or an illustration, or to a film format as a slide. Cave paintings have been 'transferred' from the walls of subterranean passages in Africa and Australia to manageable photographic images and the Parthenon remains in its natural setting while photographs represent it to the world.

This reduction of art objects or natural phenomena to a paper format provides the picture library with its raw material. A user needing to study or reproduce a fresco for some purpose can do so without necessarily visiting the site. Although it may be better to do so, it may also be more convenient to have a photograph of the original, and of others like it to study at leisure or to reproduce in a publication. Picture libraries exist to provide these opportunities for research and use.

Pictures are widely available and this is a considerable asset in this day of incompatible formats and in view of the difficulties of transporting many other audio-visual materials. It is far easier to send still pictures than to ship moving film or videotape; there are no compatibility problems and the user can more easily acquire hard usable copy. It is a simple matter to send illustrations of the life, culture, achievements, and interests of one society across national boundaries.

Over and above any analysis of the picture format there is one other factor that anyone concerned with pictures must bear in mind and cultivate. This is the value of the picture in conveying the information it contains: its immediacy and visual impact. Pictures convey some information, or expression, better than any other medium and a recognition of this fact and the occasions on which it is best achieved is an invaluable asset to the picture librarian. Books impart information through words, films through movement and speech, pictures through visual impact. A picture's ability to communicate information which cannot be expressed in words is of unique value.

PICTURE LIBRARIES

A picture library is a collection of pictures acquired or accumulated with a particular purpose in mind. This purpose may be guided only by the whim of the collector, and this is especially true of earlier private collections, but it is more likely to answer a particular need or fulfil a stated function. The purposes of collecting material are as varied as the collections themselves; the pictures may be needed for research into particular subjects, for reuse in publications, as teaching materials, for reference and redrawing, or the aim may be to ensure the preservation of the picture material itself. The scope of the material in the collection will be governed by the purpose of the collection and also the uses to which the material will be put.

The function of a picture library is to provide a source of visual information and make it available to the public, or a section of that public, for the purposes of study, research, or reuse. The wide variety of picture libraries is evident to any picture researcher and a glance at either *Picture sources 3,*[1] or *Picture researcher's handbook*[2] with its 800 or more separate entries will give some indication of the range.

Pictures may be gathered together in a collection or library for several reasons including collection, conservation, and the provision of facilities for research and use, and these reasons need not be mutually exclusive.

Collection A collection may be put together for its own sake and remain in the hands of a private individual for his own satisfaction. Often, however, this collection will be handed over by sale or donation to form the nucleus of another collection and thus become available to a wider public. At this stage it will probably be organized into a library. The material contained in these collections may be based on a particular format, such as cigarette cards, theatre programmes, posters, or confined to the work of one or two pioneers of photography or well-known photographers, or it may be material on a special subject theme.

Conservation will be the eventual aim of most libraries with a greater or lesser degree of emphasis according to the other functions of the library. It may be decided that the best way to ensure the continued existence of some pictures is to gather them into one collection with special facilities for conservation. However, pictures are nothing if not seen and the library will have to strike a balance between conservation and accessibility for research or reuse.

Exploitation Libraries act as stores of information but having acquired a collection of pictures they must make the information contained in them available to others. The library's purpose is to organize the collection so as to make it easy for people to find and use the material for as wide a range of activities as possible. By centralizing material in one collection around a particular subject, theme, or even type, the potential user is helped to locate material without having to go to several sources to find examples.

HISTORY OF PICTURE LIBRARIES

Despite the proliferation of picture libraries, their history is brief and somewhat uneventful, reflecting the fact that they cannot be considered in isolation.

There is a record, dated 1889, of the first picture loan collection, in Denver, Colorado. This indicated an interest in borrowing pictures, but not so much for reuse as for the enjoyment they gave. As for illustrations in public library collections, the New York Public Library had some 60,000 items in stock in 1906.

The next most interesting period occurred in the 1940s and records indicate the presence of pictures, other than art prints, in libraries. C H Gibbs-Smith,[3] E V Corbett,[4] and the Special Libraries Association in America evinced interest and began to produce useful literature.

In the UK, the illustrations collection became one of the general provisions of the 'free' library service, although copyright and lending restrictions kept it to a narrow base. By this stage, interest was being expressed in the organization and exploitation of pictures and during the 1940s many of the large commercial picture libraries were established for the use of newspapers and publishing houses.

The Picture Division of the Special Libraries Association was established in 1952 and from this point much of the interest has grown. By 1959 Gernsheim was calling for a 'central archive' of photography[5] and this theme was continued by John Wall in the early 1970s.[6] In view of the volume of the material and its diversity, as well as its widespread reuse, this may no longer be a feasible goal but the reader of this handbook must be the judge of that.

SURVEY OF COLLECTIONS

It is possible to categorize the types of picture libraries although the dividing lines are by no means defined and considerable overlap occurs. Picture libraries or collections in libraries vary in size, scope, function, and emphasis. They may be devoted exclusively to pictures or be part of a larger, general library containing other materials. The picture library may be a small departmental collection covering a particular subject, or part of a general resources centre, or a small adjunct to another library.

One of the major differences between commercial and non-commercial sources relates to income and function, rather than the question of charging and not charging. The commercial library has to live by its own income, whereas the non-commercial one is supported in some way by a parent institution or department, even though it will have to charge an economic rate for prints and also any copyrights.

Commercial libraries include press agencies, photo agencies both general and specialist, and individual photographers. Non-commercial ones include those belonging to public institutions, government departments, societies and professional bodies, museums and art galleries, the education sector, and industrial firms.

Commercial

The commercial picture library is usually devoted exclusively to pictures and depends upon an income from these pictures in order to maintain and improve the services of the library and strengthen the collection.

Press agencies These exist to provide photographs both nationally and internationally. They gather material nationally and exploit it abroad as well as acquiring material from abroad and exploiting it nationally. They are usually organized on a syndication basis, with cameramen in various areas feeding in photographic material. The material is topical or of news value and the main users are newspapers, weekly journals, or television. Some backfiles are kept but preservation is not the major consideration in this type of library.

Photo agencies These deal with non-topical material and frequently act as agents for groups of photographers. The photographer is left free to do what he is best at and the agency handles and exploits the material produced by the photographer. The photo agency may be a large general library covering all subjects or it may specialize in particular areas or forms, for example natural history, aerial or underwater photography. The major priority in such a library is the availability of the material and considerable organization is essential.

Individual photographers may start with their own collections and specialities and branch out into handling the material of others with the same interests. These too form commercial libraries where the main aim is to provide an income for further production of material.

Historical collections constitute another major category of commercial picture library. These contain historical material gathered from many sources but designed not to conflict with the current, topical collections of the agencies. They may specialize in particular subjects, such as science and technology or periods of time, but many are general collections of early illustrations gathered together for the purposes of exploitation by publishers and other users. The primary concern of these collections is serving their users who provide the sole source of income.

Non-commercial

Non-commercial picture libraries are even more varied than the commercial ones. They may exist to serve a general public while having some obligation to conserve material as a departmental record or they may exist to serve a particular public or institution. These collections include:

The *public collections* or large general libraries attached to major public institutions, such as the British Museum, or the Kunsthistorisches Museum in Vienna. Some exist to make available material already in their own collections while others possess additional material relevant to their collection. Exploitation is not the major priority in such libraries, as witnessed by the slower service and general approach but conservation of the objects is important. Many such collections have a major archival role.

Government departments also have large collections which may or may not be generally available. They are usually regarded as archival records of the department concerned but may be released to the public domain and in some cases become very important sources of picture information. Again, the main emphasis is on conservation, with some exploitation. Charges are made for prints and processes, as well as for some reproduction rights.

Museums and art galleries usually have picture collections of their own materials and these are made generally available. In some instances the museum will have information about other works relevant to its own collections.

Societies and institutions exist to serve their own well-defined public and maintain picture collections within this context. The pictures are available for study and research by members with some extensions for bona fide use. The same rules usually apply to professional bodies.

Education authorities and establishments make widespread use of picture material. The public is usually confined to the educational establishment involved and the use made is for the preparation of teaching materials. Illustrations, posters, wallcharts, and slides are popular in this area but it is seldom that the material is used outside the school or college. Education libraries use other picture libraries but are not themselves geared to outside usage.

Public libraries may have collections of pictures for general use in the preparation of projects or for displays and some may include art loan collections. Public library picture material available for publication or for use outside the immediate community the library serves will include material contained in the books unique to that collection.

Commercial and industrial firms may have picture collections concerned with their own products and these are usually regarded as publicity material which can be reused for the ultimate benefit of the company concerned. Most supply material free of charge, requiring only that due credit is given and that the material is not used to the detriment of the company or the product.

This survey can only indicate the broadest categories into which picture libraries can be placed. Each library will be different in purpose and scope and in the end it is up to the librarian concerned to define the parameters within which the library operates. Again and again the librarian returns to the two major questions: What is the function of the library? Who does it serve and how do they use it?

SCOPE OF THE HANDBOOK

Some limits have been placed on the coverage of this handbook, either by the material or the emphasis placed on aspects of the work.

Integral collections of art works and pictures form some of the largest constituents of picture libraries but although this is an important aspect in the present context, pictures should be regarded as a source of information or as actual pieces of visual information. There is more to art librarianship than a collection of pictures, just as there is more to picture librarianship than a collection of representations of art works. Art librarianship, if one can designate it as such, is already well covered in the literature, and information about art libraries has already been collected in such works as *Art library manual,*[7] edited by Philip Pacey, or the *Art libraries journal.*[8] Therefore, libraries devoted to the arts and fine arts are considered in this present volume for the techniques and practices which can be used in any picture library, whatever the subject coverage, rather than for the subject matter.

Again, although slides are an important aspect of picture librarianship they deserve separate detailed treatment and have received this in many publications, such as *Slide libraries,*[9] or the Mid America College Art Association guides.[10] The reader requiring detailed guidance on the handling of slides is advised to consult these other sources of information. This book will concentrate mainly on photographs and illustrations, but this is not to say that slides are excluded: they are after all alternative forms of pictures and as such must have a place in the consideration of picture librarianship. Slides, when mentioned in this handbook, are usually considered as an adjunct to other pictures, either as representations of these pictures, or as a storage method, or for cataloguing purposes.

Furthermore, the book has been deliberately aimed at librarians rather than picture researchers. The rapidly growing profession of picture research has much in common with picture librarianship, but apart from the fact that it is also being catered for by other literature, especially in recent years, the picture researcher has a different purpose to fulfil. The picture researcher is the user of the picture library, while the picture librarian is the collector, organizer, and exploiter of the material. Each should have a good understanding of the other's function and needs, but the two tasks require different skills and it is not necessary for one to be skilled in all aspects of the other's craft. This is not to say that many picture librarians are not also picture researchers and vice versa, but in carrying out the two tasks a shift in emphasis and approach is necessary, if only to avoid a confusion of aims and purpose. For example, a certain amount of picture research ability is necessary to any librarian in carrying out a selection programme: knowing where the material is and which sources are expensive, cheap or free. Also, in cataloguing, a librarian with picture search knowledge will be assisted in dating the material, recognizing which processes were likely to be available and used at certain periods, and the value of some processes to the collection: that is how they can be used and what cannot be done.

The book is therefore intended for the librarian but, as a librarian can learn from books directed towards the picture researcher, so it is hoped that the material will be of value to the picture researcher while helping to increase understanding and foster helpful working relations between the two professions.

FRAMEWORK

The purpose of this handbook is to provide a manual of techniques and practices in picture libraries. It is an attempt to provide a source to which the librarian can turn for guidance when faced with a new collection or situation, or when problems arise. A similar problem or situation may have been encountered before and described here, together with one or more solutions.

The aim is not didactic for no-one can claim to have the right answer to all situations, but rather exemplary. The ways and means described here are not the only, nor indeed the best solutions, but indicate endeavours to come to grips with particular problems in certain situations and the results.

The framework of the handbook has been designed to consider the fundamental processes and operations encountered in any picture library. After a description of the materials themselves and the development of photography and printing, the book moves into the picture library itself. The sources of the material are considered and the guides available to aid selection. A library will acquire material by various methods — either as a gift, donation, deposit, or purchase — and in most instances this material will have been selected by library staff. Selection may be governed by some deposit principle laid down by a parent body, or an active acquisitions policy may be employed, or the library may act as an agency for several other collections or individuals. Once the material is acquired it will need to be processed and the collection maintained in usable format. Storage and conservation are important considerations in any library and the special characteristics and requirements of picture material will be dealt with in some detail. Different types of material will be treated in different ways according to the intrinsic and lasting value of the items as well as to the type of usage the pictures will receive: whether they are to be made available for immediate reuse, or for archival retention and reference. The pictures need arrangement and here methods will again differ both from other library materials and from one collection to another, according to their purpose.

Exploitation and use of the collections are important factors, as well as the general administration and economics of picture libraries. Staffing of libraries includes the education, training, and career opportunities of the prospective picture librarian.

Pictures are meant to be looked at and used and no handbook would be complete without a consideration of copyright and reproduction rights. This will assist the librarian in deciding what can be safely kept and how it can be used, whether it can be resold and under what conditions, or whether it can only be retained for reference purposes.

The second part of the handbook is devoted to a series of case studies or surveys of picture libraries and is designed to build up an idea of the network of picture libraries which exist. The case studies include descriptions of unique collections and the surveys provide an overview of a number of libraries of similar type with the special policies and problems common to the type, such as the population they serve, how the material is acquired, and any other special features.

The case studies provide many interesting variations on a theme and emphasize the importance of establishing the fundamental concepts of picture libraries: deciding what is the function of this particular library, who are the users, and how is the material to be used. These concepts will govern the stock and acquisitions policies as well as helping to determine how the library is to be organized.

Pictures have been part of the library scene for many decades but have perhaps not been recognized as an important source of information. The increased use of audio-visual materials over the past decade has helped to emphasize the librarian's responsibility for pictures but they may also have been overshadowed by the gadgetry of television and many other non-book materials. This is unfortunate because pictures are one of the materials most useful to publishers of books and audio-visual materials. Mastering the craft of picture librarianship can only assist other areas of librarianship and provide an increasing recognition of the status of pictures in libraries.

Of course, not every library has or should have pictures but a recognition of the usefulness of pictures as sources of information is essential to the understanding of any librarian. Sometimes, pictures do the job of imparting information better than other materials and it is helpful for any librarian to realize this and take account of it, in general reference work as well as in the more specialized area of picture librarianship.

This book is not designed to be definitive but rather to indicate the areas of concern of the librarian dealing with pictures, and to survey the present scene. In doing this, the aim is to help develop and advance the craft of picture librarianship.

REFERENCES

1   Novotny, A (editor) *Picture sources 3.* New York, Special Libraries Association, 1975.
2   Evans, H *Picture researcher's handbook.* London, Saturday Ventures, 1979.

References

3 Gibbs-Smith, C H 'The Hulton Picture Post library'. *J Doc.* 6 (1) March 1950. 12-24.
4 Corbett, E V *The illustrations collection.* London, Grafton, 1941.
5 Gernsheim, H & A *The recording eye.* New York, Putnam, 1960.
6 Wall, J (compiler) *Directory of British photographic collections.* London, Heinemann, 1977.
7 Pacey, P (editor) *Art library manual.* London, Bowker, 1977.
8 *Art libraries journal.* London, ARLIS. Quarterly.
9 Irvine, B J *Slide libraries.* Colorado, Libraries Unlimited, 1979.
10 Mid America College Art Association. Visual Resources Committee: *Guide to photograph collections.* New Mexico, 1978; *Guide to management of visual resources collections.* New Mexico, 1979.

2

Photography and Printing

J P Ward

BACKGROUND

The application of technology to the reproduction and multiplication of illustrations and works of art was a legacy of the Industrial Revolution which became one of the great preoccupations of the 19th century. During the early part of the century there was an extraordinary interest in mechanical and optical aids to drawing and the journals and popular periodicals of the time are filled with enthusiastic accounts of new varieties of perspective machine, pantographic tracing device, and camera obscura. The principles of this last-named instrument had been known for centuries but revived interest in its portable form (to all intents and purposes, a photographic camera without the light-sensitive emulsion) was an important factor in the invention of photography.

By the time the century had run half its course technology had become intimately involved with art and design. The catalogue of the Great Exhibition of 1851 contains a host of references to methods for duplicating or multiplying drawings and works of art. It is perhaps no coincidence that this period saw the birth of the modern illustrated periodical. In England, the trend began with *Punch* (1841) and *Illustrated London News* (1842); in France there was *La Caricature* (1830) and *L'Illustration* (1843); in Germany *Illustrierte Zeitung* (1843); and in the USA *Scientific American* (1845).

The Industrial Revolution, with the accompanying great interest in the mechanical reproduction of illustrations, also helped bring innovation to the printing industry after three hundred years of relative technological stagnation. Lithography was introduced to England early in the century and electrotyping was discovered in 1839. However, the most important component in the transformation of techniques for printing illustrations which occurred in the 19th century was the application of photography.

PHOTOGRAPHY

The earliest surviving photographic image was made in France in 1826 by Nicéphore Niépce. It was produced on a pewter plate coated with bitumen of Judea a substance which hardens on exposure to light after several hours exposure in a camera obscura. Niépce died before he could perfect his process but an associate, L J M Daguerre, continued work alone and eventually devised the first practicable system of photography which was announced in 1839. Called the *daguerreotype* process after its inventor, it produced a direct positive image on a silver-coated copper plate which had been light sensitized by iodine vapour.

The announcement of the daguerreotype process prompted an Englishman, W H F Talbot to publicize details of his *photogenic drawing* process, a technique he had discovered for making photographic images on paper. Talbot had begun his investigations in 1834 and his earliest surviving image, a camera negative, was made a year later. Photogenic drawings were made by sensitizing a sheet of writing paper with solutions of salt and silver nitrate. The paper, when exposed in a camera, produced a negative image. By exposing further sheets of sensitive paper through this negative, any number of positive pictures could be produced.

At the outset both processes were imperfect and required long exposure times but the daguerreotype process was soon improved to the point where portrait photography became a possibility. The world's first professional daguerreotype portrait studio was opened by Alexander Walcott in New York in 1840. Richard Beard opened Europe's first daguerreotype studio in London during 1841. Over the next few years daguerreotype portrait studios were opened all over the world. Talbot's discovery of the possibility of developing a latent image and his announcement of the *calotype* process in 1840 also allowed him to take

The first published representation of a photograph (1839). A wood engraving, probably made from a photograph on the block. *The Science Museum, London.*

photographs of living subjects. Unfortunately for Talbot, the calotype process was never widely practised by professional photographers, although it was used by many amateurs. Talbot's place in history is secure, however, for the daguerreotype process was soon to vanish and it is the negative-positive technique that forms the basis of modern photography.

In 1851, F S Archer published details of a new negative-positive process which could reproduce images with the fine details of a daguerreotype. By combining the advantages of calotype and daguerreotype, and needing a shorter exposure time than either, Archer's new process soon displaced the earlier techniques from favour. As it involved exposing within the camera a plate still wet with sensitizing solution, it became known as *wet plate,* or *wet collodion,* photography. A new cheap form of portraiture appeared, the collodion positive or *ambrotype,* and about the same time a new printing technique, albumen printing, was widely adopted.

It was primarily these technical innovations, together with the publicity arising from the photographic exhibits in the Great Exhibition in England, which initiated the rapid growth of photography in the 1850s. Studios opened in the smallest villages. For the first time almost every member of the public was able to afford his own miniature portrait and see accurate depictions of distance lands. A craze for stereoscopic photographs arose, and later for the photographic visiting card, or *carte de visite.* Within twenty-five years of its inception, photography had become familiar to all and part of every middle-class home.

The great weakness of photographic prints of the period was their tendency to fade. In the search to find a means of overcoming this problem, discoveries were made and techniques devised which later formed the basis of several photomechanical printing processes. The most relevant of the discoveries were made by Talbot in 1852 and Poitevin in 1855 and concerned the changed characteristics of bichromated gelatin when exposed to light. These led to the development of pigment processes in which the image is made of a permanent pigment rather than silver. The most important of these was Sir Joseph Swan's carbon process.

Another revolution in the techniques and practice of photography was precipitated by a further series of technical innovations in the last quarter of the 19th century. The introduction of fast gelatin bromide dry plates and, later, roll film with factory processing, at last allowed picture taking to be divorced from the previously inescapable chemical manipulations. George Eastman, with his 1888 Kodak and the slogan 'You press the button, we do the rest', introduced the masses to photography and completely changed its character. The age of the snapshot had begun. Apparatus rapidly became smaller and metal began to replace wood as a construction material. Hand cameras were widely used for the first time and the precursors of the modern miniature cameras appeared. Enlarging was simplified when albumen printing gave way to fast bromide printing. The first modern photographic lenses were marketed in the last decade of the 19th century and practical colour processes became available in the first decade of the 20th. Although colour photography was to play a minor role for many years to come, by the outbreak of World War I, the essential elements of photography as we know it today were firmly established.

THE CAMERA AND ENGRAVING

From the earliest days of photography attempts were made to apply the new art to printing. Niépce's photographic images have much more in common with what we would now call photoengravings rather than photographs and he did in fact etch and print several bitumen pictures to produce copies of engravings which have survived to the present day. Several attempts were made to etch daguerreotypes and print from them. In September 1839, Dr Alfred Donne showed specimens of prints he had produced from daguerreotypes on which the bare silver parts had been etched with nitric acid. A similar process was announced by Dr Joseph Berres of Vienna in 1840 and by March 1841 Hippolyte Fizeau was making printing plates from etched daguerreotypes, using the new technique of electrotyping. W R Grove in England also demonstrated a method of etching daguerreotypes with hydrochloric acid and then making facsimile copies by the electrotype process. His method was mentioned in enthusiastic terms in a publication of 1841.

> ... Mr Grove has described a process, by which the pencil of nature does all the work. He has taken Daguerreotype plates — those beautiful productions 'drawn by light' — and, having submitted them to the still further operation of Nature's laws, has succeeded in 'engraving by electricity'. Though this process has not been

Talbot's printing establishment at Reading (1844) where the first published works to be illustrated with photographs were produced. *Fox Talbot Collection, The Science Museum, London.*

perfected, so far as to produce plates fitted in all respects for the printer, yet, as it is one most important application of the subject on which we treat, and as it furnishes, though not for the printer, yet for the electrotypist, plates from which he can obtain perfect impressions, ... [1]

The author was right to temper his enthusiasm with a note of caution, for Grove's process, like most other methods of printing from etched daguerreotypes, was never fully perfected.

The primary influence of the daguerreotype on printed illustrations was to act as a guide for the artist when preparing wood blocks. Many of the new illustrated periodicals carried engravings which were described as being 'from a daguerreotype'. The *Illustrated London News* in 1842, its first year of publication, promised readers who were prepared to subscribe weekly for six months that they would receive a huge engraved panoramic view of London. The engraving when finished measured 3 × 4⅓ feet, and was printed from a gigantic wood block made up of 60 component parts, the work of 19 engravers over a period of two months. The preparation of an accurate original drawing from which the engravers could work would have proved a long and time-consuming task for several artists. In fact, the engravers worked from a series of daguerreotypes taken comparatively quickly by the fashionable London photographer, Antoine Claudet. Many books were illustrated in similar manner, one such example being Henry Mayhew's *London life and London poor* (1851). The engravings within were based on a series of daguerreotypes taken by Richard Beard. As other photographic processes were evolved these too were rapidly accepted as suitable guides for the artist. Although invariably worked up and 'improved', engravings began to bear much more resemblance to events reported than had previously been the case. The photograph also had a profound influence on the artist's style. Instead of the clean rather simple lines which had characterized many engravings in the past, pictures started to appear made up of blocks of dark and light tone as in a photograph. During the second half of the 19th century thousands of photographs were taken to serve as models for the engraver.

Photography was also applied to wood-engraving in a more direct way. A little more than three months after the first announcement of photography a British weekly periodical, *The Mirror*, filled its front page with what it called a 'Facsimile of a photogenic drawing'.[2] *The Mirror*'s

The photograph used as a guide to the engraver (1859). The wood engraving on the left was copied from a photograph similar or identical to that shown on the right. *The Science Museum, London.*

readers must have been impressed by this engraving for in the next issue a further article on photography was prefaced by the following: 'The facsimile of the photographic drawing in our last number has produced a much greater sensation than we had anticipated; but still we are not surprised at this excitement, for the engraving gave a most accurate idea of the photogenic picture.'[3]

Although *The Mirror* offered no explanation as to how its illustrations had been prepared, the *Magazine of Science* of 27 April 1839 included similar facsimiles with a letter from the engraver, G Francis:

Sir, — I send you three drawings of this new art, which were impressed at once on box-wood, and therefore are fit for the graver without any other preparation. I flatter myself that this process may be useful to carvers and wood engravers, ... as by this simple means the errors, expense and time of the draughtsman may be wholly saved, and in a minute or two the most elaborate picture or design, or the most complicated machinery be delineated with the utmost truth and clearness....[4]

Mr Francis went on to explain how the block was soaked in common salt and silver nitrate solutions, making it light sensitive. These engravings appear to be the first published results of a direct association between the camera and printing press. As one commentator has noted, Mr Francis's instructions were superficial and the process was probably much more difficult than implied.[5] The soaking in salt and silver nitrate solutions was likely to damage the surface of the block.

Photographic printing on the surface of a block as a guide to the engraver was not taken up with any great enthusiasm. The technique was described in 1845 as 'a novel application of this art ... recently suggested'.[6] The problems were still being worked out in the 1850s and the first complete book illustrated with photographic wood engravings was probably Catherine Winkworth's *Lyra Germanica,* of 1861. Although there were obviously several practitioners of the art throughout the 19th century it was not widely publicized and there is little evidence that it was widely used.

PHOTOGRAPHS AS BOOK ILLUSTRATIONS

Perhaps the most obvious use of photography in publishing was to use actual photographs as a form of book illustration. Part of one of Talbot's patents of 1843 proposed a system of mass producing calotypes for publication and, in the winter of that year, he set up a printing establishment at Reading to put his plans into effect. In January 1844, a slim privately printed booklet, *Record of the death-bed of CMW,* was issued as an obituary to Catherine M Walter, daughter of John Walter, proprietor of *The Times.* Within the booklet was a calotype copy of a bust of Catherine Walter which was made by Talbot's assistant at Reading, Nicholaas Henneman. This was the first publication illustrated with camera photographs.

The first publication available to a wide public was Talbot's *Pencil of nature*. Published by Longman's and issued in six parts between 1844 and 1846, it contained in all 24 calotypes. While *Pencil of nature* was still being issued, in 1845, the next Reading establishment publication, *Sun pictures in Scotland,* was produced. One hundred and twenty volumes were bound for which Henneman had to print 2,670 calotypes. Unlike *Pencil of nature, Sun pictures in Scotland* had no text. Two further photographically illustrated words were produced at Reading. *The Talbotype applied to hieroglyphics* was issued in 1846 and 25 copies of Sir William Stirling's *Annals of the artists of Spain* a year later.

The Reading establishment finally closed in 1847. Other books illustrated by 'stuck-in' photographs soon followed. *Reports of the juries* (1852) of the Great Exhibition was illustrated with 155 photographs prepared by Henneman. In France, photographs taken by Maxime du Camp between 1849 and 1851 were printed at Blanquart-Evrard's establishment at Lille. These photographs of the Near East were published in book form as *Egypte, Nubie, Palestine et Syrie* (1852) in a project which has been compared to Talbot's Reading venture.[7]

For about twenty years, books illustrated with actual photographs enjoyed some popularity, particularly topographical publications such as *Egypt and Palestine, photographed and described by Francis Frith* (1858). However, it soon became apparent that other methods of book illustration were required. Both calotypes and the later albumen prints showed a disturbing tendency to fade. From the 1860s this problem could be overcome by the use of the more permanent carbon prints. Although several Victorian books were published illustrated with carbon prints or *autotypes,* the production of pigment prints and silver prints was dependent on good daylight. In conditions of low light intensity printing could be very slow. Sticking the prints onto suitable paper and binding them into the books could also be a slow labour-intensive operation and therefore very expensive. By the end of the 1880s the use of any form of actual photographic print as a means of book illustration had for all practical purposes ceased.

PHOTOMECHANICAL PRINTING

True photomechanical printing can be classed into three distinct groups of processes.

1 Intaglio processes or photoengraving, where the printing blocks have an image etched into them, the depth of the etching depending on the tones of the original picture.
2 Planographic or lithographic processes, where a completely flat plate bears an image on a coating capable of accepting or repelling a greasy ink according to the amount of light imported.
3 Relief or letterpress processes, where the parts of the block bearing the ink are raised up as in a typewriter.

I Intaglio Processes

Although Niépce's process and etched daguerreotypes were the earliest forms of photoengravings, the direct ancestor of photogravure was Talbot's *photoglyphic engraving* process patented in 1852[8] and 1858.[9] Mungo Ponton in 1839 had reported the light sensitivity of bichromates. Talbot followed up this discovery and found that light hardened bichromated gelatin. It was upon this property that his process was based. Talbot made his engravings by exposing bichromated gelatin on a steel plate under a transparent positive photograph. The image was developed and then the soft areas of the gelatin, which had been under the dark areas of the photograph, were dissolved away with platinum chloride (later ferric chloride). The resulting intaglio plate could be used for printing.

It was soon found necessary to use a screen between the photograph and the plate during exposure in order to produce a print with a range of tonal values. Talbot's first screens were of gauze or muslin. Later, he borrowed the aquatint engravers' technique of spreading a fine powder of gum or resin over the gelatin to act as a screen. Details of Talbot's process and examples of photoglyphs were published in the *Photographic News* during the autumn of 1858[10] and later in 1859.[11] Unfortunately, even in its most sophisticated form, the photoglyphic engraving process did not produce consistent results. Many of the innovations made in devising the process were pointers to the future but, not for the first time, commercial success eluded Talbot and his process was never widely adopted.

Another early intaglio process, *photogalvanography,* devised by Paul Pretsch, made use of the fact that bichromated gelatin not exposed to light will swell when treated with water. It involved making an intaglio mould of gutta-percha from a swelled gelatin image and from this a copper printing plate was produced by the electrotype process. Pretsch formed a company in England in 1856 and made prints for about two years but the process was difficult to work and the plates usually required retouching by hand. Photogalvanography soon vanished, along with the similar *dallastype* process which was based on (or stolen from)[12] Pretsch's process.

A process which enjoyed much greater success was patented by W B Woodbury in 1864.[13] Like Talbot, Woodbury was concerned about the fading of conventional photographs. He became interested in Swan's carbon process and investigated the possibility of making a mould from the slight relief image characteristic of pigment prints before devising the process which he called the *woodburytype* process. Briefly, this involved using a negative to form a relief image in colourless bichromated gelatin. The thickness of any part of the gelatin image corresponded to the density of the original negative. The relief image was used to make a lead mould into which pigmental gelatin was poured. A sheet of paper was placed over this and the pigmented gelatin image transferred to the paper in a press. The resulting print closely resembled a carbon print.

The great defect of the system was that, like photographic prints, woodburytypes required hand pasting onto the page when used for book illustration and could not be printed with type. Despite this limitation, the prints produced were permanent, of high quality, and could be made at the rate of 120 an hour. From the 1870s until the end of the century, the woodburytype process was used to illustrate several transient publications and numerous books. One of the latter, *Men of mark, a gallery of contemporary portraits,* 1876-83, included no less than 252 woodburytypes. The patent rights of the process were sold to Goupil and Co. of Paris in 1867 and the process introduced on the Continent as *photoglyptie.* The *stannotype* process was a variation of the woodburytype process introduced in 1879. It was not widely practised.

The most significant intaglio process of the period included elements of Talbot's 1858 process and Swan's technique of carbon printing. It was invented by Karl Klic in 1879 and called *photogravure.* A polished copper plate was coated with a fine resin dust which was fixed by heat. An exposed carbon tissue was transferred onto the plate and the soluble soft parts removed by washing with warm water. The plate was then etched with a ferric chloride solution, the depth of the resulting etching being proportional to the tones of the original photograph which had been exposed over the carbon tissue. When cleaned, the plate was ready for printing. After further experiments, Klic devised a means of replacing his resin dust ground with a cross-lined screen of opaque squares and clear lines which was printed onto the carbon tissue before exposure. This modified *rotogravure* process enabled rotary cylinders to be used for printing and speeded production up from about four hundred prints a day to around five thousand. The first books illustrated with photogravure plates appeared in the 1880s and by the turn of the century the process was widely used.

The printing industry now had a means of mass producing good quality photographic illustrations for periodicals and the first British paper to be printed by rotogravure was *The Illustrated London News,* in 1895. In 1912, it introduced a regular eight-page rotogravure section with the type set alongside the picture. Photogravure prints have been reproduced under a wide variety of names: *autogravure, goupilgravure, mezzotinto-gravure, rembrandt intaglio* prints, *vandyke-gravure,* etc., but all derive from Klic's process. The plates were often retouched by hand, and colour printing, by careful hand inking of the plates, appears to have been practised before the end of the 19th century.

2   Planographic or Lithographic Processes

Photolithographic printing processes have a history which begins with the early unsuccessful experiments of Nicéphore Niépce. In 1839, Dr Andrew Fyfe of Edinburgh described a method of reproducing photogenic drawings using lithographic stone coated with silver phosphate. Subsequently, many photolithographic processes were devised and for twenty years most were quickly abandoned. Of the short-lived processes perhaps that of John Pouncy deserves a mention. In 1857, he produced the first book published in Britain to be illustrated by photolithographs: a four-part work, *Dorsetshire photographically illustrated.* Several artists were involved at some stage of the production of the plates which must have made it a rather expensive project, and no more publications were produced.

The development which finally led to the establishment of photolithography as a practical process was announced by Alphonse Poitevin in 1855. He had discovered that bichromated gelatin when exposed to light hardens and will not absorb water; the parts unaffected by light retain the property of absorbing water. In a patent of the same year, Poitevin describes what happens when stone coated with bichromated gelatin is exposed to light under a negative.[14] The gelatin when moistened with water, accepts greasy printing ink only on the hardened parts, the ink being repelled in those parts where water has been absorbed. The gelatin reticulates during drying producing a fine grain making it possible to print directly from the gelatin. The process came to be known as *collotype.*

Although F Joubert produced collotype copies of a negative by Camille Silvy for publication in the *Photographic Journal* during 1860,[15] he refused to reveal details of his process and it was not until the end of the 1860s that a completely practical method of collotype printing became available.

In 1868, Josef Albert introduced the *albertype* process which differed only in detail from Poitevin's collotype. Albert was able to produce over 2,000 prints from a single plate at the rate of 200[16] a day, using one small printing press. By careful selection of inks he was able to produce pictures virtually identical in appearance to contemporary photographs and which cost about a shilling to make. Albert was later able to increase his rate of production and bring costs down even further by employing rapid rotary presses. Albertypes, as such, were little used in England but the technique was practised by Spencer, Saywer, Bird and Co., who seem to have been a subsidiary of The Autotype Co. Several books were illustrated by the process, sometimes being described, rather confusingly, as 'mechanical autotypes'.

The *heliotype* process was a variation of the albertype process, patented in England by Ernest Edwards in 1869. By printing from metal plates which could withstand far greater pressure in the presses than the glass plates favoured by Albert, Edwards was able to obtain 1500 prints from each plate and produce up to 300 impressions a day.[17] The first of many books to be illustrated with heliotypes was Darwin's *The expressions of the emotions of man in animals* published in 1872.

All collotype processes are comparatively expensive and require some skill to practise but it is generally accepted that prints of the very highest quality can be produced. Perhaps because of patent restrictions, it was only slowly taken up at first but by the turn of the century, the collotype and similar processes had become an established part of the printer's art.

The discovery of the properties of bichromated gelatin led to many other photolithographic processes, including several devised primarily for quickly and accurately reproducing maps. Among these was *photo-zincography* introduced in 1859 by Colonel Sir Henry James, FRS, of the Ordnance Survey, Southampton. As well as reproducing maps, the Ordnance Survey department used the process to produce facsimile reproductions of a number of books. Others include the *papyrotype* process, invented in 1873 by Captain (later Sir) W de W Abney, of the School of Military Engineering, Chatham, and the *vandyke* process of 1901.

Offset-lithography was invented by Robert Barclay in 1875 but did not come into general use until the early years of this century. In this technique, the inked plate is first rolled onto a rubber 'blanket' cylinder and the image then transferred (or offset) onto the paper. Although the quality of the image produced by offset methods does not match that of direct printing from the plate, it does mean that images can be readily transferred to the poorest quality paper, or indeed a surface of almost any material, rough or smooth.

3 Relief Processes

Half-tone relief printing is the process most commonly used today for reproducing photographs in books, magazines, and newspapers. The photograph is converted into a printable form by breaking up the image into a series of dots. The broad principles of the process are as follows. A photographic exposure is made through a glass screen made up of small squares formed by intersecting dark lines and this yields a negative dot image. The negative is next exposed to light over a metal plate coated with bichromated gelatin. When the plate is washed, the areas not rendered insoluble by the action of light are removed, leaving an image made up of dots of gelatin of varying sizes. Treatment with an etching solution which removes the non-printing part of the plate leaves the dots standing in relief. The finished plate is then ready for mounting so that the image is at the same height as the type. When inked, the large dots of the image take the most ink and make up the dark areas of a photograph, the small dots take the least ink and will print the light areas of the photograph, and the intermediate size dots represent the half-tones in between.

The screen is the key to the half-tone process and the first suggestion of the use of a screen to break up a photographic image came from the fertile brain of W H F Talbot. In the patent of 1852 he mentions using gauze[18] and a year later '... a glass plate covered with an innumerable quantity of fine lines...'.[19] Talbot's ideas were pursued by a number of investigators but progress was slow for there was little incentive. One of the great advantages on the half-tone system is that photographically based pictures can be printed within a column of type. However, the daily illustrated newspaper had yet to appear and for books and magazines, wood engravings, and later collotypes, woodburytypes, and photogravures were perfectly satisfactory.

In 1882, George Meisenbach patented a single-line screen method, which had in part been anticipated by Swan. He was soon working the system successfully in Munich and, from 1884, in London. Cross-line screens were suggested in England and America but the process was perfected by Max Levy of Philadelphia. In 1890 he introduced an improved cross-line screen by etching the lines into the glass and then filling them with black resin, a development which advanced the technique to its present-day form.

The perfection of the half-tone process was perhaps the most important single factor which led to the change in character of the popular press at the beginning of this century. Almost for the first time, topical picture material could be printed quickly and simply. The first step towards the future was taken on 4 March 1880 when the *New York Daily Graphic* carried a picture of 'Shantytown' — a squatters' camp. The half-tone black of this photograph was made by S H Horgan. Horgan spent several years trying to convince newspaper owners of the advantages of including half-tone photographs in the press but had little success until 1897 when the New York *Tribune* finally began to print half-tones on speed process.

But it was in Britain that the new process was first exploited fully. Evidence that the possibilities of half-tone printing were appreciated at an early date can be found in *The Photographic News* during 1884 which included examples of half-tone prints and commented: 'Not only is the engraved block made entirely by photographic agency, but it represents current news, and what is perhaps of more importance, it was printed satisfactorily along with the rapidly machined letterpress.'[20] By the turn of the century several British periodicals and newspapers were including topical half-tone prints.

In January 1904, a newspaper which had appeared for the first time just two months earlier, the London *Daily Mirror,* became the world's first daily newspaper to be illustrated exclusively with photographs. In 1907, the *Daily Mirror* enjoyed another 'first' when it became the world's first daily newspaper to put into operation a regular 'wire service' whereby it could receive photographs by telegraph. The age had arrived, prophesied by George Eastman in 1885, when he suggested that the camera would be as necessary to the newspaper correspondent as the pen.[21]

PHOTOTYPESETTING AND DOCUMENT COPIERS

Photography revolutionized the reproduction of the printed illustration in the last quarter of the 19th century and it seems likely that it will help revolutionize the reproduction of the printed word in the last quarter of the 20th. The idea of phototypesetting was probably anticipated by Talbot in the 1840s when he appears to have photographically copied a stanza of verse assembled from individual letters. It is only in recent years that phototypesetting techniques, such as the *monophoto* machine, have been introduced at all widely but already these have led to several labour problems in the printing industry. Photographic and, more importantly, xerographic copies now offer a quick and cheap means of duplicating documents and illustrations that would formerly have been reproduced by the printer. There seems little doubt that the industry will again undergo radical changes in the next few years.

REFERENCES

1 Walker, Charles V *Electrotype manipulation, Part II.* 3rd ed. London, George Knight and Sons, 1841. 30.

2 *The Mirror* XXXIII (945). 20 April 1839. 242.

3 Anon 'The new art — photography' *The Mirror* XXXIII (946). 27 April 1839. 262.

4 Francis, G 'Important application of photogenic drawing'. *The Magazine of Science* IV. 27 April 1839. 28.

5 Wakeman, Geoffrey *Victorian book illustration: Great Britain.* David and Charles Limited, 1973. 76.

6 Fisher, George Thomas. *Photogenic manipulation, Part I.* 2nd ed. London, George Knight and Sons, 1845. 28.

7 Thomas, D B *From today painting is dead* (an exhibition catalogue). Great Britain, The Arts Council, 1972. 59, No.893.

8 Talbot, W H F 'Engraving pictures obtained by photographic process on steel, etc.' British Patent No.565, 28 October 1852.

9 Talbot, W H F 'Improvements in the art of engraving etc.' British Patent No.875, 14 October 1858.

10 Talbot, W H F 'Description of Mr Fox Talbot's new process of photoglyphic engraving'. *Photographic News* 1(7) 22 October 1858. 73. (Examples of photoglyphs published in *Photographic News*, 12 November 1858.)

11 *Photographic News* III (54) 16 September 1859.

12 Eder, J M *History of photography* English language ed. New York, Columbia University Press, 1945. 583.

13 Woodbury, W B 'An improved method of producing or obtaining by the aid of photography surfaces in relievo and intaglio etc.' British Patent

No.2338, 23 September 1864. (See also Patent No.1918, 26 July 1866 and Patent No.947 30 March, 1867.)

14   Poitevin, A L 'Improved photographic printing'. British Patent No.2815, 13 December, 1855.

15   *Photographic Journal* VI (98). 15 June 1860.

16   Seamoni, G *Handbuch der Heliographic.* St Petersburg, 1872. 30. (From Gernsheim, H & A, *The history of photography.* rev. ed. London, Thames and Hudson, 1969. 548.)

17   Gernsheim *History.* p.549.

18   Talbot: British Patent No.565, 1852. (See ref. 8.)

19   'The Athenaeum'. 30 April 1853. (From Gernsheim *History.* p.549.)

20   Quoted by Gernsheim. *History.* p.551.

21   Ackerman, C W *George Eastman.* London, Constable & Co. Ltd, 1930. 51.

This list of references is linked to the text, but for anyone interested in pursuing the subject an additional guide to further reading is appended.

APPENDIX

A brief outline of the history of photography and printing can be found in T K Derry and Trevor I Williams *A short history of technology* (Oxford University Press, 1960). A similar but more extensive treatment is given in the seven-volume set edited by Charles Singer, E J Holmyard, A R Hall, and Trevor I Williams, *A history of technology* (Oxford University Press, Vols I-V, 1954-8, Vols VI & VII, 1979).

Detailed accounts of the evolution of photography and photo-mechanical printing appear in the three classic histories of photography: J M Eder's *History of photography* (Trans., Epstean, Columbia University Press, New York, 1944), Beaumont Newhall's *The history of photography* (Museum of Modern Art, New York, 1964), and H and A Gernsheim's *The history of photography* (rev. ed., Thames and Hudson, 1969).

Useful concise descriptions of early photographic and photo-mechanical techniques are included in D B Thomas' catalogue *The Science Museum photography collection* (HMSO, 1969) and in 'The focal encyclopedia of photography' (various eds., Focal Press, London and New York). Geoffrey Wakeman's *Victorian book illustration* (David and Charles, 1973) is an interesting and readable broad account of 19th-century developments in the techniques of printing illustrations and H J

P Arnold's biography *William Henry Fox Talbot* deals authoritatively with the work of Talbot and his contemporaries.

Those interested in consulting contemporary sources will find a wealth of detail and examples of processes in issues of *Photographic Journal* and *Photographic News* published between *c.* 1860 and *c.* 1914. A useful simple guide to many of the 19th-century photomechanical processes and which includes several examples is A Brothers' *Photography* (Charles Griffin and Co., 1892). Numerous splendid examples of photomechanical processes can be found in the yearly *Penrose Pictorial Annuals* of the first decade of this century.

3

Sources

Anthony J Coulson

INTRODUCTION

The discovery and acquisition of useful pictures is a skill that can only be gained by experience and a certain amount of speciali- zation. The core of this skill lies in the apt choice of sources. In this section I will try to introduce some of the guides to sources and techniques useful to a librarian, particularly a librarian who has to develop a picture collection as part of a larger library complex.

From this it follows that the first questions the librarian should ask relate to the purpose and function of the picture library within an individual library or organization. Answers to these questions will go a long way towards selecting the appropriate format, quality, and content of the material to be obtained. Does the collection need to provide illustrations that will be good enough to publish? Are the pictures mainly for class-teaching? Should the collection act as a bank of images for designers or students to use directly in their own work? Are the pictures needed as a quick reference collection or are they needed for detailed research? Are there other picture collections within the same organization? Where, how, and why do their needs and functions differ? What budget and manpower resources will be available to support the picture collection?

Although the next section (Section 1.4 on Selection) deals with priorities and details of selection at much greater length, it is absolutely essential to be clear about the financial implications of using external

35

sources before approaching any of them. Quite apart from the cost of time, paper, and postage, the librarian needs to be aware in advance of the expensive sources that the budget cannot afford. Many commercial agencies are very expensive and impose a lot of restrictions which put them well out of the reach of most libraries. They may have superb material but this is not much use if it is not available.

RELATION TO BOOKS AND OTHER STOCK

In many libraries the most obvious but also the most undervalued picture resource is the book stock. Quite a few books could be seen as ready made, organized collections of pictures at the lowest available cost. Compared with the cost of selecting, mounting, and organizing individual pictures, books will often provide a far better return and choice for the same financial outlay. From the outset the librarian needs to be clear just how much time and effort can be spared for a separate illustrations collection and precisely which sort of material will best meet the particular needs of the library and its public. In small libraries where time and money are often inadequate this is an acute problem. Unless there is a clearly identified need, such as class-teaching requiring transparencies, or publications needing best quality photographic prints, there is little point in duplicating subjects already well covered and illustrated by books in the library.

But, how can you find illustrations in books and periodicals easily without having to check individual works one at a time? There are some published indexes to reproductions in books and magazines[1] but they refer mainly to American editions. Many of these editions may not be available worldwide or are now out of print. These indexes are also very selective but, if the library has a large book stock, it may not be too difficult to trace English or European editions of the works cited. Many of these will have the same plates. Some journal indexing services note the existence of illustrations in articles and a very few, such as *Art index*[2], have selective entries for some individual reproductions. In a more general way, the detailed published catalogues of large specialized libraries may help reveal well-illustrated articles, pamphlets, and books. Printed catalogues that deal with some of the special interests of the library might be a worthwhile investment. For example, a library with extensive collections of art, architecture, and more general arts journals might find the Art Institute of Chicago, Ryerson Library's *Index to art periodicals*[3] extremely useful. Most published catalogues and indexes do not list individual illustrations but they do indicate heavily illustrated works clearly.

Many sumptuous and expensive 'coffee table' books are of doubtful value even as bundles of illustrations but the librarian should think hard before deciding *not* to acquire inexpensive books that consist mainly of plates or subscribe to heavily illustrated and well-indexed journals. If staff time is at a premium and if the picture collection needs to serve the widest range of general needs, it may be cheaper for the library to subscribe to journals like the *National Geographic Magazine,* or buy the appropriate Dover Pictorial Archive publication or the relevant Time-Life volume. This may help free resources and time for the picture collection to concentrate on more detailed materials. The acquisitions policy devised for the picture collection needs to be an integral part of general library acquisitions policy, unless the collection has to be housed in a remote location or has to serve a radically different purpose. If it is not closely related to the other parts of the library the picture library cannot make the best use of the collecting, editing, cataloguing, and indexing activities that already exist. Most librarians need to get the best return from the limited resources available.

On a more detailed level, both librarian and user may need to know something about the historical development and technical processes of illustrations to make effective use of the collection. An earlier section of this book (Section 1.2 on Photography and Printing) makes some useful suggestions and, unless the picture collection has to be very specialized, the library should contain some books to provide this historical and technical background. These may include general historical surveys,[4] dictionaries of illustrators, engravers, photographers,[5] studies of methods of reproduction.[6] Increasingly, photographs and older illustrations of all types are becoming collectors' items and so it might be useful to have some books to help with valuation and conservation.[7] Books that relate to particular interests and special problems of the collection should be available. For example, a picture library that concerns itself with detailed high quality photographs of works of art should include books and data on this specific type of photography and reproduction.[8] Although this body of information will not necessarily indicate specific illustration sources, it will help the libarian avoid misunderstanding and anticipate technical problems.

The librarian would also be wise to anticipate some of the difficulties that arise from users trying to translate abstract or literary concepts into visual terms. A few illustrated dictionaries and encyclopedias, such as *I see all*[9] or the *Bettmann portable archive,*[10] provide the browser with a visual aid. The latter has an idea and image index and the pictorial alphabet ranges widely from 'Absurdities' to 'Zoology'. In a more general way, many of the larger and lavishly illustrated encyclopedias can provide this valuable pictorial introduction and the few pictorial dictionaries should not be ignored.[11] Exhibition catalogues are often even more valuable. Not only do they have up-to-date information about the location of objects and photographs, but frequently they demonstrate how a subject can be explained visually and reflect something of the range of different attitudes and visual treatments that exist.

FREE OR INEXPENSIVE SOURCES

Perhaps the first place to check is the library discard pile. Plates from old books, cuttings from magazines, advertisements, sales catalogues, dust jackets, brochures, duplicates, old posters may be cut up and given a new role, provided that they are clean and well printed on materials that are chemically and biologically stable. The clearer and larger the image the better. A regular look at this redundant material will soon provide a basic stock of general or thematic images for no cost beyond staff time. Even so, remember to keep a careful note of the distinctive facts of the illustration — title/identification caption, creator, source of the clipping, date, and any copyright holder acknowledged. This information will make the tasks of accurate classification and replacement much easier. It may be worth topping up these free materials by actively encouraging donations and keeping an eye open for cheap or free second-hand materials — old illustrated books with useless texts, damaged books with intact plates, odd copies of magazines, out-of-date textbooks, greetings cards, postcards, plans, designs, perhaps even wallpaper and textiles, as well as the more obvious photographs, slides, and posters. Most collections need to cover a very wide span of subject matter and so it is prudent to range as widely as possible from the outset. Even the most unlikely material could be some use. For instance, an out-of-date school textbook could yield portraits, designs, plans, diagrams, maps. *But* it is very important to be critical and selective. Material that is vaguely identified, misleadingly described, incorrectly credited, visually unclear, or confusing will create difficulties in the future, particularly when pictures need to be replaced or upgraded.

Bearing in mind points made previously about the book stock of the library, the librarian should pause before dismembering some old books and journals. Might they serve the user more effectively in one piece or in a new binding? Most exhibition and sales catalogues are best kept complete as self-contained information sources. Files of many journals, such as *Picture Post, Punch, Illustrated London News, Scientific American, Nature* are now valuable archives in their own right. Even if they are incomplete they would be more useful bound and indexed rather than dismembered and scattered through a general collection.

Another rich but often neglected source of good illustrations might be advertising matter — published advertisements, sales promotion handouts, brochures from public relations and information departments of companies, tourist organizations, and local, national, and international public bodies. The competitive pressure of advertising often guarantees bright and vivid images, well printed and freely available. For the cost of only stamps and letters a large collection of pictures of local views, brand images, consumer products, technical data, and graphic design of all sorts can be assembled to add to the siftings of unsolicited advertising leaflets. Names and addresses can be found easily by looking through telephone directories, commercial and public yearbooks, and directories,[12] as well as trade literature.

Resource packs and teaching aids of all sorts are another easy source of inexpensive illustrations. There is a growing range of cheap facsimile reprints, such as 'Jackdaws',[13] as well as the more conventional charts and audio-visual aids that can be traced by scanning the catalogues of educational publishers and suppliers. There are many specialized collections, such as the school documents packs produced by some County Record Offices, which can generally only be discovered by local enquiry. A surprisingly large number of organizations have teaching packs covering subjects as diverse as silk and York Minster but they can generally only be found by writing to the bodies publishing them. Fortunately, there are some national listings of audio-visual aids[14] and some national bodies, such as the Design Council and the Historical Association,[15] publish their own guides to audio-visual aids for teachers. Some time spent building up a collection of these lists and catalogues will soon create a valuable mine of information for acquiring detailed but relatively inexpensive materials.

PICTURE COLLECTIONS, MUSEUMS, LIBRARIES, ARCHIVES, AND OTHER INSTITUTIONAL SOURCES

So far I have suggested only those sources most suitable for general reference and illustrations that can be obtained for little or no cost but, if the library needs to support more specialized work, more detailed and higher quality material will be needed. These photographs may have to be individually searched, specially commissioned and bought at current market prices. Negotiations may also involve problems of language and copyright (discussed in Section 1.11 on Copyright).

Before setting out on this expensive voyage of discovery it might be wise to try and find out what already exists in organized photographic collections. They may be able to supply a duplicate or enable you to contact a specialist. Sadly there is no comprehensive international directory of collections and the searcher soon becomes aware of their enormous diversity. There are many thousands ranging from large independently organized photograph libraries, to sections of company public relations departments, to the life-long accumulations of individuals and small neglected corners of local repositories. As well as these there are millions of items in museums, art galleries, research organizations, companies, and private collections which may have been photographed or could be made available through their own photographic services.

International efforts have been made to document at least part of the field. In 1950, UNESCO sponsored *The international directory of photographic archives of works of art*[16] but, apart from the much less ambitious lists of widely available reproductions of well-known paintings,[32A] there has not been a successful attempt to bring even this directory up to date on a comprehensive international scale. Nevertheless, there are now some very useful national listings. The *Directory of British photographic collections* and the American *Picture sources 3* provide a lot of very helpful information on public collections, while the *Répertoire des collections photographiques en France* includes some commercial and personal collections as well.[17] For a wider international but very selective directory, there is Hilary and Mary Evans's *Picture researcher's handbook.*[33]

These concentrate on photographs. For details of slide collections and suppliers the librarian will need to turn to predominantly American published listings and directories. The College Art Association has taken a lead with its very useful *Slide buyers' guide* and other publications. On a smaller scale, there are a number of lists that concentrate on college and museum collections, as well as a growing number of more general audiovisual guides.[18]

In practice, the librarian will find that for ready-made slides and photographs of the quality and detail suitable for specialist work he or she will have to rely on a fairly small number of specialist commercial suppliers or the products of a much greater number of museums and galleries. There are now a few useful national bibliographies of the products of public and college collections,[19] but there can be no effective substitute for building up detailed knowledge of the resources of individual institutions and their publications relevant to the librarian's own picture collection. Some large museums, such as the Science Museum in London, have detailed photographic subject lists which specify negative numbers for photographs that can be obtained from their own photographic department. Other institutions, such as the Courtauld Institute of Art and the Victoria and Albert Museum,[19A] are beginning to make some of their photographic archives available in print or in microfiche through separate commercial publishers. Arrangements differ from institution to institution and many of these products escape published lists altogether.

The sources detailed so far are likely to lead to either ready-made illustrations or material that can be duplicated fairly easily. More detailed work may lead one to less obvious sources and the organization of special photography. In most cases this will involve the librarian in one of two distinct types of search — either a hunt for a particular type of collection that might yield the sort of illustration required, or a detailed search for the present location of a specific object. Both types of search can be very time-consuming and may need a wide range of directories and background information that can only be provided by the largest libraries.

Let us look at some of the books that may help with the first type of search. One of the large international directories of museums[20] may suggest a number of possibilities. Apart from the obvious facts, such as address and availability, content details are extremely brief and so the librarian may need to hunt for a specialized international list of collections, such as Cecil Lubell's *Textile collections of the world,*[20A] for more information. Unfortunately, there are still very few international directories of more specialized museum collections and so he or she will need to turn to the larger national and regional museum directories[21] for fuller and more up-to-date information on the scope and personnel of individual collections. Keeping track of museum and gallery additions is only possible in a general way[21A] unless the librarian has the time and opportunity to search files of annual reports and internal museum lists.

Many libraries of all sorts have very valuable collections of photographs, prints, engravings, and other visual materials. *The world of learning* and some of the national and international directories[22] may help give some idea of special collections and local interests, but more detailed work will often necessitate research among local publications, indexes, and information files, together with specific personal enquiry. Formally organized company and public archives are potentially rich sources of illustration but the problems of locating individual items and groups of documents may be even more complex. Directories of archives and associations[23] may help indicate particular collections and even sections but the availability of individual repository guides and lists is so patchy that a personal visit is generally necessary. Wide-ranging surveys of largely unpublished documents on particular subjects, such as the recent survey of natural history[23A] and Maurice Barley's *Guide to topographical collections,*[23B] are still fairly rare but well worth searching for. Company archives, information and publicity services are other rich fields best prospected after checking the *ASLIB directory*[24] or more general commercial and product lists[12] to sort out names, interests, and locations.

So far, I have only discussed books that will help locate subject areas and collections. In the search for an illustration of a particular object the librarian may need to draw on published sales records[25] and lists of collectors, experts, and dealers, such as those conveniently provided for the art world by the *International directory of arts* and the *Arts Review yearbook.*[26] Many dealers keep illustrations of objects that have passed through their hands and some of these are becoming available in published form.[25A] If the librarian is fortunate to discover a published illustration of the object sought, with a clear acknowledgment, the hunt for a fresh photograph may not be so cumbersome. A letter to the named source may be all that is needed, provided that the name and address of the source or contact can be found.

This may not be quite as straightforward as it seems. Different sorts of illustrations pose different sorts of problems. I cannot hope to deal with all these in the short space available and so I will confine the final stages of this section to a brief examination of the guides and sources that may help the librarian in searches for illustrations of two of the most popular sorts of material: portraits and paintings. Great Britain and the United States are fortunate to have a number of meticulously prepared dictionaries and surveys of portraits, based mainly on central national collections,[27] which provide ready access to images of the famous. Many of the long-established seats of learning, professional bodies, and museums also have very extensive and well-catalogued collections.[28] In addition, there are quite a few well-known portrait photographers with very rich and detailed historical collections. Contacting them may be much easier than hunting through *Who's who* or *Burke's peerage, baronetage and knightage,* or worrying individuals and relations.

Locating photographs or slides of paintings may present many more difficulties. There are lots of valuable encyclopedias, biographical dictionaries, specialist directories, censuses of particular sorts of paintings,[29] with meticulous details of location but they tend to cover works in public or easily accessible collections only. Unless a comprehensive catalogue of an individual artist's work has been prepared, there may well be no indication where paintings are held privately or any clue how an illustration may be obtained through an agent if the private collector wishes to remain anonymous for security reasons. There are a number of fine summary and detailed catalogues of public galleries[30] but for less obvious and rarer works the librarian may need to search exhibition catalogues. Fortunately, some of the larger art libraries with big collections of exhibition catalogues have also published lists of their holdings[31] and these make useful retrospective indexes, particularly now that companies such as Chadwyck-Healey[31A] have embarked on ambitious programmes of microfiche republication of a lot of the most important catalogues.

COMMERCIAL SOURCES

As the photographs and slides provided by public collections and other institutions or their agents can vary so much in quality, it may be necessary to draw on more expensive private photographers and picture agencies for pictures that can provide the clarity and detail needed for research, teaching, or publication. This can be very costly and the librarian needs time and patience selecting agencies and then details. Some long-established art photographic companies and foundations, such as Bulloz and Giraudon in France, Scala and Alinari in Italy, Foto Marburg in Germany,[32] have produced extensive and detailed catalogues and their work is widely available in many picture collections. Many specialist photographic companies and agencies, such as Aerofilms, publish their own catalogues or topic lists. Publishers of reproductions, such as Medici, also have detailed sales catalogues and some of the most accessible individual reproductions are listed in the UNESCO catalogues[32A] mentioned earlier.

In addition, there are many specialists who are less well documented. Finding them can be a problem. There is a useful introduction to the more important sources in *Picture researcher's handbook*[33] which sets out details of specialities and services, based on information provided by the sources themselves. However, the librarian must realize that many of the agencies detailed in this book are geared primarily to serve publishing, film and television work. Many will not permit their work to be copied or used for any other purpose. They also charge for searching and for borrowing time and their reproduction fees may be very high indeed.

Apart from the agencies and individuals covered by *Picture researcher's handbook,* there are many other photographers (working or retired) who may have their own private collections or files of negatives and be willing to supply the librarian with photographs. Finding these people may not be as difficult as it might seem. As well as the classified sections of telephone directories, the librarian could check the directories of professional organizations, such as the Institute of Incorporated Photographers,[34] or more general market guides, such as the *Writer's and artist's yearbook.* The American market is particularly well served by the *Stock photo and assignment source book* and *Photography market place.*[35]

PROFESSIONAL PICTURE RESEARCH

The further the librarian has to go into investigating the enormous range of likely picture sources, the more he or she will have to tangle with the daily problems of the professional picture researcher (styled 'picture professional' in America) who works in publishing or film and television. Hilary Evans's book, *The art of picture research. A guide to current practice, procedure, techniques and resources,*[36] provides a concise and practical introduction to this type of work. Based on a wide range of experience and contacts, it is the first published 'textbook' for this sort of researcher and contains a lot of advice and guidance that will help the librarian as well as the professional searcher.

Professional organizations are developing on both sides of the Atlantic and the librarian might find their publications, meetings, and contacts extremely useful. In America, there is the American Society of Picture Professionals[37] and the Special Libraries Association[38] has a Picture Division. The latter sometimes discusses picture issues in the columns of *Special Libraries* and its occasional publications,[39] while the Picture Division publishes its own quarterly, *Picturescope.* In Britain, there is SPREd (Society of Picture Researchers and Editors)[40] which holds meetings, publishes a regular newsletter, maintains a freelance register, and attempts to codify professional conduct and contracts. Although founded only very recently, it is now the main forum for picture researchers in the United Kingdom and may eventually sponsor courses.

Both picture researcher and acquisitions librarian of a picture library share a need for systematic knowledge and appreciation of sources. Any move to encourage this and promote more effective documentation of existing resources must be welcome.

REFERENCES

1   Monro, Isabel Stevenson and others *Index to reproductions of European paintings. A guide to pictures in more than three hundred books.* New York, H W Wilson, 1956. 668p.
      Monro, Isabel Stevenson and others *Index to reproductions of American paintings. A guide to pictures occurring in more than eight hundred books.* New York, H W Wilson, 1948. 731p.
      Vance, Lucile and others *Illustration index.* Metuchen, New Jersey, Scarecrow Press, 1957 (with later supplements). 192p.
      Thomson, Elizabeth W *Index to art reproductions in books compiled by the professional staff of the Hewlett-Woodmere Public Library.* Metuchen, New Jersey, Scarecrow Press, 1974. 371p.

Smith, Lyn Wall and others *Index to reproductions of American paintings appearing in more than 400 books mostly published since 1960.* Metuchen, New Jersey, Scarecrow Press, 1977. 931p.
Havlice, Patricia Pate *World painting index.* Metuchen, New Jersey, Scarecrow Press, 1977. 2 vols, 2130p.
Parry, Pamela Jeffcott *Contemporary art and artists. An index to reproductions.* New York, Greenwood, 1978. 327p.
Clapp, Jane *Sculpture index.* Metuchen, New Jersey, Scarecrow Press, 1970. 3 vols.
Havlice, Patricia Pate *Art in Time.* Metuchen, New Jersey, Scarecrow Press, 1970. 350p. ('An index to all the pictures in the art section of *Time* magazine.')
Clapp, Jane *Art in Life.* Metuchen, New Jersey, Scarecrow Press, 1959 (with later supplements). 504p.
2   *Art index.* New York, H W Wilson, January 1929-. Quarterly with annual cumulations.
Other useful indexes and abstracts:
Art bibliographies modern. Oxford, Santa Barbara, Clio Press, 1970-. (1969, 1970 title = *LOMA*).
Art, design, photo. London, Alex Davis Publications/Art Book Company, 1972-. Annual.
Répertoire international de la littérature de l'art (RILA). International Repertory of the Literature of Art. Williamstown, Massachusetts, Sterling and Francine Clark Institute, 1973, 1975-.
The Studio: a bibliography. The first fifty years 1893-1943, with an introduction by Bryan Holme. London, Sims and Reed, 1978. 142p.
3   Art Institute of Chicago, Ryerson Library *Index to art periodicals.* Boston, G K Hall, 1962. 11 vols.
Other G K Hall library catalogue reprints:
Columbia University *Avery index to architectural periodicals.* 2nd ed. 1973. 15 vols with supplements.
Victoria and Albert Museum *National art library catalogue. Author catalogue.* 1972. 10 vols.
Museum of Modern Art, New York City *Catalog of the library.* 1976. 14 vols.
Metropolitan Museum of Art, New York *Library catalog.* 25 vols with additional supplements.
New York Pubic Library; Astor, Lenox and Tilden Foundations; The Research Libraries *Dictionary catalog of the Prints Division.* 1975. 5 vols.
New York Public Library; Astor, Lenox and Tilden Foundations; The Research Libraries *Dictionary catalog of the Art and Architecture Division.* 1975. 30 vols with annual supplements entitled *Bibliographic guide to art and architecture.*
4   Evans, Hilary and Mary *Sources of illustration 1500-1900.* Bath, Adams and Dart, 1971. 162p.
Slythe, R Margaret *The art of illustration 1750-1900.* London, Library Association, 1970. 144p.

References

Bland, David *A history of book illustration: the illuminated manuscript and the printed book.* London, Faber, 1969. 459p.

Bland, David *The illustration of books. Part 1: History of illustration. Part 2: Processes and their application.* London, Faber, 1951. 200p.

Garrett, Albert *A history of British wood engraving.* Tunbridge Wells, Midas, 1978. 416p.

Levis, Howard C *A descriptive bibliography of the most important books in the English language relating to the art and history of engraving and the collecting of prints...* London, Dawson, 1974 (first published 1912, 1913). 141p.

Hunnisett, Basil *Steel-engraved book illustration in England.* London, Scolar Press, 1980. 256p.

Weber, Wilhelm *History of lithography.* London, Thames and Hudson, 1966. 259p.

Tooley, R V *English books with coloured plates 1790 to 1860. A bibliographical account of the most important books illustrated by English artists in colour aquatint and colour lithography.* Rev. ed. London, Dawson, 1978. 452p.

Newhall, Beaumont *The history of photography.* 4th rev. ed. London, Secker and Warburg, 1972. 216p.

Gernsheim, Helmut and Alison *The history of photography from the camera obscura to the beginning of the modern era.* Rev. ed. London, Thames and Hudson, 1969. 600p.

More specialized types of illustration:

Knight, David *Zoological illustration.* London, Dawson, 1977. 192p.

Blunt, Wilfrid J W *The art of botanical illustration.* London, Collins, 1950. 304p.

5 Baker, Charles (editor) *Bibliography of British book illustrators 1860-1900.* Birmingham, Birmingham Bookshop, 1978. 186p.

Houfe, Simon *The dictionary of British book illustrators and caricaturists 1800-1914.* Woodbridge Antique Collectors Club, 1978.

Engen, Rodney K *Dictionary of Victorian engravers, print publishers and their works.* Cambridge, Chadwyck-Healey, 1979. 245p.

6 Brunner, Felix *Handbook of graphic reproduction processes.* London, Academy Editions, 1962. 379p.

Dalley, Terence (compiler) *The complete guide to illustration and design techniques and materials.* Oxford, Phaidon, 1980. 224p.

7 Witkin, Lee D and others *The photograph collector's guide.* London, Secker and Warburg, 1979. 458p.

Castle, Peter *Collecting and valuing old photographs.* London, Bell and Hyman, 1979. 176p.

Plenderleith, H J and others *The conservation of antiquities and works of art. Treatment, repair and conservation.* 2nd ed. Oxford, Oxford University Press, 1971. 414p.

8 Gross, Anthony *Etching, engraving and intaglio printing.* Oxford, Oxford University Press, 1970. 172p.

Sources

Wright, John Buckland *Engraving and etching: techniques and the modern trend.* New York, Dover, 1973. 240p.

Chamberlain, Walter *Woodcut printmaking and related techniques.* London, Thames and Hudson, 1978. 184p.

Chamberlain, Walter *Etching and engraving.* London, Thames and Hudson, 1973. 200p.

Vicary, Richard *Lithography.* London, Thames and Hudson, 1976. 152p.

Yule, John Arthur Carslake *Principles of color reproduction applied to photomechanical reproduction, color photography and the ink, paper and related industries.* New York, Wiley, 1967. 428p.

Lewis, John N L and others *The graphic reproduction and photography of works of art.* London, Faber, 1969. 144p.

Encyclopaedia of photography. London, Focal Press, 1965. 2 vols.

Gotlop, Philip *Professional photography.* London, Thames and Hudson, 1973. 208p.

Photo-Lab-Index. London, Morgan and Morgan. Looseleaf.

9   *I see all. The world's first picture encyclopaedia.* London, Amalgamated Press, 1928. 5 vols.

10 Bettmann, Otto *Bettmann portable archive... a graphic history of almost everything.* New York, Picture House Press Inc., 1966. 229p.

11 Daniel, Howard *Encyclopaedia of themes and subjects in painting.* London, Thames and Hudson, 1971. 252p.

Hall, James *Dictionary of subjects and symbols in art.* London, Murray, 1974. 349p.

Winternitz, E. *Musical instruments and their symbolism in western art.* London, Faber, 1967. 240p.

12 **Commercial**

Register of British industry and commerce. London, IPC (Kompass). Annual. Similar directories available for other countries.

Guide to key British enterprises. London, Dun and Bradstreet.

Kelly's manufacturers and merchants directory. London, IPC (Kelly's).

Stock Exchange yearbook official yearbook. London, Stock Exchange.

Who owns whom. London, Roskill. Annual. Separate editions for North America, United Kingdom and Republic of Ireland, continental Europe.

Public

The Civil Service yearbook. London, HMSO.

The municipal yearbook. London, Municipal Journal.

13 Jackdaw Publications Ltd, 30 Bedford Square, London WC1B 3EL.

14 *Audiovisual aids: films, filmstrips, transparencies, wall sheets and recorded sound.* London, National Committee for Audio Visual Aids in Education, 1971-. Eight separate sections.

15 Sykes, Jane and others *Design resources for teachers.* London, Design Council Publications, 1976. 26p.

Williams, Gwyneth A (compiler) *Guide to illustrative material for use in teaching history.* London, Historical Association, 1962 reprinted 1969. (Helps for students of history no. 65.)

16 *International directory of photographic archives of works of art.* Paris,

Dunod; London, Crosby Lockwood, 1950, with supplement 1954. 668p.

17 Wall, John (editor) *Directory of British photographic collections*. London, Heinemann for Royal Photographic Society, 1978. 268p. and the earlier:
Nunn, George W A *British sources of photographs and pictures*. London Cassell, 1952. 220p.
Picture sources 3. Collections of prints and photographs in the US and Canada. New York, Special Libraries Association, 1975. 387p.
Répertoire des collections photographiques en France. Paris, Documentation Française, 1980.

18 DeLaurier, Nancy (compiler) *Slide buyer's guide*. 3rd ed. New York, College Art Association of America, 1976. 135p.
Petrini, Sharon and others *A hand list of museum sources of slides and photographs*. Santa Barbara; University of California, 1973.
Irvine, Betty Jo *Slide libraries: a guide for academic institutions, museums, and special collections*. 2nd ed. Littleton, Colorado, Libraries Unlimited Inc., 1979.
Hoffberg, Judith A and others (compilers) *Directory of art libraries and visual resource collections in North America*. Oxford, Clio Press, 1979. 310p.
Audiovisual market place: a multimedia guide. New York, Bowker. Annual.

19 *Bibliography of museum and art gallery publications and audiovisual aids in Great Britain and Ireland*. Cambridge, Chadwyck-Healey, 1980.

19A *Courtauld illustration archives*. London, Harvey Miller, 1976-.
Victoria and Albert Museum departmental collections. London, Mindata, 19/8-. Microfiche.

20 *Museums of the world. A directory of 17,500 museums in 150 countries including a subject index...* 2nd ed. Pullach bei München, Verlag Dokumentation, 1975. 808p.
Hudson, Kenneth and others *The directory of museums*. London, Macmillan, 1975. 864p.
Cooper, Barbara and others *The world museums guide*. London, Threshold/Sotheby Parke Bernet, 1973. 288p.

20A Lubell, Cecil *Textile collections of the world. Vol 1: An illustrated guide to textile collections in United States and Canadian museums. Vol. 2: United Kingdom and Ireland. Vol. 3: France. An illustrated guide to textile collections in French museums*. London, Studio Vista, 1976-7. 336p, 240p, 240p.

21 **Great Britain and Ireland:**
Museums and galleries in Great Britain and Ireland. Dunstable, ABC Historical Publications. Annual.
Museums yearbook. London, Museums Association. Annual.
What is where in national museums? London, British Tourist Authority, 1975/6. 32p.
London:
Standing Commission on Museums and Galleries *Guide to London museums and galleries*. London, HMSO, 1974. 162p.

Sources

Brooke, Brian (editor) *Art in London.* London, Methuen, 1966. 223p.
United States:
Official museum directory. New York, National Register Publishing Company for American Museums Association, 1981.
France:
Guide des musées de France. Fribourg, Switzerland, Office du Livre, 1970. 220p.
German speaking countries:
Kloster, Gudrun B (editor) *Handbuch der museen: Deutschland BRD, Osterreich, Schweiz.* New York, Bowker, Pullach bei München, Verlag Dokumentation, 1971. 2 vols. 1300p.
Israel:
Rahmani, L Y *The museums of Israel.* London, Secker and Warburg, 1976. 239p.
Japan:
Roberts, Laurance P *Roberts' guide to Japanese museums.* Tokyo, Kodansha International Ltd, 1978. 348p.

21A *On view. A guide to museum and gallery acquisitions in Great Britain and America.* London, Plaistow Publications. Annual.

22 *The world of learning.* London, Europa. Annual. 2 vols.
Internationales bibliotheks handbuch. World guide to libraries. Pullach bei München, Verlag Dokumentation, 1970-. 4 vols.
Libraries, museums and art galleries yearbook. Cambridge, J Clarke, 1976. 254p.
American library directory, edited by Jaques Cattell Press. 33rd ed. New York, Bowker, 1980. 1698p.
Subject collections: a guide to special book collections and subject emphases as reported by university, college, public, museum and special libraries in the United States and Canada. 5th ed. New York, Bowker, 1978.

23 *Annuaire international des archives. International directory of archives.* Paris, Presses Universitaires de France for *Archivum, Revue internationale des Archives,* 1975. 480p.
Royal Commission on Historical Manuscripts *Record repositories in Great Britain. A geographical directory.* London, HMSO, 1979, 33p.
Scientific and learned societies of Great Britain. London, Allen and Unwin, 1964. 222p.
Directory of British associations and associations in Ireland. London, CBD Research.
Directory of European associations. London, CBD Research. 2 vols.
Encyclopedia of associations. Detroit, Gale Research. 3 vols.

23A Bridson, Gavin and others *Guide to natural history manuscript resources in the British Isles.* London, Bowker, 1978. 600p.

23B Barley, Maurice W *A guide to British topographical collections.* London, Council for British Archaeology, 1974. 159p.

24 *ASLIB directory. Vol 1: Information sources in science, technology and commerce. Vol 2: Information sources in medicine, the social sciences and the humanities.* London, ASLIB, 1977, 1980. 634p. 849p.

References

25   *Annual art sales index.* Weybridge, Art Sales Index Ltd. Annual.
     Art at auction. The year at Sotheby Parke Bernet. London, Sotheby Parke
     Bernet.
     Christie's review of the season. London, Hutchinson/Christie.
25A *Christie's pictorial archive.* London, Mindata, 1979-. Microfiche.
26   *International directory of arts.* 15th ed. Frankfurt, Art Address Verlag
     Müller GmbH; London, G Prior, 1981/82. 2 vols.
     Arts Review yearbook. London, Eaton House. Annual.
27   Ormond, Richard and others (editors) *Dictionary of British portraiture. Vol.
     1: The Middle Ages to the early Georgians: historical figures born before
     1700. Vol. 2: Later Georgians and early Victorians: historical figures born
     between 1700 and 1800. Vol. 3: Victorians. Vol. 4: Twentieth century.*
     London, Batsford, 1979-.
     Neumaier, Linda *National Portrait Gallery, Smithsonian Institute.
     Permanent collection illustrated checklist.* Washington, Smithsonian Press,
     1979, 172p.
     Richter, Gisela M A *The portraits of the Greeks.* Oxford, Phaidon, 1965. 3
     vols. A magnificent earlier survey.
     National Portrait Gallery catalogues:
     Hill, Maureen (editor) *National Portrait Gallery, Concise catalogue
     1856-1969.* London, National Portrait Gallery, 1970. 346p.
     Strong, Roy *National Portrait Gallery. Tudor and Jacobean portraits.*
     London, HMSO, 1969. 2 vols.
     Piper, David *Catalogue of seventeenth century portraits in the National
     Portrait Gallery 1625-1714.* Cambridge, Cambridge University Press,
     1963. 410p.
     Kerslake, John *National Portrait Gallery, Early Georgian portraits.* London.
     HMSO, 1977. 2 vols.
28   **British Museum:**
     O'Donoghue, Freeman *Catalogue of engraved British portraits preserved in
     the Department of Prints and Drawings in the British Museum.* London,
     British Museum Publications, 1914-1925. 6 vols.
     Stephens, Frederick George *Catalogue of political and personal satires
     preserved in the Department of Prints and Drawings in the British Museum*
     (to 1832). London, British Museum Publications. 9 vols.
     University:
     Goodison, J W *Catalogue of Cambridge portraits: the university collection.*
     Cambridge, Cambridge University Press, 1955. 212p.
     Poole, Mrs Reginald Lane *Catalogue of portraits in the possession of the
     university, colleges, city and county of Oxford.* Oxford, Clarendon Press,
     1912-25. 3 vols.
     Yale University portrait index 1701-1951. New Haven, Connecticut, Yale
     University Press, 1951. 185p.
     Learned societies and foundations:
     Catalogue of American portraits in the New York Historical Society. Yale
     University Press, 1974. 2 vols.
     Driver, A H *Catalogue of engraved portraits in the Royal College of*

Sources

Physicians of London. London, Royal College of Physicians. 1952, 219p.

Burgess, Renate *Portraits of doctors and scientists in the Wellcome Institute of the History of Medicine.* London, Wellcome Institute of the History of Medicine, 1973. 459p.

Wolstenholme, Gordon and others *The Royal College of Physicians of London. Portraits. Catalogue II.* Amsterdam, Oxford, Elsevier, 1977. 237p.

29 **A few encyclopedias:**

Encyclopedia of world art. New York, McGraw Hill, 1968. 15 vols.

Encyclopedia of art. London, Pall Mall, 1971. 5 vols.

Biographical dictionaries:

Bénézit, E *Dictionnaire critique et documentaire des peintres, sculpteurs, dessinateurs et graveurs de tous les temps et de tous les pays par un groupe d'écrivains spécialistes français et étrangers.* Paris, Librairie Gründ, 1976. 10 vols.

Kindlers malerei lexikon. Zurich, Kindler, 1964-.

Thieme, Ulrich and others *Allgemeines lexikon der bildenden künstler von der Antike bis zur gegenwart.* Leipzig, Seemann, 1907-50. 37 vols.

Vollmer, Hans *Allgemeines lexikon der bildenden künstler des XX jahrhunderts.* Leipzig, Seemann, 1953-62. 6 vols.

Johnson, J and others *The dictionary of British artists 1880-1940.* Woodbridge, Antique Collectors Club, 1976. 567p.

Some more specialized dictionaries:

Fisher, Stanley William *A dictionary of watercolour painters 1750-1900.* London, Foulsham, 1972. 245p.

Mallalieu, H L *The dictionary of British watercolour artists up to 1920.* Woodbridge, Antique Collectors Club, 1976. 299p.

Grant, Maurice Harold *A dictionary of British landscape painters from the 16th century to the early 20th century.* Leigh-on-Sea, F Lewis, 1952, reprinted 1976. 236p.

Burbidge, R Brinsley *A dictionary of British flower, fruit and still life painters.* Leigh-on-Sea, F Lewis, 1974. 2 vols.

Wood, J C *A dictionary of British animal painters.* Leigh-on-Sea, F Lewis. 76p.

Lewis, Frank *A dictionary of British bird painters.* Leigh-on-Sea, F Lewis, 1974. 47p.

Wilson, Arnold *A dictionary of British military painters.* Leigh-on-Sea, F Lewis, 1972. 58p.

Wilson, Arnold *A dictionary of British marine painters.* Leigh-on-Sea, F Lewis, 1970. 90p.

Lewis, Frank *A dictionary of British historical painters.* Leigh-on-Sea, F Lewis, 1979. 70p.

Some more detailed surveys and censuses:

McCoy, Garnett *Archives of American art. A directory of resources.* New York, Bowker, 1972. 163p.

The Marburger index. Photographic documentation of art in Germany. Munich, K G Saur, 1977-81. 5,000 microfiches when complete.

References

Wright, Christopher *Old master paintings in Britain. An index of continental old master paintings executed before c. 1800 in public collections in the United Kingdom.* London, Sotheby Parke Bernet, 1976. 287p.

Fredericksen, Burton B and others *Census of pre-nineteenth century Italian paintings in North American public collections.* Cambridge, Massachusetts, Harvard University Press, 1972. 678p.

30 Abse, Joan *The art galleries of Britain and Ireland. A guide to their collections.* London, Sidgwick and Jackson, 1975. 248p.

Blunt, Anthony and others *The nation's pictures; a guide to the chief national and municipal picture galleries of England, Scotland and Wales.* London, Chatto and Windus, 1950. 300p.

Beall, Karen F (compiler) *American prints in the Library of Congress. A catalog of the collection.* Baltimore, Johns Hopkins University Press for the Library of Congress, 1970. 568p.

Vanderbilt, Paul *Guide to the special collections of prints and photographs in the Library of Congress.* Washington, Library of Congress, 1955. 200p.

National Gallery *Illustrated general catalogue.* London, National Gallery, 1973. 842p.

31 *Catalogs of the art exhibition collection of the Arts Library, University of California at Santa Barbara.* Cambridge, Chadwyck-Healey, 1977. Microfiche.

Victoria and Albert Museum. *National Art Library catalogue.*

Catalogue of exhibition catalogues. Boston, G K Hall, 1972. 623p.

31A *Art exhibition catalogues on microfiche.* Cambridge, Chadwyck-Healey. Series.

32 **Some addresses:**

Photographie Giraudon, 9 rue des Beaux Arts, Paris 6, France.

Ets. Bulloz, 21 rue Bonaparte, Paris 6, France.

Fratelli Alinari, Via Nazionale 6, 50123 Florence, Italy.

Scala, Via Chantigiana, 50011 Antella, Florence, Italy.

Bildarchiv Foto Marburg, Ernst von Hulsen Haus, 355 Marburg, Lahn, Federal Republic of Germany.

32A *Catalogue of colour reproductions of paintings prior to 1860.* 10th ed. Paris, UNESCO, 1977. 525p.

Catalogue of reproductions of paintings 1860-1973. Paris, UNESCO, 1974. 549p.

33 Evans, Hilary and Mary *Picture researcher's handbook. An international guide to picture sources – and how to use them.* 2nd ed. London, Saturday Ventures, 1979. 328p.

34 *IIP register.* Ware, IIP. Annual.

35 *Writer's and artist's yearbook.* London, A & C Black. Annual.

McDarrah, Fred W (editor) *Stock photo and assignment source book. Where to find photographs instantly.* New York, Bowker, 1977. 481p.

McDarrah, Fred W (editor) *Photography market place. The complete book for still photography.* 2nd ed. New York, Bowker, 1977. 502p.

36 Evans, Hilary *The art of picture research. A guide to current practice,*

procedure, techniques and resources. Newton Abbot, David and Charles, 1979. 192p.

37 American Society of Picture Professionals (ASPP), Box 5283, Grand Central Station, New York, NY 10017, USA.

38 Special Libraries Association, 235 Park Avenue South, New York, NY 10003, USA.

39 Shaw, Renata V 'Picture searching 1: Techniques'. *Special Libraries* 62 (12) December 1971. 524-9.

Shaw, Renata V 'Picture searching 2: Tools'. *Special Libraries* 63 (1) January 1972. 13-24.

Fetros, John G 'Cooperative picture searching and collection development'. *Special Libraries* 62 (5/6) May/June 1971. 217-27.

Shaw, Renata V 'Picture professionalism'. *Special Libraries* 65 (10/11) October/November 1974. 421-9.

Shaw, Renata V *Picture searching techniques and tools.* New York, Special Libraries Association, 1973. SLA Bibliography no. 6.

40 Society of Picture Researchers and Editors (SPREd), c/o The Secretary, Box 259, London WC1N 3XX.

4

Selection

Robert F Looney

Picture collections are certainly nothing new but, as library resources, the concept of what a picture is changes from the purely decorative object to the richly informative document. Library users thus rediscover a resource they have been accustomed to all their lives, yet never deliberately viewed as such, and find what appears to be a new source of information. This extraordinary fact is validated almost every day at the Free Library of Philadelphia by users who come into the 50-year-old Print and Picture Department and exclaim with astonishment and delight, 'I never knew you were here!' Let it be said quickly that this is not due to any lack of publicity. The crux of the matter lies in the thinking of the ordinary library user that pictures are for walls alone. Suddenly, a whole new world opens up upon the realization that files of pictures, or visual images, on any one of ten thousand subjects are available upon request! The logic of the existence of such a department has eluded them heretofore, even though they are aware that we live in an age in which visual communication is so vital and widespread as to become commonplace.

Many patrons become curious about the construction and maintenance of the picture collection and ask about the sources of the material, who selects it, and who organizes it. Again, they register surprise on discovering that the answer to these questions is standing in front of them. This of course leads to one of the central aspects of the matter: picture collecting, or choosing images for a specific resource collection, and all of the inherent problems and considerations involved in this job.

FUNCTION OF THE LIBRARY

It is the essential purpose of a picture library to provide visual reference materials for its patrons, and to this end the creative efforts of the librarian or curator are directed. The kinds of visual reference that are selected are determined first of all by the type of library of which these materials are to become a part, whether it be specialized or general, public or private, and secondly by the physical properties of the images themselves. The third major concern is the community that the library serves. Into these three broad categories fall the principal concerns of the picture librarian.

The first consideration is the type of library or the type of collection that is to be built up. Types of picture collections and their specific requirements are legion; there can be as many as there are subjects. Consider, for example, the picture morgue of newspapers and other communications media and the importance of the range of subject matter it collects: events, persons, places — whatever is of current interest finds its place and is useful, not only momentarily, but as future reference. In this way the newspaper morgue takes on historical significance while its concentration is in the facts, the events of the moment.

The collections of historical societies on the other hand are depositories of unique and socially important documents of the past, and their pictures form a vital part of all regional, historical, geographical, and genealogical resources. The growth and development of areas, cities, and settlements of other kinds (religious encampments, industrial complexes, natural resources) attract the concentration of the collector as recorded in visual images. Families and persons of importance to regional as well as natural history are likewise documented.

Institutional and special libraries in most cases contain a bank of visual images. Universities and all types of educational institutions are interested in the record of their growth and activities, out of historical consideration as well as for purposes of future development, for pictures can play an important part in matters of fund raising. This same point is raised in support of industrial development and its relation to the region it occupies and to the economy of the nation. A picture history of a specific industry and a visual record of its operations is frequently called upon to demonstrate the uses and advantages of the industry to the general community.

Scientific organizations, government-directed as well as private, are concerned with reflecting their own image in terms of progress and specific details of accomplishment (programmes, inventions, contributions to the community and society in general) as they relate to the community they serve. A noteworthy example is the federal space research programme and the visual record of all their activities and achievements. As with any other government-sponsored agencies in the forefront of national attention, a picture collection is a necessary part of communications as well as documentary programmes. The nation demands information concerning an agency that it supports with its taxes, and the agency for its own security and knowledge requires a record, visual and written, of its claims toward achievement. The visual material thus collected becomes an integral part of an agency library.

Special libraries of many kinds are to be found throughout the industrial, scientific, and cultural communities. Separate agencies and organizations frequently contain within the corporate structure a library established for their own use, which if developed can serve the community. The public library, however, is called upon to serve the community at large in all its varied aspects and seemingly endless requirements. Again, in an age in which visual communication is as universal as verbal, the relevance of a picture collection is obvious. Indeed, the practicality of a department devoted to visual images is a foregone conclusion. However, such departments existing as separate and independent agencies in public libraries are relatively rare.

In the United States, among the most noteworthy picture collections as described above are those located in the Boston Public Library (Boston, Massachusetts), the New York Public Library (New York City), the Free Library of Philadelphia (Philadelphia, Pennsylvania), and the Library of Congress (Washington, DC). The character of each of these large libraries differs radically. The common characteristic is that all four are open to the public.

In Boston, the concentration is upon original American graphic art while there exist files of reproductions and other types of pictures for study and use in various ways. None of these items is available for loan;

they exist as a reference resource prepared for the academic and cultural community.

In the New York Public Library, the vast picture collection of over two million items is necessarily separate in every sense from the richly stocked original print collection. The former is universal in its subject coverage and contains images in all media. It is a collection widely used by the general public and its materials are used for a multitude of different applications. Its founder was fond of saying that every production in the Broadway theatres since the time of its inception around 1930 was researched in this collection. The materials in the Print Room, on the other hand, constitute one of the great collections in the United States, and its function as a source for study in the fine arts and for works for exhibition in the museums and other cultural institutions throughout the country and indeed the world, is indication enough of a service altogether different from the usual picture collection.

The Print and Picture Department of the Free Library of Philadelphia is organized differently, and its service to the general public therefore varies accordingly. It is primarily an educational resource and its collections combine original art and reproductions and images in all media. The requirements of the public have dictated the selection of material throughout its 50-year history.

The Library of Congress is not a public library in the traditional sense, though the general population of the United States has access to its holdings. Its Print Division contains only original material in all media; every conceivable type of printed image can be found in its seemingly limitless resources. It represents the penultimate collection that exists by public demand.

Thus, the four largest public picture collections are the result of an interaction between the institution of which they form an important part, and the broadest general community in whose service they are specifically engaged: that is, between the server and the served. Therefore, the two basic principles that govern the selection of materials for a picture collection are: the character of the library of which it is a resource agency and the character of the community it serves.

SELECTION PRINCIPLES AND LIMITATIONS

The character of the library, whether general, public or special, determines in part by virtue of the range of its general collection, what visual images are included in its picture files. Such files frequently exist as adjunctive, and reflect the content of the book collection and other resources. In the case of a general public library, the subject coverage approaches the universal, and ideally its picture collection aims at the inclusion of anything a reader *might* request. The paradox here is that such a goal is in itself impossible; however, it is approachable insofar as there is a reasonable limit to the variety of subjects that the average reader *will* ask for, regardless of the range of the picture collection.

Libraries devoted to special subjects, however, quite naturally contain picture files that are limited according to the range of the speciality. Limitations may also be set by the particular community that a library is designed to serve. In the case of an industrial community, for example, the needs of the readers who use the library can be expected to be dominated by the industrial specialities. Where there is a large automobile industry, one will expect to find an extensive collection of visual material related to automobiles and the manufacture thereof. Beyond this, the cultural and recreational needs of a community will likewise be reflected in whatever collections the local library might contain.

The character of the library is in many cases the determining factor in selecting visual material for inclusion in its files. The most obvious examples here are historical and genealogical societies whose express purpose is to act as repositories for all types of material relating to a city, a country, a region, etc. Such archives are meant to contain not only the written record of a given area but also the visual. The concern of the collection is with any material that might relate to the history of the area and, in this way, pictures become documents, just like letters, records, books, or any other permanent source of information.

One discovers, then, that a necessary approach to selection is on the premise that pictures, whatever else they might be, are also documents. The problem of choosing thus becomes less intense and the librarian or curator has increased latitude in the matter of selection. Pictures need not be the highest form of the art of image-making so long as they convey to a varied audience the information that is sought, accurately and clearly. The image need not be suitable for purposes of decoration, so long as it documents its subject reasonably well and educates the viewer honestly.

It is often difficult and sometimes impossible to reorient a particular viewer as to the true nature of a subject when he brings to it a fixed, carefully learned notion of what he believes it to look like. But so long as the librarian knows that the image he presents to the reader, or viewer, is accurate and true, his responsibility is fulfilled.

A second principle in the matter of selection is therefore the quality of the picture. Accuracy of representation is of prime importance. A photograph of a rhinoceros, for example, can be expected to be as true a representation as it is possible to achieve. However, the famous woodcut of the same subject by Albrecht Dürer, or the popular painting by the poster artist who signs his name 'Hug' are also true representations, but in a different sense. Dürer's picture is a *tour-de-force* of detail showing, with the artist's precision, the great beast as he saw it. It is an accurate scientific conception. 'Hug' on the other hand also presents an accurate likeness; he conveys a sense of strength and ferocity in the living animal — a psychological conception. The viewer is thus educated on three levels by these types of image, all accurate and forthright. The photograph is absolute in its presentation; the woodcut shows details that might escape into the shadows of the photograph; the painting conveys a feeling for the nature of the subject.

Further consideration in selecting pictures should be given to the clarity of the image, to the many angles from which the subject may be shown, and to the most appropriate tones, whether in colour or black and white.

The accuracy of any representative image is inherently dependent upon its clarity. To be sure, vague or foggy pictures have their place and are circumscribed by their own qualities of accuracy. But here, the concern is for pure objectivity. To return to the rhinoceros, the clearest image is the most educational and is the starting point for any interpretation of the appearance, or for any understanding of the actual qualities of the subject itself. The student may learn in the most fundamental sense what a rhinoceros is; an artist may determine the approach for his specific interpretation; the scientist may look for precision for his instruction. Clarity of image is thus a necessary consideration in selecting pictures on whatever subject, and determines the usefulness of the file devoted to that subject.

At the same time, the angles from which an image may be shown are important to a true understanding of the actual object. To all viewers the proportions of the subject, whether animal, vegetable or mineral, person, place, or thing, are of the utmost importance. Through the representation of an object from as many points of view as possible, the viewer is able to discover its proportions. A subject cannot be known without an idea of the relation of its parts to the whole.

An artist might be interested only in the torso of an animal, or in a head-on view, or the rear end. A straight view of the side, either in repose or in action, is often called for. This brings to mind the extraordinary photographic studies of animal locomotion made by Edweard Muybridge in the 19th century, as a case in point. Also, the aerial views of landscapes, of buildings, of events in progress, or of small objects, or people at rest, are further examples of the angles to be aware of in selecting images for a collection. There would seem to be no limit to the possibilities of this kind of image, regardless of the subject, hence its importance.

In many instances the colours, or lack thereof, of a given image must be considered. Colour, and light and shade go hand in hand in the depiction of an object. Depth perception is of course dependent upon how well an object is shown in all the variations of its planes, curves, surface textures, by means of the play of light and the colours that are natural to it. It is, therefore, appropriate to select pictures that show the subject in both colour and varying degrees of monochrome. Both are useful, both called for.

Think, for example, of architectural subjects upon which the light falls at various hours of the day and night, and how the shadows cast by angles and walls change character with each passing moment. Think also of sunsets and the richness of colour with which the sky is tinted. There is hardly any scene more dramatic than the forest at mid-day with nearly tangible bands of sunlight piercing through the leaves and lighting the ground in great pools, or the pure white marble of the Acropolis under a full moon. It is easy to judge the importance of tone in views such as these. The physical characteristics of the picture, such as size, format, paper, and medium play an important part in its durability and usefulness.

It is obvious that size is related to clarity and is significant in the use of an image. Very often a small picture is appropriate to a file built around a specific subject because of its crystalline definition; it is so clear an image that it is just as useful in many instances as a much larger one. Yet, the larger images command attention by virtue of their easy visibility. No-one wishes to have to use a magnifying glass, for whatever reason. On the other hand, a picture can be larger than is practical for a given collection, depending of course upon the size of the storage units that are in use. Some flexibility in this regard is in order, however, to prevent the exclusion of large pictures of high quality relevant to the collection.

As for format, experience in this matter seems to indicate that the average size that is most practical is about 8 ½ × 11 inches or 22 × 28 cm. Similarly, if pictures are mounted, the average size of items in the collection as a whole may extend to the dimensions of the mount, which are in turn cut to the dimensions of the storage containers. It would seem that the containers determine the size of the pictures in use, though in actual fact, it is the reverse that is true in most cases.

The paper upon which an image is drawn or printed determines to a large extent the durability of the picture, especially when the particular item becomes part of a collection that is available for loan. Ideally, the images that are printed upon archivally sound papers have a life in excess of 500 years. This means that 100% rag or synthetic stocks are the most desirable but how many commercially produced images come thus? Not many. Hard surface, flat finish papers are next best. But usually the collector must accept whatever he can get! Glossy papers of a weight such as those used in the annual reports provided to stock holders of large corporations are good too. Photographic papers are durable to the extent that the photograph has been carefully processed to relieve it as much as possible of chemicals used in developing. Ordinary book and magazine papers, in spite of their poorer quality, are in most cases surprisingly durable.

The handling of individual items and the use to which they are subjected, especially in regard to loans, are crucial factors. Despite attempts at controls to protect pictures that are lent out, wanton damage and carelessness perpetrated even by some of the most respected institutions, businesses, and individuals, are responsible for their early destruction.

The medium — the technique by which an image is produced, be it an etching, engraving, lithograph, silkscreen print, one of the various types of drawing or painting, or a commercial mechanically-produced print or half-tone — is an important consideration in all phases of selection and the choice is governed by the uses for which an image may be singled out. For the ordinary copyist, the medium is of less concern; he or she is interested in the image as an example or model from which to draw. But for those interested in direct reproduction, as in photography, the medium is of paramount importance. For them, the most useful media are photography, etching, engraving, and such graphic media that are themselves not mechanically reproduced. This leads to a consideration of the uses of a picture collection, which in turn raises the question of the needs of the community which it is built to serve.

First of all, it is the lifestyle of a community that determines the presence or absence of a library — and of course it determines the contents of the library when it exists. The broader the scope of community activities, pursuits and outlook, the larger the population, the range of its cultural development, the greater will be the need for a library and the resources it is required to offer. Even today, a library agency devoted solely to pictures (or printed images) is considered an extra and unnecessary resource, something in the category of a luxury, by the community at large. But this is never the case with those library patrons who discover for themselves its particular uses, and find to their increasing satisfaction the areas of study and research that this visual storehouse enhances so extensively — to say nothing of the sheer pleasure to be gained from it.

A picture collection lists among its users teachers and students of all kinds, designers, theatre, film and television personnel, writers, biographers, artists, cabinet-makers, mechanics, persons from all the professions, etc. Where then is the limit to just what to collect? The answer rests not in subject matter, unless the picture collection in question specializes, but in availability and availability of picture material may be in turn limited by budgetary concerns, staff (or lack thereof), location or inaccessibility, and rarity. In other words, the sky is the limit, unless the collector is found to fix his attention on matters closer to hand!

'WEEDING' THE COLLECTIONS

Once a picture collection has matured, so to speak, like a tree, it must be pruned to ensure a fuller and more refined growth. There are several criteria to govern the process of 'pruning' or 'weeding' as it is called. The first of these is the saddest, the most automatic, and the most frustrating to the public librarian and that is the natural attrition of accidental destruction and loss. This is self-explanatory and affects private, special, and public libraries alike.

A second criteria is unnecessary duplication. Public librarians are less concerned about duplication, however, than keepers of collections that are not open to the heavy use of the general public. It becomes only a question of space, which can be of vital importance to the growth of a collection. The lesser copies of the same image may then be pulled out to allow for newer and different images of the same subject.

Another criteria is condition. The public librarian is concerned daily with the wear and tear to which materials are subjected by visitors and borrowers. This is unavoidable and the results must be dealt with. There are two ways of handling worn-out pictures: the first is to withdraw them from the collection altogether and to discard them, the second is to withdraw but save the image whenever possible (especially if it is in any way valuable to the collection) through photocopying. Pictures are never superseded, except when a better image of the same subject comes along. Then the older one may be discarded provided it has no intrinsic value: for instance, it might bear a signature or other autograph or constitute part of a series of images, etc.

The limitation of storage space is probably the most insistent cause for forced weeding. The frequency of use made of certain pictures gives them some priority over others that have proved to be less valuable to a given file. In this way, the decision as to what to discard becomes easier to make. It is advisable in any case, before discarding any picture, to determine its relation to the collection as a whole and the degree to which it might be rare, or even unique. Weeding is not a job for a novice, but for a seasoned librarian who not only knows from experience how a collection has been used, but also has the vision to foresee future possible uses for specific images as well as for the collection as a whole.

5

Processing

Helen P Harrison

This deals with the preparation of material for inclusion in any collection and involves procedures such as accessioning, captioning, protection or mounting where this is carried out, handling and general preparation of the picture for filing, storage, and subsequent use. The amount of processing required depends upon the function of the library and the way it is used: archive material will probably require more preparation for long-term storage, including some restoration, while copy prints for use in a commercial library may require less preparation for storage and more for usage, such as additional captioning. As with almost all considerations in picture librarianship, the procedures, details, and amount of processing carried out relates directly to the purpose and function of the library. Once these have been clearly defined the librarian can turn to a consideration of the details of preparing the material acquired to suit his particular purpose.

Before deciding on the processing to be carried out the librarian needs to consider the material itself. Is it original or irreplaceable? Is it a copy print which can easily and economically be replaced or will it be difficult to acquire replacements? Is the material for reference, loan, or sale? How long is it hoped that the picture will be kept and how will it be used? Will it be handled frequently and in what situations — inside the library, outside, sent through the mail, used by printers, and so on? All these questions will help to determine the sort of information which must accompany the picture and whether it should be protected or mounted to help prolong its useful life. Against these considerations the librarian should remember that the amount of processing expended on the picture should not exceed the value of the illustration to the particular library, and pictures are not all worth the same to every institution. A poor print may be as valuable for reference purposes, if it is unique or the only example available in a library serving research, as it is useless for reproduction purposes in a library serving a publishing house. Time and effort expended in processing a picture with little useful life is time wasted. There are too many other useful pictures to be dealt with.

This said, however, it is important to retain perspective and another useful maxim for the librarian is that conservation is far less expensive than restoration and procedures for preventing deterioration are much simpler than those for repairing damage.[1] The initial processing of photographs will do much to extend their useful life and a careful selection of materials by the librarian will help to prevent, or at least not exacerbate deterioration.

HANDLING PICTURES

Processing inevitably involves handling the pictures and one of the first lessons any picture librarian has to learn is how to handle the material to do the least damage. A short time spent with a new recruit in order to inculcate habits of clean handling in him or her will pay dividends in a picture library; it is surprising how many people do not understand the basic principles of handling, usually through lack of explanation.

Folding, bending, fingermarks, and the use of most writing materials on pictures are all to be avoided. Folds and bends on photographs are at best semi-permanent and will show if there is any reproduction of the print. Fingermarks, especially if not detected quickly, will deteriorate the surface of the print and ruin a negative. Paperclips or staples are an anathema — they leave a mark on the material initially and if they rust the mark becomes indelible. Anything but the softest lead pencil mark on the back of a print will show through to the surface of the print and on negatives, apart from being indecipherable, cannot be erased. Inadvertent damage can be done by writing on top of photographic materials — the surfaces are very hospitable to pressure and lines from ballpoint pens or hard pencils.

Photographs should be held by the edge wherever possible and the wearing of lint-free cotton gloves, as film editing and cutting staff do, can be recommended if a lot of material is being handled, especially negatives. Clean, dust-free areas should be used for the handling and sorting of pictures, sited well away from likely spillage. Food and drink do not go well with photographic material and prevention is better than cure. Illustrations and photographs should be carried in some protective covering when being taken from one area to another, and never by hand alone. A folder, box, or tray can be used to prevent direct handling. Plastic see-through covers are useful but unless the plastic is inert these should not be used for long-term or permanent storage.

ACCESSIONING

Accessioning involves adding material to a collection and in many libraries it further implies numbering the item with a stock or accessions number. Picture libraries are not uniform in using numbers to identify their prints and if an accessions number does appear it may do so in many guises. Other picture libraries have decided against accessioning by number, sometimes because of the sheer volume of material or because the collection is so small or specialized that another method of identifying prints by place, artist, designer, or architect may suffice.

An accession number may appear as a negative number. This is one of the commonest numbers and if prints are tied in any way to a collection of negatives the number is essential for reference purposes. Each print produced from a negative will have a number unique to that negative and as long as the number is retained the prints can be filed under other headings and manipulated in a subject index. A user requiring the print will then quote the negative number and the negative can be retrieved for processing. This means that handling of the negative can be kept to a minimum and negatives can be kept in secure storage conditions and retrieved quickly from a straightforward numerical sequence, while prints constitute a visible index for selection purposes. Materials on the same negative film or produced in the same job can be referred to by a running number within the negative number, e.g. 5093/1-n. This is sometimes called a job number, particularly if the material is copy photography from original prints. It is useful also for citing frame numbers in a complete roll of contact prints. Each negative frame has a number printed into the edge of the film which is also used as a reference when printed onto the edge of the contact print, e.g. 5095/7a-7, indicating frame 7a-7 of negative 5095.

Other accessions numbers appear as catalogue numbers, for example the Science Museum or the Library of Congress, where numbers from the printed catalogues are associated with the items and reference made from the catalogue number. Shelf numbers are used for material from books in such libraries as the Bodleian or the British Library and again these appear printed on the item. Others, especially art galleries or museums may use collection numbers for reference.

If a library acquires material from several sources these source numbers should be retained for future reference and in order to obtain new prints. Renumbering for the new file is a waste of manpower and destroys the link back to the original. If both negative and positive files are acquired, for example when a complete collection is donated or bought, the original numbering should be retained, although the library may well want to use a prefix or suffix to identify the collection within its own system. Some libraries which lend a great deal of material and do not have a negative file may use only an issue number for the material. This can be confused with a negative number but it refers to a transaction rather than a print.

It is not essential to keep a separate accessions file of the numbers assigned to prints unless it is intended to use it as a negative file or catalogue, or even in the studio as a work record, but it is always useful to have a record of the material. If the accessions record can serve more than one purpose it will be an advantage, although not necessarily to the library. The studio file may provide an adequate record for both departments, especially if the two areas are linked as part of the same institution.

CAPTIONING

Unidentified pictures are almost useless. In a library which exists to provide information and material for publication they are even dangerous. It is necessary to have some accompanying information, such as a title, source, subject, or finding device, to aid both the user and the staff. A caption can range from a full description of the subject of the picture to a note about its subject and source, including a finding device for the negative, depending upon the collection concerned. The picture should carry a note as to the ownership of the print or negative or the number of the original material, with its date, source, copyright — which may be different from the ownership — and the subject, title, or other information about the picture, the photographer where this is relevant, and a filing device if this is different from the numbers already given.

In addition to this, several other pieces of information may be helpful to the specialist user, such as the generation of the material, whether it is original or a print from the original negative or a second or even third-generation print. The process of the original may not be evident from the photograph and is of some importance. Special effects, magnifications, and other pieces of information are necessary for specialized use. Several art libraries use cuttings from catalogues attached to the illustration mount with details about the work concerned.

CAPTION LOCATION

Some captioning or titling is necessary for each picture but there is wide variation in the detail and placement of the various captions. Both prints and negatives need some captioning but they require different treatment. A print may be mounted and if so the caption should appear somewhere on the mount. Negatives also need identification and any numbers should be put on the protective sleeves and never on the negative itself, unless they are applied by a photographic process, such as an edge or key number on 35 mm. roll film which can then be transferred as a frame or key number to a contact print.

In the case of mounted prints a stamped or typed caption can be attached, but rubber stamps and ink pads should be used with care on any prints and should not be used on original or irreplaceable archive copies. In storage the ink may transfer to other materials and damage any prints with which it comes into contact. Many collections of file prints cannot afford to take full precautions against this and have to compromise, only taking due care that the stamp does not foul other material.

Other collections make use of a typed caption which is then tipped on to the edge or back of a print. This method is used particularly by the large photo press agencies such as Camera Press or Keystone Press. The advantages here are those concerned with current use: several copies of the same caption are prepared and these are usually very detailed, giving background information to the shot for use by newspapers or journals. The captions can then be attached to prints and shipped off to syndication customers. The disadvantages for long-term retention are that the glue used may cause deterioration of the print after a period of time in storage, and that the caption may become detached or torn in handling.

The caption should be positioned on the mount so as to facilitate filing and retrieval. Some large picture libraries put the more relevant details on the front of the mount, especially if it is to be filed upright in a cabinet. The user can then flip through the items guided by captions on the top of the mounts and stop where the subject looks interesting to study the print. This helps to reduce unnecessary handling of the material. Other libraries put information on the leading edge of a print for lateral filing. This causes more wear and tear but it also provides more room for the information and greater detail is possible. Others put the information on the back of the print. But whichever way is selected it should be uniform throughout the collection.

Slide captioning is always a major problem because of the small area available. The use of microtypewriters and more than one label allows for technical and library identification and some judiciously abbreviated subject detail.

MOUNTING

One of the major decisions in a picture library is how to display and protect the material to best advantage. This may involve mounting and there are several arguments for and against this. Decisions on whether to mount or not involve questions of handling, access, and retrieval, as well as the use to which the picture will be put in a syndication, loan, or reference situation.

Handling

Pictures which are handled a lot may benefit from a mount which will take the heaviest wear of fingers and pressure. If the mount is of sufficient size the print need never be touched, and a mount can often be used to set off the print to advantage.

Mounting

Access

Material on closed access may not require mounting although some provision must be made for captioning and indexing identification. Material on open access and therefore subject to handling will often have to be mounted to carry the necessary information and prevent undue direct handling by the user. The method of storage will influence the choice of mount as well as the size.

Retrieval

A standard size mount will assist retrieval. If all pictures in a collection are reduced to a common size mount there is less likelihood of the smaller illustrations being lost in among the larger and the uniformity facilitates searching — a uniform system is easier to search than a varied one. If mounting is adopted it is helpful wherever possible to choose a standard size and fit the picture to it, rather than have a series of different sizes, although this may not always be feasible, especially if you are dealing with very different types of material in the same collection, for example wallcharts or posters, standard photographs, and journal illustrations. Reducing the mounts to as few sizes as possible may be the best solution, but in these cases they may require separate filing, especially the large posters and the normal standard photographs.

Syndication

The picture collection in a syndication library may have two functions: the storage of file prints for future use and the immediate syndication of additional copies. In nearly every case prints offered on a syndication service are unmounted but carry a detailed caption. Such photographs are intended for current use and not as part of a library or collection. To spend additional time mounting them would remove any profit from the service, cause delays, and increase shipping costs. But do those prints which are retained for the library for possible future use require any additional treatment? They act as a reference to the negative file of the organization and can be loaned out to other non-syndication users. The sheer volume of prints housed in these libraries normally precludes any additional work on mounting and it is more reasonable to regard them as expendable copy prints to be used with reasonable care so as to avoid unnecessary duplication from the original negative.

Loan

Many of the larger picture libraries work with file prints which they lend out to the user for specific periods, usually ensuring that they retain a master copy in the library in case of accident or loss. The question of whether to mount these loan copies or not has to be considered in the light of the volume of prints, the postal charges involved in shipping prints and mounts as against prints only, the probable wear and tear on the items sent out on loan, and the subsequent replacement costs of damaged items. The librarian must do his or her sums and if the cost of constantly replacing unmounted prints far outstrips the cost of staff time and materials, the case for mounting may be made. If, on the other hand, the librarian considers that the cost of mounting and additional postage is unacceptably high the decision will be to regard the copy prints as expendable and replace them as frequently as necessary.

Reference

A heavily used reference collection with few back-up facilities in the way of negative files or copying facilities may consider mounting illustrations an investment. It will certainly reduce wear and tear and there are no shipping charges to consider. However, it is to be remembered that mounted prints take up more space than unmounted as a general rule and also, if the collection is archival in nature, mounting may damage or alter the original in a unacceptable way, especially if any restoration is contemplated.

To summarize this rather complicated question, the advantages and disadvantages of mounting can be listed, but in making a decision the librarian must be guided by the purpose and function of the collection.

Advantages of Mounting Pictures

1   The standard size or sizes of the mount provide uniformity for the collection, reducing pictures to a common denominator. This provides for ease of handling, storage, and retrieval.

2   The photographs and pictures if correctly mounted are flat and less liable to damage from filing and careless handling.

3   The mount adds its own protection to the material; it will take the worst of the wear and tear of handling rather the print.

4   The mount can be used for titling, an ownership device, captioning and other necessary finding aids, which is preferable to defacing the illustration itself.

5   Another less evident advantage is that the mount could, if necessary, be used for identification as a filing aid. Mounts of a distinctive colour can be used to identify material from a particular picture library, while different coloured mounts can designate different subjects, especially in junior school libraries. This has some advantages but colours fade and there are seldom enough colours to cover the areas required.

6   Lastly, it can be argued that effective, attractive mounting improves the appearance of the illustration, an essential element in the exploitation of the material.

Disadvantages

1   The worst aspect is in the use of harmful mounting materials, sometimes through ignorance, although there is now a lot more advice available to the picture librarian. Mounting board, covers, and adhesives can all contain chemicals or give off gases which are harmful to paper or photographic material.

2   Once a picture is mounted on a stiffer board any damage to the board from cracking or bending will result in cracking or bending of the photograph which may be irreversible.

3   Restoration is more difficult if the picture is mounted and has to be removed before work can be carried out. Removal of the print from its mount may do more damage than the original flaw. A dry mounting tissue is available to relieve this problem: it can be reheated to remove the print, but is more expensive to purchase initially.

4   The time and staff resources necessary to carry out a complete mounting programme are an expense which can only be offset by the anticipated longer life of the material.

5   The cost of transporting a mounted picture is greater than that for

unmounted material but again this has to be considered against the possible advantages of longer life.

MOUNTING PROCEDURES

Illustrations

As with all mounting procedures there should be a large, flat work surface in a clean, dust-free area. Illustrations will probably benefit from mounting; although they may be regarded sometimes as ephemera, they are extremely useful for reference or design reference and redrawing. They are often flimsy, for example dust jackets, or colour magazine pictures, and can be easily torn or dog-eared. Mounting gives them a longer life and makes them look most attractive. However, they have a relatively short life as a rule and the mount should not be worth more than the picture or designed to last a lifetime. Heavy mounts will defeat the object of the exercise.

All illustrations should be trimmed, preferably with a small border which makes the illustration stand out, even on a mount. When cutting, with the aid of scissors or a guillotine or a mounted cutter for stability, the assistant should produce a clean straight edge. This requires a good eye as the whole appearance of the collection can be ruined by a poor cutter, especially in combination with slipshod mounting. This may seem a small consideration, but grubby, badly cut or mounted pictures can distract the attention of the potential user from the value of the picture information. Some have advocated giving this task to one person who has been proved to have a flair and will take an interest in the general appearance of the work and material. It should never be regarded as a boring routine job. Like many other tasks in library work it *is* routine but vital work and if it is not carried out accurately the whole library service suffers. Find an assistant who takes an interest, cultivate the right attitude in him or her, and the collection is off to a very solid start.

The work should be organized in stages. If one assistant is responsible for cutting, mounting, and filing the material, these tasks are best kept separate. A number of illustrations can be prepared at each step and the same procedure applied to several illustrations. Thus, an assistant does not have to move from cutting to mounting to captioning and finally filing one piece of material at a time. Batching the work at each stage saves time. However, there is one aspect of this procedure which requires special attention and that is ensuring that all identification accompanies the illustration until the caption is transcribed to the mount and the correct print is attached to the mount. It is all too easy when cutting illustrations to lose the detailed subject information, as well as the source and date of the illustration. This may be a case for preparing the mount and caption before cutting the material.

The mount is prepared and the material cut ready for attaching. Illustrations are very often glued onto the mount. In selecting an adhesive the cost should be related to the value of the print. Dry mounting may be too expensive in terms of staff time and materials. Glue or library paste can be a quick, cheap and successful solution, although care has to be taken to ensure that the glue is suitable for the purpose. A petrol-based adhesive will stain and make the paper brittle, while a water-based glue may buckle the paper and mount if used too liberally. Adhesive can be applied to the whole surface, or to the edges of the material, or just the corners can be tipped. Of these alternatives, the whole surface treatment is most likely to result in cockling, and tipping the corners only is likely to cause the illustration to come adrift and, as there is more likelihood of something getting between the mount and illustration, there is an increased risk of damage. Pasting the edges gives more contact but care is needed to prevent the adhesive seeping out from the edge of the illustration and sticking itself to other material. One collection has found the use of glue pens helpful for spotting the edge and parts of the centre of an illustration, resulting in a reasonable adhesion without coating the entire surface. The illustration with its adhesive is pressed onto the mount and can be smoothed over with a clean cotton duster, rather than sticky or damp hands.

When mounting illustrations the picture should be centrally placed in the mount, if only one picture is to be housed, with an even space at the left and right sides. Space at the top and bottom is a matter for the library involved; if the caption or other information is to appear on the front of the mount, more space can be left at the bottom, but if other indexing details are used at the top, the spaces may be better left even. It is sometimes helpful, until the assistant gets an eye for the right position, to pencil a light mark on the mount at the corner of the illustration. It can save a messy procedure later on.

More than one illustration can be placed on one mount in some circumstances, but they should always relate to one another in subject matter and not be brought together like a collage, just because the pictures physically fit. This procedure occurs more in schools and colleges of education and usually with illustrations rather than photographs. It depends upon how the collection is to be used and filed, but if there are several versions of the same subject it can be helpful to put them together for easy comparison.

So far, we have only considered illustrations which fit standard-sized mounts, but what of the large illustration, the centrefold from a magazine or several pages of illustrations dealing with the same subject? If the material is too valuable to be folded, then an alternative to mounting has to be sought, but if it will fold, a double or hinged mount can be used and the material housed inside the mount. Similarly, centrefolds and groups of pages can be housed inside double mounts. If they can be attached to the mount this is advisable to prevent loss or damage in storage, but staples should not be used as this will damage surrounding material and mounts.

The use of glue provides a quick, economic method of mounting illustrations, but some libraries need a more permanent and protective mounting technique. Many will find that the added expense of dry mounting is viable for a heavily used, semi-permanent collection, or a commercial library which lends material out or uses a postal loan system. The amount of processing relates to the worth of the picture to a particular library and once again we come back to the function of the library and the needs of the user.

Photographs

Photographs can be treated in a similar way but more factors have to be taken into account because of the nature of the material. Illustrations can be damaged by glue or paste, but photographs may react to the chemicals in the glue and/or mounting materials and be badly damaged. It is possible to mount and use photographs in the same collection as illustrations, and to apply the same methods over a considerable period without noticeable deleterious results, but a library would be advised to house only copy material in this way and to maintain a separate negative file of its photographic prints for further copying. As we see in the next section on storage the procedure is not recommended for archive or 'permanent' collections of original materials.

Photographs can be mounted with adhesive or the use of 'corners' or linen tape hinges (see Section 2.23) or by a dry mounting method. The use of corners is not a permanent method for the tabs are very easy to knock off, may dry out and fall off in a surprisingly short space of time, and do not hold the photograph close to the mount, with the risk of damage to the print. Hinges have similar problems whereby the photograph can be bent or damaged on the mount. Dry mounting is the more permanent method.

The photograph is prepared for mounting in the usual way and all relevant data transferred to the mount. The dry mounting procedure involves the use of a press, mounting tissue, a tacking iron, some cover paper, a heavy weight, and a mounting or matting board. Dry mounting presses vary and the individual instructions will indicate the heat and length of time needed to mount the material. The mount is laid on the matting board, dry mounting tissue is placed and tacked into position with a heated tacking iron, and the photograph laid on the tissue. Alternatively, the tissue can be tacked onto the back of the photograph before being placed on the mounting board and trimmed to size. An added precaution is to lay a piece of cover paper over the face of the photograph to prevent its sticking to the press when heat is applied. The heated press is applied to the materials for about 20-30 seconds depending on the press being used. This method does take more time especially as the best results are achieved by cooling the mounted print under pressure.[2] The whole process can take up to 12 hours if this cooling process is used — the photograph is placed under glass and a dry mount weight — but this is not an essential part of the mounting procedure, only an added refinement to the technique.

The process as described is of course more time-consuming than the others, but it is the more permanent and for many libraries a useful tool. Some dry mounting tissues are manufactured which can be reheated on a press enabling the photograph to be removed for restoration or repair before remounting. The initial cost of the dry mounting press, which can be offset against future gains to the collection, ranges from £150 to £250 in the UK for a softbed press or from £250 to £550 for a hardbed press which can be used for heatsealing and lamination in addition. Dry mounting tissue also has to be budgeted for.

Contact Prints

When there are a number of prints on one subject it may not be economic for the owner to print up each negative frame. This is frequently the case with photographers' collections (see Section 2.34). A photographer may wish to send a wide selection of material for consideration and one of the best ways of doing this is to produce sheets of contact prints (usually black and white). These are labelled with an ownership identification and a negative or roll number. In printing the contacts the key numbers on the edge of the negative are transferred to the print for frame reference. When the user selects a picture he or she simply quotes a negative number and the actual frame number from the edge of the print. These contact prints can be mounted and filed in the normal way with other photographs in the collection, and any subject arrangement or indexing carried out using the contact prints, leaving the negatives in relatively safe storage. If there are other photographs in the collection the same method of mounting can be used, including on the mount full identification of source/photographer, negative and frame numbers covered by the particular contact, and subject identification including date and place. If there are a large number of contacts they can be filed separately in boxes or clipped into folders. These are dispensable prints and do not require the same stringent precautions as other originals or larger copy prints, although they will quickly show the results of careless handling, as will any print.

Slides

This is a topic in itself and has been dealt with fully in specialized publications, but as many libraries possess slides as part of their picture collection it is worth mentioning the procedures briefly. Further detailed information is available in the MACAA guides.[3]

Slides are usually housed as 2×2 inch transparencies in most picture libraries. A slide is a film transparency and as such is liable to serious damage from handling and especially sticky fingers touching the emulsion surface. The mounting of slides is an advisable precaution in any library situation, and these mounts can be purpose-built in specialist libraries from cardboard or plastic with glass frames to cover the slide area. The commonest type of mount used in libraries where slides are handled to any extent is the glass and plastic mount. Several manufacturers produce mounts in two parts ready for the user to insert the slide and join the two parts together, either by hand which is quite possible with many brands, or with the aid of a mounting jig if large quantities of slides are involved.[3] The mounting jig helps to align the slide image correctly and then exerts pressure on the edges of the slide mount to seal it. This process is reversible, with care, and the mounts can be used again.

The labelling of slides is something of a problem, for two reasons: the small area available for information and the rejection by many mounts of ink and/or label adhesives. Some mounts indeed are so thick that the addition of a label means the mount will stick in most projectors and, of course, if a projector overheats and melts the adhesive even further problems arise. Gepe is one of the most successful mounts in use in the UK and a permanent ink manufactured by Swan Stabilo allows fine-line indelible writing on the mount. Most people prefer to use self-adhesive labels with a microtypewriter. If enough information cannot be put on one label another can be used on a different surface of the slide mount.

Negatives

As a general rule it should not be necessary to mount negatives. They are kept as a separate collection, in most circumstances, for the following reasons:

1   They are not needed in the process of selection by the user. Copy prints are used instead.

2   They are required by the photographic studio or department for the production of copy prints.

3   They are housed elsewhere from the prints as a safety precaution. If one collection is damaged the other can be used to help relieve the situation.

Therefore, the mounting of negatives can be better described as the preparation for storage. However, there is another form of material closely allied to negatives which sometimes has to be accommodated in the library — the colour transparency (usually Ektachrome or diapositive). A major factor in the storage of all negatives and diapositives is to protect the material from direct handling up to the point where it is actually processed to produce a copy. In other words, the material should only be uncovered when in a photographic studio or processing laboratory. In order to achieve this a see-through mounting envelope should be considered for film emulsion reacts to chemicals or gases given off by adhesives, cardboard boxes, low grade or kraft paper, or glassine envelopes. A see-through envelope is desirable because the material will not need to be withdrawn from the cover for inspection and the mount can take the brunt of the handling. Polyester or polythene transparent envelopes are useful but even here some care has to be taken to avoid condensation and reaction between film and cover. Putting damp film into plastic envelopes will make them adhere to the cover and strip the emulsion off the film while high-humidity storage conditions will aggravate the situation. If the storage envelope has an adhesive seam at any point the emulsion side should be stored away from that seam, and it is better not to use such covers for long-term storage as will be seen in the section on storage.

Negatives can be stored singly or in strips according to the size. Strip mounting entails slipping a length of negative into a plastic sleeve and several strips can be accommodated in one mount. Identification is normally minimal for negative material, consisting of a negative number used as a filing tool and the use of key or frame numbers printed on the edge of the negative film. Used in association with contact prints, this is as effective an arrangement of negatives as any other and means that very little additional information has to be included on the negative mount or cover. Any additional information needed should always be put on the cover or mount and never directly onto the negative itself. Small self-adhesive labels can be typed and attached to both plastic and paper envelopes or it is possible to type or write directly onto opaque envelopes (an injunction not to do this with the negative inside should not be necessary!).

Glass negatives require special handling and storage and have become more of a conservation concern since the advent of the flexible negative. They are therefore dealt with fully in Section 1.6.

PROCESSING FOR FILING AND STORAGE

The considerations for deciding on the filing and storage systems in use can be found elsewhere in this manual but whatever system is chosen, the pictures have to be processed or visibly indexed in some way in order to fit the system. Each print or illustration needs an identifying mark or a filing aid which will serve two main functions: firstly, it will assist the user in finding his or her way about the collections and in selecting the material required and, secondly, it will aid the library staff in rapid, accurate filing of the item.

1 *Assisting the User*

If the pictures are self-indexed or dependent upon a catalogue, the filing device or subject heading should be the first thing the user sees either on a file containing the heading or on the individual item. Filing in boxes or vertical filing implies that this device should be on the face of the item or mount, preferably at the top. With lateral, vertical filing, the device can be placed on the back of the illustration or mount or folder. Each folder containing groups of illustrations should also be indexed with the subject. If boxes and folders are labelled in this way a complete box or folder can be removed from the file and taken to a nearby flat surface for closer scrutiny. In addition, each item with a box must be labelled with the filing aid for that container to aid the library staff in rapid refiling. Using the edge of the folders or guide tabs at frequent intervals for subject headings aids both user and staff, as well as reducing wear and tear on the illustration. The subject heading is probably the easiest device for the user in retrieving material and it may or may not be related to a classification number, depending upon the scheme used. If it is, both should be on the 'leading edge' of the illustration for quick reference.

2 *Assisting Staff*

For filing and refiling purposes the classification number or accessions number if this is used is the simplest and quickest device for the staff to use. Again, this should be somewhere on a 'leading edge', that is the first edge the user of the file comes to, be it top, front, or back. It has, however, been rightly argued that filing by number alone does not encourage staff to take an interest in the contents of the collection and the tendency to transpose numbers can result in misfiling.

As has been indicated in discussing captioning there is usually a great deal of data to be included in a caption and it is not argued here that all such information should be included on the face of the illustration. This detail would distract the user's attention from the picture and clutter the front surface. Rather, one should include just sufficient information in a prominent position to identify the item for user and staff and leave further expansion to the back of the material.

As much of the information as possible should be transferred to the mount before the illustration is added. This means that if the mount will accept typed information, the illustration is not damaged by going through a typewriter, nor is it marked inadvertently by written information. If information has to be put on after mounting, a typed self-adhesive label can be used, but many sticky labels will cause problems and this should only be used in emergency.

After processing the illustrations, labels are needed for any new or additional files. Boxes should be edge-labelled with appropriate subject headings indicating the contents, and vertical and lateral files have guide tabs made out for each division of the file.

Large illustrations, maps, or architectural drawings can be shelved horizontally in map cabinets with shallow drawers. This ensures that not too many plans are kept in one drawer and makes for easier retrieval of appropriate items. Marking the lower edges of drawings and plans helps to reduce wear and tear from clumsily looking for information in several places and it is the first part of the item the user will see in searching the file. Each drawer should be clearly marked to show its contents, again to save wear and tear in handling.

ADDITIONAL PROTECTION

While mounting is one means of protecting illustrations, additional protection may be necessary for many of the materials encountered. Some may be fragile and need protection from even minimal handling or the environment. Original material from which duplicates can be made, such as negatives or worse still, glass negatives, requires more stringent measures than other items. Other material may be expected to suffer rough handling or, by its very nature, be subject to tears and other damage, particularly in schools and colleges where large format illustrations like posters, wallcharts, maps, and plans are useful educational aids, designed to be hung and or pinned to walls and notice-boards.

Much additional protection falls into the area of conservation and the treatment of valuable or fragile items and is dealt with in the section on conservation. The protection of negatives has been mentioned in several areas and the main considerations noted, primarily: to cover negatives when not in use, not to allow indiscriminate reference to negatives, and to keep them away from heat and light sources.

Dry mounting of illustrations is regarded as one method of protection and after mounting the picture is often covered by another sheet of material to give further protection. This process is known as lamination and, while dry mounting is relatively expensive in a school library, lamination is even more so. However, it undoubtedly extends the life of the item by protecting it from dust, dirt, and tearing. As Nancy Schrock points out in Section 1.6 this process is not suitable for archive materials for it actually fuses the surface of the material to the plastic. A laminated poster or chart will, however, stand up to a great deal of classroom use and lamination or heat sealing may be considered worth while for the more expensive posters and charts. But many of these items are free or relatively cheap and it is not advocated that lamination is carried out indiscriminately. The cost of replacement may be less than the cost of protection and it is also worth noting that many such items are quickly outdated or updated by newer, better materials. Laminating machines are expensive and work on the same principles as dry mounts, but enclose the material in plastic or vinyl rather than forming a bond between item and mount as in the dry mounting process.

Edge binding is often carried out on plans and posters which are to be hung or pinned on walls. The use of binding tape around the edges strengthens the area and holes can be punched into the plan and tape attached ready for hanging, or as a veiled suggestion to pin it up rather than stick it on. Plastic bars with string for hanging can also be attached to wallcharts.

MAINTENANCE OF THE FILE

Material, once processed and included in a collection, requires varying degrees of maintenance, according to the usage, and the original success of the processing or acquisition policies. Maintenance of the file is also related to selection, that is weeding out unwanted material, replacing items with better prints, or the replacement of damaged or lost items. This entails the processing of the new item usually starting from the beginning and using a fresh mount. It is often a false economy to use an old mount for, in removing the original item, the mount may become damaged, or it may be in a poor state, or the caption details may need considerable alteration.

The amount of maintenance required will depend to some extent on the storage conditions and methods of handling. Cramped storage where materials are jammed into too small an area will cause deterioration to both mounts and material and rough handling will do the same. Pictures may have to be remounted if the damage is extensive or removed for restoration purposes. As we have already seen, this is often a difficult procedure and it may be better policy to try and acquire a replacement item.

Minor repairs can be carried out as part of an on-going maintenance policy by the processing staff. It is possible to clean prints and remove many minor blemishes, such as pencil marks or stains. Grease and dirt marks on the mounts can be removed by using a soft eraser or acetone substances. Distilled water can be used on the surface of photographs to remove many fingermarks before deterioration sets in. Reference to the section on conservation will help the librarian decide when to tackle the problem him/herself or when it is best left to an expert.

As has been said before, prevention is better than cure and many other aspects of picture library policy will contribute to maintaining the file in good order. Good housekeeping practices will help to prevent much deterioration. Regular dusting with lint-free cloths or brushes, the use of puffer brushes on prints and slides, vacuum cleaning with a gauze filter as added protection, as well as the use of anti-static cloths will help to minimize the build up of dust particles which cause scratching and abrasion.

REFERENCES

1   Ostroff, E 'Conserving and restoring photographic collections'. *Museum News,* May 1974. 42.
2   Mid America College Art Association. Visual Resources Committee. *Guide to photograph collections.* New Mexico, MACAA, 1978.
3   Mid America College Art Association. Visual Resources Committee. *Guide to equipment for slide maintenance and viewing.* New Mexico, MACAA, 1979.

6

Preservation and Storage

Nancy Carlson Schrock

Preservation encompasses a wide range of activities which attempt to prevent, stop, or retard the deterioration of artifacts. For the librarian, adequate storage within a stable environment is the single most important aspect of preservation. However, preservation should be an integral part of all operations in picture collections, from acquisitions and processing to handling and use. Therefore, this chapter will discuss preservation as an overall principle applied to various aspects of picture librarianship, with special emphasis on storage. In the process, it will differentiate between the needs of archival collections and those in current use.

Archival collections demand the most rigorous standards of preservation and storage since items in them have unique value as artifacts and research material. Use is secondary to their permanent retention for posterity. In contrast, teaching collections of pictures, film strips, and slides may be quickly worn out by use or discarded as the curriculum changes. Many other collections fall between these extremes: having been collected for particular purposes, in time they become valuable visual resources. For example, such ephemeral materials as early postcards record local architecture long since destroyed; soap wrappers or Christmas cards document trends in typography and graphic design. Whenever possible, librarians should attempt to preserve such materials and let posterity judge their value.

Preservation can be viewed as a wise investment in the future health of a collection. Even seemingly 'expendable' teaching materials represent a sizeable investment in library funds for acquisitions and technical processing. While the stringent requirements of archival collections may not apply to every picture library, an understanding of preservation principles and practice will help lengthen the lifespan of all materials.

To date, research into the preservation and storage of library collections has emphasized archival materials, particularly those made of paper. Because of their inherent worth and uniqueness, rare books and manuscripts have been the focus of preservation efforts which have adapted principles and techniques of museum conservation. Active, circulating collections have not received similar attention, perhaps because strict preservation and heavy use are often contradictory. Non-print media have also been neglected. For example, no standards exist for use copies of microfilm on vesicular or diazo films. Colour photography is such a new medium that information about the relative impermanence of various films and processes has appeared only recently. Several new publications on library preservation begin to fill the gap, but more research on actively used and circulating collections is required.

This chapter relies on the published recommendations for archival collections as the basis for guidelines for the preservation and storage of picture collections. Wherever possible, it suggests when and how these guidelines might be adapted for use collections. Each librarian must assess the needs and value of the picture collection and the individual situation.[31-32]

GENERAL CONSIDERATIONS

When developing a preservation policy or selecting specific storage enclosures and equipment, the picture librarian must consider the total operation of the collection.

Users

Who are the users? Are they serious researchers, teachers, students, or the general public? What are their ages and backgrounds? Do they represent a single academic discipline or do they come from many backgrounds or have an interdisciplinary approach?

Patterns of Use

Are the pictures part of a multimedia collection? Are they used individually or as sets? Are they used for teaching large groups or for individual study? How often are materials used? Do they circulate? How many people use the collection at a time? Is browsing important?

Acquisitions

How many items are added each year? What is the projected rate of future expansion? Are acquisitions decisions made by the librarian or dictated by the users?

Cataloguing and Classification

Are materials in classed arrangement or by accession number? Are pictures catalogued as individual items or as sets? Is the same system used for all media? Is it necessary to be able to interfile large numbers of new items within the collection?

Access

Is access open or closed? Does browsing or security take priority?

Long-term Value

What is the research value of the collection for future scholars? Are the pictures unique or duplicates? How much care is necessary to prevent damage during handling? How important is adequate security against theft and vandalism?

Budget

What funds are available for preservation and storage? How flexible is the total budget? Could some acquisitions funds, for example, be diverted for preservation? Can increased processing costs for preservation be justified by the length of time an object will be used?

Space

How much space is available for storage? How flexible is the space? To what extent can the shelving and physical plant be altered? Must space constraints dictate the format of pictures (for example, microforms take less space than hard copy)? Must space constraints dictate the arrangement of media (for example, integrated collections require more space)?

From the answers to these questions, a profile of the picture collection will emerge. Archival collections will emphasize the long-term value of their materials and the need to protect them. Teaching and circulating collections will emphasize use, sometimes at the expense of the materials. The recommendations that follow will examine the options available and their suitability to the needs of various types of picture collections.

MATERIALS

Pictures and their supports are organic materials which deteriorate over time. To retard this inevitable disintegration, librarians should understand the physical nature of materials in relation to the selection, processing, handling, and storage of the paper and photographic objects in their care. Whenever possible, librarians should specify that materials for their collection meet standards of permanence and durability.

Paper is a felted sheet of cellulose fibres — polymers of glucose units — formed by passing a liquid suspension of pulp through a fine screen. Early papers, made by hand from long-fibred rags, have survived in good condition to this day. Unfortunately, changes in papermaking technology since the mid-19th century have caused the quality of paper to decline, primarily due to its inherent acidity. The substitution of unpurified wood fibres for cotton and linen rags, for example, not only produced weaker fibres but also left lignins within the paper; these degrade to form acids. Acids were also added in the form of alum-rosin size. As a result, most book papers produced today should not last more than fifty years; they become yellow, brittle, and eventually crumble.

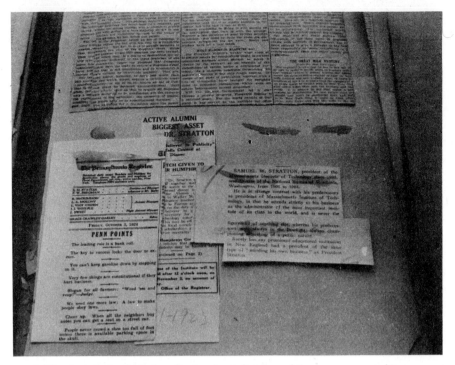

Acidic glues. Stains from the adhesives have discoloured the papers mounted in a scrapbook. *Nancy Carlson Schrock*

However, it is possible to produce modern papers which are both permanent (able to retain their original qualities during storage) and durable (able to withstand use) by using chemically purified wood fibres with a high alpha cellulose content, neutral sizing, and an alkaline buffering agent with a pH of 8.0.

Black and white photographs and negatives consist of a support base covered with a gelatin emulsion containing the metallic silver image. One must be concerned not only with the stability of the base but also with the effect of residual chemicals in the emulsion.

The base of photographic materials is normally film or paper, but can also be metal or glass. Cellulose nitrate film, which was manufactured until 1950, is a particular problem because it can spontaneously ignite at temperatures over 38°C. In contrast, 'safety film', which can be acetate or, more recently, polyester is more stable. Glass plate negatives were used extensively during the 19th century; the images are stable but the glass plates are fragile. Other more rare supports are copper (in daguerreotypes) or iron (in tintypes). However, paper has been the traditional support for photographic prints. Fortunately, photographic paper has typically been of high quality because of its high rag content. Recently, resin (usually polyethylene) coated 'RC' papers have been introduced. They are popular because they drastically reduce processing time. However, RC papers have not yet been proven to be as permanent as traditional photographic papers, especially when displayed in light.

The major cause of photograph deterioration is the presence of residual chemicals (hypo or silver compounds) in the emulsion due to inadequate processing. For maximum permanence, the photographic studio should use fresh chemicals, two fixing baths, and a clearing agent. The photographs should then be washed adequately, treated with hypoeliminator to remove 100% of the residual hypo, and air dried on a screen or between fresh blotters. Detailed instructions for archival processing appear in the publications by Weinstein,[1] Wilhelm,[2-5] and Eastman Kodak.[6-8]

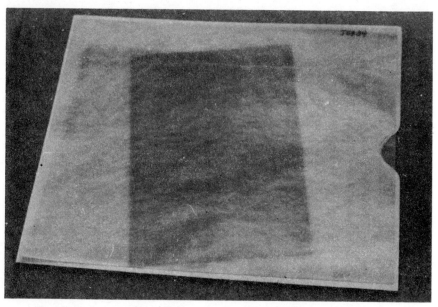

Chemicals from an improperly processed photograph have discoloured and caused the envelope to deteriorate. *Nancy Carlson Schrock*

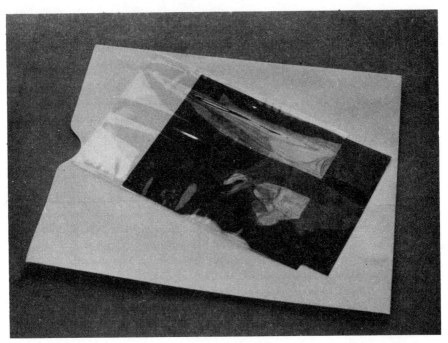

Samples of safe enclosures — polyester sleeves and acid-free envelopes for negatives or photographs. *Nancy Carlson Schrock*

Colour photographic materials present more difficult problems of preservation. Colour photography is a dye process, and all dyes fade over time. Moreover, the three primary dyes in the emulsion layers fade at different rates, thus altering the contrast and the relationships between colours. The lifespan of the film or print varies according to its type. During the sixties, many art slides were produced on motion picture film which had a lifespan of only five years; the cyan dye faded leaving magenta images. Current films, such as Kodachrome or Ektachrome slide duplicating film, have demonstrated a dark storage life of up to 50 years under proper conditions. Henry Wilhelm, who has conducted research on colour prints, notes that those on RC papers appear less stable when subjected to accelerated ageing tests. In his articles in *Afterimage*[3] and *Modern Photography,*[2] he evaluates specific films and their supports for longevity. At present, colour photographs cannot be used for archival records.

Other materials also affect pictures. Most adhesives and tapes used to mount or repair items will leave a permanent stain. Pressure sensitive tapes discolour the object and leave a gummy residue. Ballpoint pens or rubber stamps used to identify photographs can 'bleed' from the reverse and transfer a stain to the image. Paperclips rust and stain or crumple prints and negatives. Rubberbands contain residual sulphur which can leave a damaging stain. Even some plastics can be dangerous; for example, polyvinyl chloride releases hydrochloric acid.

Photographs and Negatives

For maximum permanence, photographic prints and negatives should be subjected to archival processing. Added protection against atmospheric pollutants is gained by using gold or selenium toning on prints. RC papers should be avoided. If new materials have not been properly processed, reprocess them following the directions for archival processing already described. Where the value of the items does not justify the additional cost of archival processing, use a reputable photographic studio which meets high quality commercial standards. Question the commercial photographic dealer about his films and processing. Do not purchase prints made by 'stabilization processes' which substitute chemicals for proper washing because the final prints contain large amounts of chemicals.

Microforms

Master negative microforms should be silver halide film processed for maximum permanence according to BS 1153. Copies may be on diazo or vesicular films.

Slides

Original slides (taken directly from the work of art or architecture) are best, as there is a loss of quality each time a slide is reproduced from another photographic image. Commercial slides should be purchased from a reputable dealer. Know what film and processes he uses. Information about the quality of slides and film stock is included in *Slide buyer's guide* by Nancy DeLaurier.[9] The Art Libraries Society/North America and the Mid America College Art Association have published a joint statement on slide standards which can serve as a guide.[10] Read current literature about the new colour films and their permanence.

When taking copy-slides yourself, use the best possible film. Buy it fresh, store it under the conditions recommended by the manufacturer, and use it as soon as possible. When shooting black and white images, use silver halide films.

Illustrations

There is less opportunity to influence the selection of illustrative material since the librarian must often accept the image wherever she or he can find it. Where possible, newsprint should be avoided because it deteriorates so rapidly. Material on poor quality paper should be separated from original prints or photographs. Illustrations that are soiled should be cleaned (see section on Conservation Treatment) and those with grease spots should not be added to the collection because the grease stain will transfer to other objects.

Gifts of older paper or photographic materials must be carefully inspected for signs of mould or insect infestation since these could spread through the entire collection. Rubberbands, paperclips, and miscellaneous scraps should be removed. Damaged materials should be set aside for special evaluation.

TECHNICAL PROCESSING

Once pictures have been acquired, they must be prepared for storage and use. They should be placed in a format that adequately protects against undue wear and simultaneously meets the needs of users. All materials that contact the picture should meet the same requirements of permanence and durability. Above all, they should not contribute to the deterioration of the object by introducing acidic or unstable materials.

Photographs, Prints, Illustrations

Matting and mounting flat paper objects is essential for the long-term preservation of all types of collections. Archival materials need to be processed so that the original artifact is retained intact and future handling is kept to a minimum. Any processes should meet the conservation requirement of 'reversibility'. Circulating items need to be prepared for enthusiastic and sometimes harsh handling by users. When evaluating the materials available for matting and mounting, select only acid-free, chemically stable supplies that will damage the object least and will wear well. Sources for such materials may be found in Lancefield's *Suppliers' list for archive conservation.*[11]

Historical, vintage, and original photographs (one-of-a-kind prints made at or about the same time as the negatives from which they originate), and original art prints are usually found in archival collections and deserve the care accorded museum objects. The surface should be protected from soil and abrasion, and the work should be supported so that it will not crumple or bend. Dry mounting is not recommended because removing the work from the mount in the future might damage it irreversibly. The following are alternatives:

Matting

Mount the print between two pieces of acid-free 100% rag board (four-ply thickness is usually best but two-ply is also acceptable) hinged together with linen tape. The back board supports the print which is visible through the 'window' cut into the top mount. Attach the print to the back board with Japanese paper and starch paste or secure it at its corners with pieces of acid-free paper and cloth tape. Rubber cement, gummed paper tapes, and pressure-sensitive tapes, such as masking tape, should never be used. Place a piece of acid-free tissue or polyester over the print surface and beneath the window mount to protect it against abrasion. Details appear in Clapp's *Curatorial care of works of art on paper*[16] and in Section 1.5 of this book.

Unmounted

Mounted, or matted, prints require time to prepare and take up a great deal of space. An alternative is to store the original prints unmounted in plastic envelopes. Clear polyester, polythene or triacetate sleeves protect the image while allowing it to be seen; fragile prints might need to be supported inside the sleeve by a piece of acid-free paper. The sleeves can be purchased or can be made from .005 polyester cut to fit over the front and back of the print with an additional 3/8 inch (1 cm.) creased to create a flap; the ends are left open. One also can store prints in acid-free paper

Print mounted in acid-free window mat, hinged with Japanese paper and starch paste. *Nancy Carlson Schrock*

folders. Do *not* store them in glassine or groundwood paper envelopes since these degrade rapidly and release harmful gases.

Circulating and study collections do not require the stringent precautions of archival collections. These are not original works of art — they can usually be replaced — and therefore do not warrant the additional expense of archival processing. These items usually are dry mounted or laminated.

Dry Mounting

Bonding the object onto cardboard is the traditional approach. This has several advantages: the mount board can be a standard size; it protects the object in handling; the object remains flat; labels can be placed on the board rather than the object. Whenever possible, one should use good quality, chemically neutral matt board. Poor quality board is a bad

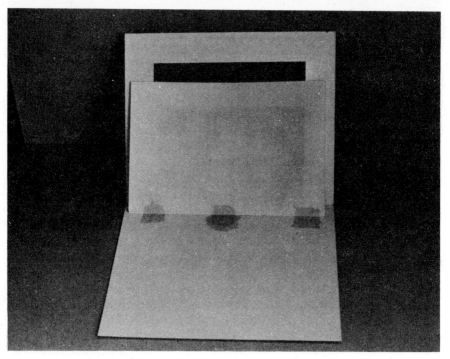

Window mat attached to back board with linen tape. *Nancy Carlson Schrock*

investment as it may deteriorate before the illustration. Its corners will become brittle and chip, and its high acid content will damage the illustration it contacts. Weights lighter than four-ply bend and curl during use; heavier weights add unnecessary bulk to store.

Attach the illustrations to the board with a dry mount press and adhesive tissue according to the manufacturer's instructions (see Section 1.5). Rubber cement, library paste, or tape should never be used. Tissues which can be used at lower temperatures or with a hard rubber roller or plastic squeegee (instead of heat and a press) are useful for colour prints and RC papers which are damaged by high temperatures. As conservation needs are recognized, 'reversible' dry-mount tissues are coming onto the market. The print can be removed by reheating. Such tissues may be preferred for research collections, but until the materials are carefully subjected to accelerated ageing tests, they should be avoided for archival collections.

Lamination

Lamination between a clear, non-glossy plastic might be advisable for teaching materials which circulate widely and are subjected to heavy class-room use, because it protects the illustration from dirt, moisture, and tears. It should never be used for archival materials because it permanently alters the image surface by fusing it to plastic. Lamination can be done with a mounting machine which is expensive. Vinyl sheets or self-adhesive sheets are cheaper but less durable. 'Archival lamination' is discussed under the section on Conservation Treatment later in this chapter.

Slide Binding

When slides are to be handled extensively over a long period of time, they should be mounted between glass to protect the film emulsion from dust, abrasion, and the heat of the projector. Slide sets which remain as a unit in a projection tray or are used infrequently may not need the extra protection, but even they become dusty. Fingerprints and dust which can destroy an unprotected slide can easily be removed from the glass surface. Although slide bindings are expensive and require staff to prepare them, they will prolong the life of a slide.

Slide bindings are available in two types of cover glass: regular and Anti-Newton glass, a special etched glass which prevents the non-emulsion side of the film from sticking to its surface and creating spectrum rings on the screen during projection. Since moisture is believed necessary for Newton rings to form, investing in Anti-Newton glass is especially wise if the storage area is humid.

Commercial slide mounts are plastic or metal. They should be easy to assemble, thin enough to work in the library's projectors, and sturdy enough to withstand the heat of an overheated projector without melting. A detailed evaluation of the brands available appears in the *Guide to equipment for slide maintenance and viewing*.[12] A G Tull has proposed a 'glass contact' binding which sandwiches the film between two pieces of glass which are held together by gummed paper strips.[13] This arrangement eliminates the air pocket in which moisture can condense. Whatever the technique chosen, the film and glass should be clean and the work carefully supervised.

HANDLING

Archival pictures should be handled as carefully as rare books and museum objects. Librarians and their staff should set good examples and instruct users in the rules of the collection. Prints should be picked up with two hands and supported from beneath. Users should have clean hands; fingers should never touch the image surface. Some repositories supply white cotton gloves. Do not allow food, drink, or smoking in the study area. Only pencils should be used when taking notes. Pictures should not be left exposed to the light for prolonged periods of time.

Users should be encouraged to respect circulating collections. They should not write on, tape, or otherwise deface the object, and should handle pictures in the fashion described above. Some libraries circulate pictures in stationers' envelopes to ensure that they will be protected during transit. These envelopes can be marked 'Do not mark, staple, glue, fold, or tear pictures', as an additional reminder. Film strips and slides should circulate in sturdy containers.

Keep equipment for viewing film materials clean and service it regularly. Encourage slide users to use the less intense projector setting and to limit projection time to less than 30 seconds. Never use an arc light or a higher wattage lamp than that recommended by the manufacturer. Prolonged exposure to the intense heat during projection is a major cause of colour fading in slides.

Photocopying

Photocopying is a popular public service usually taken for granted. Fortunately most pictures can be copied without damage, but some do require special care. Fragile items should be supported by a folder of polyester. Since oversize materials larger than the copying surface of the machine can overhang and be damaged, they too should be supported by polyester. Faded images may be damaged by prolonged or continuous exposure to the machine's light. Library staff should monitor the requests for photocopying archival materials, send rare or fragile materials to a qualified photographer, and prohibit any practices that would harm the items.

ENVIRONMENTAL CONTROLS

While the inherent chemical composition of photographic and paper materials determines their initial stability, the environment in which they are stored has a major impact on their permanence. The environmental factors which accelerate the physical and chemical reactions which degrade materials include atmospheric pollution, light, temperature, humidity, and biological agents (a detailed technical discussion appears in Wessel).[14] Unfortunately, most libraries serve centres of population in urban, industrialized areas which usually have the environmental conditions most likely to hasten the rapid demise of picture collections.

The two major types of chemical processes which deteriorate paper are oxidation and hydrolysis. Both shorten the cellulose polymer chain length and thereby make the paper more fragile. Oxidation is caused by atmospheric pollutants, such as nitrogen dioxide, ozone, and peroxides. Hydrolysis is caused by mineral acids which form when sulphur or nitrogen oxides dissolve in moisture in the paper. The rates of oxidation and hydrolysis depend on the temperature: the rate of deterioration at least doubles with every $10\,°C$ rise.

Light can cause paper to fade, yellow, or become brittle, especially in conjunction with pollutants, high temperatures, and humidity. Light of shorter wavelengths (the range of the spectrum from violet and blue of visible light through ultraviolet) enhances the rate of these photochemical reactions; while the larger wavelengths of infrared produce heat which is also damaging. The rate also depends upon the intensity of the light, the time of exposure, the absorptivity of the paper, the presence of lignin, sizing, and other additives, and the amount of oxygen and water other than the cellulose itself (inks, dyes, lignin, size, etc.) while shortening of the cellulose chain length causes paper to turn brittle.

Photographs deteriorate from the same causes which affect both the emulsion and the base. Silver is sensitive to sulphur compounds, especially hydrogen sulphide. Other gases, such as sulphur dioxide and nitrogen dioxide form acids. In areas near the sea, salt may be deposited on surfaces; because it is hygroscopic, it will attract moisture, thus accelerating deterioration.

To slow the deterioration of a collection, the library's environment must be controlled. BS 5454, *Recommendations for the storage and exhibition of archival documents,*[15] specifies conditions for 'long-term storage of archival documents in restricted access' and should be consulted for more details. For use-oriented collections too, BS recommendations can serve as ideal guidelines. They should definitely be consulted whenever a new building or storage area is planned. For a pragmatic approach see the recent recommendations by James Briggs.[33]

Temperature and Humidity

The single most important measure a librarian can take to slow deterioration is to prevent 'cycling' environmental conditions by controlling temperature and relative humidity (RH). Relative humidity over 70% allows mould to grow in photographic emulsion and paper. Insects, such as silverfish and booklice, feed on the mould and can also eat paper, glue, emulsion, etc. Excessive dryness (below 25% RH) causes brittleness. High temperatures are always undesirable; therefore, the librarian should attempt to regulate temperature and humidity within the following ranges:[15]

Paper materials	13-18°C	55-65% RH
Photographic materials (excluding colour and cellulose nitrate film)	10-16°C	30-50% RH
Small repository with a range of media	13-16°C	50-60% RH

Fluctuations in temperature and RH should be kept to a minimum since 'cycling' creates stresses within paper and can produce dimensional changes in the emulsion layer of photographs. Archives and research collections should apply for exemptions from government regulations for energy conservation which restrict the use of heating and cooling equipment. Administrators should be aware that it is false economy to turn off the environmental controls at night or over weekends.

It may not be possible to maintain a frequently used collection at the lower temperatures suggested for archives. Low temperatures are not advisable for film materials needed immediately, such as slides, because film requires time to adjust to warmer ambient temperatures before projection. If the pictures are part of an open-access collection, the conditions also must be comfortable for the users. In this case, the librarian should select a temperature that approaches the optimum for the materials, but is within the range of human comfort (for example, 18-20°C).

To meet these requirements, libraries need to be housed in buildings which provide a clean, regulated environment. Buildings should have a damp-proof course, insulated wall cavities to prevent condensation, and double-glazed windows. Collections should not be housed in damp basements where flooding can occur. Likewise, the top floor should be avoided because of potential leaks from the roof. Ducts and vents for heating and air conditioning should be kept outside storage areas whenever possible.

Libraries should have an adequate heating, ventilating, and air conditioning system. Even in a cool climate like that of Great Britain, air conditioning is desirable for picture collections because it circulates air, lowers and controls the humidity, filters the air, and maintains a constant temperature. A total system is preferable to window or household models which do not control humidity adequately. In a damp climate, dehumidifiers are necessary. An electrical refrigeration-type dehumidifier controlled by a humidistat is best. The equipment should shut off automatically when the water collector is full, unless the water can be piped automatically to a drain. Where central heating causes excessive dryness, humidifiers should be used. Temperature and humidity should be monitored regularly using a thermometer and (for RH) a psychrometer or hygrometer. Recording hygrothermographs provide a written record of fluctuations over long periods of time and, though expensive, could be considered for more valuable collections.

Air Purification

To protect materials from the harmful effects of atmospheric pollutants, incoming air should be cleaned, purified, and circulated. The BS recommendations for archival collections require a filtration system which removes 95% of the dust particles 2μm or more in diameter and reduces the sulphur dioxide content to less than 50 μg/m^3. The air should be circulated continuously, six times an hour, with a 10% intake of fresh air.

Lighting

Paper and photographic materials should be stored away from direct sunlight and fluorescent lights which are rich in ultraviolet. Ideally, they should be stored in darkness. Direct sunlight can be reduced by using heavy curtains or protective blinds. Ultraviolet filters, such as VA or VE Perspex, Uf-3 Plexiglas, or Acrylite OP-2, can be substituted for regular window glass. Ultraviolet shields of the same materials are made to slip over fluorescent tubes. Incandescent lamps generate heat and prolonged exposure to light through exhibition should be avoided (see Exhibition Planning, later in this section). Colour materials are particularly susceptible to fading. Slides should not be projected for more than 30 seconds.

Security

Archival collections require maximum protection against vandalism and theft. The repository should be used solely for document storage; there should be no unsupervised access to any of the rooms or vaults. All installations for utilities should be situated outside the storage area. Library staff should supervise use of materials and should verify their return before the researcher departs. An alarm system should be activated during nights and weekends when the facility closes and staff should check the security devices as part of the closing routine.[34]

Use collections have more problems with security, especially if users have open access. There should be a single entrance/exit where staff members can check users and inspect their belongings as they depart. Circulation systems which are efficient and accurate also promote security.

Fire Protection

Library facilities should meet national and local building codes. Automatic fire detection and alarm systems should be in accordance with CP 109. A non-aqueous sprinkler system is ideal for irreplaceable archives, since water from a sprinkler system can cause great damage, even when it extinguishes a fire. Library staff should know the procedures for fire emergencies and should hold regular fire drills. They should know the locations of extinguishers and how to operate them. The local fire department should be aware of the special needs of a library, particularly the fact that water causes serious damage (see Disaster Preparedness, later in this chapter). Special fire compartments can be constructed to provide additional protection for valuable materials.[34]

Maintenance

Libraries should have a maintenance programme for both the building and its contents. The physical plant should be checked regularly and repairs (especially leaking roof or pipes) made as soon as possible. Windows and doors should be sealed tightly against infiltration of dust or insects. Temperature and humidity should be monitored so that faulty equipment can be noticed immediately. Filtration units in air conditioning units should be checked and replaced as necessary. The fire detection, alarm, and extinguishing systems should be kept in good order.

Good housekeeping is essential to remove particulate matter which causes abrasion and staining when it contacts objects. Dust also encourages insects and vermin. Floors and surfaces should be cleaned with agents that do not damage paper or photographs and no library materials should ever be kept on the floor. Equipment should be serviced regularly. Materials should be repaired when necessary, as described in the section on Conservation Treatment in this chapter.

For small picture collections with limited budgets, the best environmental controls may be too costly. However, any measure is better than none at all. Where it is impossible to air condition an entire building, a window unit could be installed for the picture library. The unit's filters will clean the incoming air to a limited extent. Individual room dehumidifiers and humidifiers are also worth while. For a more modest programme, silica gel or calcium chloride placed within individual cabinets will absorb moisture. Silica gel lasts indefinitely, but when the colour indicator changes from blue to pink, it must be reactivated by heating. Light can be controlled by curtains and blinds on windows, as well as with UV shields on fluorescent lights. If possible, define the more valuable materials and isolate them in storage areas with climate controls. Perhaps the storage area can be separated from the study area, each with its own climate controls. If materials, such as negatives, are used infrequently, they could even be sent to a cooperative storage facility where several institutions share expenses. All librarians can practise good housekeeping — keeping surfaces free from dirt and dust, inspecting circulating items for signs of wear and tear, and keeping equipment in proper repair.

EXHIBITION PLANNING

Environmental controls are particularly important when exhibiting pictures. Exhibitions expose the public to art, encourage potential donors to contribute materials, educate users, and stimulate research. However, exhibitions can also hasten deterioration if special precautions are not taken against excessive exposure to abnormally high light intensities or heat. Colour materials are particularly vulnerable.

Librarians and curators should limit the time material is exhibited from one to three months; they should rotate objects on display; when slides or colour transparencies are exhibited on a light table, the light source should be on an automatic timer. The best solution for photographic prints is to make copies for exhibition and retain the originals in dark storage. Valuable materials should never be exposed indefinitely. When archival materials must be displayed, the guidelines in BS 5454 should be followed.

Ultraviolet light in daylight and in fluorescent light does the most damage. Fluorescent tubes can be fitted with an ultraviolet filter which eliminates wavelengths shorter than 400nm. The transparent portions of a case should likewise be covered with a UV filter. Tungsten lamps emit less UV light, but generate too much heat; a tungsten filament lantern with heat absorbing filter could be used.

The temperature in a case can become quite high, especially when the light source is within the case. Cases should be fitted with filtered vents through which air is drawn with a small fan, if necessary. The temperature and humidity in the case should be monitored with a hygrothermograph.

If prints are to be shown in frames, they should be matted and framed according to the directions in Clapp[16] and Doloff.[17] Their surfaces should be protected by glass, VE or VA perspex, or plexiglass (though the long-term effects of acrylic plastics like perspex or plexiglass on photographs is not yet known). Sectional aluminium frames are least expensive and safest; unbleached wood should never be used.

Adequate security is also important. Cases should be sturdy, locked securely, and placed away from pipes and windows. If irreplaceable documents are to be exhibited, a conservator should be consulted. If materials are to be exhibited outside the institution, they should be carefully packed to minimize damage from fluctuations in temperature and humidity, vibration, and careless handling. The borrowing institution should practise the same stringent safety precautions. Guidelines appear in Banks[18] and Stolow.[19]

Non-rare items may not require the elaborate procedures of archival documents, but many of the same principles should be practised: exposure to direct sunlight should be avoided, the items on display rotated and no object should ever be exhibited permanently.

DISASTER READINESS

Despite precautions, disasters take their toll of library collections. They may result from natural events (floods, earthquakes, fire), from accidents to the control systems (broken pipes, leaking roofs), or, increasingly, from arson or sabotage. A quick response to such crises will save the maximum amount of material.

All libraries should prepare an organized disaster plan. This should include lists of:

— library staff members with responsibilities during a disaster (and their home telephone numbers);
— priorities for salvage, including floor plans identifying the locations of items to save first;
— outside resource people with experience in salvage operations (for photographic materials, locate a professional photographic laboratory equipped to process water damaged films and prints);
— sources for emergency materials and a cold storage facility.

Copies of the plan should be posted throughout the library and kept in the homes of the disaster team members. Staff should be informed of disaster procedures and taught to handle safety equipment, such as fire extinguishers. Detailed guidelines for preparing a disaster plan can be found in Bohem[20] and Waters.[21]

The work after the Florence Flood of 1966, and more recently after the hurricane damage at the Corning Museum of Glass in 1972, has shown that freezing book and paper materials as soon as possible after water damage inhibits the growth of mould. Decisions about drying techniques and restoration can then be delayed until an organized recovery programme is established. Large batches of books and papers have been freeze-dried successfully, a relatively new method of mass treatment.

Procedures for photographic materials are somewhat different. Water-damaged photographs and their enclosures should be kept wet, immersed in plastic containers with clean cold water (18°C or below) to which formaldehyde has been added (15 ml/litre), and then reprocessed. Black and white material should be washed and reprocessed within 36 hours, colour within 48 hours, before the emulsion separates from the base. Use a commercial laboratory (Eastman Kodak provides emergency assistance in the US) or consult Weinstein and Eastman Kodak's preservation pamphlet for in-house procedures.[1-6] If reprocessing this quickly is impossible, photographic materials may be frozen, although the emulsion may be damaged as ice crystals form. At Corning, 6,500 glass photographs frozen immediately after the flood were successfully restored whereas those not frozen until four days later were so damaged by mould that they could not be salvaged.[35]

STORAGE

Besides monitoring the environment, librarians must also select the storage equipment for the picture collection. Their choice will depend upon a variety of factors. Space is a major influence, especially when considering format. Whether various media are integrated or segregated is also crucial. Storage should reflect patterns of use if it is to promote rather than hinder the effective exploitation of the collection.

The format chosen for visual collections will reflect the needs of the users and the nature of the subject matter. Slides are popular for instructing large groups. They take up less space than larger transparencies and are less likely to be damaged. When treated as individual units, they can be regrouped for a great many different talks. Film strips have some of the same advantages in presentation. For example, they are a prepackaged series of images which require no preparation time. On the other hand, they cannot be rearranged. Photographic prints and illustrations do not require expensive viewing equipment but are more difficult to present to large groups. They are more suitable for close personal study and enjoyment. Microforms allow inexpensive reproduction of large numbers of images in a compact format, though viewing equipment is necessary. Sets such as the microfiche of the manuscripts in the Bodleian Library make available research materials never before seen outside the parent institution. Long-term preservation needs should also be considered. For example, black and white photographs on silver halide film will last far longer than colour slides.

Integrated Collections

For teaching collections where pictures are one of many media available to the users, the integrated collection is often the ideal. These media centres focus on students' needs: all information on a single topic should be found together, regardless of format. Since subject content is most important, all formats must use the same classification system. Freedom to browse is essential. Total intershelving is usually possible for books, pamphlets, audio records, pictures, film strips, transparencies, and slides; it is more difficult to combine models, games, kits, motion picture films, and microforms.

Such an approach demands flexible storage and packaging, and more physical space. Although some publishers do issue audiovisual materials in packages that can be shelved beside books, these materials are not standardized. However, they can be placed in standardized containers on regular library shelves. Among the types available from library supply companies are drop-front plastic containers, zipped polyethylene wallets, pamphlet boxes, and looseleaf binders. They usually provide flexible space for slides, cassettes, film strips, and their printed guides. These binders and containers protect the materials from air, provide a compact and sturdy method for circulation, can be labelled like book materials, and can be stored on regular library shelves. Larger materials, such as kits, can be stored in classified sequence on wider bottom shelves.

An alternative to standardized containers is a modular shelving system having slanted shelves with special media inserts. Multimedia cabinets similarly offer a variety of media modules to create an individualized storage system tailored to the needs of a specific collection. However, these cabinets are expensive and awkward for a large expanding collection. Both systems require the media to be separated by format into parallel sequences. Suspended filing rails in standard office filing cabinets can be used for plastic wallets, with sections for slides, cassettes, transparencies, and notes. Any storage system selected for an integrated collection should be carefully coordinated with the cataloguing and classification system so that items can be easily retrieved. Information about suppliers appears in a survey by Davies 1976.[36]

Archival Collections

The priorities of integrated collections are reversed for archival collections: use is secondary to long-term preservation. Since different materials require different temperature and storage conditions for optimum preservation, it is essential to segregate them. Since access normally is limited, the shelving arrangement does not affect the patterns of use. For these reasons, media are rarely integrated in archival collections.

For archival picture collections in particular, where the user must see the image to decide if he/she needs that visual information, it is often advisable to create a copy for preliminary visual needs. This practice also generates copy negatives which preserve information, are available for additional copy prints, and can be used for chemical enhancement of faded photographic images. For example, the Special Collections at the University of California at Los Angeles made two negatives of each of their collection of 19th-century photographs: 4 × 5 inch archival negatives and 35 mm. negatives. The 35 mm. negatives were used to produce teaching slides and to create a visual card catalogue of 3 × 5 inch cards. These were made by printing the image directly onto double-weight semi-mat photographic paper which would also accept typing. As a less expensive solution, the City of Toronto Archives provide access to their 60,000 photographs via photocopies enclosed in polyester sheets arranged in three-ring binders.

Other types of conversion are possible. For small collections of colour prints or photographs, colour slides can serve as an index. Colour photocopies of sheets of slides or individual colour photographs are also effective. Aperture cards which allow space for a transparency can be punched for computer retrievable information. The Yale University archives are currently indexing their architectural records in this way. Microfiche can be effective when several copies are needed for different locations. The goal of all these systems is to allow the user an opportunity to do preliminary visual research without handling the pictures themselves. They promote use of the collection while limiting damage to the objects.

STORAGE EQUIPMENT

Storage equipment should be metal, preferably baked enamel over steel. The materials and finish should comply with BS 826. Wood is less desirable because it absorbs and retains moisture which can cause swelling, warping, and mildew. Wood shelves also take up more space and are more expensive. Basic requirements as stated in BS 5454, Section 8.1.1. are that the equipment:
— be strong enough to carry the potential load
— be made of durable, non-combustible material
— be easily adjustable, without mechanical aids, to accommodate units of varying size and shape, and to permit rational arrangements of records in proper relation to each other
— not have features or properties, such as sharp angles, projections or chemicals (e.g. for fireproofing), damaging to documents or people
— permit free circulation of air.
Detailed specifications for size and load capacities can be found in the Standard. Picture collections are usually housed on standard library shelving, in special media cabinets, or standard library filing cabinets adapted for use. If flooding is possible either from utility pipes or geographic location, materials should be shelved 6 inches (15 cm.) above floor level. The special requirements for each type of material are listed in the following section.

Mobile (compact) shelving is an alternative for limited access collections where space is at a premium. In such a system, moving shelves on tracks create an aisle where needed. Safety devices prevent injuries. Since mobile shelving allows over 50% more material to be housed in a smaller space, the building structure must be able to bear the greater load.

Pictures should be kept in enclosures made of permanent and durable materials. Paper and board should be acid-free (pH 6.5-8). Do not use cardboard made of ground wood. Plastics should be chemically inert and non-destructive. Kodak advises against nitrated and formaldehyde-based plastics, polyvinylchloride, and acrylics, including acrylic lacquer and acrylic enamel. Triacetate, polyester, and polyethylene seem to be safe plastics. Unplasticized polymethyl methacrylate may be used when bending or folding is not necessary.

SPECIAL STORAGE PROBLEMS

Each format has unique problems and special solutions, depending on whether the materials are part of an archival or use collection. Therefore, we will consider the needs of each format separately. The librarian with an integrated collection will have the difficult problem of balancing the storage requirements of the various media with the users' demands for comfort and easy access. The system finally selected for each picture collection will be a compromise between the demands of preservation, budget, and users.

Negatives

Negatives on cellulose nitrate film should be identified and removed from the collection because they can decompose and, in the advanced stages of decomposition, can spontaneously ignite if stored for prolonged periods at temperatures above 38°C. Nitrate film can be identified by placing a 6 mm. square piece of dry film in a test tube of trichlorethylene and shaking the tube to wet the film sample completely (do not inhale the vapours). Cellulose nitrate film sinks; acetate and polyester films float.[37]

Nitrate film should be duplicated onto safety film as soon as possible and then destroyed. Until this time, it should be stored separately in ventilated metal boxes at 21°C or lower with a relative humidity of 30-50%, preferably below 40%. Eastman Kodak advises, 'Unstable or deteriorated nitrate films present hazards similar to explosives and must be handled with the same respect.'[6] Dispose of them with great care, preferably by burning in the open air according to directions from Kodak. If it is necessary to save nitrate film, storage conditions should meet Home Office Regulations (obtainable from HMSO).

Black and white negatives on acetate and polyester film base should be placed in individual enclosures which protect the film from dust and abrasion. In the past, the frequently used kraft paper and glassine envelopes contained chemicals which stained and faded the silver images. The paper itself also became brittle over time, and the animal glues in the centre seams released sulphur and stained. Kraft paper and glassine envelopes should be used only for short-term protection. For long-term storage, paper envelopes should be made of plasticizer-free, chemically stable paper, the edge seams held with a non-destructive adhesive according

Albums of photographs stored in a motorized roll store racking. *The Imperial War Museum, London*

Selecting negatives in a negative store. *The Imperial War Museum, London*

to the American National Standard Institution specifications in ANSI 4.20 and BS 5454. The emulsion side of a negative should be positioned away from the seam for added protection. Illustrated directions for making a seamless paper enclosure appear in Weinstein.[1] Also acceptable are plastic sleeves and envelopes of triacetate, polyester (Mylar), and polyethylene (Tyvek). The added advantage of these materials is their transparency.

Glass-plate negatives are chemically stable but easily broken. They should be separated from film-base negatives, placed in individual enclosures, and stored on edge in metal boxes or cabinets with sturdy dividers which provide support and prevent them from breaking against each other.

If possible, negatives should be stored in a location separate from the picture collection in case of disaster. They should be grouped by size and stored on edge under slight lateral pressure in metal filing cabinets. The temperature should be kept below 21 °C and the RH between 30% and 50%, preferably below 40%. The British Standards Institution suggests 10-16 °C for an archival collection. Negatives deserve special attention since they are the master records of a collection and the source of additional prints and copies.

Colour Negatives and Positives

Although colour negatives and prints are inherently unstable, it is possible to prolong their useful life by careful storage. Low temperature storage in the dark at a controlled humidity is best since the rate of dye fading is thereby minimized. Archival collections of colour materials should be stored in darkness at 2 °C with a relative humidity of 25-30%. Kodak produces moisture-proof heat-seal aluminium foil envelopes which help control humidity if used according to their directions. Henry Wilhelm has suggested that a household frost-free refrigerator can be adapted to store colour materials if a humidity gauge is used to regulate conditions.[5] Colour materials should be allowed to adjust gradually to changes in temperature when taking them in or out of cold storage.

A more expensive alternative is to make black and white separation masters for each colour print or negative. These record the intensities of the three dyes on archivally processed, stable, silver halide film. Such work requires great skill and the expense probably can be justified only for the most valuable records.

113

Photographs, Illustrations, and Prints on Paper

Photographs, prints, and other types of flat paper objects can be treated in a variety of ways, depending on their value and ultimate use.

Archival Collections

These materials should be protected in individual enclosures. Like negatives, photographic prints can be placed in sleeves of inert plastic or in envelopes of acid-free paper meeting the specifications described previously. Original prints and photographs can be matted as works of art. Place illustrations and ephemera like book jackets between folders of acid-free paper. Works of art should be matted. Fragile items can be encapsulated (see Conservation Treatment). Any necessary cataloguing or classification information should be written lightly in pencil on the edge of the verso. Store the folders or individual works flat in archival boxes of buffered, acid-free material of standard sizes. Store them flat on metal shelves.

Where possible, oversized materials, such as posters, maps, and charts, should be unfolded and stored flat in acid-free folders in portfolios or in metal map cabinets. Store rolled materials according to BS 5454, Appendix A.[15] If there is no alternative to folding, follow the recommendations in BS 5454, Appendix B. To prevent unnecessary handling, alternative visual indexes such as those already described are advisable.

Use Collections

Heavily used collections are usually dry mounted on standard-sized board (28 × 21 cm. or 11 × 9 inches). Four-drawer A4 filing cabinets are commonly used. Place the materials in heavy paper folders or between guide cards of mount board (preferably acid-free) with subject headings on the projecting tabs. Unmounted materials can be placed in folders. They also can be stored in suspended folders on tracks set into the cabinets. Although the suspended folders are more expensive initially, they are easier to file and maintain in good order. Slides and other materials in plastic wallets can be interfiled. When estimating space requirements, Vanderbilt suggests 25 mounts per inch, 100 unmounted items per inch.[38] It is easy to browse through mounted materials in vertical cabinets without removing them; they remain in better order and refiling is minimized. The main problem is a tendency to bend and warp unless the mounts are tightly packed.

Another method which is possible for a well-catalogued small collection is to shelve mounts vertically on standard shelves as though they are books. This requires multiple supports to keep the mounts upright and ample guide cards. Browsing is more difficult. Integrated collections could shelve pictures in pamphlet boxes or in envelopes under a single topic within its appropriate classified location. Research collections of less frequently used materials might consider horizontal storage in archival boxes such as those described for archival collections.

Pictures larger than A4 size can be kept flat in map cabinets. The recommended drawer size is 43 (width) × 32 × 2 inches. Oversize materials also can be suspended vertically. Free-standing units are available from library supply dealers and Rodwell describes a less expensive home-made version.[22]

Large public libraries often circulate photographs, prints, and other such materials which are meant to be displayed and enjoyed. Since continued exposure to light is destructive, they normally are not originals. If they are, they should be matted and framed according to the directions in Clapp and Doloff.[16, 17] Reproductions or copies can be dry mounted, permanently framed, and stored upright in storage cabinets. Plexiglas is usually preferred to glass for reproductions because it protects the image and yet will not break under hard use. It can, however, be scratched. A less expensive solution is to store prints in flat file cabinets and supply a commercially available, adjustable frame when the items circulate; this requires more staff time. Preframed reproductions can be purchased from library supply houses or art reproduction dealers.

Slides

When original colour slides are the sole visual record (for example, of a museum collection or the work of an architectural firm), they should be kept in cold storage according to the same rigorous standards described for colour negatives. Copies should be made for use, and the originals should never be projected. However, most slide collections are teaching tools, created to meet the specific demands of faculty and students. An acceptable environment for a use collection kept in dark storage is

18-20°C with a RH of 40%. Prolonged exposure in a projector should be discouraged.

Within integrated collections where slides are purchased and catalogued as discrete sets, shelved with other media, and circulated as units, two types of storage are typical.

Slide, Tray, or Magazine Storage

If an institution uses 35 mm. projectors with slide changing trays, slide sets are most easily stored in these trays in a prearranged order. The slides may not need more expensive, permanent mounts since they are handled so infrequently. Trays are relatively inexpensive and usually come within cardboard or plastic boxes which can be labelled and interfiled with their guides and other media on the same topic. As disadvantages, the trays require a great deal of shelf space and imply a rigid approach to visual information. Therefore, they are not suitable for slide collections which must meet flexible and varied needs.

Plastic Sleeve Storage

Groups of from 12 to 24 slides can be filed in transparent sleeves made of a chemically stable plastic. Sleeves (or wallets) come in standard sizes and have various options for pockets for accompanying cassettes, texts, or other materials. They can fit into a looseleaf notebook which can be labelled and interfiled on shelves in an integrated collection. They can also be suspended in a conventional filing cabinet; a four-drawer A4 filing cabinet can hold up to 10,000 slides at a modest cost. Because the sleeves are transparent, the user has immediate visual access, and browsing is easy; they are also portable. However, there are problems if the collection is large or heavily used. It is time-consuming to refile slides after use, and particularly difficult to interfile new material if entire sheets must be rearranged. The plastic can also trap moisture and promote the growth of mould in a humid environment.

More compact and flexible storage is required for large collections which catalogue, file, and circulate slides as individual entities.

Filing Drawer Cabinets

These cabinets contain sets of drawers set on a bench, table, or custom-made base. Cabinets specifically designed for slides are commercially available or else a standard metal cabinet or wood card catalogue can be adapted with custom-designed inserts which permit either single or group slide filing. Such a system has advantages: it is easy to add new material; guide cards and shelf list information are easily interfiled; and large numbers of slides can be withdrawn at a time. Its major drawback is that browsing is difficult; each slide must be removed for viewing and can be misfiled easily when returned. Slides subjected to this type of heavy use must be mounted between glass to protect the film emulsion.

Visual Display Racks

Up to 100 or more slides can be supported on a metal frame within a display rack. Each storage unit has several racks which can be pulled out individually and illuminated by the light source which is part of the unit. Browsing is easy. However, like the plastic sleeve storage, this system is awkward for a rapidly expanding collection because it takes up more space and new material cannot be interfiled easily. It works best for material filed by accession number.

More extensive information, including names of manufacturers, illustrations of slide storage systems, and diagrams of drawer inserts, can be found in Irvine.[39] Coverage is most comprehensive for file drawer cabinets which are used by the majority of academic slide collections in the United States. The *Guide to equipment for slide maintenance and viewing*[12] also summarizes the types of storage and has a list of manufacturers/distributors which includes a few European firms.

Lantern Slides

Lantern slides, $3\frac{1}{4} \times 4$ inch slides with the black and white silver images printed directly on glass, are still found in institutional collections begun during the 19th and early 20th centuries. The images themselves are stable, though the glass can be cracked or broken during careless use. Usually lantern slides are stored on edge in specially designed wooden containers. Modern metal cabinets can also be adapted for lantern slides with custom-designed inserts. Supporting dividers every five to ten slides are essential or they may fall and crack when groups are removed.

Today lantern slides are nearly obsolete as teaching tools. In the

United States, many institutions are converting entire lantern slide collections to the 35 mm. format. However, original lantern slides should not be discarded automatically. The larger format provides a clearer and sharper image; some are valuable as documents of early photography; others record buildings or art works subsequently destroyed. If a library has no space for its lantern slides, it should offer the material to a larger research institution which can sort and retain the most valuable items.

Film Strips

Film strips are usually 35 mm. colour films with fading problems similar to slides. Although they can be cut, mounted, and treated as slides, this is usually not done. They are purchased commercially as teaching tools and are rarely treated as archival objects. They are usually kept in individual containers which are a standard size according to BS specifications. Typically, they are part of an integrated collection and are placed in the media containers along with their guides and stored on open shelves as previously described. In segregated collections, they can be stored in shallow drawers with dividers of moulded plastic or intersecting slats of wood. They should be inspected periodically and cleaned if soiled (see Conservation Treatment section). The containers should be kept free of dust and mould.

Transparencies

Transparencies are teaching tools for use in overhead projectors. They should be individually mounted to protect them from damage and make them easier to retrieve. Unmounted, they tend to stick together. Transparencies also can be bound with notes in a looseleaf binder or in a 'Flipitran' book which can be used on a projector with a Flipitran viewer. They can also be stored in plastic sleeves.

Microforms

Storage requirements distinguish between two types of microform: master negative microforms for permanent retention and service copies intended for patron use (see Darling).[25] Negative microform masters should be processed and stored according to BS 1153, *Recommendations for the processing and storage of silver-gelatin-type microfilm.*[23] These archivally processed silver gelatin films should be stored in metal cans in fire-proof vaults with environmental controls, as specified earlier for archival negative collections. Cooperative storage with other institutions or in commercial facilities may be more economical. Such films are used only to generate use copies. When the masters are removed from cold storage to a warmer temperature, several hours of 'warm-up' time should be allowed before use. Since they are the permanent archival copies, their long-term survival must be guaranteed.

In contrast, service microforms may be on less expensive and more durable diazo or vesicular films. These films have not yet been proved to be suitably 'archival'. Diazo films are damaged by light and should not be exposed to ultraviolet light for long periods. They can be replaced by additional copies of the silver-gelatin archival copy when they finally do wear out. Service copies should be stored under the general conditions for film collections: 18-20°C and 30-40% RH. Under these conditions, film can be kept in boxes and microfiche as a group in file cabinets. However, if temperature and RH fluctuate, microfilm should be kept in air-tight metal cans and microfiche in individual acid-free envelopes for added protection. Secure microfilm with acid-free paper and string; never use rubberbands. Film should have 18 inch (45 cm.) leaders and tails and be wound loosely. All microforms should be stored vertically. Service viewing equipment regularly and teach users to handle it properly. Inspect microforms after use and encourage users to report tears and scratches (see Conservation Treatment section for repair techniques). Every microform should be inspected at five-year intervals. A programme of regular maintenance will prolong the lifespan of service microforms.

A new format called 'textfiche' has recently appeared in visual collections. Pioneered by the University of Chicago Press, it combines printed text with colour illustrations on fiche. Libraries have approached this combination in different ways. Some have retained text and fiche together either in the book collection or in the picture collection. Others have split the materials, placing the fiche with other microforms or in the slide or visual collection and including a cross-reference in the pocket of the text which is kept in the book library. If the microform storage area has better climate controls, keep the fiche there because of the impermanence of colour films.

CONSERVATION TREATMENT

Conservation is 'the use of chemical and physical procedures both in treatment and in storage to ensure the preservation of a document' (BS 4971: Part 1). Its goal is to maintain each document in usable condition. A related library practice is information preservation which saves the information in a document by transferring it to a more stable material. Extensive conservation treatment is outside the scope of this book and beyond the skill of most picture librarians. Conservation is a highly specialized field which demands an understanding of chemistry and physics to diagnose problems as well as the manual skills to perform the necessary work. Extensive conservation treatment is time-consuming and costly.

Ideally, a library conservator or conservation librarian should review material and prescribe suitable treatment. However, few libraries have such a staff member, and the task falls to the curator, bibliographer, and/or processing librarian who must maintain the collection in good repair. Pearl Berger effectively points out both the difficulties of and necessity for setting up an in-house facility for minor repairs of library materials. While a few rare items may warrant professional treatment, a large volume of non-rare research material needs regular attention in every picture collection. Guidelines are necessary to decide what operations can be done in-house: 'Since the staff of such a workshop will not include a highly trained conservator, its function must be clearly delineated and limited so that there is no danger that lack of sophistication will lead to irreversible damage.'[24]

The first task of the picture librarian is to set criteria for the range of treatments based on the research value of the objects. For example, guidelines might carefully define the following categories:
—rare items with artifactual value which should be sent to a professional conservator
—research items which should be repaired in-house to conservation standards to prolong their useful life
—research items with informational value which can be copied and discarded
—high-use material with currrent interest value only which will eventually be discarded.

The librarian is responsible for diagnosing problems so that the technicians who repair the objects do not receive problems beyond their capabilities. To make these decisions, he or she should be familiar with current developments in library conservation. Publications, such as *Paper Conservation News, Repairers Newsletter, Journal of Photographic Science, Restaurator, PhotographiConservation, Conservation Administration Newsletter,* and publications of the IIC carry information about conservation. Other information appears in *Photographic Journal, Creative Camera Yearbook, Photohistorica* (Newsletter of the European Society for the History of Photography), *International Bulletin for Documentation of the Visual Arts.* Some information occasionally appears in library literature, such as *Art Libraries Journal,* or in museum literature like *Museums Bulletin* or *Museums Journal.*

Much conservation treatment seeks to repair the mistakes of previous caretakers — removing transparent tape or acid backing, reprocessing poorly fixed photographs, removing dirt or mould. Thus, the picture librarian must refrain from repair or processing practices which damage the objects and accelerate their degradation: pressure-sensitive tapes and acidic glues, such as rubber cement; marking the print surface with rubber stamps or ballpoint pen; attaching illustrations with staples, rubberbands, or paperclips; poor housekeeping; acidic mounts and storage containers.

After deciding the kinds of materials to be repaired in-house, the librarian should set up work routines and train staff to execute them. Where possible, a library conservator should be consulted and staff encouraged to attend in-service workshops, such as those sponsored by the Society of Archivists and Camberwell School of Arts and Crafts. Although there are no formal qualifications yet established for photographic conservators in either the UK or the US, an accepted course in paper conservation is probably the best starting point. The staff should be trained and supervised so that their work meets clearly defined standards.

We suggest that picture collections without a staff conservator limit their activities to cleaning and minor repairs of non-rare items in use. All work should be non-destructive and meet the conservation rule of 'reversibility' so that any repairs can be easily undone in the future. Avoid complicated procedures requiring toxic chemicals; use chemically stable and non-destructive repair materials. Although it is difficult to obtain information about new products, it is good practice to purchase from reputable dealers. Consult Lancefield's *Suppliers list for archive conservation.*[11] Set aside a separate space for repair work. The area should be kept clean and neat with large work surfaces, good light and ventilation, and ample storage space for equipment, supplies, and work in progress.

Film

Before handling film, be certain that your hands are clean or else wear disposable cotton gloves. Clean lint and superficial dirt from the film surface with a soft brush. Seemingly insignificant dust particles are annoying when projected onto a large screen. Photographic cleaning fluids can also be used with a lint-free cloth to clean film surfaces (use in a well-ventilated area). Slide film should be carefully cleaned before mounting between clean glass binders. Film lacquer can be applied to unmounted slides for added protection from fingerprints, scratches, and mould.

Film strips and roll microfilm can be cleaned manually or with the same equipment used for 16 mm. and 35 mm. motion picture film. 'Torn film can be repaired in several ways: 1) with a heat splicer which is fast and permanent; 2) with a cement splicer after which the splice should be allowed to set overnight before handling; or 3) with archival quality transparent tape (*not* ordinary cellophane tape), which is adequate for service copies which are not heavily used.'[25] If the film is not an archival master, it may be less expensive to purchase another copy.

Photographic Prints

Photographic images are fragile, and cleaning should be undertaken only if necessary and never on rare materials.[36] Remove surface dirt with a soft brush. Imbedded dirt can be removed with a soft eraser. Film cleaner will remove some grease stains. Stains within the image itself are the result of chemical deterioration of the emulsion and should be referred to a conservator.

Spot-check new acquisitions for residual hypo and silver which can contaminate the rest of the collection. Instructions for preparing the test solutions appear in Ostroff[26] and Weinstein.[1] Whenever there is evidence of residual chemicals, have the photographs reprocessed to archival standards.

Inspect the photograph collection periodically for evidence of deterioration even in storage areas with proper environmental controls. Small collections should be checked completely. Larger collections can be sampled according to type of film, age, source, and size. Examine newer prints every two or three years, older prints every five years, until assured of their stability. Look for an overall yellow stain or uneven brown stains in the silver image in negatives. Look for yellowing, fading, and discoloration in prints. Separate damaged materials and consult a qualified photographer or conservator for advice on treatment.

Paper

These recommendations apply to non-rare items. Unique works of art should be set aside by the curator for attention from a conservator. Pastels and charcoal drawings, for example, could be damaged by dry cleaning. Serious tears within the design should be handled by an expert.

Surface dirt, mould, and slight insect infestation can be removed by:

a low-suction vacuum cleaner (preferably with a gauze filter in the nozzle), moving the nozzle of the cleaner from the centre of the document to the edges, to avoid sucking in the material (use where there is a heavy layer of dirt on the document);

a very soft brush to remove the remaining surface dust or as a first treatment when the material of the document is not strong enough for vacuum treatment;

a lint-free duster to complete the removal of any remaining surface dust;

very soft erasers to remove any dirt which has worked into the material.[27]

Crumbled vinyl eraser, such as an Opaline cleaner, removes a great deal of dirt when rubbed gently into the paper, but do not rub up the fibre surface and remove all crumbs, and never use rubber erasers. Different papers require different types of erasers. Since all dry cleaning is abrasive, begin with the mildest methods.

Simple tears can be mended in-house. Do not use pressure-sensitive tapes unless they conform to BS 4971[27] and are colourless with a pH of 6-8.5 and not liable to cross-link or discolour in the future. It is preferable to repair valuable documents with long-fibred paper (Japanese hand-made papers or Barcham Green's Bodleian papers are frequently used) and starch paste. Directions appear in Clapp[16] and in *The Paper Conservator* 1978[28] volume on 'Manual techniques of paper repairs', which also lists necessary equipment. An alternative for non-rare items is heat-set tissue, such as the kind developed by the Trinity College Conservation Laboratory.

Polyester Encapsulation

Polyester encapsulation (or encasement) is an inexpensive, simple, and extremely effective conservation technique for an in-house repair workshop. When enclosed between two sheets of polyester, even the most brittle paper can be handled without damage. Encapsulation is appropriate for fragile unmounted older pictures, but also may be effective for new items, such as book jackets, which need immediate protection to keep them in their original state. It is also an alternative to lamination and has the added advantage of being easily reversible.

Before encapsulation, acidic paper should be cleaned and deacidified. If a librarian cannot afford to have materials deacidified, she/he should be aware that encapsulation does not stop deterioration. It is a holding action, allowing use of items without destruction, perhaps until mass deacidification is economically feasible. The procedure for encapsulation requires little equipment and can be quickly learned. The document is placed between two larger sheets of polyester (3 mm. thick for small and medium-sized documents, 5 mm. for larger), adhered on four sides with Scotch Double Coated Tape No. 415.[38]

Fumigation

Paper materials which show signs of microbiological or insect attack should be fumigated immediately. Fungicides can be applied directly as a solution to surfaces of shelves and documents or as a gas in a sealed chamber. Details appear in BS 4971.[27] Formaldehyde, thymol, and para-dichlorobenzene are commonly used. Libraries which regularly acquire collections of older material should consider purchasing a fumigation chamber and incorporating fumigation into their processing routine. This is far easier and cheaper than dealing with a full-scale infestation. The long-term effects of fumigation on photographic emulsions is not known. Photographic materials with fungus should be treated according to directions in Eastman Kodak Publication AE-22.[7]

Newspaper being encapsulated in polyester. *Nancy Carlson Schrock*

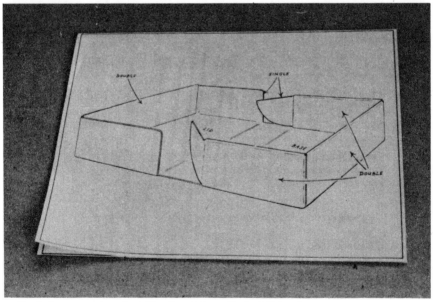

Typical construction of acid-free box. *Nancy Carlson Schrock*

Library staff should not attempt to extend their activities beyond simple cleaning, mending, encapsulation, and fumigation. When additional help is needed, consult a professional conservator. The Crafts Advisory Committee has published *Conservation sourcebook,* a comprehensive guide to conservation resources in England and Wales.[29]

A paper conservator can perform a range of treatments which stabilize the document and prolong its life. Paper can be cleaned with water or solvents, deacidified by aqueous or non-aqueous solutions, resized, and repaired. Stains, acidic backing, pressure-sensitive tape can be removed with solvents. Documents can be strengthened by lining to fabric or tissue with a transparent adhesive according to the recommendations in BS 4971: Part 1:10. At every stage, the object is tested to be certain that each treatment is appropriate and non-destructive. BS 4971: Part 1 describes such work in more detail.[27]

Photographic restoration uses either optical or chemical processes. Both procedures require a darkroom, chemicals, and extensive knowledge of photographic chemistry. Optical techniques restore faded or stained images by rephotographing them with filters and films that minimize the stains and/or intensify the contrast. The original is not touched. Chemical processes clean or otherwise treat the original image itself. When dealing with 19th-century works, it is essential to identify the photographic process since procedures vary for each. Since these treatments involve risk and are usually irreversible, a high quality negative or duplicate print should always be made before work is undertaken. Techniques for treating historical and contemporary photographic materials are summarized in Ostroff and described at length in Weinstein.

A conservation laboratory capable of extensive conservation treatment is the *final* stage in a picture library's preservation programme. It should be undertaken only when proper environmental controls have been provided; for example, an air conditioner and dehumidifier would stabilize an entire collection; treating a limited number of items only to return them to a hot and humid storage room would be short-sighted. The overall needs of the total system should take priority.

INFORMATION PRESERVATION

Not all library materials are unique artifacts which must be preserved in their original state. The enormous quantity of items and high costs of conservation prohibit individual treatment for each picture. In many cases, it may be better to preserve the information content by reproducing the images in a different, more stable format. A variety of options are available, though quality control is essential since visual materials generally demand better quality reproduction than text. The originals can then be discarded or be transferred to an appropriate research collection while the smaller institution retains a use cope more suitable to its needs.

Black and white illustrations on acidic paper, such as newsprint, can be photocopied onto acid-free paper. Several of the newer machines produce a satisfactory image. Lantern slides can be transferred to 35 mm. slides. Illustrations can be microfilmed according to specifications in BS 1153. Colour images present more problems if the colour must be preserved for colour separation negatives are too costly. Slides are possible, but since colour film is not archival, the library will probably also want to retain the originals. Early black and white photographs, especially those with fading images, can be rephotographed and copy prints substituted for use. Ultimately, successive generations of copy prints may be the only effective method of preserving photographs. Like all preservation matters, the decision to reformat and discard must be based on the value, condition, and use of the pictures.

NEW DEVELOPMENTS

If today's preservation problems seem overwhelming, technological developments offer some hope for the picture librarians of the future. The sources of these developments include adaptations of new technology to library needs, new products, and basic research into problems of library preservation.

New communication technology will have the greatest impact on information preservation, transferring visual images to new formats which enable them to be scanned and retrieved more easily without damage to the original. Microtechnology has improved so that high resolution microfilm and fiche can reproduce pictorial material satisfactorily. Colour fiches now allow high fidelity reproduction of colour illustrations at a fraction of the cost of colour printing. If the microform masters are stored under archival conditions, libraries will have a permanent source for replacement copies over the years. Libraries may be able to film their own picture collections and share their holdings with colleagues. The videodisc uses a laser to record up to 54,000 discrete images on a single disc which can be played back on a television screen. By linking the disc to a computer, users have random access to any of the images. Such a system would not only give in-depth subject access, but would also eliminate browsing among the originals and would satisfy all research needs.

Photographic conservation is a developing field. Recent work has produced new techniques for preservation treatment.[30] Neutron activation has successfully produced intensified images of faded photographs. Holographic processes use lasers to transfer colour film into Fourier colour holograms which are recorded onto archival black and white film. Mechanical techniques can separate the emulsion from its cellulose nitrate base and transfer it to safety film. Kodak reports a new technique for improved reproduction of faded transparencies on Ektachrome duplicating film. Additional techniques for treatment will evolve over the years as they have for painting and other artifacts.

As library preservation evolves into a major concern of libraries, basic research should be undertaken to test materials and develop standards for storage, environment, and treatment for libraries with both archival and use collections. Vacuum drying of water damaged books is an example of how the development of effective mass treatment procedures can solve library problems. Research on mass deacidification systems for books is underway at the Public Archives of Canada (using magnesium methoxide), the Library of Congress (diethyl zinc), and formerly at the Barrow Research Laboratory (morpholine). Mass deacidification may be the solution for large collections of illustrations on paper. Research in Great Britain is conducted at the British Museum and the Public Record Office.

REFERENCES

1   Weinstein, Robert A and Larry Booth *Collection, use, and care of historical photographs.* Nashville, Tennessee, American Association for State and Local History, 1977.

References

2   Wilhelm, Henry 'Color print instability'. *Modern Photography* February 1979.

3   Wilhelm, Henry 'Color print instability: a problem for collectors and photographers'. *Afterimage* (6) October 1978. 11-13.

4   Wilhelm, Henry *Procedures for processing and storing black and white photographs for maximum possible permanence.* Grinnell, Iowa, East Street Gallery, 1970.

5   Wilhelm, Henry 'Storing color materials'. *Industrial Photography,* October 1978. 32+.

6   *Preservation of photographs.* Technical Publication F-30. Rochester, New York, Eastman Kodak, 1979.

7   *Prevention and removal of fungus on prints and films.* Technical Publication AE-22. Rochester, New York, Eastman Kodak, 1971.

8   *Storage and care of Kodak color photographs.* Rochester, New York, Eastman Kodak.

9   DeLaurier, Nancy (compiler) *Slide buyer's guide.* New York, College Art Association of America, 1976.

10 'Slide standards'. Joint statement in *ARLIS/NA Newsletter* (6) February 1978. 26-7 and *MACAA Newsletter* 5 summer 1978.

11 Lancefield, R and others *Suppliers list for archive conservation.* Society of Archivists Conservation Group, 1978.

12 Scott, Gillian (editor) *Guide to equipment for slide maintenance and viewing.* Albuquerque, New Mexico, Mid America College Art Association, 1978.

13 Tull, A G 'Film transparencies between glass'. *British Journal of Photography* 125, 1978. 322-3, 349-51, 353.

14 Wessel, Carl J 'Environmental factors affecting the permanence of library materials'. *Deterioration and preservation of library materials.* London, University of Chicago Press, 1970.

15 British Standards Institution. *Recommendations for the storage and exhibition of archival documents.* BS 5454, 1977.

16 Clapp, Anne F *Curatorial care of works of art on paper.* 3rd rev. ed. Oberlin, Ohio, Intermuseum Conservation Association, 1978.

17 Doloff, Francis W and others *How to care for works of art on paper.* 3rd ed. Boston, Museum of Fine Arts, 1979.

18 Banks, Paul 'Preservation of library materials'. *Encyclopedia of library and information science* Vol. 23. New York, Marcel Dekker, 1978. 180-222.

19 Stolow, Nathan 'Conservation standards for works of art in transit and on exhibition'. *Museums and Monuments* (XVII), Geneva, UNESCO, 1979. IIC, 1968. 271-84.

20 Bohem, Hilda *Disaster prevention and disaster preparedness.* Berkeley, California, Task Group on the Preservation of Library Materials, University of California, 1978.

21 Waters, Peter *Procedures for salvage of water-damaged library materials.* 2nd ed. Washington DC, Library of Congress, 1979.

22 Rodwell, S 'Media storage'. *Educational Broadcasting International* 10 March 1977, 16-20.

23 British Standards Institution. *Recommendations for the processing and storage of silver-gelatin-type microfilm.* BS 1153, 1975.

24 Berger, Pearl 'Minor repairs in a small research library; the case for an in-house minor repairs workshop'. *Library Journal* (104) 15 June 1979. 1311-17.

25 Darling, Pamela 'Microforms in Libraries: preservation and storage'. *Microform Review* 5 1976. 93-100.

26 Ostroff, Eugene *Conserving and restoring photographic collections.* rev. ed. Washington DC, American Association of Museums, 1976. Originally published in *Museum News* 1974.

27 British Standards Institution *Repair and allied processes for the conservation of documents.* BS 4971, Part 1, 1973.

28 *The Paper Conservator* (Journal of the Institute of Paper Conservation). 1976-. See especially vol. 3 (1978) on 'Manual techniques of paper repair'.

29 *Conservation sourcebook.* London, Crafts Advisory Committee, 1979.

30 Orth, T W *A selected bibliography on photographic conservation, January 1975- December 1979.* Bibliography no. B 9199. Rochester, New York, Graphic Arts Research Center, Rochester Institute of Technology, 1980.

31 Swartburg, Susan G. *Preserving library materials: a manual.* Metuchen, New Jersey, Scarecrow Press, 1980.

32 Morrow, Carolyn Clark and Steven B. Schoenly *A conservation bibliography for librarians, archivists and administrators.* Troy, New York, Whitson Publishing Company, 1979.

33 Briggs, James R. 'Environmental control of modern records' *The Conservation of library and archive materials and the Graphic Arts,* abstracts and preprints. London, The Society of Archivists and the Institute of Paper Conservation, 1980, 94-103.

34 Walch, Timothy *Archives and manuscripts: a security.* Basic manual series. Chicago, Society of American Archivists, 1977.

35 *The Corning Flood: museum under water.* Corning, New York, Corning Museum of Glass, 1977.

36 Davies, Helen 'Storage of audio visual materials in the library'. *Assistant Librarian,* 69 January 1976, 6-8.

37 Rempel, Siegfried *The care of black and white photographic collections: cleaning and stabilization.* Technical Bulletin, Ottawa, Canadian Conservation Institute, 1980, 21-3.

38 Vanderbilt, Paul 'Filing your photographs: some basic procedures' *History News,* 21, 1966.

39 Irvine, Betty Jo *Slide libraries: a guide for academic institutions, museums, and special collections.* 2nd ed. Littleton, Colorado, Libraries Unlimited, 1979.

7

Arrangement and Indexing

Richard M Wright

What distinguishes pictures from other library materials, such as books, articles, or films? First, the very small amount of information contained in a picture, being momentary, local, and limited to one man's field of vision. If the visual analogue of the book is the film, and that of the film strip or slide set, the article, then the sentence or paragraph has the picture for its analogue. Second, an uncaptioned still picture is not very clearly 'about' anything, indeed it may not even be recognizable as anything other than a pattern unless captioned, for example *Eschericia coli* or 'Saudi Arabia seen from a spacecraft'. Third, pictures do not fall very readily into the framework of the traditional academic disciplines, a point to be taken up later when considering the conventional classification schemes.

Some things and concepts are not picturable, although this is not to say they cannot be symbolized. What can be pictured are natural phenomena: people and their actions and artifacts, animals and their actions. What cannot be pictured, though they can be reproduced or symbolized, include theories, doctrines, beliefs, institutions, and nations. The indexer's attention should focus on what is picturable, that is on the object in the picture and not on actual or possible uses for that picture. Consider, for example, a picture of a ship. This could be used to illustrate travel, holidays, the shipping industry. Picture files and indexes would become impossibly overloaded with cross-references or duplicates if every conceivable use were catered for, and additionally there would always be the unforeseen use. Indexing practice is conditioned by the nature of still pictures.

VARIETY OF PICTURE LIBRARIES

A glance at Part 2 of this book, Evans's *Picture researcher's handbook,*[1] or Wall's *Directory of British photographic collections*[2] will make clear the number and variety of picture libraries. They range from archival collections, like those of the Imperial War Museum or the Victoria and Albert Museum, or press libraries, like that of the Press Association, and the large commercial collections at one end of the scale, to one-man libraries or collections, or the files of individual photographers at the other. The function of the library, together with a consideration of the staff and clientele, will condition indexing practice. The archival collection may well contain prints, engravings, or original paintings, as well as photographs, and some of these will be unique items of high intrinsic value. The Scott Polar Research Institute, for example, has prints, drawings, and very early photographs of polar expeditions. Collections of this kind may have material which is difficult to file in one place because of its format, or is stored in a reserve stock, or otherwise scattered. It is in these circumstances that the provision of a descriptive record of a library item standing in place of the item is of importance when cataloguing. On the other hand, the commercial or press library often has millions of photographs of little or no intrinsic value. Access to the collection is required directly and quickly, and staff and users are not always familiar with the use of catalogues. Here, the retrieval function of cataloguing is important: and it should be designed to direct the user to the item as quickly as possible.

The provision of a separate catalogue is obviously necessary in the case of books, and even more so for films, but its validity for picture collections, except in the special cases noted above, may be doubted. Before embarking on a cataloguing programme one should consider the following points: an 'author' approach to pictures is often not possible as photographers are unknown or unsought; 'titles' of pictures are often arbitrary, unsought, or have reference to the news item or feature article for which they were taken. Additionally, a caption to a picture does not uniquely identify that picture. If a picture costs £1 to produce and £2 to put into the system using conventional methods, these methods are not cost-effective. A library with a stock of several million pictures, and a high intake of, say, 15,000 per annum, may find it impossibly costly and laborious to catalogue its stock. Finally, if a collection is accessible to users, and properly guided and displayed, what need is there for a catalogue?

Having said this, an accessions register of some kind is needed, as a means of stock and circulation control and, in the commercial picture agency, as a means of identifying pictures which have been reproduced, in order that the photographer can be paid.

CATALOGUE ENTRIES

The elements of a catalogue entry should include information under the following headings.

1   What is it about? The subject and a brief description of the content of the picture or the title if it is a named work.

2   What kind of thing is it?
   (a)   The medium, for example photograph, slide, etching, mezzotint. If an item is a copy in one medium of a work in another medium, for example a slide of an original painting, this should be stated.
   (b)   Format normally given as height × width, and increasingly given in centimetres. In the case of slides, film size may be given, or the size of the mount to indicate the type of equipment needed to view the slide.
   (c)   The hue — colour, monochrome, sepia, or tinted — should also be stated in the physical description.

3   Who is responsible for the item, and who owns the rights?
   (a)   The creator, painter, engraver, photographer, etc.
   (b)   The publisher or other body who issued the item if different from (a).
   (c)   The holder of the copyright if different from (a) and (b).
   (d)   In the case of reproductions of items in museums or art galleries, the location of the actual item.

4   Are there any restrictions on the reuse of the item?
  (a) Copyright restrictions, e.g. 'World calendar rights sold', 'Editorial use only!' It is worth remembering that in the case of a person shown recognizably in a picture a model release should be obtained permitting reproduction of the picture.
  (b) If the picture is reproduced, the copyright holder normally expects a credit, and the form or wording should be noted.

5   Administrative information such as:
  (a) the accession number
  (b) the negative number
  (c) any notes on the physical condition or reproducibility of the photographic print held.

Example:
Bignor, Roman villa-Medusa head, photographed by David Baker. Postcard 20 × 25 cm. of mosaic. Reigate, Frith & Sons Ltd. 134598.

Having considered the catalogue entry, the next step is to decide on a policy of indexing the items. Should they be indexed at all, and if so should this be according to a conventional classification scheme, or is the library in a position to adapt one of the special schemes already devised for pictures?

CONVENTIONAL CLASSIFICATION SCHEMES

Schemes, such as Dewey, UDC, or Library of Congress, may be considered for picture collections on the grounds that other media in the library are classified by them, and consequently they are familiar to staff and users. The National Library of Medicine classification has been used for slide collections in medical libraries, Radio Telefís Eireann has used UDC imaginatively for its photographs, and the Scott Polar Research Institute uses its adaptation of UDC for pictures as for other items.

But there are compelling reasons against the use of the book classifications in libraries composed wholly of pictures. Schemes such as UDC are academic and discipline-oriented, seeming always to ask the question, 'Which department in a university would deal with this topic and how would it do so?' Only the use made of a picture, as opposed to the object represented in it can fit the UDC pattern thoroughly. A picture of a person drinking a glass of wine would fit into any of the classes: ethics, religion, social life, domestic life, etc., and, of course, the act of drinking a glass of wine has or could have all these dimensions.

In order to cater for as many of these approaches as possible the picture would need to be filed in a picture library simply as a person drinking, but UDC has no place for this, or indeed for people except as subdivisions of particular subjects or in particular roles. Further, because UDC is discipline-oriented, its placings often run counter to our ordinary ways of thinking and speaking. For example, in ordinary speech we use, understand, and agree upon what falls under the concept of 'bad weather'. But this cannot be specified in book schemes. All that can be specified are meteorological notions such as 'precipitation', 'fog', 'snow'. Not all those wanting pictures of a London street in the rain have a meteorological interest in the subject; they may, for example, just want to sell raincoats.

In a conventional classification many numbers and even main classes would remain unused in picture collections. Simons[3] adduces, rightly, the example of philosophy: 'Try to imagine a picture of philosophy. I think about all you will come up with is a picture of a philosopher.' Certainly, in a picture library, main class numbers and their theoretical subdivisions would be unused because unpicturable; consequently class numbers in this type of library would tend to be more specific and often rather long.

Further, for the commercial or press library, the conventional book scheme is a non-starter. The staff of such libraries are often not trained librarians, and regard the techniques of librarianship, if they know of them, as irrelevant to their problems. Users of such libraries often want material in a very great hurry, and would prefer direct access to the pictures via easily understood natural language headings. 'User training' in the scheme used is impossible in such libraries — there is no time and no 'captive audience' as in college libraries.

Several schemes have been drawn up in particular circumstances dealing with single collections and in considering a scheme the librarian will do well to investigate existing schemes relevant to the subject matter of the collection concerned. Some examples follow showing several different approaches to the problem and indicating the differing degrees of success.

SPECIAL SCHEMES FOR PICTURES

Simons and Tansey[4]

This is described as 'A slide classification system for the organization and automatic indexing of interdisciplinary collections of slides and pictures'. It was designed at the University of California at Santa Cruz to support the programme of interdisciplinary studies there. The desiderata for the scheme were:

1. The collection, and hence the classification, should be general, encompassing the subject matter of all academic disciplines.
2. The arrangement of the collection should reflect a broad, historical, cultural approach to teaching.
3. The filing arrangement of the collection should encourage and facilitate browsing, that is, visual inspection and comparison in the files.
4. In addition to being filed for easy browsing, the collection should be fully catalogued or indexed, preferably by automated means.

Three main subject divisions are used: Art, including all man-made artifacts; Science, natural phenomena and principles, as well as the results of scientific research; and History, everything except Art and Science — people, events, the social and economic environment. Art is assigned to a major category since the scheme's compilers consider that any universal collection of slides will be heavily weighted on the side of the arts. This is just not so. The BBC Hulton Picture Library is 'heavily weighted' in social history. Mary Evans Picture Library contains works of art, such as engravings and prints, carefully organized and filed as items illustrating history. In fact, almost any picture can be considered from an art point of view, but this does not make its subject 'Art'.

Division under each main heading is as follows:

HISTORY
Field   1: Chronological Period
            2: Country
            3: Subject

    4: Subdivision of Subject
    5: Primary Key Word
    6: Format
    7: —
    8: Secondary Key Word
    9: Detail Number
  10: Additional Detail Number

ART
Field
    1: Chronological Period
    2: Country
    3: Medium
    4: Style
    5: Origin (artist or city of origin)
    6: Subject
    7: Subdivision of Subject
    8: Title
    9: Detail Number
  10: Additional Detail Number

SCIENCE
Field
    1: Science Group
    2: Country
    3: Subject
    4: Subdivision of Subject
    5: Primary Key Word
    6: —
    7: —
    8: Secondary Key Word
    9: Format
  10: Detail Number

'Field' above refers to the sort fields for the punched cards on which details of each slide are entered. These punched cards are used for cataloguing and shelf list preparation, using a computer. This provides an elaborate system of retrieval in addition to a file arrangement facility to allow browsing.

Notable is the curious facet order within history, running counter to that of all book classifications, and not, one would have thought, especially visual. The reason for this might well be that the college teaches art and social history in an interdisciplinary way primarily by period and country; but if this is so, why is the scheme advanced as a universal one, capable of adoption by other libraries?

Examples of the practical classification of slides using this method might be:

> Timber felling in the Amazonian forest
> G848E.D
> G   20th century (within History)
> 848   Amazon basin
> E   Forestry
> D   Tree felling

> Primary school classroom, with children
> G370U.E
> G   20th century (within History)
> 370   British Isles or Great Britain
> U   Education
> E   Elementary schools
> *or*
> P370E.C
> P   20th century (within Art)
> 370   British Isles, or Great Britain
> E   Architecture by building type, Education
> C   Classrooms

The class numbers used in the scheme and illustrated here have several drawbacks for others who may adopt them, including an American bias, indicated by the confusion between British Isles and Great Britain, with no means of specifying 'United Kingdom'. Also, there is no way in which the system can specify children, or indeed people in general as opposed to people in occupational roles.

In the second example there is no decision procedure for putting pictures under Art or History. One has to guess that a full classroom would go under History and an empty one under Art.

The Science part of the classification is broken down quite conventionally by subject as follows:

R   Mathematics
S   Astronomy and Space Sciences
T   Earth Sciences
U   Physical Sciences
V   Life Sciences
W   Medical Sciences
X   Technological Research and Engineering

There is provision for country subdivision but if this cannot be done, the number 000 is used.

The classification in this section is a fairly conventional hierarchical one which would not be out of place as a book classification scheme. But, having rightly said in the introduction 'The greater part of a typical book classification... has no meaning for picture classification' and given an example from the Dewey scheme at 320, followed by the statement 'in no case could the listed subject be the visual content of a picture', the authors then break their own principle by including, for example:

RS.P   Probability Theory
RA.A   Numbers, Number Theory

Probability theory cannot, indeed, be the *visual* content of a picture, although the subject can certainly be illustrated by several means including a picture of a formula.

Medical and life sciences are classified in the conventional way known to those familiar with book schemes. This leads to difficulties where, for instance, an ordinary picture of an oak tree would go under *Fagaceae* in a system which is meant to facilitate browsing!

All told, the scheme is a conventional hierarchical one, heavily biassed towards the arts, with an odd facet order, and retaining the traditional academic disciplines and theoretical subdivisions which, as already indicated above, cannot be pictured. It is not especially visual, despite a clear and repeated recognition that visual and printed matter differ as library materials. Simons and Tansey's scheme has no apparent advantages over traditional book schemes as a means of classifying pictures.

Post-coordinate Indexing

Pictures may be considered candidates for coordinate indexing for a number of reasons. For example a picture may be put under a number of different descriptions; a portrait may be described as of a banker, a patron of the arts, or a Renaissance man. Further, many unconnected objects may appear in the same picture. A picture of Regent's Park Canal may have a child cycling along a towpath, people drinking outside a pub, a barge, spring flowers, and so on. Compound subjects occur in pictures as they do in other documents, for example, police cars or primary school buildings. Furthermore, the same reasons for using this form of indexing for other types of collection apply to picture collections. It is possible to bring together material scattered by conventional schemes, and the problems of collocation, significance, and citation order are solved by abolishing them. Coordinate indexing neatly separates the intellectual and clerical tasks in indexing.

Diamond[5] has developed what is in effect a coordinate indexing system, although it is not called such, for the State University College, Fredonia, New York. Wishing to cater for an interdisciplinary approach to slides, Diamond devised a pilot project on European 17th-century history. The objects of the project were to evolve a list of identifiers and test them on a random sample of 150 slides. To this end lists of identifiers were drawn up by specialists in the fields of history, literature, and art history, evaluated by an advisory committee, and then a final list was prepared at a joint meeting. The identifiers were divided into six major areas:

1 What is it? Applied art, architecture, drawing, painting.
2 Who made it? Artist.
3 When? Date of production and date of subject.
4 Where? Where produced and where currently located.
5 Subject. Content and/or function, e.g. if the slide is of a silver saltcellar with a picture of Achilles on it, both 'saltcellar' and 'Achilles' would be indexed.

To put a slide into the system Diamond suggests assignment of the 'maximum number of identifiers that describe its characteristics'. There is no logical upper limit to this, especially as Diamond wants to build into his system a subject's relations with other subjects.

If a person portrayed figured in a sonnet by a named author, Diamond would want to index the author, date, and other details of the sonnet. In one example he gives 23 identifiers assigned to a single slide, which seems an inordinately large number, and which would make both indexing and retrieval very time-consuming and expensive. Moreover, in the pilot project teaching staff were responsible both for compiling the list of identifiers and assigning them to slides, and it was envisaged that they should do so when the system was operational. Teaching staff would surely be better employed in teaching and research. Nowhere in the paper does Diamond quote the annual intake of slides in his collection, but if it is at all large the indexing and assignment procedure does not look cost-effective.

Where Diamond has got the problem right is in realizing that a picture, even if it is a work of art, has different applications in different disciplines, and is not necessarily restricted to any one of them. But he seems to want to build *uses* of pictures into his system, and as previously stated, this must necessarily fail: a picture normally has more than one use. Additionally, as we saw when discussing Simons and Tansey's work, attempts to bring together considerations of the object in a picture as an object and as a work of art are fraught with difficulty.

Shell Photographic Library

The setting up of a coordinate indexing system at this library has been described by McNeil,[6] and its scrapping, together with the reasons for this move, by Scoones.[7]

The coordinate indexing system replaced an inadequate alphabetically arranged scheme. The requirements for the new system were provision for both broad and narrow subject searching and infinite expansibility in all subject areas. A system of keyword indexing using translucent 5,000-hole aperture sheets already in use elsewhere in the Shell organization was selected as meeting these requirements. The 60,000 photographs in the collection were placed in groups according to the main areas of activity within the organization, in effect using these areas as a system of role indicators. This grouping produced nine sequences:

G   General Matters
H   Historical
K   Manufacturing — Chemicals
L   Marketing — Chemicals
M   Manufacturing — Oil
R   Research

S Marketing — Oil
T Transport and Storage
X Exploration and Production

Within these nine sequences photographs were arranged by running number.

The thesaurus was one which was common to all the sequences, specially designed for the photograph library. When completed it reached a total of some 1,200 terms, a total kept deliberately low by using semantic factoring, e.g. 'multigrade' use ('multiple' + 'grade'). In addition, references were used to indicate hierarchies. The library was transferred from one system to the other in about fifteen months using temporary staff from an agency for punching and filing. As for the detail employed in the index, on average 15 keywords were necessary to describe a picture, the range being between 5 and 30. For retrieval purposes the average was about 5 keywords. It appears from this that indexing at too great a depth was being attempted.

Scoones was asked to investigate the efficacy of the keyword system. He states that the cost of punching the aperture sheets was uneconomic and that temporary staff employed on punching increased the likelihood of punching errors. Much of the punching was of a repetitive nature, since photographs were processed in batches from common coverages, and in the case of a new installation, 20 pictures might have been taken, resulting in considerable overlap in the keywords assigned to them. Various solutions were costed out, including the purchase of a Keydex drill for punching many sheets at one time, but none proved satisfactory. Moreover, Scoones contends that a user's choice of a picture involves elements other than the subject, elements such as aesthetics and personal preference which are not amenable to indexing. Therefore, a browsing facility is needed, and this can only be given by a well-classified and displayed collection.

For these reasons it was decided to discontinue the keyword system and revert to a more conventional system of classification. But keyword indexing was continued experimentally for six months, during which period staff were instructed to use the system only when all else failed. At the end of the period it was found that eight out of ten requests had been satisfied without recourse to the index, while one out of ten used the index and one was not satisfied at all.

What appears to emerge from Shell's experience is that the pictures were probably indexed to an unnecessary level. First, the Shell Photographic Library has strong links with the Publicity Department, and less in the way of detail was probably required by these users than would be the case with scientists or technologists. Second, the users and staff greatly preferred a browsing facility to asking questions of an index. A picture is a visual object and there is no genuine or adequate verbal substitute for a picture. Also, each user may be able to employ the picture for a different purpose and without seeing it may not realize its potential. Finally, as a test case for keyword indexing, the Shell experience was not truly representative, since a broad arrangement by subject and by country was available as a back up. Library staff have memories and can retain the general outline of a classification scheme. This means they can often go direct to a file where they know the required material will be, which impresses the user, is good public relations, and is quicker than the necessarily slow process of comparing entries on aperture sheets. Hence, other things being equal, a classified arrangement is preferable.

Some general conclusions on the value of coordinate indexing applied to picture collections can be summarized.

— The facility to browse is sacrificed. This is certainly an important disadvantage in a general picture collection, especially the press and commercial collections, but may be less important in the small specialized library.

— There is a tendency, as we saw with Diamond's scheme, to build the uses of pictures into an index. This bulks the index, makes retrieval slower, and is self-defeating, since there will always be an unforeseen use for a picture.

— Costs, if one may judge from the examples of Diamond and Shell, are very high.

— Coordinate indexing may be most useful for small specialized collections where a great deal of detail is required.

ALPHABETICAL SUBJECT ARRANGEMENT

This method of arrangement is almost universal in commercial and press picture libraries, and it is easy to see why. An alphabetical list of ordinary language terms seems simple and obvious — 'as easy as ABC' — and it should be remembered that many staff, and most users, in these libraries are not library trained. Nevertheless, alphabetical arrangement does present problems.

Users often expect material which is related in some way, for example, all animals, all birds, or all flowers, to be at the same place in the files. This appears to be in accordance with common sense. In certain categories, Sport and Agriculture for instance, users are often interested in a broad sample from the category, for example, *all* winter sports, sheep *and* cattle farming. But if, say, weddings were placed under some broad heading, such as Customs, this would run counter to the consensus of ordinary users. If a part-alphabetical arrangement is adopted then an index is needed to show which subdivisions go under each main heading.

Place Versus Subject

Many libraries in the United Kingdom put non-UK subject pictures under place, giving rise to a series of headings, such as: France — Agriculture, Army, Education, Law, Police. This of course scatters material on the subject, and it is a well-known paradox of classification that bringing material together scatters it as well. Some subjects divide more easily into countries than others. Agricultural pictures typically have characteristic landscapes and policemen wear different uniforms in different countries. However, there are certain borderline cases where the place-versus-subject decision is difficult. In picture libraries, Industry may be filed by country, but such pictures are often more suited to subject division — after all, what visual difference is there between an English and a German car factory or steel mill? Even if there are people in the pictures they will look no different. In other cases, such as Art, Entertainment, Science, Religion, or Sport (with the possible exception of ethnic sports like *boules*) no library would contemplate filing by country.

Personalities

The most convenient arrangement for this type of picture is one alphabetical order, although royalty and royal associations are often filed separately, especially if there are many items under these headings. Sporting personalities present something of a problem since action shots tend to be asked for separately and often have other well-known personalities in them, while sportsmen frequently develop different careers later in life, e.g. Roger Bannister, David Sheppard. One solution to these problems would be to place action shots under Sport and reserve portraits for the Personalities file, with appropriate cross-references.

Form of Name

It would be pointless in this context to reiterate the well-known rules for forms of names as given in the AACR. Picture libraries should adhere to the simplest and best-known form of name, using only commonly-known given names, e.g. HEATH, Edward *not* HEATH, Edward Richard George. For foreign names normal practice in the media should be followed, and an authority file of preferred forms of name should be maintained. Chinese names will cause difficulty for some time to come, now that the media are turning to pinyin romanization.

Geographical Names

A problem which has arisen, especially with the independence of former colonial possessions of Western powers, is that of changes in names of countries. In some cases, as boundaries or groupings are redefined several changes of name may occur in one country, e.g. Zimbabwe-Rhodesia, or new countries may appear, e.g. Bangladesh.

The librarian has the option of dealing with this situation by relabelling every picture each time a name changes but this could be an impossible, laborious, and expensive task in a large library. Alternatively, pictures taken before the change of name can be filed under the old name and a file can be opened under the new name, containing 'see also' cross-references.

Another problem which arises with geographical names is that of subdivisions within countries. English counties (even the new ones) and the states of the USA are relatively straightforward, although there should be an index showing what is commonly included in 'New England' or the 'Mid-West'. But there is difficulty with French *départements,* or German *Länder,* since few people know what these are, and in these instances a division into major cities, towns, and general views is probably more helpful than detailed country divisions.

AUTHORITY FILES

A list of subject headings used in the library should be maintained and
constantly updated, although surprisingly many commercial and press
libraries neglect this. There should be an indication of the scope of each
heading, with a note of alternative headings and when they are to be
used, e.g:

> TREES
> File here trees growing singly or in groups of up to about six.
> Woods, forests filed under WOODLAND SCENES. Logging, tree
> felling under TIMBER INDUSTRY. Tropical forests under
> TROPICAL FORESTS.

Additionally, authority files for names or persons and places should be
maintained.

Standard Subject Headings

Can a standard list of *visual* subject headings be produced, suitable for
adoption by all types of library? The advantages of this would be obvious
in terms of the interchange of staff and users between libraries. But it can
be argued that there are so many picture libraries of varying types and
functions, with differing needs, that this is both impossible and
undesirable, and that each library should create its own *ad hoc* list on the
basis of requests received. Nearly all commercial and press libraries
operate in this way, which has the advantage of flexibility and
adaptability to change, although it lacks consistency and predictability —
the need to know where new subjects fit into the framework.

Standard subject heading lists available include the Library of
Congress, Sears, and the Newark system. The two former are, of course,
book schemes, have a heavy American bias, and in many cases an odd
and outdated terminology. Newark is specifically intended for picture
collections but has an inadequate number of terms and, again, an
American bias. In the United Kingdom subject heading lists remain
unpublished and there is no particular standard list in use.

Consequently, each individual library has to decide on its own subject headings, sometimes based on an existing standard list, but more often a unique list of terms. This is an area in which picture librarians could cooperate in compiling a list of terms which, with minor local adaptations, could be used by all libraries.

One example of an alphabetical subject heading scheme in the United Kingdom is the BBC Hulton Picture Library (previously the Radio Times Hulton Picture Library), and a brief indication will help to point out some of the disadvantages of such schemes.

The system in use here was originated by C H Gibbs-Smith, Hulton's first librarian. The picture field is divided into Personalities (P), Modern (M), Topography (T), and Historical (H). Material in these categories is then broken down into main headings, each being given a three-letter abbreviation, e.g., BIC Bicycles, this being broken down into four-letter abbreviations, and then into the full word. Thus, a picture of the Great Eastern would be labelled, within the H section, 'SHI-MERC-Great Eastern', meaning 'ships–merchant-name'. The three-letter abbreviations are not always intuitively obvious: TRA could be Travel or Tramways to the uninitiated, instead of Transport. Examples of some of the main headings used are:

MAP	Mapping and Surveying
MEA	Meat
MED	Medical
MEN	Men (misc.)
MET	Meteorology and Natural Phenomena
MIL	Mills and Milling
MIS	Misery and Poverty
MON	Monuments (misc.)
MOT	Motor Transport
MUS	Music
MYT	Mythology

It will be seen from the above that the headings are not developed according to any systematic plan; they are in fact generated in response to requests. Scope notes and cross-references are plentiful and very detailed, and are actually in the files, so that the pictures are truly self-indexing. An example of the cross-referencing is:

JUVENILE — JUV
Here: Juvenile activities, baptisms, scouts, motherhood, creches, baby shows, children's costume.
Away: Toys in TOY, juvenile labour in LAB, customs in CUS, childbirth and child welfare in MED, juvenile crime in LAW, day nurseries in EDU, native and primitive children in TYP.

Now, this example can be criticized in detail. Why, for example, is children's costume separated from other kinds of costume, and on what principle are creches separated from day nurseries? And it is high time old-fashioned concepts, such as the description of people as 'native and primitive', were removed. But the cross-referencing system serves as a model for other libraries.

Gibbs-Smith and his successors at Hulton have felt that direct access to the files can only be allowed to those trained in the library. Reasons for this include security when misplaced photographs could be lost for years, and the complexity of the system where the headings are not obvious. Many picture researchers feel that they cannot do their job properly unless allowed to inspect picture files almost at random, and this is certainly true, for serendipity plays a great part in the make-up of the successful picture researcher. In another major collection in the UK, the founders of the Mary Evans Picture Library made a deliberate decision to allow researchers direct access to their collection, and this has paid off handsomely.

ILLUSTRATIONS IN BOOKS AND PERIODICALS

Many picture libraries try to extend their range of materials by referring to art books or bound volumes of picture materials to avoid destroying the original volumes by cutting. If a pictorial index to a book collection is provided it should be very detailed, since every enquiry would have to be made *via* the index. Broxis[8] has suggested that the following details should be included in such an index: caption, size, colour or black and white, angle from which the object is viewed, full book details.

CONCLUSIONS

From this analysis, the evidence suggests that conventional classification schemes cannot, in general, be used for the larger picture libraries. Multimedia libraries however, where several different forms and materials are housed and organized in the one collection, may be able to adapt the existing schemes successfully. Attempts to use coordinate indexing for pictures have not on the whole been successful. The field seems open, therefore, to alphabetical subject headings, which at least at present, need to be compiled by the individual library.

REFERENCES

1   Evans, H and others *Picture researcher's handbook*. Newton Abbot, David and Charles, 1975.
2   Wall, J *Directory of British photographic collections*. London, Heinemann/ Royal Photographic Society, 1977.
3   Simons, W W 'Development of a universal classification system for two-by-two inch slide collections' *in* Grove, P S and others *Bibliographic control of non-print media*. Chicago, American Library Association, 1972. 362.
4   Simons, W W and others *A slide classification system for the organization and automatic indexing of interdisciplinary collections of slides and pictures*. Santa Cruz, University of California, 1970.
5   Diamond, R M 'A retrieval system for 35 mm. slides utilized in arts and humanities instruction' *in* Groves, P S and others *Bibliographic control of non-print media*. Chicago, American Library Association, 1972. 346-59.
6   McNeil, R J 'The Shell Photographic Library'. *ASLIB Proceedings* 18 (5) May 1966. 128-37.
7   Scoones, M A 'The Shell Photographic Library'. *Audiovisual Librarian* VI. 1 (3) February 1974. 95-105.
8   Broxis, P F *Organising the arts*. London, Bingley, 1968.

8

Recent Technological Developments

Arlene Farber Sirkin

In the last few years several new technologies have been developed that will have a significant impact on the future of photographic collections and archives. These technological developments can significantly reduce the clerical, labour-intensive portions of the workload and help make the images more widely available. Below is a brief description of three of these technologies and their potential benefits for photographic collections.

AUTOMATION

One of the on-going problems for the individual supervising a photographic collection (photo archivist, librarian, or historian) is how to maximize the availability (i.e., the location of and access to) of items within the collection. The availability problem is the same whether the collection contains hundreds, thousands, or millions of items; it is simply much more pronounced with the larger collections.

This is not an easy problem to overcome. Its scope can best be understood by imagining that each page of a book is separated from the book. It would be quite difficult to locate one specific page. Now multiply this by hundreds or thousands of books. To find one page out of this maze of material without mechanical help would be quite time-consuming. This example may create for you a visual picture of the problems faced daily in photographic collections as they deal with the volumes of materials that must be organized, described, and hopefully retrieved.

Added to the problem of quantity is that of accurately describing visual images with words. This is a continuing challenge for all who deal with visual information. If one picture is worth 10,000 words, how can anyone truly do justice to a picture in under 50 words? This is normally the maximum for the description of images in any collection.

The use of computers to process data quickly can help photo specialists take a quantum leap in gaining control over the large volumes of material in their care. Automation provides the tool to make an impossible manual task a realistic one for insufficiently staffed photo collections. It can enhance access by creating a situation in which it is practical to assign a greater number of identification points and subject descriptors to each image. The computer, properly programmed, can manipulate these characteristics or subject descriptors and sort out those items that simultaneously have two or more specified criteria or subjects, e.g. an image of both Prime Minister Churchill and President Roosevelt. In most manual systems it would be necessary to search for Roosevelt in all the files on Churchill, or for Churchill in all files on Roosevelt. Since both of these men were prominent and frequently photographed it would be a very time-consuming task.

If access is in the form of a card file, one more term means one more card — just adding to the housekeeping problems that are concomitant with larger and larger manual files. With a computer the search can readily be reduced to only those images containing both of these famous personalities. Similarly, such searches might consist of the photographer's name and a date or place, or any two descriptors that are part of the system.

In this move towards automation there are two challenges — the definition of standards and conversion of the material to a machine-readable format.

Definition of Standards

Rules and parameters are obviously necessary for cooperation and exchange of information between systems. Standards are even more crucial in automated systems because computers require a high degree of precision. The recently introduced MARC format provides standards for the automation of information about monographs and journals, but no standard has yet been agreed for visual resources. Instead, many different automated systems for visual resources have been designed and implemented. Little effort has been made to reconcile incompatibilities in these systems because of differences in mission and focus of museums, archives, libraries, historical societies, and government agencies.

In recent years, however, there has been general acceptance of the idea that, in spite of the disparities, the overlap in categories of information necessary to identify an image warrants the creation of a national standard. The library monograph and journal standards models, if examined thoroughly and critically, may serve as bases for developing standards for pictorial material. Since many of the large collections are in libraries it makes sense to consider the library model as one alternative and to learn from its mistakes and successes. Work is underway by a Joint Committee on Specialized Cataloguing from the Library of Congress in cooperation with the Council on National Library and Information Associations. They are developing a manual for graphic materials (prints, photographs and drawings) to supplement AACR2 which will provide the basis for a national standard.

Standards for pictorial automation need to be established in order to allow those who wish to establish compatible systems to do so. A standard format would enable interested persons in the future to search simultaneously and easily in many systems. A researcher could easily locate, for instance, all the work of a given photographer or all the work on a given topic. Ready access to many collections would be achieved without the researcher having to go through the time-consuming task of learning each system. Such uniformity of access would encourage the use of visual resources and hopefully heighten the researcher's awareness of the usefulness of photographs as historical documentation.

In most collections information on the photographer or process (film, paper, etc.) is not deemed worthy of note even if it is available. Economic reality seems to be the primary reason for the decisions to ignore certain information. It is evident that there is enough consensus among collections, as to the fields or categories of information deemed important in order to identify the collection's image, for standards to exist. However, they must be established to meet a range of institutional needs. It would be up to each institution to determine for itself which fields within the system to use and which to skip. A standardized system offering alternatives would allow each institution to adopt the appropriate categories to meet its needs while remaining compatible with other institutions. This would include standards as basic as defining a field of information for size, in which height is listed before width.

It cannot be stressed strongly enough that future access to photographic collections depends on standards that must be adopted *now*. Economic reality dictates that institutions which have invested heavily in developing a system are not apt to change to another. Many institutions are just starting to explore automation alternatives. Some of these institutions and groups would be very willing to accept an established standard but if no standard exists, each will reinvent its own system with resulting incompatibility of systems.

Conversion to a Machine-readable Format

Just as people must have books in a language and format they can 'read', computers can only utilize information they can 'read'. This language is usually referred to as 'machine-readable format' and is stored on magnetic tapes or discs. In order to translate or convert information into that format, there are a variety of options which include the use of a keypunch or a computer terminal. With the innovation and increasing sophistication of word processing equipment, it is now also possible to use some sophisticated word processing equipment to create a manual card catalogue on 3 × 5 inch cards while simultaneously creating a machine-readable file for future use in a computerized system.

The importance of the conversion process of data into a machine-readable format cannot be overemphasized. It is useless to teach someone a new language if there are no books or materials in that system to 'read'. Likewise, it is useless to create an automated system without considering how to provide it with material (information/data) to 'read'. Some institutions faced with this problem are identifying the most important items based on their own institutional priorities. In some cases, they use historic importance as the test; in others they adopt usage statistics.

Usage may seem a peculiar criterion, but studies have documented that a high percentage of requests often relate to a small portion of a file or collection. It therefore makes sense to invest time and resources in making this small percentage of photographs the most accessible, since they will fill most user requirements. This is especially true of photographs reproduced in publications. As most people in charge of collections can document, the publication of a photograph is almost guaranteed to increase the demand for it drastically.

Another difficulty is that since the images in most collections are unique, cataloguing information cannot be shared as it has been done with books. This makes the conversion task an even greater burden.

Yet, although the conversion costs in terms of resources and time are initially high, in the long term they are the most cost-effective alternative for a large file. The realities of ever-increasing labour and personnel costs, together with the simultaneous decrease in relative cost of computer capabilities, are facts of life in the 1980s.

VIDEODISC

The second technological development that will have a profound effect on photograph collections is the videodisc. A videodisc looks like a long-playing photograph record. Twelve inches in diameter, the disc is made of a low-cost plastic. Usually the information from the disc is 'read' by a person viewing it on a TV set in a similar manner to a videotape or videocassette. The videodisc has the capacity to store up to 54,000 individual frames or 30 minutes of information on one side. Each one of these frames is identified by a number from 1 to 54,000. With the programmable model, any of these 54,000 frames can be called up within seconds.

The easiest way to understand the storage capacity is to use our comparison to a book once again. Each page of the book is numbered and may consist of a picture, a page of print, or a combination of images and text. The videodisc is the same. If you know the exact page number of what you want in the book or the frame number on the videodisc, you can go straight to it, by-passing all the other pages or frames. This is known as random access. The primary difference between books and videodiscs is that the information happens to be stored electronically and 'read' by means of a television screen rather than via a printed page. Additionally, it is possible to program a string of frames so that the viewer can automatically go from frame 201 directly to frame 607, to frame 708, etc. Such programming can link images in numerous

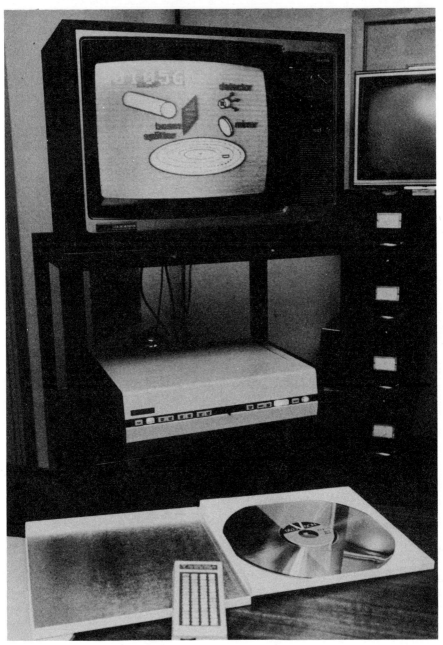

Videodisc equipment. *US Army Audio-Visual Center, Washington DC.*

Videodisc. *US Army Audio-Visual Center, Washington DC.*

patterns for a variety of purposes, such as linking frames relating to one subject or arranging material for programmed instruction.

One good example of the possibilities that videodiscs offer is a mapping project that is being done at the Massachusetts Institute of Technology (MIT) in Boston, Massachusetts, USA. The MIT group filmed every 9 feet of Aspen, Colorado, a town that was laid out on a grid (i.e., the town has only vertical blocks and horizontal blocks). They then programmed or 'linked' the frames of film on the disc. As a person looks at a television screen, the disc relays the view he or she would get looking out of the front window of a car while driving down the street in Aspen. At each intersection the car keeps going down the street unless the viewer indicates otherwise. However, the car can be asked to turn left or right at the intersection. This is interpreted by the videodisc system as a choice to switch frames in non-linear order. Thus, instead of going from frame 101 to frame 102 to frame 103, as would be the case if the car was to go straight through the intersection, the choice is to switch to frame 167 for a left turn and to frame 193 for a right turn.

Again, to use a print model, this is similar to a programmed text. In such a text the person keeps working through it question by question and page by page until a section is incorrectly answered. At that point the program might require that the section be repeated or that another section be completed for extra help. On the other hand, if a person does well in a pretest, the programmed text might miss out a whole section.

The videodisc has limitations. The most prevalent make currently available commercially, Discovision, is not reproducible, i.e. you cannot get a hard copy reproduction from a videodisc image: it provides purely a reference copy. Such a limitation is an inconvenience, but does not negate its other features. It still has great advantages, particularly for large picture collections. The videodisc would allow, for example, large portions or the entire collection of the Imperial War Museum or of the US Library of Congress Prints and Photographs Division to be reproduced on videodisc and distributed worldwide. In addition to providing multisite reference access to the collection, image identification numbers could expedite the order and purchase of prints from the original depository. This would greatly increase worldwide access to collections. A researcher would no longer have to travel great distances to view unique images in these national depositories.

Videodiscs are not practical for all institutions and collections. As with an audio record, the cost of producing the original master is high, currently running into several thousands of dollars. Also, like an audio record, most people do not have access to equipment to produce the original or master locally. Videodiscs are based on the same mass-market concept as audio records. They are practical primarily for producing large numbers of copies for a mass market, priced to sell at $15 to $25 per videodisc. For collections of national or worldwide interest with high volume demand, or those so valuable and unique that they are worth the expense of reproduction for use in several sites by scholars for research, videodiscs are a viable proposition.

Videodisc vendors predict that most households now owning stereo equipment will purchase the consumer models of the videodisc. These, however, will be used primarily for viewing movies. Vendors expect to be selling movies the way they now sell audio records.

This new dense storage medium will probably replace 16 mm. film in most institutional collections, especially with the fluctuating price of the silver that is needed for films. The film base, and therefore the medium of film, is getting so expensive that alternative ways for distributing the contents of collections by videodisc are becoming more and more practical. Further, the life expectancy of the disc is predicted to be significantly higher than that of film. Its outstanding features — density of information, i.e. 54,000 pages on one side, and durability — make it a technology that must be further explored by those with large and specialized photographic collections.

Another system of high-density storage is the microform and for a full discussion of this system the reader is referred to the next section of the handbook.

WORD PROCESSING EQUIPMENT

Word processing equipment (WPE) basically takes a mechanical typewriter and expands its potential up to and including sophisticated computer capabilities. Whereas every action on the regular typewriter is a mechanical gesture, the WPE has electronic retention that can repeat the mechanical movements. WPE systems vary greatly in sophistication in direct relation to their cost; normally the more expensive the system, the greater the number of features and computer capabilities. One of the most popular and prevalent uses is for text editing. The user can quickly and easily change, omit, or insert letters, words, lines, or paragraphs into the body of a report or letter. WPE can facilitate and significantly speed the merging of a mailing list with form letters to give the impression of a personalized document. Additionally, WPE can provide the same name and addresses on a label or envelope with no additional typing of the information. Standard information necessary for filling in forms, such as a request for photo services, can also be filed so that repeated standard information can be added automatically. Additionally, it can be invaluable for bibliographies or lists of numbers that are continually changed and updated.

However, the most important feature and benefit is for a collection anticipating conversion to an automated system. Certain WPE systems can provide a tool to produce both a hard copy (index cards or sheets of paper) for present needs, while simultaneously creating a machine-readable file for future use in an automated system. This would in effect build a data base. As explained above, this is basic to building an automated system. Some WPE models also provide simple sort-and-search functions, i.e., items entered into the system can be later sorted or retrieved.

Many institutions are considering purchase of WPE for administrative purposes, primarily for text editing. If the requirements of the photography collection can be defined in terms of specific WPE features, this should be brought to the institution's attention for input to be used in defining criteria for the future purchase. If your institution already has WPE, do check with the unit administering it to determine its features, computer capabilities, and availability to help meet the photo collection's requirements. In many instances, WPE is purchased for one specific purpose and its potential is not being fully exploited. It is possible that if time and space permit, it would be readily available to the photo collection.

This technology provides another vehicle to reduce the labour-intensive and time-consuming clerical tasks involved in the operation of a picture collection. By reducing the time element, the availability of staff time which can be diverted elsewhere is effectively increased.

CONCLUSION

It is time for those managing photo collections to be realistic and pragmatic. The new technologies discussed have the potential to reduce dramatically some of the most labour-intensive, repetitive portions of the workload in photographic collections. Faced with the pressure of the economic realities of the 1980s, there seems to be little hope of increasing staffing levels. Many of these new technologies require initial capital expenditures, but these can be justified by long-term savings and efficiencies. Such are the priorities and concerns of those heads of institutions and individuals making decisions about the funding and future of most of our photographic collections. They differ in outlook from the concerns of those actually running the collections. Their priorities are more likely to lie in improving access to the collections. Yet, these technologies can satisfy the priorities of both groups. For some collections in addition to being cost-effective, they provide tools to improve access and an increased opportunity to share resources never before available through the dense storage capability of videodiscs; multisite availability of access to the images of national and other important collections is now possible. Automated systems allow access and the eventual exchange of bibliographic information via the telephone or other data communication channels.

The technologies have another positive by-product. They precipitate communication between photographic collections that was largely absent until just recently. This in turn leads to increased sharing and the building up of formal and informal networks of information that result in less duplication of effort and more progress. This is an instance where technology has led to an increase in *human* interaction and communication.

Finally, technology provides the means for picture professionals to reduce redundant clerical operations, thereby releasing more time to be spent with the images themselves. Hopefully, it will lead to a reduction in the boxes and piles of photographs that sit untouched in all collections because there is never the time available to get to them.

The views expressed in this chapter, written in March, 1980, are solely those of the author and do not reflect those of the US Army.

9

Microforms

Charles Chadwyck-Healey

I t is only since 1975 that microforms (the generic term for microfilm and microfiche) have come to be recognized as a suitable medium for the reproduction of visual material. Shortly before then a major American microform publisher announced a series of art theses reproduced on microfiche, taking care to point out that the series was confined to titles without illustrations. Perhaps this attitude was borne out of the unfortunate experiences many researchers have had when using microfilm — poor quality images on outdated and badly maintained readers. Or perhaps there has been a tendency to associate microforms with certain types of research material, newspapers, government documents, or typed theses. Neither of these explanations is entirely convincing if one looks at the close similarities between slides and microforms. Slides have been with us for almost a hundred years. The lantern slide was a relatively large piece of glass, but as time went on slides became smaller until after the war the ubiquitous 35 mm. or 2 × 2 inch slide displaced all larger formats. This reduction in size has been accepted as the natural development of advancing technology, bringing with it the benefits of cheapness, convenience, and the saving of space with little or no discernible loss of quality.

Is not the microfiche the logical successor to the 35 mm. slide (35 mm. microfilm being none other than an unmounted version of the latter)? Certainly, the reduction of the image from the 35 mm. format to the format of a single frame on a 60, 84, or 98-frame microfiche produces the same benefits as described above, again with no significant loss of quality.

The acceptance of microforms in the picture library is happening slowly. Limited amounts of material available on microform, the lack of suitable readers and projectors, and misconceptions about microforms have held back development, but this is now changing and the two most important factors bringing about this change are the rapid growth in the amount of visual material becoming available and the increases in film costs in 1980 due to the fluctuations in the cost of silver used in film. This will affect the price of both slides and microforms but because slides use proportionally more film per image the increases will have a more marked affect on slide prices than on microfiche prices.

Comparisons with Slides

Comparisons between slide and microform prices are worth making because few picture librarians are aware of how many more images they could acquire for the same amount of money if obtained on microform rather than as slides. Currently, a colour slide costs between £0.20 and £0.75. An image on colour microfiche costs from £0.08 to £0.10 and this will probably include the cost of a printed catalogue or index to the collection of which the image is a part. A monochrome image is much cheaper — about £0.025 and is worth mentioning because many collections of visual material on microfiche are monochrome rather than colour. The difference between the unit price of an image on colour microfilm and on a slide is even more striking considering that the image area is as large if not larger. An average price would be £0.06, a third of the price of the cheapest slide, and presumably reflects the saving in cost in not having to mount each image individually. It may be said that these comparisons are not entirely relevant in that many slide librarians buy relatively few slides, making most of the slides themselves. But in the early 1980s, at a time of inflation and cuts in spending on education in most developed countries, slide librarians are already finding that their slide-making unit which is intended to supply 'free' or highly subsidized slide copies to lecturers 'on demand' is becoming so expensive to maintain that they are returning to buying slides from commercial producers.

The prevalence of the 'home-made' slide has some bearing on the

Eye-Com microfiche projectors. *Charles Chadwyck-Healey.*

question of acceptable quality of microforms. There are so many thoroughly badly made slides in use today with distorted colour values and fuzzy, out-of-focus images that users have become conditioned to standards below that obtainable from a good quality microform image. Furthermore, the same problem is unlikely to happen with microforms, since the cost and complexity of the processes needed to make either monochrome or colour microforms are such that production will always remain in the hands of a few professional suppliers with a vested interest in producing images of a consistent quality.

During the 1970s there was a trend towards the standardization of microform formats. Unfortunately the use of microforms for the reproduction of visual material has reversed this trend in that it has brought into use new formats and formats that were previously going out of use. The standard format for microfilm remains the 30 metre roll of 35 mm. wide film. Because microfilm is unperforated the image can be taken to the very edge of the film (as opposed to the 24 mm. width available on perforated slide film), and there are an average of 800 frames on each roll of film. The standard microfiche format for printed matter is the 105 × 148 mm. sheet of film carrying 98 images designed to be read at a magnification of 24 times image size. Some very large collections of visual material have been produced on this internationally accepted format but the author must accept some responsibility for bringing back into use the old COSATI European format of 60 frames per sheet designed to be read at 20-22 ×. Improvements in monochrome film quality meant that this format was being displaced by the 98-frame format but colour film has a lower resolving power (i.e. is less 'sharp') than monochrome microfilm and the larger size of the 60-frame image is fundamental to the production of high quality colour images. We have extended the use of the 60-frame format to collections of monochrome material in which special films with lower resolving power but greater tonal range than standard microfilm are used. Here again the 35% larger image area makes all the difference in the production of a high quality image.

While it is unlikely that the resolving power of colour microfilm will increase significantly over the next few years, Eastman Kodak are planning to bring in a new microfilm which combines a high resolution with an extended tonal range which will be eminently suitable for the reproduction of visual material and may enable us to return to the 98-frame format. The other non-standard format is the 84-frame format adopted by the University of Chicago Press for their *Text Fiche* series (see below). The main advantage of this format is that both vertical and horizontal images can be read without having to rotate the microfiche. Many libraries now have microfiche in this format. It has been widely and effectively advertised and has even had a special microfiche reader[1] designed for it, but few if any other microform producers have adopted this format so it may be destined to remain 'a speciality'.

Potential users alarmed by this situation may take comfort from the fact that all of these formats can be used on standard 24 × microfiche readers, particularly those with a large screen. Book publishers too, from the birth of printing, have met the problems of reproducing visual material by the uninhibited use of non-standard formats — the landscape format, the elephant folio, the fold-out.

These are some of the physical characteristics of microforms and their similarities to slides but one can claim that the microfiche format is not just as good but is superior to all other formats — books, slides or original pictures themselves — in bringing coherence and true accessibility to very large picture collections. One should stress *large* because when dealing with a few hundred pictures, the book and the slide formats have advantages of convenience and flexibility that cannot be ignored, but collections of 10,000 images upwards are too large to be included in any series of books or considered as a single slide collection and are as laborious to use in their original form. Some of the collections which have been reproduced have contained from 50,000 to 90,000 photographs. Apart from the space occupied by the photographs and the amount of curatorial time required to maintain the collections, researchers are put off by the sheer physical effort and time required to search through them systematically. Reproduction of such collections in book or slide form is usually impossible on economic grounds alone but the microfiche scores both through ease of handling and through its capacity for image reproduction at different magnifications. Ease of handling is self-evident — it is easier to use 60 images on one piece of film than 60 separate slides that have to be individually refiled after use.

The advantages of variable magnification are not so obvious and yet are much more important. The microfiche can be scanned with the naked eye, it can be viewed full size on a microfiche reader, or it can be projected onto a screen before a group. When the microfiche is scanned with the naked eye an enormous amount of information can be gained without having to put the microfiche in the reader. Put five colour microfiche on a light box and within a few minutes you can scan and visually compare 300 images, gaining enough information from them to know which are worth closer study. After initial selection the microfiche images can be studied full size on a microfiche reader and then be further enlarged on a screen in a class or seminar. In this way a researcher can scan thousands of images in a matter of hours with the minimum of physical effort, thus encouraging more thorough use of large picture collections which may be inaccessible to all but the most determined researcher through their very size.

Picture Collections

Examples of large picture collections made more inaccessible in this way include the Index of American Design,[2] a collection of 15,000 renderings reproduced on 291 colour microfiche. The paintings occupy a very large area in the National Gallery of Art, Washington; the microfiche occupy one small box. The very size of the paintings many of which measure 1×1.5 metres means that comparisons are limited to three or four renderings at a time. Now this collection is available in many libraries throughout the world it is likely to be more thoroughly explored in one year than it has been in the previous forty years.

The Farm Security Administration and Office of War Information photographs in the Library of Congress[2] form another large collection — 87,000 photographs in 135 file drawers. It is not surprising that most researchers have until now confined themselves to the few hundred photographs that are well known through having been frequently published, leaving most of the collection, generally considered to be one of the most famous collections of photographs in the world, virtually unknown. It must be pointed out that even on microfiche the collection would remain unknown and unused if it were not arranged systematically by subject and were not accompanied by a printed subject index. As with collections of manuscripts and printed material on microform, the inclusion of a printed guide or index is almost essential if photograph collections are to be fully usable. The Marburger Index[3] is another well-known collection of 500,000 photographs of German art and architecture; a collection of this size and diversity needs extensive indexing and while no index exists at present the publisher plans to produce computerized indexes at some time in the future.

Most slide libraries contain large numbers of slides of works of art in individual galleries so it is to be expected that the complete collections of galleries will be published on colour microfiche. One of the first major collections to be reproduced on microfiche was the portraits in the National Portrait Gallery in Washington[2] in which over 5,000 portraits are reproduced on colour microfiche, the microfiche being keyed to the printed catalogue. But visual material on microform need not be confined to the arts; scientific and medical material have been published on microfiche, while for theatre historians there is the Vandamm Collection,[2] a collection of some 30,000 photographs of New York stage productions from 1919 to 1961. Access is through an unusually comprehensive card index reproduced on microfiche, while the photographs themselves are reproduced on microfiche by production in alphabetical order, enabling the reader to go straight to a production without using the index.

The University of Chicago Press *Test Fiche* series[4] has been a pioneering attempt to establish microfiche as a medium for the reproduction in colour of visual material. The high editorial standard of the texts and the care that has gone into the production and presentation of each title has done much to make microforms more widely accepted.

The term *Text Fiche* describes a hybrid format of conventional printed text with illustrations on colour or monochrome microfiche kept with the text (in a wallet at the back of the book) which, while convenient for the private user, may create security problems for the librarian.

Equipment

The success of microforms in a picture library depends as much on suitable equipment as on the choice of suitable titles. Libraries sometimes buy expensive collections and then look around for a microform reader as an afterthought. The prevalence of readers in many libraries for reading the library catalogue on COM microfiche can be a mixed blessing because the picture librarian may be supplied with a 'spare' reader only to find it quite unsuitable for reproducing visual material, with its high magnification lens, and tinted screen of the wrong size and shape. At a time of budget limitations it needs a strong-minded librarian to hold out for the right equipment when the nearly right equipment is already there but it is just that difference which will decide whether microform collections are used or not.

Before discussing suitable microform readers in detail one important factor should not be overlooked — the storage of microfiche. This does not refer to temperature and humidity, important though these are, since the majority of picture libraries are already within the limits required for storing processed photographic film, but to physical damage and contamination by dust. If the microfiche are stored in purpose-built steel cabinets[5] they will last indefinitely; if they are left in piles on a shelf or in open cardboard boxes (probably the boxes they arrived in) they will deteriorate quite quickly. Furthermore, if they are kept in the librarian's office without ever getting into the catalogue everyone will soon forget that they are there. Microfiche collections costing hundreds of pounds have been found stored in this way in libraries in the UK and USA, and one can go so far as to say that microfiche collections should not be bought if the library cannot also afford a suitable reader, a storage cabinet, and an area in the library that can be set aside for microform users.

A suitable microfiche reader should have high quality optics including interchangeable lenses so that $18\times$, $20\times$, and $24\times$ magnifications can be used; the screen should be a neutral grey for the accurate reproduction of colour and a large screen with a square or vertical format

Microfiche from *America 1935-1946. Charles Chadwyck-Healey.*

is best.[6] Image rotation and projection facilities are desirable additional features. More specialized readers include reader printers[7] which enable photocopies to be made from microform images, and readers which enable two images to be looked at simultaneously. The former is not necessary for most picture libraries since the reproduction of images with a continuous tonal range is generally not very satisfactory; the latter answers the criticisms of those users who say that images on microfiche cannot be compared in the way that images in two different books can be laid side by side; the dual platen microfiche reader[8] is particularly useful in the picture library since, either images on two different microfiche can be viewed simultaneously on the same 'double'-width screen, or an index on microfiche and an image can be used side by side. The alternative to this is to use two separate microfiche readers side by side.

Microfiche can be projected by removing the viewing screen from the reader so that the image is projected onto a separate screen. This is most suitable for use in a small group since the size of the image is limited by the relatively low power of the reader light source. However, there is now on the market a purpose-built microfiche projector[9] with a more intense light source enabling an image to be projected large enough to be seen in a medium-sized class room or lecture hall. This projector will in itself do much to further the use of microforms for visual material since lecturers are more interested in using such material to illustrate their lectures than for private study in the library. Once lecturers understand that microfiche can be projected as effectively as slides and provide access to far larger collections of images than is possible with slides, it is likely that the use of microfiche for the reproduction of visual material will rapidly grow.

REFERENCES

1   The Bell and Howell PMR VIII microfiche reader with projection facility — see item 6 below for address.
2   Published by Chadwyck-Healey Ltd, 20 Newmarket Road, Cambridge CB5 8DT and distributed in the USA by Somerset House, 417 Maitland Avenue, Teaneck, NJ 07666.
3   Published by K G Saur Publishing Inc., 175 Fifth Avenue, New York, NY 10012.
4   Published by the University of Chicago Press, 5801 S Ellis Avenue, Chicago, IL 60637.
5   Ranges of microform storage cabinets are made by Microstar, Castle House, Old Road, Leighton Buzzard, Beds. and Microphax Ltd, Canterbury House, 393 Cowley Road, Oxford OX4 2DF.
6   There are many good quality readers available though the majority are designed for COM and tend to have a landscape screen (not good for vertical images) and a $42\times$ or $48\times$ lens. Suitable readers used by the author include:
— NCR 456-200 Universal Microfiche Reader with $18\times$, $20\times$, and $24\times$ interchangeable lenses, a grey screen, and projection facility. Supplied by NCR, Microform Systems Division, 206 Marylebone Road, London NW1 6LY.
— Bell & Howell PMR VIII Microfiche Reader with interchangeable lenses including $18\times$ and $24\times$ and projection facility. Supplied by Bell & Howell Ltd, 33-35 Woodthorpe Road, Ashford, Middlesex.
— Kodak 321/323 Microfiche Reader/Printer, reader with interchangeable lenses including $18\times$ and $24\times$ and image rotation and a facility for the addition of a photocopier for conversion into a reader printer. Supplied in the UK by Kodak Ltd, Micrographic Sales, PO Box 66, Station Road, Hemel Hempstead, Herts HP1 1JU; in the USA by Eastman Kodak Co., 1133 Avenue of the Americas, New York, NY 10036.
— Carl Zeiss Dokumator DL2 Microfilm/Microfiche Reader. Image is projected onto a flat white surface rather than through a translucent screen

and so provides particularly accurate colour reproduction. Choice of four lenses mounted in turret include 17×, 20×, and 24×, image rotation, and projection facilities. Will also accommodate 35 mm.microfilm. Supplied by Carl Zeiss Ltd, Boreham Wood, Herts, UK.

7   There are many reader-printers on the market usually costing over £1,000.

8   The Microcomparator reader allows two microfiche to be viewed simultaneously on a single screen. Interchangeable lenses including 18× and 24× and different magnification lenses can be used at the same time. Supplied in the UK by the Mike Fraser Group, 225 Goldhawk Road, London W12 8ER.

9   The Eye-Com Microfiche Projector for 60, 84, or 98-frame michrofiche is supplied by Eye Communication Systems Inc., PO Box 278, North Lake, WI 53064, USA, and is available in the UK from Chadwyck-Healey Ltd, 20 Newmarket Road, Cambridge CB5 8DT.

10

Exploitation

Hilary Evans

GENERAL CONSIDERATIONS

A picture is doing its job only when someone is looking at it and with rare exceptions (the secret plans for a new missile, say) it is doing its job best when the greatest possible number of people are looking at it. It is to enable pictures to do their job as well as possible that picture libraries exist.

It is at once evident that this comprises two basic functions:
— conservation — the creation and maintenance of the picture collection, and
— exploitation — making the pictures available to the, or a, public.

In some picture libraries the first of these functions will dominate: in a library such as the British Museum Print Room the role of custodian will, understandably, take precedence. Elsewhere it will be the other way about: in a reference library attached to an art college, that of giving students access to visual documentation will more probably be seen as the primary role.

This is as it should be but, while it will sometimes happen that a library will get its priorities topsy-turvy, most will be aware of their double duty to conserve and to exploit. Most of the problems — and the excitements — of the picture librarian's job arise from the challenge presented by these conflicting aims for, as will be seen, conflicting, alas, they frequently are. Indeed, it may be said that it is on the success with which a library resolves this dilemma that it will ultimately be judged. There is clearly something sadly amiss when those who wish to use material from a great state archive have to wait weeks or even months before they can obtain the material they require; equally, there is something wrong when valuable pictures are put at risk by a librarian who, preoccupied with the short-term benefits of making material readily available, fails to reflect that unless that material is properly safeguarded, it will not survive to serve future users.

Before we examine how, in material and everyday terms, the dilemma can best be resolved, let us see if there exist any criteria to which the librarian can refer as he strives to implement this dual function.

PURPOSE OF THE COLLECTION

Every picture library was created with a particular purpose in mind. Sometimes that purpose may appear obscure — perhaps it was only to gratify an individual collector's private whim. Sometimes the original purpose will have changed over a period of time — the growth of the heavily illustrated popular education book, for example, created an enormous new field for picture exploitation and caused many picture collections to adjust to meet the demand. In nearly every case, however, the purpose was either:

> — to gather in a convenient place visual reference material related to a particular subject or theme, or
> — to make available to a given body of people the kind of visual material they are likely to require in the pursuit of their study or profession.

In most cases, moreover, the function of the collection will be evident enough, and will either dictate, or be dictated by, the kind of user who makes use of it. This in turn will determine the way in which the material itself is used, which will generally be:

> — as visual reference for artists or designers, or
> — for reproduction as illustration in books, periodicals, audio-visual items, television productions, etc.

There are of course many other uses, but they are generally either derivatives of these, or so marginal as not to constitute a major factor when establishing the design and procedure of the library. In most libraries, both purposes must be served to a greater or lesser degree, so that the librarian's second function, that of exploitation, can be further divided into:

— access — making it possible for the user to *inspect* the material, and

— availability — making it possible for the user to *borrow* or *copy* the material for reproduction purposes.

Of course the execution of this second function must not override the first function of conservation by putting the material itself at risk.

All of this remains broadly true whether the library is a picture collection attached to a college of art, used almost entirely for visual reference, or a print room attached to a great public collection, used chiefly by academics for study purposes or by publishers of art books and histories, or a commercial photo agency, where the collection is geared almost wholly to the needs of those seeking illustrations for reproduction purposes. What happens, though, is that the basic principles will be interpreted in different ways to meet different circumstances. Also contributing to determine the practical expression of these abstract principles will be such limiting factors as these:

— The material may be available only to a limited public, e.g. members of a specified society, professional body, or educational institution. Insofar as access is limited only to people of high trustworthiness, particularly where all users are individually known to the library staff, greater latitude as regards access can be granted and the need for close supervision and security will be reduced.

— The material may be used only in certain circumstances, e.g., it may be used only for educational purposes, or may not be used for commercial purposes. This will require tight scrutiny of users as to their purpose in using the library.

— The material may be of great intrinsic value, e.g. a great public collection may possess a legacy of ancient manuscripts which cannot in the normal way be made available even for casual inspection, but must somehow be made accessible to users who will probably wish to use the library precisely for the sake of such material. This will dictate specific procedural arrangements.

— The material may exist in such quantity that only a highly sophisticated retrieval system can ensure effective access, e.g., a modern press agency, where every day hundreds of new photos of the day's events, world-shaking or trivial, are arriving from all directions, and where instant retrieval is a *sine qua non* of the library. In such a case, the entire design of the library will be subordinated to the function of making the material available.

These are just a few of the factors which can influence the character of a library and dictate its procedural system. It is absolutely essential that the librarian, before setting out to exploit his material, should be absolutely clear in his own mind what are his aims and objectives and what it should not attempt; what priorities may exist which will dictate the way in which the library is planned and the procedural system applied; what limiting factors he must, for good or ill, take into account; and above all, who the library's users are, and in what way it can serve them best.

On one side of the stage we see the librarian, jealously clutching his pictures as a doting father holds his beloved daughter, pleased that others desire them too, but fearful of what may befall them — and over there, confronting him, is the library user, the lover, ardent and impatient, more concerned with immediate needs than with future consequences. How can we help these two to come together as friends rather than foes, recognizing each other's fears and claims?

Let us be quite clear about one thing: every library is in the risk business. The only way in which a library can ensure the safekeeping of its pictures is by withholding them from the very public it exists to serve. So, whatever is done will be a compromise. Accepting this, how can the librarian, within the parameters he has set or has been set, make pictures available as freely as possible, to help the user as much as possible, without placing too great a burden on the staff, and without putting the material at too great a risk?

ACCESS

Most picture collections consist of pictures printed on sheets of paper, either by graphic or photographic processes. (The exceptions — books, periodicals, ephemera, etc. — are a matter for separate treatment.) So, we are concerned with many thousands of individual pieces of paper.

Paper is a remarkably durable material, considering how fragile it is.

Any child can ruin a work of art in a fraction of a second, yet even loose sheets of paper have an incredible survival value. (I acquired an original print of the first depiction of dowsing, from Munster's *Cosmographia* of 1553, from a bulldog clip in the Portobello Market: it is in perfect condition.) But preservation must always be a very high priority, and unrestricted access to original prints is asking for trouble. So, the obvious solution is to keep the prints in a suitably safe place, and let the user ask if he wants to see them...

...which is fine, except that a user of pictures is unlikely to know in advance *which* picture is going to meet his or her needs. And while it is theoretically possible, and indeed one's right as a taxpayer, to go to the Victoria and Albert Museum and ask to see all their pictures of the English countryside until a suitable one is found for the book jacket which is being designed, in the process both the user's patience and the goodwill of the staff will be tried beyond endurance. So, what is to be done? The alternatives are as follows:

1 Closed Access

Library users do not have access to picture files, but to indexes, from which they ask for pictures by artist's name, title, or subject. This has the merit of keeping the pictures in maximum safety, but calls for a heavy investment in indexing if the indexes are to be really useful for, while the first two categories mentioned are relatively easy, the third is by no means so, and it may well be that a single picture will have to be indexed under several different headings. Furthermore, it calls for laborious retrieval work on the part of the staff, unless the user happens to want a specific picture. If he requests a photograph from the 1920s showing 'bright young things' behaving in a frivolous manner — a perfectly legitimate subject — this could well mean that the staff would have to bring him a large number of items, perhaps taken from several different files, each of which would subsequently have to be returned one by one to its place. And this, remember, is simply to give the user sight of the possible material, let alone any question of lending or copying. Clearly, except in the case of works of art or other items of substantial intrinsic value, this is not practicable for most picture libraries.

There is of course one way in which such a system could be made effective, and that is by keeping the pictures themselves on closed access but placing a small contact print, sufficient for identification, on open access; from this users could either request to see the original, if they wished, or order copy prints if they were confident that this would satisfy their needs. This would effectively safeguard valuable items while giving users the opportunity to inspect as much material as they wished, with the additional advantage of facilitating the ordering of copies, a separate matter which we shall be considering later.

The one drawback to this suggestion is that for all but the most munificently endowed collections it would be totally prohibitive in terms of both money and time and would in effect amount to duplicating the entire collection.

There is, however, a compromise, whereby this process can be implemented on a gradual basis. If the policy of the library is to allow its material to be copied, it would be easy enough to arrange things so that every time a picture was copied, a contact print was placed in the files and over the years a visual reference file would be built up of all those items which had already been copied. This could be a parallel file, or the cards bearing contacts could be substituted for purely verbal ones in the same file so that it would become an increasingly visual record. Though perfectly practicable, however, there can be no question that this is very much a second-best solution.

2 Open Access

Library users have immediate access to pictures in files through which they may browse at will. This eliminates the need for indexing, reduces staff work to a minimum, and gives the user maximum opportunity to find what he wants. At the same time it results in maximum damage through wear and tear, not to mention misfiling, theft, and other hazards. Consequently it is only practicable in the case of material of relatively low intrinsic value, whose loss or damage can be faced with comparative equanimity, or which is easily replaceable.

3 Discretionary Access

(a) By User

It is theoretically possible to envisage a two-tier structure of usership, by which certain types of user would be allowed direct access to the material while others would not. It might be felt, for instance, that members of a learned society could be trusted to handle items in their library with proper respect, while some doubts might be felt about granting the same licence to researchers from outside. Such a procedure would in some respects be the worst of both worlds, for the material would still need to be indexed for the benefit of outsiders even though the index would not be required for the trusted users, and staff would be required to provide the necessary retrieval facilities. Except in the case of a very small and highly selective collection, with limited material and restricted usership, such a compromise arrangement hardly seems practicable.

(b) By Material

It is, on the other hand, quite feasible to separate the material itself into classes of greater or lesser value, and to treat each in a different way. Material that is considered suitable for open access can be filed accordingly; valuable or fragile or classified items can be available on request and subject to whatever limitations are appropriate. While this places an additional burden of decision making on the library staff, it offers such a combination of advantages that in many cases it represents the ideal arrangement.

In such a system:

— The main bulk of the collection is available on open access.
— Valuable, fragile, or classified material is subject to closed access, stored in albums, portfolios, boxes, etc.
— Cross-references to the closed-access material are filed along with the open-access material, wherever possible, so that the user is made aware of it at the same time as doing his primary search, and may request it if he so wishes.

Which of these forms of procedure is adopted will depend on the nature of the material and the character of the usership: there is no question of one being 'better' than another. However, it will probably be most helpful if we take as our model in the pages which follow the most complex of the four, the last — *discretionary access by material*. Moreover, I believe that this is likely to be the most practicable model for most general picture collections, and has certainly proved its efficacy in practice in at least one working picture library in Britain.

However, before we can consider how such a policy can best be implemented in concrete terms, we have one further fundamental decision to make: what is to be the library's policy as regards lending and/or copying?

LENDING POLICY

There is perhaps no issue on which picture libraries are more divided than in their answer to the question, 'To lend or not to lend?' There are libraries that will lend every item they possess at the drop of a hat; there are those which will never part with a single item under any circumstances; and there are libraries which lend some items and not others, or lend to some users and not others, or lend some items to some users and others to others.

Yet again, this is not an area where one policy is to be regarded as 'better' than others, but is related, as before, to type of material and type of user. Here are some examples:

— A press agency, dealing entirely with photographs of which it possesses the original negative, will almost invariably prefer not to hold extensive stocks of prints for possible loan, but will make and sell copy prints on demand.

— A colour transparency collection, in view of the cost of making duplicates and the inevitable slight loss of quality, will generally lend its material.

— The print room of a big public collection, where every item is of some value, will lend none, but require users to purchase or arrange for copies.

In the mixed, general library which we have agreed to take as our model, it is probable that a flexible policy will be adopted, whereby some material is loaned — items that are neither too valuable nor too fragile, or are in transparency or copy-print form — while the rest must be copied. But of course this doesn't complete the decision-making process, for the librarian must now decide whether the *copies* are to be loaned or sold.

Here, the decision will generally be contingent on a further factor which has yet to be considered: *who is paying for the service?* If the library is charging for the use of its material, then it may well choose to carry the cost of copying material itself, reckoning it as part of the service it is contracted to provide, and amortizing the copying cost from the revenue derived from the fees paid for the use of the picture. On the other hand, if the basic service is provided free of charge, then it is only reasonable that any user who requires more than that basic service should bear the cost of providing that service. This will probably be a decisive factor in the matter of whether the picture is loaned or purchased:

— Where a user has paid for a picture to be copied so that he may make use of it, he will purchase the copy outright.

— Where a user is not required to carry the cost of copying the picture he wants to use, he will merely borrow the picture and return it when he has finished with it.

Lending pictures brings in its train a number of administrative problems. A copy-and-purchase collection has merely to arrange for a picture to be copied, or for its photographer to provide a further copy print of a picture which has already been copied. A loan collection, on the other hand, has to introduce a system of checking the pictures out and in again, keeping track of each individual transaction. This entails maintaining files of users and files of pictures supplied, with a note regarding holding periods and other pertinent information. This is of course basically the same as with any other type of lending library, so there is no practical difficulty. It does get more complicated, of course, if a charge is made for the loan service, and for the use of the picture, for in such a case the system needs to be a watertight one so that a proper check can be maintained, not only as to who has the picture, but as to what use is being made of it.

We have now elaborated our model library in one further respect, and decided that while some of its material may be loaned to would-be users as it is, other items will have to be copied as they are too valuable or fragile or otherwise unsuitable for loaning. Next it has to be decided, who is to do that copying?

COPYING FACILITIES

A few picture libraries still allow users to do their own photography, or to send in their own photographers. This, which until fairly recently was standard practice at many of the big public collections, is becoming less frequent, and we may expect to see it disappear completely in the very near future. Reluctant as many libraries may be to take on the burden of responsibility for copying, there can be no question that it is overwhelmingly to their advantage to do so. The reasons are obvious enough. First, the risk of damage, which is inevitably greater when an outsider is left free to do the work. Second, the fact that when an outsider has taken the photograph he will probably feel free to make what use he likes of his picture, giving the library no control whatever over what is, still, in some respects its property, in the sense that because it owns the original of the picture it retains certain rights even though the picture has been copied. A further discussion of these points occurs in Section 1.12.

A widespread practice, particularly among public collections, is to contract the work to outside photographers on a regular basis: they come into the library as frequently as the volume of work demands, and do a batch of copying, retaining the negatives from which additional copy prints can be made as they are required. It is up to the library to decide who retains titular ownership of the negatives: librarians should remember that they may, if they choose, insist on retaining ownership and/or possession, though it is important to remember that this must be a matter for negotiation in the first instance as the photographer will otherwise assume, in the light of what is normal practice, that he has the right to retain the negative. Note, too, that the photographer may expect to be paid more if he is not to be the owner of the negative, as this potentially reduces his income — the library, needing further copy prints, could get some other photographer to make them.

These details can, however, be sorted out easily enough when the arrangement is made, and many libraries manage perfectly happily along these lines, saving the cost of maintaining their own facilities which might not be economically justifiable in terms of volume of work.

Nevertheless, there can be no doubt that the best possible arrangement is for the picture library to have its own copying facilities, and these should be incorporated wherever practicable. Every library that requires copying, on however modest a scale, should carry out a feasibility study in this matter, for it will often be found that the enormous savings, when the copying is done in-house, easily recoup the cost of installing equipment and taking on additional staff. Moreover, it will be found that the possession of an in-house photographic department makes it possible for the library to do many things it would not otherwise consider practicable, for example:

— build up a visual index or catalogue, as suggested earlier in this chapter;

— make copies of items which could be filed under various headings — e.g., copying a picture of Saint George so that it can also be filed under 'dragons' — which is much more effective than a verbal cross-reference;

— produce illustrated brochures, catalogues, newsletters, and so on at very low cost;

all this in addition to providing a copy-print service to users of the library at a very economic rate.

Many libraries will no doubt shrink from the step of installing their own photographic facilities, not only on grounds of cost but also of complexity. There is, of course, some justification for this attitude, but technology in the copying field is making such remarkable advances at present, that what used to be a highly skilled practice is steadily becoming one that can be managed even by people who know nothing about photography. For a few hundred pounds, equipment can be purchased on which any member of the library staff, however inexperienced, can quickly learn to make colour transparencies at a fraction of the cost charged by professional photographers; for about £1,200, equipment is available for making perfect facsimiles, enlargements or reductions of black-and-white line material; and it can only be a matter of time before someone develops similar equipment to handle the most difficult type of material — black and white photographs. (Black and white photographs are more difficult to make than colour because the latter are subject to a one-stage process — the film taken *is,* after processing, the picture — whereas black and white photographs have to undergo a second operation — printing from the negative.)

The decision about copying is the last of the 'theoretical' decisions which must be taken before a picture library begins to make its material available for exploitation, and it is appropriate to present, at this point, a summary of the decision-making process so far (see below).

The six items on the lowest level of the chart represent the six types of actual material which the library could make available to users for exploitation purposes. Some libraries — the British Library, for example — would be dealing with only the second, *purchased copies of valuable originals,* while a more flexible establishment, such as the Mary Evans

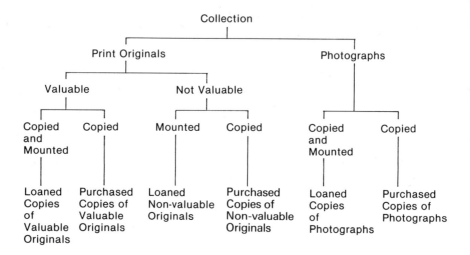

Picture Library, is liable to find itself handling all six at one time or another, according to users' needs.

ACCESS PROCEDURES

Open Access

We have now reached the stage where our imaginary library has made a succession of decisions and, according to those decisions, has a picture collection which is more or less accessible, whose contents may be inspected either in their original or in copy form, and which — unless it is purely a reference library — has facilities whereby it can make available, on a loan or purchase basis, and in original or copy form, its material for exploitation. In what follows it will be assumed that we are concerned with a library which is willing for as much of its material as possible to be available on open access, but recognizes that some of its material must be reserved on closed access, requiring special procedure.

The next question, clearly, is how can the open access material be made available to users as readily as possible yet with minimal risk of damage or loss?

Transparencies

The 35 mm. transparency is the librarian's dream come true — a small, lightweight item, easily protected despite its inherent vulnerability, and easily captioned, especially if stored in one of the many ready-made wallets or files now available. Enormous numbers can be stored in a tiny corner of a room, requiring no specialized furniture — a standard A4 filing cabinet will meet the requirement perfectly. All that is needed is to devise a classification and numbering system, provide a lightbox to enable viewers to see what they are looking at, and you are in business.

Printed Items

These should be separated according to size. Larger items should not be available on open access because of the risk of damage: a reasonable size limit is approximately 25 × 20 cm. Pictures larger than this should be on closed access, and will therefore be considered in the following section.

Pictures up to this size can be conveniently stored in several different ways — in an envelope in a suspended file, in flat drawers, or in box files. If kept in any of these, there is no necessity to mount them, except from the point of view of preserving them from wear and tear. On the other hand, none of these methods offers maximum ease of access, and all necessitate the handling of a number of items before the user reaches the specific item being sought. So, while such storage methods may be adequate for material which is rarely referred to, they are not suited to a collection which is deliberately geared to exploitation.

For such a collection, undoubtedly the most satisfactory method is to place the pictures upright, in a filing cabinet, so that they can be flipped through like a large card index. For this purpose, they must be rigid rather than flimsy, from which it follows that most items will have to be mounted onto a stiff material (see also Section 1.5). This is of course tiresome. On the other hand, it has many secondary benefits. It provides substance, so that the picture is less easily bent or torn; it creates wide margins in most cases, so that the edges of the picture are not folded or scuffed; it makes space available for captioning; and by using mounting cards of a standard size, irrespective of the size of the picture itself, pictures of varying sizes can be presented in a uniform format, diminishing the risk of loss or damage, simplifying filing, and making the task of flipping through a collection of pictures relatively easy.

The optimum size is 28 × 21 cm. which happens to be an economical size relative to the sheets of card from which the individual cards are cut. This is slightly larger than the 25 × 20 cm. standard photographic size, and comfortably accommodates most printed pictures, such as the half-page *Illustrated London News* wood engravings which are the mainstay of so many historical collections. The purist may well prefer a straight A4 format, but he will find that this frequently leaves him with an embarrassingly wide margin at either end of the picture.

Photographs

The librarian whose collection consists entirely of photographs will probably not consider mounting them, for it would add enormously to both cost and labour. Even so, if the library reckons to loan its material, it is worth considering whether the protection provided by mounting will not in the long run justify the expense. An unmounted photograph can seldom be lent more than two or three times before it has become useless through handling, whereas a mounted photograph can expect a much longer life.

Of course many collections contain mixed material, printed items as well as photographs. In such cases, if the decision has been taken to mount the printed items, the librarian will do well to grit his teeth and mount the photographic material also, for this will mean that both classes of material can be filed together, rather than as two separate systems.

It takes an act of courage on the librarian's part to resolve to mount a picture collection. But once the decision has been made and the new system tried, the librarian will wonder why he ever hesitated.

Closed Access

Even in a picture library which is basically open access, there will be a certain amount of material which is unsuitable for open availability along with the main bulk of the material. This is most likely to be because it is too valuable but it may also be because it is too fragile, or too large, or in book or periodical form.

Despite these inconveniences, it should be the policy of the library to make it available to users, albeit on somewhat stricter conditions than the rest of the collection. Even though the materials be of considerable value, they should be accessible to bona fide scholars who can show good cause why they should inspect the original rather than a copy — to act otherwise would be to behave like people who buy jewellery or postage stamps only to keep them in a bank vault. A picture library is not in the investment business.

Consequently, wherever practicable, the material should be housed in a form which facilitates retrieval by the staff, and inspection by users of the library, with a minimum of handling. This subject will have been considered at greater length in another chapter of this book; for our present purposes it is enough to recommend that as much of the material as possible should be housed in plastic see-through files, folders, or display albums, which allow the item to be clearly seen while preventing direct contact.

The greater danger with closed-access material is, of course, that people forget that it is there. This is especially likely to be the case when the bulk of the collection is immediately accessible on open access. Consequently, unless the library has good cause to conceal the fact of the existence of closed-access material, there should be some indication, at the same time as the user is inspecting the open-access material, that there is supplementary material available on closed access. The obvious way to do this is to file a card, the same size as the open-access pictures but perhaps of a different colour, bearing the relevant information. If the closed-access item has been copied, then it will be possible to include a contact print showing the item, so that the user will have a clear guide as to whether he should ask to see it.

Copied Items

It may be thought that, once a picture has been copied, there is little point in keeping the original in the open-access files. However, this is not really the case. The original will always have a specific quality which the copy will not possess, even though — as can happen — the copy is actually superior, from a reproduction point of view, to the original. The original should therefore be retained for purposes of inspection, although there may be some indication that it is there only for that purpose, and may not be borrowed.

Contact Prints and References

When a picture has been copied, some kind of reference should be kept so that, should further prints be required, the appropriate number can be given to the photographer.

It is a good idea, at the same time, to get the photographer to provide a small contact print, which can be filed as a visual reminder of the copied picture. This will mean that, if by any chance all the existing copies of the picture are out of the library, there is still a visual reminder to work from. Naturally, the best place to keep this is not in a separate file, where its existence can easily be forgotten, but in the same file as the rest of the material, mounted on another card, the same size as the others, and serving as an immediate indication of the existence of the additional item. Naturally, such a card should never be allowed to leave the library under any circumstances; to order another print from the photographer, one should simply quote the reference number or send a photostat of the picture.

Similarly, references to items in books or periodicals can be housed in the open files, whether the material itself is on open or closed access. Thus, if an interesting item is found in such a publication, a verbal reference — on yet another card — will direct the user to the source.

If all these recommendations are followed, the result will be an open-access file consisting of a variety of standard size cards, possibly colour-coded to their differing functions:

- the print original
- copy print(s) from the original
- contact print of the copied original, with photographer's reference number for reordering
- reference card to closed-access material
- reference card to transparency file if appropriate
- reference card to related items in books and periodicals, and other items which, though not on closed access, are for one reason or another unsuitable for filing with the primary collection.

COSTS AND CHARGES

In order to make it possible for our material to be exploited, we have come a long way from the packets full of variegated pictures with which the collection in all likelihood started. The individual items have been cleaned, identified, and captioned. They have been mounted on protective mounts, stored in wallets or envelopes, or placed in albums or portfolios, in box files or plan chests. They have been classified into convenient categories and labelled accordingly, and filed in such a way as to make their retrieval as convenient as possible. If they are valuable they have been photographed, their negative numbers recorded, and reference prints filed where they may be readily inspected. At the same time, on the administration side, a procedural structure has been created so that users may either borrow items or order copies of them. In short, a number of people have done a great deal of work. Who is going to pay for it all?

Costs

Some picture libraries will have been created as an adjunct to some institution which has a need for such a service: an obvious example is a picture library created to meet the needs of an art college. Here, the library is evidently part of the service facilities of the establishment, and the financial authorities will have taken this into account, hopefully fairly realistically. All costs will be met out of whatever budget has been allocated, and those who use the facilities of the library will not be expected to pay for its services unless they make exceptional demands on it.

At the other extreme are those picture libraries created, if not specifically in order to provide a source of income, at least on such a basis that they depend entirely for their survival on the revenue that they can derive from the exploitation of their material. While all such libraries are inevitably classified as 'commercial', and there is a clear division between them and the 'public' collections, this is often largely a technical distinction. In practice, the collections may be very similar both in their material and in the way they operate, the difference consisting in the way they are financed. Many public collections start as the work of a single enthusiastic collector, just as most 'commercial' ones do: the fact that the collection was subsequently donated or otherwise taken over by a public institution does not necessarily mean that its character has changed greatly. The reason why many so-called commercial collections *are* commercial is so that they can be self-financing when no other source of financial assistance is to be looked for.

Between the wholly-tied collection whose facilities are not available outside a clearly demarcated public, and the commercial collection which is generally available to all comers, are all gradations of picture library which are funded either by a public authority or by some specific institution, such as a learned society, and whose resources, though primarily intended for a specific group, are probably also available to a wider public provided certain conditions are complied with. In such cases, basic running costs for the creation and maintenance of the collection are paid by the institution in question — but it is also reasonable to require that those who not only use but actually profit from the library should also contribute to its upkeep by paying for the service they receive.

Once this principle has been admitted, the implementation of the decision is a relatively straightforward, if somewhat remorselessly logical process, in which the librarian will become inextricably involved in a commercial web of ever-increasing complexity. It will be well for him to face this from the start and build the necessary commercial structure, in all its gruesome logic, from the outset, rather than seek to persuade himself that it is not all necessary. For, alas, it *is* necessary, and only by starting out as he will have to go on will the librarian's existence be bearable.

Next, comes the complex question of what charges should be made for the services. Will there be an overall standard fee, or will it be flexible — if so, to what extent? (See Section 1.12 for detailed discussion of charges.)

Lastly, the fact has got to be faced that when services are being formally charged and paid for, they have got to be worth the money. The library now has a new dimension of responsibility towards its users. So long as a service is being provided free of charge, the user has no cause for complaint if he gets something less than the highest standard, but a professional operation implies professional standards — prompt delivery, meticulous paperwork, constant attention to detail.

All this will inevitably add to costs and make greater demands on staff.

Before embarking on such an operation, the library must be sure that the income to be derived from it will be sufficient to cover these additional costs and still make it economically viable. There is no point in setting up a complex system if it does no more than cover its own cost: it must bring in additional revenue to the library which can be put to good use, either in the improvement of services or enlargement of the collection.

Charges

Those who use pictures professionally expect to pay for that use, but they do not expect to pay the same amount regardless of how the picture is used. They expect to pay more for a modern photograph than for a historical print; they also expect to pay more for a 'known-name' photographer like Cartier-Bresson than for a young unknown from East Grinstead; and even if the pictures themselves are of equal value though coming from two different sources, they expect to pay more to the source which gives them the better service. They may consider it worth paying more to a commercial source, which provides material in a matter of hours, than to a public source which may not supply the requested item in less than two or three months.

Consequently, it is largely up to the librarian to decide what quality of service, particularly in the matter of time, he is prepared, or able, to give those who use the library. It is not an easy decision to make and many factors will influence it. Other things being equal, however, the librarian should aim to provide a quality of the highest standard, for in so doing not only will the library be justified in charging more for the service provided, but the library's reputation will be enhanced. So, though of course it costs a lot more to provide a really good service, it is generally well worth the extra investment.

Whatever the library has to offer, either in terms of material or service, once a librarian has made the decision to exploit a collection, he should enter into the task in a whole-hearted and totally committed fashion.

THE MEANING OF EXPLOITATION

Underlying the various practical aspects of exploitation that have been discussed, a more fundamental message has pervaded this chapter: that message takes the form of a warning, that a library cannot hope to enjoy the rewards of exploitation without paying the price.

We have spoken of costs, of the need for equipment, of staff time, of the necessity for rigorous procedural methods, and so on, but these are only the material expressions of a more basic change. For, quite simply, exploitation changes the character of a library, not just in its immediate and outward aspects, but in its very nature.

Properly controlled, this change can be almost wholly for the better. It means that the library enjoys an added dimension of vitality, that its pictures benefit from a new lease of life by being used, not simply as relics of the past, but as elements in creations of the present. To see a *Punch* cartoon on the subject of the polluted Thames resuscitated from the 1840s because of its relevance in the 1970s is a reminder that pictures in a library are human documents, not dead scraps of paper.

And so the dialogue between library and user will animate the working life of the library, awakening staff to new possibilities, opening up new attitudes to the material itself, breathing new life into a static collection. For the most part this stimulus will work unvoiced and unnoticed, but by the nature of their requests and by the way in which they use the material and services, those who use the library will, in time, change it.

This is something to welcome rather than fear, but the librarian should be aware of it because it will from time to time constitute a threat to the library — for example, if so many requests were received for a certain type of material, or a certain service, that the essential quality of the library would have to be modified in order to meet them. In such a case the librarian would have to consider whether it would be detrimental to the fundamental character of the library to make such changes, and whether, by meeting demands from a specific quarter, the services provided in other respects might suffer.

But such negative possibilities can be dealt with as they occur, and the prospect of their occurrence is not so great a threat as to discourage the librarian from taking positive steps to broaden the scope of what the library has to offer. Exploitation is a positive step forward which, if taken prudently and in full knowledge of the pitfalls, can carry the library into new fields of activity and new dimensions of relevance which will have an invigorating and stimulating effect on the library, on those who use it, and those who work in it.

REFERENCES

1   *Reproduction fees, photography, etc; guidelines for museums.* Museums Association Information Sheet number 20, 1975.

2   For information about BAPLA, write to PO Box 93, London NW6 5XW.

3   *Picture researcher's handbook,* Saturday Ventures, 1979. Enquiries to 11 Granville Park, London SE13 7DY.

4   Evans, Hilary *The art of picture research.* Newton Abbot, David & Charles, 1979.

11

Copyright in Artistic Works

Geoffrey Crabb

INTRODUCTION

The law of copyright is designed to give legal status to the principle that the creators of certain types of material should have the right to control, and to derive financial benefit from, the use which society makes of the material. Few will contest the validity of this principle. Not only does it represent a fundamental human right but it has the more pragmatic effect of encouraging the creation and production of more material for the general benefit.

Although the principle is positive, the law of copyright, which in the United Kingdom is determined by the Copyright Act 1956, adopts a negative approach. It does not, for example, provide that every new novel must be published or that every composition must be performed. It merely gives the owner of the copyright the sole right to do, or authorize others to do certain acts in relation to the work. In other words, before a protected item may be legally used in certain ways the permission of the owner of the copyright must be obtained. The copyright owner has the right to refuse permission or, in giving it, to demand remuneration usually referred to as a royalty.

CURRENT LAW

The Copyright Act of 1956 (the Act) grants protection to literary, dramatic and musical works, sound recordings, films, broadcasts, and published editions, i.e., the typographical layout of a literary, musical, or dramatic work. It also protects artistic works and it is these which are of interest to picture librarians and which form the subject of this article.

The Act defines artistic works as including:

— paintings
— sculptures
— drawings (including diagrams, maps, charts, plans)
— engravings (including etchings, lithographs, woodcuts, prints)
— photographs (including any product of any process akin to photography other than a cinematograph film).

All these items are protected irrespective of artistic merit. In addition protection is given to works of architecture (buildings or models for buildings) and works of artistic craftsmanship, the meaning of which is unclear but which would include jewellery or other artifacts not produced from drawings.

Protection is given provided the work is original and either the 'author' was a qualified person or, if published, the work was first published in the United Kingdom. These conditions need some explanation. The term 'original' is not meant to imply novelty, only that the work is not copied from an existing one. For example, a photograph of Big Ben is hardly novel but each new photograph, not copied from an existing one, is original and acquires copyright protection. 'Qualified person' means a British or Irish citizen or one who is resident in the United Kingdom. In practice, because of this country's adherence to international conventions artistic works will, with few exceptions, be protected here irrespective of the country of origin.

It is commonly supposed that copyright exists only if the c-in-a-circle symbol appears on works, but this is not so. Provided the conditions of original work by a qualified person are met then protection is automatic from the moment of creation. Although the symbol is internationally recognized as an indication that protection is claimed, it has no legal standing in this country and its absence in no way weakens the copyright status of a work.

This is an appropriate point to mention a common mistake in assuming that ownership of a work as a physical object goes hand in hand with the ownership of the copyright. This is not the case in law and rarely in practice. If an artist paints a picture of St Paul's and then sells it to a collector or art gallery, the artist retains the copyright unless, in selling the painting, the copyright in it is implicitly or explicitly transferred as well.

If the conditions for protection are present and copyright exists in an artistic work, the period of protection lasts until the author dies and for 50 years thereafter. Here again there are some exceptions to this general rule. Engravings are protected until the author dies or until first publication, whichever comes last, and for 50 years thereafter. Photographs are protected until first publication and for 50 years thereafter.

From this it will be appreciated that in order to determine whether, say, a drawing is out of copyright it is only necessary to discover the year of death of the artist but an engraving made by an engraver who died more than 50 years ago may still be in copyright if it remains unpublished or was first published only within the past 50 years. Similarly, the death of the author of a photograph is immaterial since the term of protection is determined by the date of first publication and unpublished photographs remain protected in perpetuity. Librarians with an interest in old photographs will wish to know that photographs taken before 1957, when the Act came into force, are protected for 50 years from when they were taken and publication is irrelevant.

The Act also deals with the ownership of copyright in artistic works, or rather stipulates where ownership lies at the time a work is created. The distinction is important because copyright, as a moveable property, can be bought and sold, given away and left in a will and during the period of protection the ownership of copyright may change many times. For example, an artist may sell his copyright to a book publisher who, subsequently, may sell it to a greetings card manufacturer, and so on.

So, the ownership of copyright at any one time depends on the contractual arrangements that have been made since the work was created. All that the Act can do is to state where ownership lies at the start and this is generally with the 'author', a term used by the Act to cover painters, engravers, and sculptors although in respect of photographs it is the person who, at the time the photograph is taken, is the owner of the material on which it is taken.

However, there are some important exceptions to the rule that the first owner of the copyright is the author. These are:

1   Where an artistic work is made by the author in the course of employment by a newspaper, magazine, or periodical under a

contract of service, then the proprietor has the copyright insofar as use in these types of publication is concerned but the author keeps the copyright insofar as other use is concerned.

2   If (1) does not apply, then where a person commissions the taking of a photograph, or the making of an engraving or the painting or drawing of a portrait, the person commissioning the work is entitled to the copyright in it, provided there is no agreement to the contrary.

3   If (1) and (2) do not apply, then where an artistic work is made in the course of employment under a contract of service, the employer is entitled to the copyright provided there is no agreement to the contrary.

The term 'in the course of employment' means the work is created as part of the duties for which the author is employed and 'a contract of service' means the normal employer/employee relationship.

Finally, the Act specifies those acts which can be legally performed only with the prior consent of the owner of copyright. These are called 'the restricted acts' and the number and style vary from one type of material to another. The copyright owner of an artistic work has the sole right to do, or authorize, the following restricted acts:

1   reproduction of the work in any material form
2   publication of the work
3   inclusion of the work in a television broadcast
4   transmission of a television programme which includes the work to subscribers to a diffusion service.

The implication of (1) is that the copyright in a painting is infringed, not only if another painting is made from it, but if it is reproduced in some other form, such as a photograph, or included in a film. The term 'publication' in (2) has caused considerable interpretative problems but it means a distribution, whether for sale or otherwise, sufficient to satisfy the reasonable demands of the public, so it is immaterial how many copies are distributed provided it is available to anyone who wants it rather than to a private group. The other restricted acts are of less interest to librarians and more the concern of the makers and transmitters of television programmes. Note that to display an artistic work in public is not a restricted act.

It is important to understand that the copyright status of a work is not diminished by its inclusion in another work. For example, if a copyright painting is photographed there will, in the finished photograph, be two copyrights, one in the photograph itself and another in the painting. So, anyone intending to copy the photograph will require the permission, not only of the copyright owner of the photograph, but of the painting also and they may possibly be two different people. To copy a photograph of a painting, where the painting is out of copyright, will require permission only in respect of the photograph. Conversely, to copy a photograph taken in 1920 of a painting by an artist who died in 1950 will require the permission only of the owner of the copyright in the painting.

Summary

Before continuing, it may be helpful to summarize what has been covered so far.

1 A wide range of artistic works are protected including photographs.
2 No formalities are necessary in order that works may be protected in the UK but they must be original and originate from the UK or another country with which the UK has reciprocal arrangements.
3 Ownership of copyright will probably change as a result of commercial deals but the first owner is normally the 'author', although the first owner of the copyright in a photograph is the owner of the material on which it is taken. There are exceptions where authors are employed by newspapers, where certain works are commissioned and where works are otherwise produced as part of an employee's duties.
4 Copyright lasts for at least 50 years from either first publication or the death of the 'author' but photographs taken before 1957 are protected for 50 years from when taken.
5 There are four acts which only the copyright owner of an artistic work may do or authorize others to do but only two, reproducing in material form and publishing, are of direct interest to librarians.

STATUTORY CONCESSIONS

In seeking to protect the originators of artistic works, the Act recognizes that there are circumstances where too rigid an application of the restricted acts would be unreasonable. It therefore provides a range of concessions whereby to copy without the authority of the copyright owner is not an infringement. In order to infringe copyright a substantial part of the work must be used and, although there are no definitions in the Act, litigation has shown that not only must the proportion of the part copied to the whole be considered but also the importance of that part to the whole. Using this guide, if the Mona Lisa was still in copyright it would probably not be an infringement to copy six square inches of the background but it might be if the same area of that famous smile were copied.

Generally speaking, if the part taken can be said to be significant then it is probably substantial and permission is required. It is easy to fall into the trap of regarding an illustration in a book as just part of the book and to copy it as an unsubstantial part, whereas in fact the whole of the artistic work is being copied and the relationship of the illustration to the book is irrelevant.

In addition, the concept of fair dealing is extended to artistic works. This provides, *inter alia,* that artistic works may be copied for the purposes of research or private study and for the purposes of criticism and review on condition that the circumstances are 'fair' to the owner of the copyright. Librarians will be familiar with the Library Regulations which permit them to provide copies of literary, dramatic, and musical material to applicants wanting them for research or private study and to fellow librarians for their collections. It is only appropriate here to mention that artistic works are not included in the Library Regulations, except where they comprise illustrations to literary, dramatic, or musical works. Similarly, the provisions of the Act which permit certain manuscripts to be copied and published do not extend to artistic works except where they illustrate or explain the manuscript.

These provisions reveal rather muddled thinking on the part of the legislators because artistic works may be copied for research or private study but, whereas librarians are permitted to copy literary, dramatic, and musical material for applicants, they are not permitted to do so in respect of artistic works unless they form part of a literary, dramatic, or musical work. The practical result is that a student may copy an artistic work on a photocopier at a railway station but a librarian cannot make one on the student's behalf.

Against this, the British Copyright Council in 1970 issued a statement, 'Photocopying and the Law'. While this dealt primarily with literary material, it did acknowledge that previously artistic works were often displayed on a screen by use of an epidiascope and the making of a slide or transparency was merely a modern equivalent. The Council stated that artists and publishers would not object to the making of a single copy of an illustration from a book, if in the form of a slide or transparency, for teaching purposes. In practice, it is doubtful if the owner of the copyright in an artistic work would object to librarians making a copy for projection purposes, either in the library or on behalf of an educational establishment requiring it for teaching purposes. They should not, however, supply copies to applicants requiring them for research or private study unless, as already stated, the work illustrates a literary, dramatic, or musical work.

On the other hand, artistic works are covered by some special regulations because they are frequently displayed in public places:

1   The copyright in a sculpture or work of artistic craftsmanship which is permanently situated in a public place or in premises open to the public is not infringed by the making of a painting, drawing, engraving, photograph, or film of it or by its inclusion in a film or television broadcast. This concession applies also to works of architecture.

2   The copyright in an artistic work is not infringed by its inclusion in a film or television broadcast if only by way of background or incidentally.

3   Where a painting, engraving, film, etc. is made as under (1) and (2) the copyright in the artistic work is not infringed if the painting etc. is subsequently published.

4   The making of an object of any description which is in three dimensions shall not be taken to infringe the copyright in an artistic work in two dimensions, if the object would not appear, to persons who are not experts in relation to objects of that description, to be a reproduction of the artistic work.

PRACTICAL IMPLICATIONS

The foregoing, rather potted, summary of the law of copyright in artistic works can now be related to the field of picture librarianship. This can be divided into two areas, the acquisition of material by the librarian and the use which is made of it while it is deposited in the library. It will be seen that, provided artistic works are acquired legally, there is nothing in the law of copyright which prevents their being stored, catalogued, displayed, or loaned to the public. The circumstances under which librarians acquire material may incur limitations as to its use, or common courtesy may imply the need to ask the permission of benefactors even where the work is out of copyright.

Librarians should be careful not to ask permission to do something which they have a legal right to do and to resist pressure to pay copyright fees when what is really being demanded is a fee in exchange for access to a work. Such arrangements are not copyright matters and only cause confusion when used in such a way that a copyright interest is suggested.

PERMISSIONS

Copyright is of relevance where librarians wish to make copies of artistic works and to distribute them. Permission to do this will be needed unless the following circumstances apply:

1   The work is not protected by copyright because it is not original or it originates from a country with which the UK has no reciprocal rights (very few of these).
2   The work is out of copyright because of its age.
3   The part to be copied is not substantial in terms of proportion or importance. The librarian must decide this and it is for the copyright owner to challenge the decision, in court if necessary.
4   The artistic work illustrates a manuscript which is covered by the library provisions of the Act.
5   The artistic work illustrates a literary work which is covered by the Library Regulations for the supplying of copies to other libraries and to researchers and private students.
6   The copying is permitted under the provisions which apply to works of sculpture or to artistic works generally.
7   The copying is covered by the statement of the British Copyright Council or, by implication, is merely the production of a single slide or transparency for lecturing or teaching purposes.

These apart, there are no statutory provisions for librarians to make

copies of artistic works and the permission of the copyright owner or owners must be acquired in each case. It has already been mentioned that an artistic work may represent two or more copyright elements (a photograph of a painting) and permission is needed for both. Likewise, the individual restricted acts will have to be cleared and not necessarily with the same copyright owner. For example, if a librarian wishes to make copies for exhibition use only, the right to reproduce will be required, but if the copies are for general distribution then the right to publish will be required in addition. It is therefore essential, when seeking permission, to be very explicit as to:
— the number of reproductions to be made
— the use to which they are to be put
— the method of distribution and whether for sale or gratis.

A standard letter form is a useful and time-saving device if a lot of clearance work is done. This can take the form of a standard request letter on one side, with provision on the reverse for the details to be inserted. Copyright owners do appreciate being able to sign a release slip at the foot of the letter which saves them time and effort. Here is a possible form of wording for such a letter.

Dear Sirs,

Request for permission to reproduce copyright material

Would you please confirm that, as the owner of the reproduction rights, you will permit the Library to reproduce the material listed overleaf for the purposes stated. Full acknowledgement of the source will be made. If you are not authorized to grant these rights would you please let me know whom I should contact.

To save you time and trouble, may I suggest you return this letter or a photocopy of it, duly authorized in the space provided.

Yours faithfully,

Librarian

(Reverse)

Description of material

Reproductions required for

I/We, as owners of the reproduction rights, agree that the Library may reproduce the material for the purposes stated. We require no fee/We require a fee of   for these rights. (Please delete whichever is inappropriate.)

Dated............   Signed............

Note: Fees are payable if and when the right granted is exercised.

Tracing the names and addresses of copyright owners is sometimes difficult and occasionally impossible. Illustrations in books and periodicals frequently cause difficulty where the authors and publishers do not own the rights but have only acquired from the copyright owner a limited permission to include them in the publication. Sometimes several approaches to different people are necessary before the right one is tracked down. Failure to trace the copyright owner is no justification for proceeding without permission but in a court action evidence of an attempt to clear may support the library's case, so all correspondence, even if it is one-sided, should be retained.

INTERNATIONAL COPYRIGHT

Finally, a word about 'international copyright'. This is a misnomer because there is no such thing as 'international copyright'. Most countries include copyright in their legislative structure but the provisions, and even the philosophies behind the provisions, vary considerably from one to another. For example, it would not, in the UK, be an infringement to mutilate an artistic work but it might well be in France which includes in its copyright law the conception of the '*droit moral*', or the moral right of the author, an idea quite alien to the rather commercial and down-to-earth approach of the 1956 Act. All countries provide for a term of copyright after which a work loses its protection and becomes public property, but the term varies quite considerably, being 50 years in Britain but 70 years in the German Federal Republic. It follows that a work can still be protected in one country when it has already expired in another.

However, most countries adhere to either, or both, the Berne Convention or the Universal Copyright Convention. These do not seek to impose a uniform law in every country but instead lay down certain minimum standards which member countries accept. Having become a signatory of a Convention a country agrees to extend to the nationals of other member states the same degree of protection as it gives its own nationals. This means that a French painting in Britain is treated in the same way as a British painting and in France a British painting comes under French law.

Since Britain is a signatory of both Conventions and between them they represent about 100 countries, it follows that most artistic works from abroad are protected to the same extent as domestic works and the concessions apply equally. It is really only when domestic works are sent abroad that the copyright laws of foreign states become relevant but, as it is impossible to deal in a helpful way with this vast subject in a short article, librarians concerned with distribution overseas are advised to seek legal advice when in doubt.

US COPYRIGHT

Librarians in the United States benefit from special provisions contained in the revised legislation which came into force in 1978 and replaced the outdated legislation of 1909. The Act introduces into American law the concept of 'fair use' but, like its British counterpart, provides no definition of the term. It does go a little further than the 1956 Act because, not only does it list the purposes for which fair use may apply (criticism, comment, teaching, scholarship, and research), but also lists four examples of factors which a court must consider when faced with a defence plea of 'fair use'. These include whether the use is for commercial purposes, the amount copied in relation to the whole, and the likely effect of the copying upon the potential market or value of the work. All categories of protected material are included, so pictorial, graphic, and sculptural works may be copied under the 'fair use' exemption.

Quite apart from the 'fair use' provisions of Section 107, there are special arrangements for libraries and archives in Section 108. They are complex and do not all refer to pictorial, graphic, and sculptural works but American public libraries may reproduce these types of material for non-commercial purposes:

1   Where the item is unpublished and is reproduced in facsimile form for purposes of preservation or security or for deposit for research use in another library or archive.
2   Where the item is published and is reproduced in facsimile form for the purposes of replacing a lost, damaged or stolen item, provided that a replacement copy cannot be obtained at a fair price.
3   Where the item is an illustration, diagram, or similar adjunct to a journal article or collection or other printed work which the library is copying on behalf of someone requiring it for private study, scholarship, or research.

So, although pictorial, graphic, and sculptural works may be copied, under certain restrictions, for preservation, security, or replacement purposes, copies may not be supplied to applicants unless they are required for private study, scholarship, or research *and* they form part of a printed work, such as a book or periodical, which librarians are permitted to copy for these purposes on conditions laid down in Section 108.

Libraries and archives may also make off-air videotape recordings of daily newscasts for lending to scholars and researchers. This is an example where the new American law provides greater latitude than does the 1956 Act but, conversely, the American law gives the owner of copyright the sole right to display his work publicly, a provision not found in the 1956 Act. This means that libraries not only need permission to copy but also to display pictorial, graphic, and sculptural works in public. On the other hand, Section 109 (b) provides that the owner of a copy which has been lawfully made is entitled, without the authority of the copyright owner, to display the copy either directly or by projection to viewers present at the place where the copy is located.

The precise meaning and implications of Section 108 must await court decisions or the agreement of guidelines between librarians and copyright owners. Arrangements are already in hand to hold a series of public hearings to evaluate whether the section has achieved the aim of balancing the needs of libraries and copyright owners.

Further advice on general matters of copyright in the UK may be obtained by writing to The Rights Development Officer, CET, 3 Devonshire St, London W1. The following publications may be helpful:

Council for Educational Technology
— Five leaflets on copyright matters. Free.
— G Crabb *Copyright agreements between employers and staff in education.* Free.
— G Crabb *Copyright clearance – a practical guide* (for teachers). £3.25 + postage.

Museums Association
— Charles H Gibbs-Smith *Copyright law concerning works of art, photographs and the written and spoken word.* 3rd ed. London Museums Association, 1978.

12

Administration

Helen P Harrison

The administration of picture collections is closely allied to administration in other libraries. It incorporates the same range of activities as well as the same diversity of libraries. In managing resources and stock, planning, budgeting, and staffing, the administrator of a picture collection whether he or she is called a library manager, photo librarian, picture librarian, curator, or director will need to apply general management practices and adapt a specialist knowledge of pictures to running a collection. The range of job titles given to picture librarians is as varied as that applied to most managers of resource collections, whether these resources are books or audio-visual materials. Most managers of picture collections start with a specialist knowledge or interest in the materials themselves and it is seldom that a collection is run by a manager *per se*. What is more important is that the librarian, whatever his or her title, should have some grounding in management principles in addition to technical skills or special subject knowledge. This can be the subject of short courses or part of the general training of picture librarians, but it is important to introduce the concept of management training to librarians in charge of collections to enable them to organize and exploit these collections to advantage. An interest in pictures is a good starting point for a picture librarian, but without the ability to manage a collection and to accept a great many administrative chores the librarian will not effectively exploit the materials in his or her charge.

One of the first principles of management is to establish the aims and objectives of the collection. What is its purpose, either standing on its own as a commercial venture or as part of another institution? Following directly on from this, who are the users of the material and what do they use it for? A librarian coming to a collection needs to seek out answers to such questions and establish policies which will achieve the objectives of the library or institution in an efficient way. This will apply to all libraries whether large or small and, in the long run, it is up to the librarian as a professional to draw up the policies and procedures appropriate to the library concerned and the public it serves.

Mention has been made of different types of picture libraries and some basic functions can be drawn from the range. A picture library may exist for reasons of conservation, collection around a particular subject, exploitation — that is providing material primarily for reproduction by publishers and others — or for information about the picture material itself. These categories are not of course mutually exclusive, but priorities have to be established, for example between conservation and use. Policies must be formulated according to whether the material is to be preserved in as good a state as possible or whether usage of, for example, current news material is of more importance than long-term preservation. Is the user likely to want the material for illustration or for study purposes only? The answer will influence access conditions.

One of the most important functions of the librarian is to form the collection into a coherent whole rather than just a collection of pictures, or to give it a purpose, whether this is a central theme or an objective. This will help to give the collection a special identity according to subject, material, or the services rendered.

Having established the function of the library and its clientele it is essential for the librarian to establish the extent of his or her authority. Who is responsible for the collection and at what level does responsibility rest? Is the librarian in sole charge of stock, budgets, and staff or is there a structure within a department or institution which spreads responsibility? If so, the librarian must understand his or her own position within this hierarchy and where to go for financial and other support.

STAFFING

There are four main areas of work in a picture library:

— Administration
— Professional
— Clerical
— Technical.

Administration   Duties carried out by the administrative staff include the current management of the collection, future planning and the formulation of policies and procedures, whether the collection is an independent unit, or part of a larger organization, according to the needs and objectives of that organization. Supervision of all areas is necessary to ensure the work is carried out within the guidelines. Staff recruitment, training, and supervision also comes within administration, as well as budget control, the management of funds, and the general exploitation of the collection, including contacts with users and suppliers to achieve a balanced service.

Professional staff are responsible for areas of acquisition and selection, including the evaluation of materials and the ordering of reference materials, photographs, and illustrations. Cataloguing and classification of the collection and enquiry work also form a major part of the professional duties. Staff in this category have a great deal of contact with the users and can explain the scope and content of the collection, as well as instruct the user in the most effective methods of finding material and the regulations of usage and reproduction: in other words user education is the responsibility of this section of the staff. Finally, they have some responsibility for selection and evaluation of equipment.

In the larger picture libraries especially in the commercial area there is a need for accounting staff.

Clerical staff carry out clerical and secretarial functions, such as record-keeping, typing, filing, and issue desk or circulation control duties. They also process photographs and slides, including accessioning where applicable, mount both photographs and slides, label and file the materials. The operation of office machinery, as well as some of the processing equipment such as mounting presses, should be delegated to the clerical staff.

Technical staff are responsible for the production of material for the collection, either in the form of original or copy photography, the duplication of slides, the printing of photographs, for the collection or for supply to users, and the maintenance of the photographic and laboratory equipment.

Number of Personnel Required

Inevitably there is considerable overlap in the function of different members of staff, according to the size and type of library, the growth rate of the collection and the issue systems in use whether postal or internal, and the complexity of the cataloguing systems. In smaller libraries employing few people there may be only one or two to perform the whole variety of jobs, while in other libraries with large stocks jobs are more clearly defined. In other libraries, some aspects of the work are absent, for example where the library sends processing work to outside photographers or laboratories and maintains no technical staff of its own, or where other departments within the parent organization exist to provide technical or accounting support. However, whatever else the collection lacks it needs clerical support, for the amount of paperwork produced by illustrations is considerable and the filing and general control of the material is the single most essential part of a picture library's function. An untidy, ill-housed, badly filed library is worse than no library at all. It cannot be exploited if no-one can find the material and the visual indigestion resulting from being let loose in a large, badly controlled collection in the hope that 'browsing' will reveal all is enough to turn even the most conscientious picture researcher away.

The different types of library also reflect the spread of staff in the above categories. Those libraries with an archival function require more professional staff to identify and index the material, as well as conservation staff to preserve the stock. Commercial libraries with large stocks and distribution turnover need enquiry staff and administration. Technical staff are needed in large self-generating collections and those which sell prints for outside usage. Previously, much of this work was done by outside agencies, but it has become increasingly obvious that with a growing volume of use in-house facilities for printing and processing are more economical.

The size of the staff also relates closely to the purpose and size of the collection and it is not possible to lay down rules for the relation of size of stock to number of staff. In small collections one person may be able to cope, and in the education library sector, frequently has to attend to the illustrations as part of other general duties. Larger collections may have a range of staff all attending to specific functions, or each member may do a little of everything. Part of the task of management is to decide on the workload and the organization of the work, bearing in mind the ultimate objectives of the collection and the welfare of the staff involved. Some of the jobs in picture libraries can be tedious, as they can in any profession, and it is sensible to try and spread the load among as many staff as possible to prevent any one member becoming bored and making mistakes. However, as a general rule, the larger the staff the more specialized they can become and a staff structure can be established. Once this is done, job descriptions can be written up and recruitment can be related to specific areas.

The Mid America College Art Association has published some useful data on average workloads related to collection size, and although they are primarily concerned with slide libraries the figures can be transferred to photographic collections also. MACAA plots the following figures for the average hours per week devoted to specific tasks related to collection size.[1]

Collection size	Filing	Labelling & typing	Mounting
under 25,000	4.5	8.5	7
25-75,000	10	13	12.5
75-125,000	17	14	14.5
125-175,000	16	17	17
over 175,000	32	41	27

On the basis of these figures they recommend that any collection over 15,000 items, with a 1,000 plus growth rate per annum and a wide circulation, needs a full-time person in charge. Collections of 30,000 to 75,000 with a growth rate over 2,500 p.a. and average circulation, need one full-time professional and one full-time clerical assistant, with part-time help in addition. Collections of 75,000 to 125,000, with moderate growth of 5,000 p.a. and about 50,000 circulation need at least two full-time professionals, one full-time clerical assistant, and several part-time workers. There are many other examples in this handbook of staffing patterns related to type of library, size of stock, growth, and circulation rates from which the reader can glean useful guidelines.

The part-time workers referred to can be other members of library staff delegated to the picture collection for the appropriate periods of time. One feature of many colleges of art or other educational institutions is the use of student assistance. Such assistance can be useful and beneficial to both sides, but it should not be relied upon too heavily. There is often an imbalance between the amount of staff time necessary to train students to a useful standard and the amount of time such students remain with the library.

Selection

The selection of staff is an important part of management. The administrator of a collection must decide how many staff and what sort of staff he or she needs before attempting to recruit people to fill the posts. Having adequate job descriptions and clear ideas about the type of staff being sought is helpful to both management and candidates. Managers who embark on interviews with the vague notion 'we will see what turns up' and then try to fit candidates into imaginary situations are doing a disservice to themselves and the prospective employee. As with other areas of management, to have clear aims and objectives is the first step. The interview should present the opportunity to find a suitable candidate to fill a particular job and carry out a stated range of duties. Of course, there must be some flexibility for growth, but if candidates have a clear idea of the range of duties to be performed at the outset, there is less likelihood that they will present themselves for unsuitable jobs or become bored by lack of opportunity.

Qualifications

It is seldom, if ever, that a picture librarian or a librarian has any special formal qualifications in picture or any other audio-visual techniques. Indeed, the current trend in librarianship training is to include mention and study of non-book materials as part of the general educational programme, not a separate line of study. This is the most logical development as the general principles of librarianship can and should be adapted to all materials and the setting up of a separate branch of librarianship would only dilute the usefulness of the qualification. The qualifications which can be sought realistically include formal degrees in librarianship, formal degrees in special subjects or general studies, short-course training, experience and, lastly, the very informal understanding of picture material — sometimes referred to as 'having an eye or a feeling' for the special materials.

Librarianship qualifications are useful for staff concerned with picture libraries. A good grounding in the basic principles of indexing, information retrieval, the use of reference tools, as well as the encouragement of what Hilary Evans calls 'the state of mind of librarianship': namely tidiness, orderliness, preservation sense, exploitation, and a genuine regard for the material. Most librarians will not quarrel with these principles when applied to their job, but it is another matter if they are applied to their persona. A qualification in librarianship is becoming recognized as relevant to picture libraries and in many is an essential tool, especially in a multimedia situation in which pictures only represent one aspect of a resource collection.

Subject knowledge is very relevant in more specialized collections, such as art libraries, medical or science collections. As well as giving the student a grounding in the special subject, it helps to produce an enquiring mind and a familiarity with the techniques of information retrieval. This can be gained from a general degree, but it is more usual for graduates in fine arts to gravitate to art collections. Subject knowledge and a degree will therefore help in many of the specialized collections. Post-graduate training for archivists or museum curators is another specialized area which can be valuable for some types of work in picture libraries attached to museums, national and some university libraries.

A wide general knowledge, not necessarily gained from a degree, may be an essential requirement in other collections, and allied to the techniques of information retrieval. General knowledge may be a sign of an open mind and this is an important attribute in a general collection where users often present a startling diversity of requests. The ability to switch from one subject to another with facility and to get to the bottom of the actual question being asked are essential attributes in many a picture librarian.

Language training is another asset for the picture librarian who may be dealing with works of art or general pictures from all over the world.

Informal Qualifications

Librarianship qualifications and degrees provide the formal grounding and qualifications but there is a large area of informal training which is also useful to the picture librarian. This can be regarded as continuing education or an updating of knowledge. It may take the form of adult education programmes, such as art appreciation or a specifically designed short course to introduce particular library techniques — for example the courses run in the University of Missouri, Kansas City each summer by Nancy DeLaurier and Nancy Schuller, on Slide Librarianship. Any short course which improves either technical or special subject knowledge can be regarded as an asset.

In addition to formal qualifications much informal training can be acquired by experience. This means actually doing the job for a while, including any in-training that is given, and attending any related short courses and professional meetings to exchange experience and information.

In-training

Once the candidate takes up a position a further period of in-training is necessary, and the nature of this will be related to the previous experience and qualification of the recruit. It is necessary to introduce the collection to the new member of staff so that he or she can become familiar with the policies and procedures in force, as well as the strengths and weaknesses of the particular collection. Some technical training in particular procedures is necessary and a general introduction to the type of material and the uses made of it by the public it serves. One of the more important things to be acquired at this stage is to develop an awareness of what makes a picture useful for the collection and also its possibilities for the user.

In addition to in-training, staff can be sent on visits to other collections to compare methods, procedures, and stockholdings, as well as to printing houses to see what can be done with the pictures themselves. A knowledge of the stockholdings of other libraries will enable the staff to help the users more fully. No picture library can be complete and in a position to satisfy all users, but a knowledge of other accessible material will assist the staff to inform the users of alternative or additional sources of materials and information — one of the basic tenets of librarianship.

Organizing Workloads

In addition to a responsibility for staff recruitment and training, the administrator of a collection must organize the work pattern of the department according to the work to be carried out, the number of staff available, and the jobs to which they are particularly suited. The librarian must calculate the amount of work which can be achieved with the resources available, using figures of time spent on processing one item by different levels of staff and considering the expected intake of material. Allowance has to be made for the experience and abilities of the staff and training periods should be built into the calculation. A new recruit will seldom achieve the facility, accuracy, and speed of a longer established staff member and time has to be allowed for a trainee to achieve maximum efficiency.

As well as organizing workloads the librarian is responsible for what might be called the professional welfare of the staff. Professional interests can be fostered by allowing scope for initiative and involvement in planning the work of the unit — either the person's own activity or that of the wider group. Delegating parts of the training programme of new members of staff is helpful and provides the established staff member with an opportunity to take a fresh look at the work and rethink processes or procedures. Outside professional or related activities can also be encouraged, especially in the form of updating meetings, short courses, and visits to other picture libraries. Professional training in picture librarianship often has to be gained after formal training is complete, and refresher courses for new ideas and techniques form much of the continuing education programme of a librarian in this and many other areas, both general and specialized.

PLANNING

The responsibility for planning and the layout of a picture collection should be that of a librarian. Seldom, however, does a picture librarian have the luxury of starting from scratch with a new collection and new premises; the situation is more likely to be one of redesigning current layout to achieve maximum efficiency or better utilization of existing premises. Alternatively, as the collection expands and its functions develop as the number of staff increases and a larger working area is required, the library may acquire new premises.

Preplanning is an important phase of any reorganization, and at this stage the objectives of the library should be considered, together with the size of the collection, the expected growth rate and the storage space required, the size of the staff and its expected increase, as well as the number of users and potential users, especially if accommodation is provided in the library for users. The equipment required by the staff and users should also be taken into account before the space is allocated. An analysis of the activities of the library will gather facts about space requirements, what equipment is required in certain areas and how much space it will take up, the number of staff and users needing access to the equipment, how much storage space is required for the present stock and how much should be allowed for expansion in the foreseeable future.

Guidelines which have been suggested by government departments in the UK should be taken into account in planning spatial requirements. For example, one accepted guideline is 150 square feet of space for each member of staff, 70 square feet for each activity, and storage can be calculated according to the type of filing adopted and the space taken up by existing files, as well as the amount of space required around these files in order to utilize them fully. Suspension filing cabinets which pull out need at least double their area as well as space for the user and this basic factor should be included in the calculations. When considering space requirements for picture libraries, one maxim should be borne in mind: picture librarianship needs space and plenty of it, both for preparing the materials, handling and selection by users. Large flat table areas are needed so that pictures can be spread out for comparison or processing rather than piled one on top of the other. This helps to alleviate some of the damage to corners, edges, and surfaces of the prints. Picture libraries should therefore attempt to be more generous with space than other libraries.

Once the spatial requirements have been calculated the relationship between units within the library and the special needs of each unit can be considered. Layout can be done on a theoretical basis before practical arrangement is put into operation. Staff functions and needs can be analysed with reference to the equipment and supplies they require. Enquiry staff need to be close to the materials or the catalogues, and the telephones. Cataloguing staff should be within easy reach of the catalogues and the materials on which they are working. They may require access to special equipment for studying the materials, such as lightboxes or viewers for transparencies, and they probably need quick access to the collections of reference books for checking facts and dates.

Staff preparing materials for mounting and filing need large work areas and easy access to mounting equipment; preferably these areas should be separated from the rest of the library to prevent damage from accidental spillage onto other materials. In a picture library with open access a number of user spaces will be required near the catalogues and picture files to facilitate consultation. Planning a picture library within another library or a resources area should take account of other activities and the needs of other areas. If equipment is used by more than one area easy access should be arranged for all users of particular services and/or equipment.

Once all the data about functions, spatial requirements and proximities are gathered an actual layout can be designed. This layout will in all probability not be the final answer but with consultation between staff administrators and architects a solution can be arrived at and committed to paper before the actual moves of staff and equipment are made.

The diversity of picture libraries precludes any suggestions for layout in the present context, but the reader can refer to several sources to fit particular needs and functions.[1-5] The MACAA booklet contains many planned layouts for slide libraries which could easily be adapted to picture libraries.[1]

BUDGETING AND ECONOMICS

Where does the money come from? How is it spent? What accounting procedures are necessary to run the library? Any picture librarian is likely to become involved in budgeting and costing, although the degree of involvement will vary. The librarian in a commercial library is dependent on income from the sale of services and material, others have to work within a set budget granted by a department or institution, and others have to make a case at regular intervals for an injection of resources. Whatever the case, budgets have to be balanced and presented and services costed realistically. A commercial library offsets expenditure against income to achieve cost-effectiveness, while a more conventional library will have to balance expenditure against services provided to its public. An institution paying for the provision of services will quickly curtail its investment if those services are not provided in a cost-effective manner and, in effect, the librarian in a non-commercial library will lose this investment and therefore his income. Wherever the income comes from and in whatever guise it appears, it must be balanced against the expenditure of resources.

Costing the Service

When costing a service, any or all of the following have to be considered: premises, staff, stock, processing, equipment, stationery, furniture, and any ancillary services such as technical support or accounting for which the library itself has to pay.

Premises

The cost may be absorbed by the parent institution, or the library may have to pay the rent, rates, electricity, and telephone charges out of its own budget.

Staff

Salaries are the other large item in the overheads and, again, they may be paid by a parent institution or an education authority.

Stock

Budgeting for stock may be the most difficult item to predict accurately, especially in libraries which buy in older material. Such material may appear at most unexpected times and the library has to consider having a contingency fund to fall back on in an emergency. Very tight budgeting of commercial collections can result in important opportunities being lost. The budget for stock should therefore be as flexible as possible within set limits and the librarian or administrator should be in a position to provide for contingencies or have recourse to other funds to supplement the budget for stock. The normal stock budget can be calculated on the amount of material to be acquired, the cost of the items expected to be purchased, and a healthy regard for the factor of inflation. For budgeting purposes, reference materials can be considered as part of the stock or as a separate item.

Processing

Processing costs may be part of the stock fund or a separate item. A library which sells copy prints or produces file copies from its own negatives incurs processing costs whether this is done in-house or by an external agent. Costing for an in-house operation is done on the basis of the capital expenditure on equipment and the running costs for the materials used in processes. By using an external agent the library will pay more than for in-house work, but the difference may not be sufficient to justify an in-house operation. More and more libraries are finding it convenient to have in-house facilities but these have to be viable propositions and the amount of use should justify the expenditure before they are installed.

Equipment

Equipment costs include photographic and copying equipment where appropriate, lightboxes, slide-mounting and dry-mounting equipment, and storage files, and also allow for maintenance, and the repair and replacement of items.

Stationery

Stationery includes materials for mounting illustrations, caption labels, headed and ownership labels, envelopes for storage of prints and negatives, as well as invoices and delivery notes.

Furniture

Furniture such as desks, tables, chairs, catalogue drawers, and office files should appear as capital outlay.

Other costs include services rendered by other departments or outside accountants, solicitors, and insurance agents and the less obvious costs of providing services, recovering fees, and so on. In many picture libraries these have to be built into the budget.

The MACAA *Guide for the management of visual resources collections* has some useful advice for anyone planning a budget.[1] The main recommendations are to list all activities and obtain costings for each, this to include a unit price for activities actually carried out, such as the preparation of material, indexing, accessioning, and filing. These unit costs are obtained by considering the staff salaries, breaking down the work into the individual activities, and costing staff time against the activities carried out. Using the information of unit costs, production rates, and the other factors a budget can be itemized.

Charges

There can be no hard-and-fast rules about the charges made by picture libraries for their materials and services and a librarian in control of a collection should investigate other similar institutions before deciding on the scale of charges and fees to be adopted in his or her own situation. In some cases no direct charges are necessary, especially if the library acts as a resource centre, for example in a school or college of art. However, in days of escalating costs, even in such educational establishments consideration has to be given to charges for copy materials, whether this is absorbed by a department as a transfer charge or paid for by the individual requiring the material. Three main questions have to be answered when discussing the charges:

1 Should a charge be made?
2 What charges should be levied?
3 At what level should the charges be set?

If the collection is a commercial one then it must be self-financing and charge for both the materials and services provided. Unless it charges economic rates it cannot continue to acquire material or provide it for later use. Such a library is dependent on its own materials as a sole source of income and charges for usage of that material and other services it may provide.

Other non-commercial libraries may be supported by public institutions or education authorities, all funded in turn from the public purse. These are designed to serve a public, whether this is general or a particular section of the public, and users may think to argue that they should be allowed to use all the services of the library free of charge on the basis that they are taxpayers and therefore their money is being used to fund the library. This argument does not bear close scrutiny and it can equally be argued that non-users should not have to subsidize users of a picture collection by their taxes. Every institution has to try and run its services within a budget: if it runs at a loss which cannot or should not be absorbed by other areas of the institution it will be the first in line for closure.

There is usually a marked contrast in the pattern and level of fees charged between commercial and non-commercial libraries. Commercial libraries exist or die by their own endeavours and they have to charge full economic rates for the pictures they provide as well as rather higher reproduction fees than those charged by non-commercial libraries. Reproduction fees represent the major source of income and arise from the use of library material. The setting of realistic reproduction fees helps to ensure that the library can continue to acquire stock and provide the standard of services the user expects. Non-commercial libraries are less dependent on reproduction fees and their charges tend to be lower; nevertheless, they charge full cost price for copies of the pictures. In certain libraries there are no charges for prints or reproductions as these are considered to come under the umbrella of publicity or public relations, tourism or diplomacy. Such pictures may advertise a product or place and as such, it is argued, should be made freely available. Perhaps, the collection is merely an extension of another area of the organization and costs can be absorbed in the promotion programme.

Having decided to charge for pictures and/or services the next step is to consider the categories of charges to be made. The librarian must decide how the material is to be used, whether the original should be loaned out or copy prints made for each potential user. If copy prints or photographs are provided who is to make them and what charges should be levied? Pictures out on loan may be subject to holding fees either at the time the loan is made or after a set period. The following fees can all be considered according to the circumstances and function of the library.

Print Fees

Where a library provides copy prints or photographs to the user, using its own collection of prints or negatives, the user can expect to pay the cost of making that copy. If the library does not already have a negative or print and has to make one or photograph new objects in its collection, for example in an art gallery or museum, it may treat this as a one-off request and require the user to pay for both the negative and the print. If it is envisaged that the photograph will be used in the collection, the library may choose to absorb the cost of photography and charge the user for the print only. In either case it is perfectly reasonable for the library or its agent to retain the negative.

Facilities Fee

This is sometimes called a disturbance fee and may be charged by a museum or gallery if the user takes his own photographs of objects or sends in a photographer as his agent. This fee is charged for providing things like extra lighting, barriers to keep others away while photography is in progress, or allowing the photographer in outside normal opening hours and therefore having to provide members of staff for supervision or security reasons. It can also apply if material has to be removed from storage or special collections for photography.

Lending Fees

Material may be loaned out to users for set periods and charges can be made for this loan under some circumstances. A commercial library does not usually charge for loan as this may reduce the user's incentive to refer to the library's material in the future; if a library relies on the use of its material for an income such a charge would be self-defeating. A loan fee may apply in cases where a library does not wish to sell its material. This particularly applies to large colour transparencies available from art galleries or museums. The gallery may make one, or better still a few, colour-corrected originals from objects in its collections — the point of having more than one is to prevent constant photography of the object or painting which may be of considerable value and subject to damage or deterioration from photography, especially the extra lighting required. In order to ensure that the user has a correct colour rendering of the material to start with, these originals are loaned out against a fee. The gallery normally requires that the original on loan is used in any printing process and that no duplicates or copies are made, on the assumption that the colours would suffer to some extent.

Fees for the loan of such material are usually charged at an economic rate to absorb the cost of original photography, materials and processes used to produce the transparency, and the time the user will need to retain the transparency to ensure good reproduction. The loan period is normally at least one month, but as a user is unlikely to have an accurate idea of the time required for the printing processes, the custodian should expect the material to be absent from the collection for at least three months. Fees are therefore usually charged at a basic monthly rate until the material is returned, hopefully undamaged. The loan fee may take account of the subsequent usage of the material and be set against the final reproduction fee, especially if the material is out of copyright or in the public domain in which case the loan fee is normally higher than other institutions that charge both loan and reproduction fees.

Holding Fees

Closely allied to loan fees are those charged against long retention of the material by a user. If a user retains loan prints for a considerable time he is effectively depriving the owner of the material of the opportunity to exploit that material elsewhere and should compensate the owner in some way, especially if he has acquired several prints for selection purposes in the knowledge that only one or a few will be used. Libraries often require a user who receives several prints to return those not to be used immediately after selection and only allow the user to retain a few likely prospects out of a large batch of material. This leaves the returned material free for other users while allowing the first user some leeway with the few prints he has retained. In such instances only one or two prints may eventually be used but it is usual for the library to charge reproduction fees only on those prints actually used. If, however, the user retains all prints for some length of time and then returns all unused, some holding fee should be levied to compensate the library for the retention of prints. This can be levied on a weekly or monthly basis after a set period of time determined by the librarian. Usually, a one-month leeway is allowed, after which holding fees apply and the fees may be calculated by transaction or by the number of prints retained.

Penalty Fees

Holding fees can be considered as penalty fees for long retention but there are other penalties which a library may have to apply. Material which is lost, damaged, or irrecoverable for whatever reason should carry a penalty. This should be clearly stated in the conditions of supply and can be charged at the current rate of replacement. The charges should be assessed according to the difficulty or feasibility of repeating the photograph or item. This may involve a quick visit to a local museum or gallery to replace the material, the organization of a photographic session with facilities fees, or it may mean releasing or commissioning a photographer to go round the world to reshoot the item. Black and white material is less subject to high charges because the library probably has a negative in stock from which to replace copy prints. Colour material, as we have seen, is different in that it is very often the original material which is lost or damaged. Higher penalties inevitably apply to the loss or damage of transparency material.

To take account of all these possibilities would be a difficult task for the librarian and the resulting sliding scale of penalty charges confusing to the user. It is therefore usual to fix a penalty charge on the high side to cover all the possibilities. A user may feel annoyed if he has to pay high replacement charges for something he could easily go out and photograph himself, but equally a librarian would be failing in his job if the penalty charges did not begin to cover the cost of replacement. This might be a matter for negotiation when the situation arises but clear penalty charges should always be stated in each transaction.

Search and Service Fees

These fees may be levied for special reasons or as a normal part of the library's practice. If the staff devote a considerable amount of time and effort to providing material for a user, then a fee for these staff services could be levied. If the user removes a large number of items from the library, again, a service fee can be charged. Such fees are normally kept fairly low, sufficient to cover the services rendered but not to provide a source of income. They can also be regarded as a small compensation in the event of no material being used.

Reproduction Fees

All the preceding fees are necessary to a greater or lesser degree to pay for the services which a picture library provides. The reproduction fee is a charge made for the use of the material and varies widely according to the type of library involved and the restrictions placed on some libraries by the copyright ownership of the material they hold for, as explained in Section 1.11 on Copyright, the owner of the copyright and the owner of the material are not necessarily the same. Basically, the reproduction fee is the charge made by the owner of the material for supplying the user and allowing him to reproduce the material in some form. Although the fee paid is loosely termed the copyright fee, in most instances it is better referred to as a reproduction or usage fee. The law of copyright is so complex and even nebulous that it is often difficult to establish or defend copyright in an item and the librarian would be well advised to refer to 'reproduction rights'.

While the fees mentioned so far are levied as they are incurred, for instance, the cost of supplying a print or loaning a transparency, or penalties for damage, loss, or long periods of loan, the reproduction fee is usually incurred only on material used and in some instances only on publication of the document in which the material is used. Publishers who use illustrations are loath to pay before publication as they can never be certain that the material in question will appear in the final work. Difficulties may be met in the printing process which preclude the use of some material, the emphasis of the text may change, or the cost of the work mean that some of the more expensive material and processes have to be withdrawn. The librarian must therefore be prepared for long delays between supply of the material and payment of the reproduction fees. Libraries may require earlier payment but it is more usual to pay on publication rather than on supply.

Reproduction fees vary widely according to the use of the material. They can be fixed according to the size of the final photograph, whether colour or black and white, the number of copies printed, the type of publication, or usage by film and television. To cover these eventualities most libraries have a sliding scale of reproduction fees, some of them very complex. But a moment's thought about the different possible applications of the material, from the front cover of a prestige publication with a wide market to a small margin illustration in an educational publication with restricted sales, will serve to indicate that all markets cannot afford similar rates and to exploit the material to the full the librarian must take the users' ends and means into consideration. Of course, there are libraries which charge a set rate for reproduction regardless of usage, but these are usually controlled by an outside authority, such as a government department or public institution, and do not depend on reproduction fees to remain viable.

Copyright Fees

The material to be reproduced may be owned by the library while the copyright is held elsewhere, in which case a double fee is incurred for usage. The copyright fees may have to be collected by the library on behalf of the rights owner, but it is more usual for the user to apply to the copyright owner for clearance and to pay any fees direct to the owner or his agent. The library must inform the user of the rights owner and may require clearance before releasing the material, but it is up to the rights owner to set the copyright fee. This fee can be waived or set at a prohibitive level by the copyright owner who is perfectly entitled to do either, but a library should take the attitude of the copyright owner into account before agreeing to hold the material. If the fees charged are going to prohibit reasonable use of the material, should the library continue to stock that material?

Royalties

If a library collects fees on behalf of the owner of material or the original photographer it may come to an agreement with the owner to pay a percentage of the reproduction fee on each usage. This is especially the case with commercial picture libraries which depend on staff or freelance photographers for the supply of current material and pay a commission on work used. This can be regarded as a royalty and the agreed percentage is usually incorporated in with the reproduction fee charged.

Level of Fees

The level of charges made brings us back to the purpose and function of the library. Clearly, a commercial library dependent upon usage of its material for an income must charge more than a subsidized library or one used for education purposes. The level of the fees for printing, use of facilities, and penalties should relate to the cost of these services; those for reproduction, search, and service can be graded to provide an economic income for the library concerned. The actual levels at which reproduction fees can be set are limited by the market involved and here the librarian has some assistance in the form of rates set by agencies or associations related to his or her particular library.

The Museums Association in the UK has a scale of charges applicable to museums, art galleries, and other government institutions, while an association of picture libraries, BAPLA, relates to the commercial scene. Neither of these bodies can lay down definitive charges, but they both provide useful guidelines for libraries allied to their aims and objectives. Any librarian would be wise to consult either one of these associations, or at least investigate the area of particular concern in order to match his or her library's rates to those of competitors in the field. Users quickly distinguish between a library overcharging for poor services or material and one charging reasonable rates for services, and the usage figures will vary accordingly. Conversely, the cheapest is not always the best but users are prepared to pay economic rates for good service allied to a useful collection and libraries fitting this description should be able to exploit their collections to the best advantage. Any fees charged should take account of the paper and clerical work involved in recovering those fees and should at least cover the cost of the services involved.

PAPERWORK

Administration and the keeping of records engenders paperwork and picture librarianship is no exception. Records have to be kept for stock, issue, and other transactions including sales of prints and payments of fees. Other records are necessary if the library uses outside processors or suppliers. Most of the paperwork involves keeping track of the photographic material in the library and is therefore to be regarded as an essential part of picture librarianship, not just an unnecessary clerical chore. As in any lending library a picture library must know who has the material at any time and under what conditions. Non-commercial libraries need to keep an issue record with information about the material on loan and the name, address, or department of the borrower, together with a signature for the material taken out. Commercial libraries probably require much more detail than this to cover all the possibilities of use.

The library needs to know what material is out, who has it, when it should be returned, and any fees payable. The user needs to know what he has, how long he can keep it, and the conditions of supply, including any fees and penalties accruing. The issue record or a delivery note can be designed to include all the necessary information even if the result is a lengthy document.

The delivery note is usually in at least three sections, one to be retained by the library, two to be sent to the user who should sign for the material received and return one copy. The user then has a record of the material he has retained, together with the conditions of usage and the date of return. Delivery notes usually include details of material supplied, details of the borrower, conditions of supply including date of return, any holding fees payable, any immediate charges such as search or loan fees, notes as to any penalties likely to be levied for loss, damage, or delay, and whether reproduction fees are required. Actual fees can either be shown on a separate rate card, or a note can be made on the record to the effect that reproduction fees of X amount are payable each time the material is used. The delivery note can also be a source of information for the library if a space is made available in which the client can inform the library of the intended use of the material, so that fees can be calculated. If as much information as possible is given at this stage, there is less likelihood of disagreement or time-consuming discussions later on. Sample forms for delivery notes are set out in McDarrah's *Stock photo and assignment source book.*[6]

The library must keep strict records based on these delivery notes, with details of material retained by a user and the conditions under which the user has the material, including dates of return. This is one of the major problems of a library: having set a date of return the library must be prepared to follow this up and chase the material. A duplicate of the issue record can be filed under the date of return and when that date comes round the staff should send out reminders for outstanding items. The process of selection from a commercial library may mean that pictures are returned in stages, one batch after initial selection, others on the same assignment being retained for further selection, while the material finally selected may not be returned until on or after the publication date. Delivery notes should allow for this method of working and the follow-up system be flexible enough to handle it.

Information required on the library record includes the transaction or delivery note number, name and identification of the user, date material borrowed, the number of items, and any agreed conditions of supply or fees to be paid including any special arrangements made with the particular user. The method of identifying material varies from one library to another. Some number the items 1-n on the back of each print and cancel these numbers as the prints are returned. Others use negative numbers and a brief description but this only applies where a negative collection exists parallel to the print collection.

Some other record number, such as a classification or catalogue number can be used if the negative collection is housed outside the library, to facilitate access to the material to identify missing or lost items which need recall or replacement. Accession numbers can be used alone if they refer to an accessions register with subject details of the individual items. This is often the method adopted in slide libraries where a considerable number of slides may be issued at a time. There are several methods available for issuing picture material according to the type of material, the back-up procedures, and existing collections in the library.

Further paperwork is necessary for invoices and reproduction rights or copyright declarations. A library which sells prints including reproduction rights may issue an invoice stating the fee and the conditions under which it is released. For example, the Metropolitan Museum of Art, New York uses this procedure when releasing material for one-time editorial usage. Some libraries may require the user to sign an agreement granting specific rights to reproduce the material on payment of the fee and quotation of the source in a particular manner, for example, publishing houses like Macmillan, Oxford University Press, or W H Freeman. Others require a reproduction declaration to be made giving full details before calculating the fees. This requires some additional paperwork, but may be necessary for those with complicated usage rates.

REFERENCES

1   Mid America College Art Association, Visual Resources Committee *Guide for the management of visual resources collections.* New Mexico, MACAA, 1979.
2   Beswick, N *Organising resources.* London, Heinemann, 1975.
3   Shifrin, M *Information in the school library.* London, Bingley, 1973.
4   'Planning the special library' in *Blueprint for the 70s: a seminar on library planning.* New York, SLA, 1972.
5   Metcalf, Keyes D *Planning academic and research library buildings.* New York, McGraw-Hill, 1965.
6   McDarrah, F W (editor) *Stock photo and assignment source book.* New York, Bowker, 1977. 427-9, 430-4.

13

Education and Training

Antje Lemke

Whenever new cultural patterns emerge and society's information needs change librarianship has reflected this development and library schools have responded by adding new courses to their curriculum. Law and medical librarianship are early examples of this subject specialization. As the use of pictorial images in all areas of our life is steadily increasing, education for the management of visual resources has become an issue of concern for librarianship.

As we review the development and current status of courses in non-book media, art librarianship, and visual resources management, we must remind ourselves that, while law and medicine have been relatively well defined disciplines for some time, 'visual documentation' or 'art' are broad concepts and the systematic development of education and training programmes require much careful consideration. Pictures do not just represent one medium but they come in ever-increasing forms and materials. Picture collections do not serve art-related purposes only but practically all subject areas and disciplines. Postcards, posters, and many pictorial items that were not created for documentation purposes, have turned into highly desirable resources, used in education or in documentary films, and in many other contexts. For example, 50 years ago a French civilization course would have been taught from lectures and textbooks. Today, slides, photographs, and films have become an integral part. Naturally, the context in which the pictures are used affects decisions about the organization of the collection. The journalist, the advertiser, the teacher, and artist all require different points of access, sometimes to the same image.

An awareness of these factors, combined with an insight into the great variety of institutions that have developed picture collections, are as important in any education programme, as familiarity with various media and processing methods.

ART LIBRARIANSHIP

In past centuries pictorial collections developed primarily in connection with the arts and were administered by art historians or connoisseurs. The first effective advocate of the importance of organized picture collections for the purpose of visual documentation of nature and all human endeavours may well have been John Cotten Dana. When he initiated the establishment of picture files related to community interests and, in 1898, opened an art room at the Newark, New Jersey, Public Library, he also instructed his staff in the organization and maintenance of these files. Librarians who worked at the Newark Public Library in Dana's days learned about picture subject headings as well as the cutting of mounts for the more valuable prints. From Newark came the first recommendations, in the USA, for the cataloguing and arrangement of picture files, and these were perhaps the first tools in the training of picture librarians beyond the acquisition of skills by direct experience.

A broader professional interest in picture librarianship and the background desirable for work in this field developed in the 1920s. The American Library Association founded an Art Reference Roundtable in 1924, and the Special Libraries Association a Museums Group in 1929, and a Picture Division in 1952. For the next decades organization and bibliographic topics were the predominating interests of these groups. It was not until 1972 when, following the British initiative of founding the Art Library Society of the United Kingdom, ARLIS/UK, art librarians, art publishers, and others interested in the arts and in visual documentation formed the first independent professional organization, ARLIS/North America.

Immediately, the question of education for art and picture

librarianship in the USA and Canada was included in the discussions at annual meetings, recommendations were drafted and, in 1978, an Education Committee was created.

An organization of direct interest to picture librarians, and encompassing all those interested in the production and use of images, from graphic artist to publisher and librarian, was founded in 1967, the American Society of Picture Professionals. Through its newsletter, as well as through meetings and seminars, this organization contributes constantly to the education of picture librarians.

The timing in some other countries has been similar. In Australia, for example, at the 1978 meeting of ARLIS/Australia, and in New Zealand, at Hobart, Tasmania, a session was devoted to the topic of art library education. Questions of dual degrees in librarianship and a subject area, of integrating art library courses in existing library curricula, and/or the development of workshops were discussed.

Slightly preceding the founding of ARLIS/NA, a few library schools had already offered individual courses and field experience in art librarianship in the late 1960s, for students who wanted to specialize in this area.

CURRENT PROGRAMMES

Currently existing opportunities for education in art and picture librarianship in the USA can be divided into five categories:

1   *Courses offered in accredited graduate schools* of library and/or information science.

2   *Apprenticeship arrangements and internships* in various art and picture libraries from the National Gallery in Washington, DC or the International Museum of Photography in Rochester, NY to local museums and historical societies.

3   *Seminars and workshops* for periods from one month to one weekend. Sponsored by a great variety of private and public institutions from the Federal Government to small community colleges, by professional organizations of librarians or archivists.

4   *Professional meetings*   ARLIS/NA, the College Art Association, and the Art Section of the Association of College and Research

Libraries devote major sessions of their annual meetings to panels and lectures of experts that contribute to both the introduction of new subjects and the continuing education in art and picture librarianship. Regional chapters often have their own educational programmes.

5 *Professional literature,* especially journals and technical reports. Prior to the development of professional organizations and academic programmes, picture librarians depended in their daily operations almost entirely upon their experience. Increasingly, journals began to provide information, and today they serve a major education function. In addition to the publications of professional associations, including the Society of American Archivists, and the American Museum Association, the *Technical Leaflets* of *Historical News, Leonardo,* the International Journal of Contemporary Visual Arts, and *Visual Resources* (an International Journal of Documentation that began publication in the Spring of 1980) are rich sources of information and practical examples. Many other countries have comparable publications.

According to a 1979 survey in the United States, 10 out of 60 accredited library schools currently offer regular courses in art librarianship. Some emphasize art bibliography and the needs of academic art history programmes; some emphasize the library needs of museums and art schools; others concentrate on the production dissemination, and organization of non-book material: photographs, slides, films, and ephemeral picture sources.

In addition to the ten library schools, some universities offer courses in slide and photograph librarianship. Best known among these are those of Margaret Nolan, Chief of the Photograph and Slide Library at the Metropolitan Museum of Art in New York, and of Nancy DeLaurier Slide and Photograph Curator at the University of Missouri, Kansas City.

In the design of our educational programme it is important to note that these pilot courses are given by practising professionals, within an academic graduate credit programme. According to student responses, the broad context of the graduate programme, combined with the specialized current experience and professional vision of recognized authorities in the field, constitutes a most effective course.

STAFF QUALIFICATIONS

Without devoting a chapter to education, Betty Jo Irvine does mention the qualifications for professional staff in her book, *Slide libraries*.[1] She stresses that 'Slide collections are highly sophisticated instructional resources libraries' that need 'preparation in the management of non print media, in the operational requirements' and in 'the subject concentration of a given collection'. These collections are, naturally, not limited to the fine arts, and what is said about the background needed for slide librarianship can be applied to all other collections of visual documents.

It is a reflection of the enormous growth of slide collections that, in the USA, slide librarians are among the most vocal special interest groups in art librarianship today. General picture collections have, perhaps, grown more steadily, and they are usually arranged by broader subjects. Many do not yet require the intricate classification systems needed for the retrieval of details from architectural monuments like the cathedral at Chartres, or the innumerable versions of a singular theme by a prolific painter. Picasso, alone, could serve as an example for a seminar on organization and retrieval of various media, styles, art movements, and social issues.

With the variety of uncoordinated offerings of courses and workshops, most of which developed in response to the need for a formal background in this specialization, it was natural that ARLIS/NA should establish an Education Committee in order to work towards the implementation of its standards. These were published in 1977 as *Standards for staffing art libraries*. Concerning the education of art librarians, they state:

The Professional
The mandatory mark of an art librarian is a master's degree in library science from an American Library Association accredited school or a recognized equivalent graduate school. This degree equips the librarian with the technical and bibliographical knowledge necessary to direct the basic functions of a library.

An art librarian must have a knowledge of the basic literature, of the major reference sources, of the primary indexes and abstracting services thereof, of community resources, and of network systems

— their capabilities and potential as applied to art libraries.... An art librarian must have a knowledge of the periods, schools, styles, and movements of art history and a knowledge of the techniques of art forms and media. For certain careers in art librarianship it may be necessary for the librarian to hold a master of arts degree in art history or in the subject field covered by the library.... It is essential for the art librarian to participate actively in specialized professional organizations as a manifestation of career commitment and as a means of continuing education.... .

The Para-Professional

The major function of the para-professional is to release the librarian from routine technical tasks. The para-professional ought to have a bachelor's degree, preferably with some hours of art history on studio art. The para-professional acts as a general assistant and should have basic skills such as typing and filing. A reading knowledge of at least one language other than English can be very helpful. It is important to encourage para-professionals in career development and to afford them the opportunity for continuing education.

A separation of professional tasks, those that demand knowledge and commitment, from the para-professional functions was given special attention. In a field in which, for example, the intellectual activity of classifying and indexing is not always seen as distinct from sorting and filing, it is important to analyse all library activities carefully as standards and educational programmes are designed.

COURSE CONTENT RECOMMENDATIONS

The *Standards for the staffing of art libraries* constitute the basis on which the ARLIS/NA Education Committee is currently developing its *Recommendations for educational programs in art library and related information resources and services.* Because of the current changes in art libraries, art archives, and related documentation centres, and because of the beginning rapprochement in professional exchange and education in these fields, it was decided not to develop an accreditation system based on fixed standards. Instead, the Committee suggested recommendations in order to achieve uniformity of content and a high quality of instruction.

The recommendations address themselves to the curriculum, i.e. course content, independent study, fieldwork and internships, as well as to the environment necessary to provide instructional excellence and the necessary resources.

One area in which the recommendations of the Education Committee go beyond the scope of the ARLIS/NA staffing standards, is that of management. While the standards emphasize subject knowledge and bibliographic skills, and while they require 'Knowledge of community resources and network systems', there is no mention of necessary prerequisites for the administration of art libraries, or the participation in network activities.

Because librarians who are responsible for the organization and services of visual resources often are also responsible for the administration of staff and resources and for effective network arrangements, the Education Committee included courses in management in the recommendations for educational programmes. The following draft recommendations are currently under discussion:

1 *Programme for library school curriculum in art librarianship*
   (a) Core courses with content generic to the practice of library and information service, such as reference, management, and the organization of knowledge.
   (b) Background for art specialization should include arts resources and services; archival, manuscript, and rare book collection; non-book media; conservation and preservation; cataloguing, indexing, and abstracting; research methodology.
   (c) Subject specialization should include information resources and services; art bibliography; management of art resources and services; directed reading, research, and practical experience in art librarianship.
   (d) Cognate fields include history of art, visual communications or museology.

2 *Institutional qualifications*
   (a) A resident faculty member should coordinate art specialization. Subject specialization courses should be taught by resident or

adjunct faculty members qualified in the subject area. Coordinators and/or subject instructors should act as student advisers.

(b) On-site facilities should include an art library with professional staff. A History of Art graduate programme should be part of the institution's curriculum. Art centres and museums should be easily accessible.

(c) Schools offering the specialization in art librarianship should affiliate with ARLIS/NA.

(d) Students in art librarianship programmes should be encouraged to attend professional meetings and join organizations such as ARLIS/NA, Special Libraries — Art Section, College Art Association, American Association of Museums.

RELATED PROFESSIONS

Some of the ten library schools mentioned earlier have developed course sequences for students specializing in art librarianship and related visual resources fields. The following list of courses represents a sample list of those recommended for this specialization.

In all of the introductory and general courses, e.g. Management, or Government and Information, those interested in art librarianship can concentrate on, and select, projects related to the arts and visual resources.

1   *INTRODUCTORY COURSES*
    The information environment
    Contemporary agencies, industries, and services involved in the production, organization, and distribution of recorded information.
    Reference and bibliographic services
    Basic reference sources and the reference function of the librarian.
    Organization of information resources
    Cataloguing, classification, and indexing systems and practices.
    Development of library resources
    Selection, evaluation, and preservation of collections in response to the clientele and the mission of the library.
    Management principles for information services
    Contemporary management theories and practices, as they apply to libraries and other information agencies and networks.

Information systems analysis
Methods and techniques of contemporary information systems.
Includes computer and microform technologies in libraries.
Introduction to non-book media
Contemporary audio and visual resources, their availability, quality,
organization, use, and preservation.
Basics of computerized retrieval systems
Introduction to programming language and on-line information
storage and retrieval systems.

2 *RELATED GENERAL COURSES*
   Humanities resources and services
Bibliographic sources and their organization in literature, the arts,
religion, and philosophy. Includes commercial, private, and
government programmes and services.
Archive and manuscript collections
Principles, methods, and techniques of archival management.
Includes preservation, organization, description, and service of
collections.
Rare books and special collections
Principles, methods, and techniques of rare book management.
Includes the antiquarian book trade, special bibliographic services,
and physical aspects of books and other print media.
History of books and libraries
Development of the book and recorded information in general; the
role of the librarian from ancient times to the present. International
in scope.
Governments and information
International, federal, state, and local governments and
intergovernmental agencies. Their publications and services.
Information needs of society
The librarian's interaction with political, social, and cultural
agencies to meet specific individual and societal needs. International
in scope.
Community analysis for designing library services
Evaluation of existing services in terms of user/non-user survey, and
analysis of community characteristics. Design for new library
services.

Indexing and abstracting
Introduction to existing manual and computer-based systems and services; includes practice in basic indexing and abstracting skills.

3   *SPECIAL COURSES FOR THE ART LIBRARIAN*
Art and museum librarianship
Production and dissemination of art publications, including non-book materials. Documentation and access to resources; acquisition, organization, and preservation of library collections and general management issues of art libraries and visual archives.
Visual resources
Sources, selection, processing, and conservation of slides and photographic material (the subjects covered in this Handbook).
Art bibliography
In-depth study of bibliographic organization, services, and research methods in the arts, with emphasis on art history and theory.
Reading and research in art and visual resources
Selection of a specific subject for in-depth research resulting in a bibliographic essay, a bio-bibliography, or recommendations concerning a specific issue in the fine arts and visual documentation.
Fieldwork in art and visual resources
Practical work in selected art libraries and visual documentation centres, under the supervision of a staff member and the instructor.

In the development of programmes along these or similar patterns, the commonality of all professions involved in the organization of visual resources must be considered. As more librarians are responsible for original or unique materials, and as more archivists open their resources to a wider public, issues of description, of classification, and of access and preservation often become identical. We can use similar keywords or subject headings and coordinate our methodology. From broad conceptual issues to small technical details the professions can learn much from each other.

This process of exchange, of joint exploration, joint meetings and publications is just beginning, and new education programmes should be based on this concept. An indicator for the recognition of common interests is the change of title and scope of the former *UNESCO Library Bulletin*. Since 1979 it appears under the title *UNESCO Journal for Information Science, Librarianship, and Archives Administration.*

Any review of the education of the picture librarian, and of the significance of visual resources today, reveals the vital role of this profession in our society. As we develop academic programmes of a highly specialized nature, we must also strive to increase the public's awareness that this specialization and the total spectrum of contemporary life, in which visual images can more than ever before inform and enlighten, are mutually interdependent.

REFERENCE

1   Irvine, Betty Jo *Slide libraries.* 2nd ed. Littleton, Colorado, Libraries Unlimited, 1979.

EDITOR'S NOTE

This section has concentrated on education available in art librarianship with special reference to the USA. There are several reasons for this emphasis, not least the fact that the USA is in advance of the UK and other countries in providing education for picture librarianship.

The concentration on art librarianship is natural in that it is in this field that the beginnings of picture librarianship as a craft were first established. It would be difficult to avoid a consideration of pictures in dealing with an art library and the growing reproduction of pictures or artworks as photographs and slides has led many art libraries to establish separate collections of these pictures in forms other than the originals, or books about the originals.

In the UK this factor is reflected in the pattern of employment. Most of the people who fill posts in collections based on art libraries and in education are library trained in addition to having a degree in a specialist subject, whether relevant or not. In the past, few picture librarians in other areas have had any library training; rather, the training or qualification has been in a subject relevant to the field in which they work, whether in science, journalism, museums, archives, or publishing. It is a further indication of the point made by Antje Lemke that there is a commonality of all professions involved in the organization of visual resources.

The section on administration has already discussed the question of qualifications in considering staff selection and mention has been made of both formal and informal qualifications as well as in-training possibilities. In the UK the pattern of education for picture librarians reflects the commonality for there are no courses available in picture librarianship as such, but there are opportunities to acquire education or training in specialized areas of picture librarianship.

The accredited library schools and university departments give a grounding in library principles and in certain cases present options to the student, if not in picture librarianship at least in dealing with all non-book materials including visual resources. Two universities in the UK run courses in Museum Studies and these include consideration of visual resources in a museum or gallery setting.

Other than these formal courses there are occasional short courses, seminars, and workshops run by interested associations, such as ARLIS/UK, the ASLIB Audio Visual Group, the Library Association Audio Visual Group, and the Publishers Association.

Thus, although there are no formal courses in picture librarianship, the prospective picture librarian has a range of related courses to follow and can adapt principles to suit the particular needs of picture libraries.

It can be argued that a specialist course in picture librarianship would not be helpful to the student in finding employment. The job market for picture librarians is not wide and to educate a student in so limited a field is to do him or her a disservice. A wider education in librarianship or museum studies is more helpful and the principles can then be applied to a variety of jobs.

Part 2

CASE STUDIES AND SURVEYS OF PICTURE LIBRARIES

Preface

Helen P Harrison

Having considered the fundamental processes involved in the handling of pictures in Part 1, we can now turn to a consideration of the network of existing picture libraries. Part 2 consists of a series of case studies of individual, even unique, picture libraries, interspersed with some survey essays which cover a range of libraries devoted to a particular subject or type of material, or with a similar purpose and outlook.

This section looks first at examples of important national collections, starting with the Library of Congress in Washington whose collections include some 10 million pictures — surely one of the largest to be found. The subject coverage concentrates on the USA, as befits a national collection, but includes many other items of interest to life and culture in America and indicates how a large collection can be organized, preserved, and made available to as many people as possible, both within and beyond the national boundaries.

Not all national collections, however, have as catholic a taste as this. Some are devoted to particular subjects concentrated within a national setting, for instance, the pictorial collections of the Imperial War Museum in London. Here, the subject matter is clearly defined, as is the 'national' interest, but the range of material within that definition makes this an important example of a national as well as a museum collection. Even more specialized in terms of subject matter is the National Film Archive which is concentrated on film and many of the important aspects of the archival function of a national library are represented within the smaller scale of the subject speciality.

There are still many collections to be described which could be designated as 'national' collections, but the three examples given have introduced the concept of archives and it is this idea which is developed in the next section, devoted to the 'archival' functions of picture collections, with a special reference to one archive of material housed in a university.

It is time to mention the art galleries of the world for, as well as having the most art-orientated picture collections, they frequently house national collections, either with a primary geographic or subject interest. A survey of the main national galleries of the UK is followed by a description of one of the more important museum collections in London — the national museum for science and technology: the Science Museum. The US scene is covered by a contribution which surveys both art galleries and museums.

No survey of national libraries could be complete without a consideration of the large collections contained in government departments. These include materials collected through national activity and interests, and many hold invaluable archival records. Photography carried out by government departments in the USA has found its way into many libraries, as well as the Library of Congress instanced in Section 2.14. A résumé of activity at state level indicates how widespread picture collection and conservation can (and should) become.

In addition to government departments, many institutions, learned societies, and quasi national departments have their own picture collections. National or government authorities may delegate the housing and organization of their collections to others. One particularly interesting example is the deposit of much of the NASA material in the Lunar and Planetary Laboratory of the University of Arizona. Not only is the subject matter of interest to all those living in the twentieth century, but many of the methods associated with modern technology are being tried out in this particular collection.

Architecture is one of the most pictorial subjects we see everyday; it is a part of our lives, and therefore a subject worthy of serious study. In picture terms it is a 'special' subject well catered for by the existence of both a national institution and a learned society in the UK. The Royal Institution of British Architects as a professional institution is devoted primarily to the interests of its members. There is a wider obligation involved as it is a national institution, but users have to respect the aims and objectives on which it was founded, although much of the material is widely distributed. The Architectural Association is a learned society and material is only available to its members for use in the pursuit of their chosen profession. This is an interesting example of a library which relies on its book stock, as opposed to pictures *per se;* it is also of interest in that it reproduces pictorial material from a variety of sources, in order to keep a record of architectural constructions for the future.

Closely associated with the national and institutional libraries are those concerned with education. These range from the archival type to those intended for immediate use by the student. Universities include the archival type, as instanced in Section 2.17, as well as reference collections, such as the one created for the benefit of publishing and design use by the Open University. Polytechnics, colleges of education, and colleges of art provide material for their students and staff to exploit. Much of the material in these collections is restricted in distribution to the institution concerned, although in some instances, especially in academic libraries, it can be made available to a wider public.

Furthering the educational concept, public libraries in both the UK and the US are described. Picture loan collections are an important aspect of the public library service and details are included. The section covering the US goes a step further, however. It shows in no uncertain terms what can and should be achieved by any picture librarian worthy of the name. There must be a commitment, an interest, an opportunity, and, what is more, a sure eye for the goal.

The commercial picture library has to be more aware of this goal than most: it will live or die by its ability to provide services and achieve sales. The network of picture libraries takes shape as the book progresses, with a description of three of the many collections available in the UK, dealing with historical rather than current material. Commercial libraries can span the ages from the historic material discussed here to the even more 'historic' material represented by the case study of an art library service in London.

Of the commercial sources of pictures, none is less or more so than the independent photographer with his or her individual collection by subject or type which could in the future become a small or significant part of a larger collection. Many a collection is founded on one photographer's work and when material is incorporated into a larger collection it may be indexed by the photographer's name or by his or her own method; therefore it is important to most picture librarians to know how photographers organize their material in a working collection.

Advertising agencies deal with commercial products and have a special interest in pictures for design purposes in promotional literature or other media. The advertising agency library described here has been created for the benefit of the limited public of the staff of the agency involved and represents an amalgam of a commercial end-product based on a special collection dealing with its own defined public. The end is commercial, but the means appears not to be.

A special area of picture librarianship includes libraries whose pictures are free to the public: those who promote products, services, and facilities, such as companies, industrial firms, and tourist boards. Companies and industrial firms of course only promote the products with which they are concerned, but may well provide promotional literature in the hope of a favourable mention to a wide public. Tourist boards promote the area with which they are concerned but there is usually a difference in emphasis: industry promotes a product, tourist boards a place. The materials are usually free for promotional reasons, but the products seldom are!

All picture libraries can be thought of as communicating information to a general or specialized public, but the last three studies are closely connected with the communications industry itself and exemplify the special materials and organization required to provide information for three facets of communication.

Publishing houses often specialize in particular subjects or areas and the case study quoted features a publishing house concerned mainly with fine art books, which requires access to stocks of pictures and in turn may produce a picture collection of its own, which would need to be organized for reuse, either by the publisher concerned or by others with the same interests.

Newspapers also use pictures for printing purposes and here a system which permits fast, accurate retrieval is even more important than in many other picture libraries, where perhaps browsing is an important feature. Pressing deadlines have to be met and this may make for a different emphasis or approach in running the picture library.

Broadcasting, especially television, is also a great consumer of pictures and many picture libraries exist in broadcasting services to help provide material quickly for use. Television is not the only user of pictures in broadcasting, but it has its particular requirements, in that pictures have to be transferred to another medium for transmission. Broadcasting also uses a great deal of material from outside sources, and both aspects are covered in the concluding essay.

14

The United States Library of Congress, Prints and Photographs Division

Renata V Shaw

The visual collections of the Prints and Photographs Division are universal in scope. Pictorial images have been collected since the early 19th century when the first pictures arrived in the library as copyright deposits. Today, the collections have grown to over 10,000,000 items.

The library acquires prints and photographs by gift, transfer from other federal agencies, domestic and foreign exchange, purchase, and direct solicitation, in addition to copyright deposit.

1 COLLECTIONS

The collections are divided into six major areas differentiated by artistic medium or format: fine prints; popular and applied graphic art; master photographs; documentary photographs; architecture, design and engineering collections; and posters.

(a) Fine Prints

The fine prints collection includes over 100,000 prints produced during the last 500 years. The older European prints initially came to the library through two large donations: the Gardiner Greene Hubbard (1898) and the George Lothrop Bradley (1906) bequests. The Joseph and Elizabeth Robins Pennell donation of Whistleriana and 19th and 20th-century prints was augmented by a later Pennell bequest, which allows the library to purchase fine prints by artists active during the last 100 years. This fund has helped the library build an extensive collection of 20th-century American and foreign prints. It includes examples of contemporary art by artists working in widely varying techniques and styles. The most recent prints are used primarily for exhibitions and research since copyright laws prevent their reproduction without permission of the artist. The older prints, however, are frequently reproduced for use in publications.

The library owns 2,000 Japanese Ukiyo-e woodcuts produced before and during that country's first contact with the West.

The fine prints are arranged alphabetically by century under the artist's name regardless of the nationality of the printmaker. There is a partial subject index to iconographic themes. A printed catalogue is available for United States prints only: *American prints in the Library of Congress: a catalog of the collection of fine prints,* compiled by Karen F Beall and published for the Library of Congress by the Johns Hopkins Press, Baltimore and London, 1970.

(b) Popular and Applied Graphic Art

When the subject matter of a print is of prime importance and the reason for its creation, the image can usually be found in the popular and applied graphic art collection.

Popular Graphic Art (PGA)

In the 19th century numerous American lithographic companies supplied an eager public with a great variety of popular prints. These realistic or romanticized images of mass appeal can be located by searching for them under the name of the printmaker or publisher when the artist is unknown. American popular prints were long neglected by collectors and students alike. They were rediscovered in the 1920s by researchers newly interested in Americana, the 19th century, and popular culture. This collection includes 12,000 images in all the media used in the 18th to 20th centuries.

Exhibition installation for caricature show, 1977. *The Library of Congress, Washington DC.*

Political Prints (PC)

The library owns 15,000 political cartoons illuminating historical figures and controversies from the 18th century to the present. These are arranged by country, century, and printmaker. British political prints are keyed to the holdings of the British Museum. Unique Library of Congress holdings can be located in *British cartoons in the Library of Congress* — a checklist compiled by Elena G Millie of those cartoons not found in the catalogue of Prints and Drawings in the British Museum, Washington, US Library of Congress, 1970 (typescript).

Applied Graphic Art (AGA)

The applied graphic art collection consists of 82,000 advertisements, labels, sheet music covers, calendars, and examples of typography arranged by designer or printer. This collection is an important visual archive for the study of the growth and development of commercial graphic art during the last century and a half.

'Posada's Mexico' Exhibition, entrance, November 1979-December 1980. *The Library of Congress, Washington DC.*

The Cabinet of American Illustration (CAI)

The Cabinet of American Illustration was organized in 1932 as a collection of over 4,000 original illustrations created between 1880 and 1910, primarily for *Harper's Magazine, Scribner's, Collier's, Cosmopolitan,* and *Century.* The artists worked in ink, gouache, and watercolour. A card file by artist gives access to the collection; no subject analysis of the collection as a whole has been undertaken, although some of the drawings have been indexed in the division's subject files when they were used for specific exhibition or publication projects.

The Cartoon Drawing Collection (CD)

The cartoon drawing collection consists of 2,200 political, social, and satirical cartoons. These were produced for magazines such as *The New Yorker, Collier's,* and *Puck.*

This collection, arranged by artist, is growing annually by the acquisition of outstanding examples of editorial cartoons commissioned for newspapers and periodicals.

The American Drawing Collection

The American drawing collection includes about 700 Civil War drawings; there is partial subject access to the events depicted. Other drawings are preliminary sketches for prints or topographic views. There is a card catalogue arranged by artist to aid in finding specific items.

(c) Master Photographs

The master photographs collection contains 3,500 photographs by primarily American photographers, from the pioneers of the early 19th century to contemporary young artists. Unless a photograph is protected by copyright, it can be reproduced by the library and used in publications. The newest photographs are used only for exhibitions and for research. This collection is arranged by photographer with no subject access to the images.

(d) Documentary Photographs

The documentary photograph collections form the backbone of the visual archives. These include 6,000,000 photographs and 5,000,000 original negatives. The subject coverage is universal although the emphasis is on every aspect of American life, from the early years of photography to the present. Some of the most frequently requested photographs are those from the Mathew B Brady collection pertaining to the Civil War, the Detroit Publishing Company photographs of American cities, resorts, and landscapes, the Farm Security Administration/Office of War Information files documenting the depression and World War II era in the United States, and the *Look* magazine collection of over 3,000,000 photographs and slides which cover the period 1937-71. Access to the *Look* photographs, however, is restricted to the published material in the collection; photographs are not available for trade, commercial, or advertising purposes, but are for personal and research use only. Two large collections recently received by the library are those of the Alexander Graham Bell family and of Theodor Horydczak, a local Washington photographer who documented social change in the city during the first half of this century.

Photographs in these documentary collections are not individually catalogued. Many are arranged in 'lots' by subject, photographer, period, collector, sponsoring body, or other common denominator. These different groups can be located by readers through a divisional card file arranged like a dictionary catalogue with access through author/creator, title, and subject.

(e) Architecture, Design, and Engineering Collections

The two oldest collections devoted to architecture consist of the *Pictorial Archives of Early American Architecture* and the *Carnegie Survey of the Architecture of the South.* Both started in the 1920s, spurred by a newly emerging interest in Americana and by a desire to record structures before they were destroyed by the growth of modern cities.

The *Historic American Buildings Survey (1929-)* and the *Historic American Engineering Record (1969-)* differ from the earlier collections in that they systematically incorporate data pages documenting the background of each structure, as well as photographs and measured drawings prepared by professional staff to the specifications of the US Department of the Interior, the American Institute of Architects, and the Library of Congress.

The architecture, design and engineering collections also include architectural renderings acquired from individual American architects or architectural firms. All the materials in different formats are keyed to the geographic locations of the structures. At present there are 13 state catalogues of the HABS in print, but additional catalogues will be produced as the recording of buildings proceeds state by state.

(f) Posters

The poster collection includes over 70,000 American and foreign posters from the 1850s to the present. These are organized by country of origin, designer, and promotional goal. The collections include a representative selection of international posters of the art nouveau period and of Austrian and German expressionists. The United States Works Progress Administration (1936-41) is represented by 750 original silk-screen display posters.

The library is actively collecting outstanding posters by designers working today. It has an on-going programme of exchanging posters with institutions in the United States and abroad. Many recent posters are protected by copyright law; older ones can be reproduced for use in publications.

2 PROCESSING

The processing of new acquisitions to the Prints and Photographs Division takes place in the division itself. After a group of pictures has been accessioned, it is integrated into the holdings according to guidelines established in the division. Portraits of personalities, and pictures associated with these individuals, are mounted on acid-free board, captioned, and placed in self-indexing files open to the public. Geographic pictures are accommodated in the same manner. Single photographs are placed in a specific subject file where they can be located under one subject only. This browsing file leads the user to simple categories, e.g., kiosks, turkeys, whisky, etc.

Another basic research tool is the graphics file in the reading room. This consists of illustrations from many different sources arranged under subject headings, such as Fires and Firefighting, Money Crises, Transportation, or Western Life. The file also includes 8 × 10 inch reproductions of oversize graphics. This arrangement saves time and effort by allowing readers to choose needed pictures from copy prints rather than originals, while wear on the originals is minimized.

Pictures which cannot be simply filed in self-indexing drawers are described as 'lots' on cards and stored in archival document boxes or in metal cabinets (some examples are shown below). Large groups of newly accessioned pictures, e.g., those received from the library's Manuscript Division on transfer, are divided into logical groups and catalogued as 'lots'. The example of the Herbert Putnam Collection illustrates this principle.

Lot 11490
Putnam, Herbert, 1861-1955, *collector.*
[Portraits, mostly uncaptioned, of Herbert
Putnam's family and friends. Includes photos
of Brenda Putnam and Herbert Putnam.]

Approximately 350 photos, including 5
family albums and 2 tintypes.
From Herbert Putnam papers.
Transfer, Manuscript Division, 1971.

Lot 11491

Putnam, Herbert, 1861-1955, *collector.*
[Portraits, mostly formal, of Herbert Putnam;
as a child; with family; as librarian at Boston
Public Library (in uniform); as Librarian of
Congress, in LC settings, with staff; with
honorary degree recipients at Princeton
University; at class reunions (Harvard '83);
at ALA dinner honoring him (Boston,
1950).]
Approximately 65 photos and 1 pencil
sketch. From Herbert Putnam papers.
Transfer, Manuscript Division, 1971.

Lot 11492

Putnam, Brenda, 1890-   , *collector.*
[Photographs of Brenda Putnam and her
sculptured works. Announcements of
classes, exhibits. Magazine articles and
advertisement of her book, *The sculptor's
way.*]
Approximately 125 items, including 6 pencil
sketches.
From Herbert Putnam papers.
Transfer, Manuscript Division, 1971.

Lot 11493

O'Hara, Eliot, 1890-   , *collector.*
[Photographs of the O'Hara family and
friends. Mostly informal snapshots.]
Approximately 200 photos.
From Herbert Putnam papers.
Transfer, Manuscript Division, 1971.

'Lot' numbers are purely arbitrary and refer to shelf location only. Individual catalogue cards can be easily duplicated and filed under several subject headings in order to provide the user with as many access points as seem necessary for full exploitation of the collections.

Drawings, fine prints, master photographs, and posters of artistic, historic or intrinsic value receive individual cataloguing. Architectural drawings also are individually catalogued and the resulting cards filed separately.

An illustrated shelf-list card has recently been introduced for cartoons in the popular and applied graphic art collection. It bears a 2×3 inch photograph of the print and a call number leading to the specific location of the original picture. The visual cards are filed chronologically to aid users in documenting a specific historical event or political crisis of the 19th century.

An unpublished draft for the 'Organization and cataloguing of pictorial material in the Library of Congress, Prints and Photographs Division' was prepared in 1978 by Elisabeth W Betz, picture cataloguing specialist. We hope that one day this publication will be expanded to become a general guide for picture cataloguers in different types of institution.

An extensive list *Subject headings used in the Library of Congress Prints and Photographs Division* was prepared by Elizabeth W Betz in 1980. This is based on the diverse holdings of universal scope and is intended to bring subject headings for visual materials into conformity with those for books and related materials.

Glass and film negatives are stored separately, protected by acid-free Permalife paper jackets in vertical files arranged by alpha-numerical codes which derive from the source and size of the negatives. These files are closed to the public, but prints from the negatives are available for consultation by researchers in the files described above.

3 PRESERVATION AND RESTORATION

The Preservation Office of the Library of Congress is responsible for the overall preservation effort in the library. Within the Preservation Office, the Restoration Office has a Paper Conservation Section which repairs works of art on paper sent to them from different divisions of the library. Large posters are protected by Mylar encapsulation which allows them to be handled without damage to the surface. Newly printed file photographs are dry mounted and caption strips attached to them by this office. Special boxes of archival board are constructed for oversized pictures or collections which cannot fit into standard size containers.

There is an on-going programme of converting nitrate film negatives and glass negatives to safety film in order to preserve the image if the original were to decompose or be broken. Old crumbling negative jackets are being replaced by Permalife jackets to protect negatives from deterioration. Plans call for storage of all photographs and negatives in air-conditioned and humidity-controlled storage facilities in twice-filtered air to remove atmospheric pollutants.

4   REFERENCE AND USE OF THE COLLECTIONS

All patrons above secondary school age are allowed to use the collections. On average, over 600 readers visit the reading room monthly, studying an immense variety of subjects from sports to religion and advertisements to viticulture. The majority of these readers finish their research by placing an order for photographs with the Photo-duplication Service of the Library of Congress. The Reference Section does not sell ready-made photographs; all photographs are made to order for a specific client.

Readers usually request 8 × 10 inch glossy black and white photographs or 4 × 5 inch colour transparencies because these sizes are preferred by most publishing firms. The Photoduplication Service also produces exhibit quality prints if these are needed for display purposes. A price-list for different photographic services is mailed to interested readers by request.

The reading room houses a reference collection of 2,000 volumes relating to the collections. Picture books based on the holdings of the Prints and Photographs Division are annotated with negative numbers and thus serve as finding aids to the library's pictures.

The reference staff answer picture requests by mail provided that these include photocopies of the needed images or otherwise precisely identify them by bibliographic citation. As a general rule, staff are unable to search more than 10 pictures for correspondents, but the division maintains a list of qualified picture researchers who have many years of experience working at the Library of Congress and who can assist with lengthy projects. These specialists can be engaged to work for an hourly or weekly fee agreed upon in advance between reader and researcher.

5 BIBLIOGRAPHY

The Prints and Photographs Division does not have a single up-to-date guide to all of its resources but the following publications are of help to a researcher:

America, 1935-1945 The Photographs of the Farm Security Administration and the Office of War Information. 83,000 photographs at the Library of Congress, arranged by subject and region and reproduced on microfiche. Cambridge, England, Chadwyck-Healey, 1980.

A century of photographs, 1846-1946 Selected from the collections of the Library of Congress; compiled by Renata V Shaw. Washington DC, Library of Congress, 1980.

Graphic sampler Selected from the collections of the Library of Congress; compiled by Renata V Shaw. Washington DC, Library of Congress, 1979.

Historic American buildings survey Microfiche reproduction of the photographic and written records. Cambridge, England, Chadwyck-Healey, 1981.

The Middle East in pictures A Photographic History, 1898-1934. Four volumes by G Eric Matson. New York, Arno Press, 1980. [in press]

The American revolution in drawings and prints A check-list of 1765-90 graphics in the Library of Congress, compiled by Donald H Cresswell with a foreword by Sinclair H Hitchings. Washington DC, Library of Congress, 1975.

Special collections in the Library of Congress A selective guide compiled by Annette Melville. Washington DC, Library of Congress, 1981.

Viewpoints A selection from the pictorial collections of the Library of Congress. A picture book by Alan Fern, Milton Kaplan, and the staff of the Prints and Photographs Division. Washington DC, Library of Congress, 1975.

6 FUTURE DEVELOPMENTS

The Prints and Photographs Division has recently moved into expanded, modern quarters in the James Madison Memorial Building. The new address is:

Library of Congress
Prints and Photographs Division
The James Madison Memorial Building
Washington, DC 20540
USA

15

The Imperial War Museum, London

Penny Ritchie Calder

T he Imperial War Museum illustrates and records all aspects of the two world wars and other military operations involving Britain and the Commonwealth in the 20th century. The museum was founded in 1917 and was established by Act of Parliament in 1920. It has been in its present home in London (formerly Bethlem Royal Hospital, or Bedlam) since 1936.

The museum is responsible for acquiring and preserving a very wide range of material. Within this range are the many three-dimensional objects in the exhibits and firearms collection, varying in size from medals to aircraft; the national reference library of 20th-century military history and a rapidly growing documentary holding, both of which are used extensively by students, researchers, and other interested individuals; a major film archive; a growing collection of sound recordings; a major art collection; and a national photographic archive.

Other departments within the museum include the Research and Information Office, the Department of Information Retrieval, the Department of Permanent Exhibitions, which is responsible for the design and execution of most of the displays in the museum's galleries, and the Department of Education and Publications, which provides a variety of educational services, mounts special exhibitions, and deals with all aspects of publicity and the production of museum publications.

The museum also has two out-stations, the former Battle of Britain airfield at Duxford, near Cambridge, which houses many of the museum's historic aircraft, tanks, and other large exhibits, and HMS *Belfast,* the 11,500 ton cruiser moored in the Pool of London as a floating naval museum.

Of particular interest to picture librarians is the work of the Department of Art and the Department of Photographs. The Department of Art is responsible for 10,000 paintings, drawings, and sculptures illustrating many aspects of war in the 20th century, 50,000 war-time posters of all nations from 1914 to the present day, ephemeral material such as postcards, charity flags and badges, and a fine collection of First World War French prints and wide-ranging examples of postage stamps, censor marks, paper money, coins, and medallions.

These have been acquired over a considerable period of time from various sources. Many of the works of art were officially commissioned by the Ministry of Information during both world wars as part of the War Artists Scheme, including outstanding works by artists such as Paul Nash, Sir Stanley Spencer, Graham Sutherland, and Jacob Epstein. Among the drawings acquired by the museum are groups by Muirhead Bone and Adrian Hill of the Western Front, watercolours of the Middle East by James McBey, portraits by Francis Dodd, and aviation drawings by Richard and Sydney Carline. The large poster collection (30,000 from the First World War and 20,000 from the Second World War onwards) contains such famous examples as 'Women of Britain say go', 'I want you for the US Army', and 'Dig for victory', as well as works by Brangwyn, Spencer Pryse, Flagg, Fougasse, Bert Thomas, and Abram Games.

Other items have been acquired by gift or purchase and by these means the collections are constantly being enlarged and improved. Some of the more important gifts in recent years have come from artists and their families — 'Vietnam requiem', a mixed-media work, was given by Philip Hicks, and Edward Ardizzone presented four volumes of his war diary, which include sketches and descriptions of scenes in Italy, Normandy, and Germany, upon which are based many finished works held by the museum. Purchases, within the museum's limited funds, are made from private owners, dealers, and at auction, and a useful network of communication has been built up which provides the museum with information about works relevant to the museum's field currently on the market, and often results in favourable purchasing arrangements.

As many works of art as possible are put on display in the museum's galleries, and regular special exhibitions allow a variety of material normally kept in store to be shown. The remaining paintings are housed in a large store in the museum fitted with racks of purpose-built mobile screens on which paintings, prints, and drawings are hung for easy access and viewing. Because of the tendency of pastels and watercolours to fade, lights have UV filters, and the levels are kept deliberately low. The temperature of the store is also kept constant. About 4,000 of the most frequently viewed posters and items of ephemera are kept in plan chests and on shelves in the Department of Art's reference room, but the larger part of the poster collection is stored away from the museum.

Many works of art are lent to other museums and galleries. Some major exhibitions are mounted or shown outside the museum, such as *Stanley Spencer in the shipyard,* a joint exhibition held at the Science Museum in 1979, and *Rose of death,* (paintings by Albert Richards), which became a touring exhibition through the Arts Council. Complete travelling exhibitions of about 40 frames of posters or prints are available through the Area Museums Services or, occasionally, direct through the museum. A limited number of loans are also made to military establishments and government departments. Pastels, however, are never lent because of their fragile nature and watercolours only if display conditions meet required standards. Any damage sustained by a work of art, either whilst on loan or as a result of age, has to be treated outside the museum by professional conservationists, since the museum does not have the facilities to carry out anything other than minor repairs.

The cataloguing of paintings is by artist and is published in the *Concise catalogue of paintings, drawings and sculpture of the First World War,* and in an edition for the Second World War. Some cross-indexing has been completed, for example of portraits, and this will eventually cover the whole collection. The cataloguing of posters is organized thematically under headings, such as First World War Russian Posters or British Home Front Posters.

The art reference room, equipped with desks and large surfaces suitable for laying out posters and prints etc., is open to the public and is intended mainly for the use of researchers and students, individually or in groups of up to 12, who are interested in viewing works of art not on public display. The opportunity to use this facility has been taken up by increasingly large numbers in recent years. Visitors are asked to make appointments in advance so that material can be gathered together for

Staff of the Department of Photographs at work in the Reading Room. *The Imperial War Museum, London.*

them. If a particular item is not available, there is normally an archival copy of a photograph of the work which can be seen during a visit. The majority of pictures officially commissioned during the First and Second World Wars and a smaller number of posters have been photographed; black and white copies of these photographs can be ordered. In order to extend this scheme, the use of microfiches is currently under consideration as an aid to visitors wanting to identify posters of which they want to see the originals. The Department of Art also runs a transparency loan scheme, primarily for use by publishers, which gives a choice of about 1,000 5 × 4 inch Ektachrome transparencies.

In contrast to the relatively straightforward procedures for handling acquisitions, conservation, and cataloguing of the museum's art holdings, those for maintaining the collection of over five million photographs and negatives are more complex.

The Department of Photographs is a national archive, largely concerned with the two world wars, but also with other conflicts involving the armed forces of Britain and the Commonwealth. Since 1917, the department has been the repository for the work of official war photographers who worked in many theatres of the First World War, and this collection, together with smaller groups of photographs acquired through an exchange programme, amounts to over a quarter of a million photographs. A further two million photographs of the Second World War were added in 1947, most of them taken by official war photographers attached to the Allied and Axis forces. There are also a large number of photographs depicting the war in Eastern Europe and the Pacific, and a quantity of material relating to other conflicts, including the Korean War and the emergencies in Malaya, Kenya, Cyprus.

Since 1966 the museum has been the repository for those official photographs of the British Army which are considered to be of historical significance. Moreover, the photographs and negatives taken by professional, press and amateur photographers of both world wars and the inter-war years form an increasingly important feature of the archive. This material is acquired as a result of donations, loans, and, to a much lesser extent, purchases. It includes, for example, albums of photographs taken by Lawrence of Arabia, Field Marshal Rommel, and Cecil Beaton.

The storage of photographs and negatives, as for works of art, requires considerable care. The main point of access to the collection is through photographic prints mounted into hard-backed looseleaf albums or kept in individual envelopes, and stored on shelves in sliding racks and in the visitors' room. If, as is often the case, these prints have been copied from originals, the latter are then stored to protect them from frequent handling. Negatives are stored at a constant temperature in acid-free envelopes inside multidrawer cabinets. A long-term negative duplication programme is being carried out so that original negatives (which may be up to 80 years old) are no longer used for making prints. This, and a great deal of other processing and printing work, including the large-scale production of copy prints for users of the collections, is carried out in the museum in a suite of fully equipped darkrooms staffed by professional photographers.

Because of the size of the archive and the way in which sub-collections have been added to it, it has not been possible to introduce a single classification system which will cover accurately the entire holding. Instead, there are a number of different cataloguing systems which operate within the department, largely as a result of the retention of original cataloguing systems transferred to the museum along with official photographic collections. Air Ministry, Admiralty, and War Office photographs of the

Enlarging a photograph in the Laboratory of the Department of Photographs. *The Imperial War Museum, London.*

Second World War, for example, all have separate internal classification schemes. These schemes are not entirely satisfactory since they were evolved to fit specific short-term needs related to the war, and their original finding aids were not of the standard required by a large historical archive, but modifications carried out by the department have improved the retrieval methods. Similarly, the captions accompanying each photograph are mostly the original captions written by the photographers themselves and subject to the excisions of war-time censorship. Although these are, in themselves, of considerable historical interest, recaptioning to provide more accurate information for users of the collections is necessary.

Despite the apparent complexity of the existing cataloguing systems they can be used very efficiently by members of staff trained in their operation. Every photograph held in the museum has a prefix letter denoting its major category ('Q' for instance is used for photographs taken during the First World War and immediately afterwards, 'H' covers the Home Front 1939-45) and is given an individual number to identify it. Although it does not necessarily follow that every photograph of a particular event or personality is classified in the same category, a card index, compiled from indexes accompanying collections transferred to the museum, provides a quick reference to photographs relating to certain popular topics, such as the Blitz, Lancaster aircraft, El Alamein, etc.

To devise and execute a completely new method of cataloguing the millions of photographs in the collection would necessitate the total closure of the Department of Photographs for a period of perhaps several years. As it is a national archive, this would not be acceptable and therefore reorganization of the collections is limited to small-scale improvements, with the possibility of introducing some kind of microform to aid retrieval.

The Department of Photographs provides a variety of services, both internal and public. It is used extensively by other departments within the museum in connection with publicity, research, and the mounting of exhibitions. In addition, like the Department of Art, it offers facilities for study and research to all members of the public in its visitors' room. These facilities are used by researchers, including students and authors, who are generally looking for photographs of specific subjects; by people interested in seeing photographs of friends or relatives, or of aspects of the war in which they were involved; and by browsers, who have no particular enquiry but enjoy looking through the wealth of material contained in albums in the collection. The department also deals with many enquiries and orders for photographs by telephone or letter. When copies of photographs are ordered by visitors and other users, prints or 35 mm. transparencies are made for a relatively small fee. Original prints or negatives are never lent. In some cases, for researchers using material held by the Department of Film, it is possible to make a still print from film footage, but this is a lengthy process and is not widely used. A colour transparency hire scheme has recently been established in order to make available the extensive colour material covering the services in the Second World War and up to the present day.

The reproduction of photographs or works of art from the museum's collections in books, magazines, or other publications is permitted at the discretion of the keepers of the relevant departments, and upon payment of a fee (which varies according to the type and circulation of the publication) and the crediting of such reproductions to the Trustees of the Imperial War Museum. Both the Department of Photographs and the Department of Art can advise on any copyright issue which may arise.

In addition to the loan exhibitions organized by the Department of Art, the Department of Photographs has also set up various travelling exhibitions, which provide interesting displays in many parts of the country, as well as attracting wider publicity for the museum's collections. A recent travelling exhibition on the theme *Women at War, 1914-18,* for example, highlighted the wealth of material held in the archive on the Home Front and civilian activity during the First World War.

Aside from their responsibilities for acquisitions, conservation, and exhibition work, both the Department of Art and the Department of Photographs place a high priority on the public services they offer. It is the aim of the Trustees of the Imperial War Museum to make the contents of the archives (films, documents, and printed books, as well as photographs and works of art) available to as wide a public as possible, and to encourage their use by scholars, researchers and other individuals and groups. Indirectly, this generates a good deal of publicity for the collections, which not only increases revenue through sales of photographs and transparencies, and reproduction fees, but also leads to donations of private material to add to the collections. Having seen at first hand the way in which items are preserved and used for practical purposes by researchers and others, many visitors look upon the museum as a secure and worthwhile repository for their own or relatives' possessions which come within the museum's terms of reference.

The Department of Art and the Department of Photographs, in common with policies pursued throughout the museum, seek to promote a high level of practical scholarship, so that their staff are completely familiar with the content of the collections and are aware of the scope of the museum's field. This enables any gaps to be identified and gradually filled by initiating donations, loans or purchases; it facilitates cataloguing and the devising of efficient methods of retrieval; and by being able to supply all available material relevant to a particular enquiry and advising on further sources, it provides the public with as professional a service as possible. As a national museum and archive, the Imperial War Museum aims to maintain these standards in its many curatorial and administrative functions, as well as in all aspects of picture librarianship.

16

The National Film Archive, London

Michelle Snapes

INTRODUCTION

The stills, posters, and designs collection of the National Film Archive, London, is one of the largest and most comprehensive of its kind in the world, its aim being to illustrate the development of world cinema from its origins to the present day. It started its life as a special collection in 1948 when the stock amounted to a mere 25,000 black and white stills. It is now considerably larger and includes two types of pictorial film material: pre-production artwork drawn before a film has started, e.g., set and costume designs and designs for animation films; post-production material issued for publicizing a film, e.g., stills and posters. The collection services the archive and the various departments of the British Film Institute of which the archive is a department. It is also open to all film researchers and students as well as specialists in film, such as writers, journalists, directors, producers, and film technicians.

The Stills Collection

The stills collection consists of 1,500,000 black and white stills, 10 × 8 inches in size, and 200,000 colour transparencies and negatives of varying format, (10 × 8 inches, 4 × 5 inches, 2½ × 2½ inches, 35 mm.) representing some 50,000 different films made throughout the world. It also contains 9,500 publicity photograph files of film

Viewing a newsreel film and selecting frame stills for illustration in a book at the National Film Archive. *National Film Archive/Stills Library.*

personalities — actors and actresses, directors, producers, cameramen, and others — and a technical section showing the history of cinema buildings, film studios, and apparatus at different periods. Stills are illustrations from a particular film and are of two kinds: those issued by film companies and individuals for the promotion of a film, which are called 'production stills', and 'frame stills' which are reproductions of a single frame from the film itself. Production stills are taken while the film is being shot and are basically posed photographs of scenes from that film using special lighting and composition in order to produce the best effects. In the great day of the 'star system' when the art of still photography was at its peak, it was said that many a star would not sign a film contract until the name of the stills photographer had been agreed, so great was the impact this could make on their image.

Production stills are therefore often of great artistic beauty but their value may be limited for those researchers who are studying the structural analysis of a film. For these special projects it is necessary to select, during a viewing of the film, certain frames which illustrate the point to be made, such as the special film and editing techniques employed by film directors and cinematographers to produce certain effects. This process is both costly and time-consuming. Some well-known and popular examples of frame stills produced are those of horrific actions, such as the cutting of a human eye with a razor in Buñuel's *Un chien andalou* (1928), or magical transformations, such as Spencer Tracy changing from Doctor Jekyll to Mr Hyde in the film *Doctor Jekyll and Mr Hyde* (1941).

The Posters Collection

The posters collection comprises some 7,000 items which relate mainly to British and American film releases, although it also contains fine examples of French, Polish, Czech, and Russian posters. Some of the earliest examples dating from 1897 onwards are in the form of playbills. Posters come in a variety of sizes and their visual and artistic impact varies considerably according to the type of film presented and the designer commissioned for it, as well as the type of printing technique used, varying from silk screen to lithography.

The Designs Collection

This collection comprises mostly set and costume designs and some examples of 'cels', as used in animation films, and silhouette paper puppets and background scenes, as used in the films of Lotte Reiniger. Set design is a general term that describes the types of artwork illustrating various aspects of the film to be made. These can be drawn in pencil, charcoal, or ink, or elaborately painted with gouaches and water-colours. They can attempt to show a general view of the set, its interior decoration and furnishings, or exterior architectural outlook. These are usually referred to as scenic drafts. Another type of design is the ground plan similar to that produced by an architect, showing in accurate scale all the elements of the sets, the positioning of the action about to take place and the camera movement and angle to be used for the scene. Lastly, an even more intriguing type of design is the 'continuity sketch' which, through a series of drawings of different scales, captures certain phases of movement, spelling out visually the camera distance and angle of each shot to be filmed by the cinematographer. These drawings, of course, correspond to the analytical breakdown referred to earlier in the context of frame stills.

270

ACQUISITIONS

The acquisition of items presented in the collection is, of course, complex since these are not published and their availability is limited to a small circle of people working in the film industry. Consequently, librarians working in this field, in the UK or abroad, have to devise a method of acquisition based on the relationship they have developed with the film industry in their country. So far, no legal deposit of stills, posters, and designs exists in Britain or elsewhere, although colleagues abroad, working within the framework of a nationalized film industry, find it easier to acquire material of their national productions.

Traditionally, material is acquired by donations from film companies, individuals associated with the industry, and allied bodies; by purchase from private individuals, specialized film shops and antique dealers, auction sales, galleries, and publicity agencies used by film companies for the promotion of films in cinemas; by exchange of duplicates with collections of this type abroad, usually attached to film archives, institutes, or museums.

The policy at the National Film Archive in the UK is to acquire illustrations of almost all films released in Great Britain, with special attention to the coverage of all British films as well as material on foreign films presented at the National Film Theatre, London. Advance notice of films is picked up from trade magazines through advertisements or lists of production schedules. Stills and posters are then acquired directly from the various film companies concerned through their press offices. These procedures could not exist without understanding the special relationship that the National Film Archive and the British Film Institute have established with the film trade in Great Britain over the years. The archive has relied on the generosity of the film industry for the growth of its collection and, in exchange, it undertakes to safeguard the material collected for the future and also make it available to the donors when necessary, by means of copies. This cooperative policy has generated a large and successful collection. The same cooperative spirit exists internally among the staff of the British Film Institute and National Film Archive, and among external users who provide a useful, informal source of communication, enabling the librarian to secure many acquisitions. Information about auction sales is gathered through contacts with the various auctioneers and through a study of their catalogues; much the same is done for specialized film shops, galleries, and antique dealers.

ORGANIZATION AND INDEXING

The collection is organized into three main groups: alphabetically by original film title, cross-referenced from useful alternative titles, e.g., British release title; alphabetically, by name of personalities; and by alphabetical subject headings for the technical area.

Identification

When material is acquired it does not always carry a caption or an identification by film title, name of person, etc. Consequently, the first task is to identify the material, while information about it can be provided from its source of acquisition, e.g., the donor, vendor. Identification of old material can present problems even to experts in the field. Generally, various sources of information are used, such as film directories and annuals, cast-lists of actors and actresses, national filmographies, and histories of film companies. Stills can be identified by their serial numbers (usually printed at the bottom corner) used by most companies. Keys to these numbers are difficult to obtain but a few are circulated among archivists. Alternatively, decoding work is undertaken! Genre, style, and size of stills can be a starting point for the identification work and may indicate the country of origin and approximate date, which can lead to further research. The Sherlock Holmes spirit is never far away in this enterprise.

Indexing

Three indexes to the collection have been compiled for stills, one by names of actors and actresses, one by names of directors and technical cast, such as cameramen, producers, etc., and one by subject headings for technical aspects of film-making and apparatus. The posters and designs are indexed by film title with information about their size, location numbers, designer, and printers, as applicable.

When other categories are called for, staff and users can research these at the Information and Documentation Department of the British Film Institute or the Film Cataloguing Department of the National Film Archive. These two departments provide an in-depth analytical approach to film study essential to the collection.

Published Catalogue

So far no printed catalogue of the collection is available but work is now in progress for computerized production of a title list with an index by director's name, and indicating under each entry the type of material held, i.e., black and white stills, colour transparencies, posters, and designs. When it is published, it will be the only one of its kind available and will provide an introduction to the scope of the collection.

STORAGE AND PRESERVATION

The Stills Collection

A modern automated filing system with rotating shelves has been installed to house the collection, files being stored vertically in acid-free folders, held flat by metal partitions on each shelf. Its main advantage, apart from the obvious ones like easy and painless retrieval of material (hitherto contained in 82 filing cabinets), is that of safeguarding the collection from light and dust; the rotating movement of the shelves creates an in-built ventilation system which has had a surprisingly beneficial effect on the photographs. For example, stills which had curled up are recovering their original shape, but, most important, the air ventilation has slowed down the fading or 'yellowing' of some stills.

Stills can be damaged in a number of ways but some of the worst problems are those caused by mishandling by users, and fading of image or 'yellowing' due to excess hypo deposit on positive prints which has not been washed out properly at the time of production. Further similar damage can come from the presence of chemicals in the glue used for labels and captions on the back of stills. At present, stills showing signs of deterioration are quickly retrieved from their original file and copied so that gases emanating from chemicals do not affect others. A more

273

One member of staff chooses stills required by enquirer whilst another is filing stills into the automatic rotating storage. *National Film Archive/Stills Library.*

thorough and important preservation programme which involves copying the whole collection onto master preservation negatives is now being discussed and will be implemented in the near future.

The Posters Collection

Posters are grouped by size and stored flat in planchests, by numerical accession numbers. Items showing signs of decay are repaired. This work is carried out on behalf of the National Film Archive by the Preservation Department of the Public Record Office. It consists of stabilizing the colour dyes used in the printing techniques through a de-acidification process and backing the poster with a linen cloth. In order to reduce the handling of originals and their deterioration and to increase ease of retrieval and access, items in the collection are copied onto 35 mm. colour transparencies which are kept in the main library.

The Designs Collection

Designs are grouped together in art portfolios under name of designer and alphabetically by title of films. They are stored flat, away from dust and light. So far the collection has not required special preservation apart from the general precautions taken when collecting this type of material. Again, the material is available for consultation in the form of colour transparencies, filed by film title.

USAGE OF THE COLLECTION

The collection is used extensively in Great Britain and abroad. It is used in the publication of most film books, film magazines, newspapers, compilation films on the cinema, and television programmes. Consultation and research on the premises must be made by appointment and priority is given to serious researchers of film, who can call on staff knowledge and expertise. Requests in writing are also answered and pictorial research by staff is available. Increasingly, the collection is used by film and television designers, make-up artists and production staff for research on new productions where it serves as a unique social and historical record.

An exhibition illustrated with posters, stills, scripts and pressbooks at the National Film Theatre. *National Film Archive/Stills Library.*

Film companies also require copies of their old material for publicizing film sales on 16 mm. film, television, and videocassettes.

Copying fees, search fees, and delivery time must be agreed in advance and there must be a clear understanding of the copyright situation. The strict requirements of the archival nature of the collection mean that use of the material is made through copies of originals. Stills, posters, and designs are copied in the form of black and white positive prints or colour transparencies. The copying work is done by the library's Photographic Department which is also responsible for the preservation work and has thus developed strict control over quality and handling of the material. It can undertake various types of cleaning jobs and repairs in the case of damaged originals with due consideration to preservation policies.

Copyright

This problem is particularly crucial to the collection and its survival, given the stated collaboration and cooperation maintained with the film trade. Therefore, users are briefed on the subject before using the collection and have to sign a declaration agreeing to comply with these regulations or state this in writing. At present, stills are not supplied to advertising companies and users who do not fulfil these conditions. In addition, all copies produced are stamped with a similar declaration on copyright. Specific advice and help are provided to prospective users and names and addresses of copyright owners can be given on demand.

Exhibitions

Increasingly, the collection is being used for exhibition display in museums and galleries dealing with the subject of cinema, or on the social and artistic developments of the 20th century. Original material can be loaned provided that requirements for preservation and insurance of the material are complied with. In addition, the department mounts its own exhibitions at the National Film Theatre, London, to correspond with seasons of films shown there.

17

Archival Libraries in the UK

Robert N Smart

INTRODUCTION

Archivists, like librarians and museum curators, have in the last decade shown a new awareness of pictorial material. Nevertheless, visual records are to be found in archival collelctions from an early date. Those of which we speak are to be distinguished into three main classes: (1) those which are original drawings or paintings, (2) those which are the result of some mechanical process, and (3) those which can be grouped as the result of a photographic process. Hybrids between these classes exist but are relatively rare. Other exotic visual records, such as tapestries, reliefs, sculptures, coins, medals, and seals and seal matrices which occur from time to time in record repositories must be excluded, as must photographic methods such as microfilm, microcards, or microfiche for keeping, preserving, or reducing the bulk of records which have affected archivists for a generation. A final exclusion must be architectural, technical, and engineering drawings which at times come very near the pictorial.

What distinguishes, most clearly, the pictorial material in the archive repository from its preservation in other kinds of institution is, first, its normal occurrence as part of an archive group, as one kind of document dependent on and essentially interconnected with the other documents in the group and, second, the archivist's attitude to the material — where he or she is primarily responsible to the depositing authority and its individual parts or to private depositors and only secondarily to the general public wishing to make use of the material, and where the archivist's primary interest lies in the preservation of the historical context of the archive and not in its organization to meet the needs of current users.

THE ARCHIVES NETWORK

The general guide to record repositories is the Royal Commission on Historical Manuscripts *Record repositories in Great Britain*. Both the 5th edition and 6th edition of 1979 should be consulted as a new editorial policy has excluded many offices listed in the earlier edition. The British Records Association intends to remedy the 6th edition's omissions by publishing a supplement in its journal, *Archives*. Entries for some but by no means all of these offices with relevant material can be found in the *Directory of British photographic collections,*[1] or in *A guide to British topographical collections,*[2] but only a very few appear in the 1979 *Picture researcher's handbook.*[3]

PICTORIAL RESOURCES OF THE RECORD OFFICE

Because of the diversity of archive-keeping institutions and the uniqueness of their individual histories, it is presumptuous on the part of any individual with only limited experience to speak for all of them; nevertheless, certain broad categories can be distinguished even though their stock *per se* is unique and not in any measure duplicated from one institution to another.

The pictorial resources of an archive repository relate in the first place to the administrative unit, governmental department or institution which it serves (and with some will be limited to this) and in the second to the geographical area in which it operates, but many repositories hold important material relating to other areas and subjects which would be unsuspected were it not for entries in the directories cited above.

Because of the diverse nature of record repositories themselves and differing policies in record keeping and archive preservation, it is not possible to be particularly specific about visual material likely to be held. But in general the presence of pictorial material in record keeping is a phenomenon of the last thirty years, and the build-up is slow. This material may not be available to the public; access will be subject to the decision of the archivist and must depend on whether the files are administratively dead or active in some degree and whether the depositing department still retains some control over access.

Records which may contain visual material and necessarily, in the normal course of events, subject to restrictions on access, are court and prison records, personnel files (in many administrations these are only selectively preserved and in others not at all), planning files, and development office files. These, with press office files, are some of the possible sources of visual material within an administration. In the case of official files containing visual material, retention or destruction is not a question faced by the archivist once they have become accepted as archives. This is only a problem at the records management stage and the preservation or destruction of visual material will depend on a judgement of long-term usefulness and historical importance of the entire series of files, rather than on the nature of an individual item.

SECONDARY SOURCES OF VISUAL MATERIALS IN THE ARCHIVE REPOSITORY

However, the main available sources of visual materials in record offices are usually deposited papers — family papers, business records, private papers, particularly of scholars and those with scholarly interests, and of course the records of photographers of all types.

1 Family Papers

These may even occasionally include oil paintings as part of the deposit, but in the main they may be expected to be sources for travel diaries embellished in the late 18th and 19th centuries (much earlier examples are known in the Stammbucher), with topographical drawings and/or water colours, sometimes extensive and even on occasion of first-rate artistic merit by artists of reputation.

Family photograph albums and scrapbooks of variable quality also frequently form part of such a deposit, ranging from those containing little more than processions of carte-de-visite size portraits completely without identification, to massive carefully documented albums containing the splendid imperial-size commercial prints with which wealthy tourists commemorated their progress through Britain and the Continent and even farther afield in the latter part of the 19th century. The snapshot albums often found with family papers are frequently so poor in quality that the archivist may have serious problems in deciding whether to retain them. His decision, where he has discretion, will often be influenced solely by considerations of bulk and space.

2 Private Papers

These are distinguished from family papers in that they focus on the activities of a single individual who may be either a local antiquary or scholar. In the context in which the present writer works these are normally scholars with a more or less national or even international reputation. Photography came to be recognized early on as an important scientific aid and photographic evidence, together with the earlier tradition of scientific drawing, forms a feature of such collections, which may take the form of survey records, experimental records, or lecture illustrations and may also include illustrations of a personal or family nature.

3 Business Records

Such records, particularly for the larger enterprises, may contain visual material of considerable bulk and diverse nature. The important collection of 20,000 early glass plate negatives which are to be found among the records of the Upper Clyde Shipbuilders are an outstanding example of the historical importance such records may have. But all types of visual record may be found from prints and negatives to slides and cine films — selling and promotional films, photographic work in connection with catalogues, training films, films and pictures relating to processes and machines, historic and ceremonial occasions including staff social occasions, even large framed photographs of directors dating from the early days of photography.

4 Photographic Archives

The special business and other records which are the most important source of visual materials are in themselves essentially photographic archives and range from the records of the international photographic publisher, through the local photographer, to the compilations of a host of dedicated amateur photographers. All of these archival collections have one important feature in common: they have or have had a discipline imposed upon them in their creation which the archivist should preserve or attempt to restore as this is partly what makes such collections historically valuable.

Registers and a system are an essential part of maintaining any large photographic business, and, in the early days of photography, it became customary even for local photographers to advertise 'negatives preserved — additional copies or enlargements may be supplied' and to provide a number whereby that negative might be identified. Systematic preservation of negatives in an occasional market soon disappeared and very few of the early negative files of local photographers survive.

Successful national and international photographic publishers appear to have entered the postcard business sooner or later and they had policies of discarding 'obsolete' views from an early period, although some of them had particular views which they continued to sell for upwards of a century. The records of these large firms very often provide the best evidence to reinforce many archivists' suspicion of visual material as historical evidence. It is certainly demonstrable that the artist or photographer very often only records what he wants to be seen, that subjects are 'arranged' for artistic effect, that it is the unusual rather than the norm which is recorded, and that the original photograph is very often deliberately sophisticated to an astonishing degree. Valentines of Dundee at its peak employed a staff of no fewer than 40 artists engaged on the touching up and altering of photographs. The amateur photographer (and this excludes the family snapshotter) of whatever period (but more common post rather than pre-1860) naturally provides work of variable quality, but it does not normally raise the problem of whether to preserve or not as the family snapshotter's work frequently does. Very often these photographers pursued particular lines — recorded, for example, the family's agricultural and stock-rearing business, experimented with the more exotic photographic processes like the carbro process, or undertook local architectural surveys.

5 Non-archival Visual Materials in Repositories

Many archive repositories have collections of visual material which accumulate apart from that preserved within its archival groups, and some have deliberate policies of assembling such material as part of their role in the preservation of local documentation which has lost its original archival context. Schemes elaborate or simple may be devised to handle what is a complex and unwieldy material. The writer's system is:

(a) a portrait sequence arranged alphabetically
(b) a sequence for groups, i.e., prints showing more than one person, arranged chronologically
(c) a topographical sequence arranged alphabetically by place and then chronologically for individual locations
(d) a subject sequence
(e) a sequence for albums.

CONSERVATION IN AN ARCHIVE CONTEXT

The basic problems and solutions of conserving visual materials in an archival institution are little different from those in any other kind of institution. The archivist should place particular emphasis on the permanent preservation of his material. This is theoretically simpler with photographic materials because of the possibility of storing the original negative and print where appropriate and producing a print for normal consultation. The archivist should use his or her judgement as to the use made of the file which contains the visual material, the general attitude being to control this in such a way that the permanence and integrity of the original is in no way jeopardized; the ultimate decision as always is conditioned by what money is available. (See also Section 1.6 for details of conservation.)

LITERATURE ON ARCHIVAL VISUAL MATERIALS

There is almost no direct specialized writing on the subject in British sources. For general principles of archive treatment which, as explained above, extend to visual materials as to any other kind of document, consult the *Manual of archive administration* by Sir H Jenkinson,[4] or J H Hobson's *The administration of archives.*[5] T R Schellenberg's *The management of archives*[6] presents an American view which singles out visual materials for special treatment (pp. 332-43), but few British archivists would agree with his remarks on the unimportance of provenance and functional origins in relation to visual records. For archive conservation of visual materials, see Kathpalia's *Conservation and restoration of archive materials.*[7] A general guide to photographic archives in a particular country can be found in Clavet's *Guide to Canadian photographic archives.*[8]

A list of significant mentions of the subject in the *Journal of the Society of Archivists* follows:

—A general 'Bibliography of archival literature'[9] has no entries relating to visual materials preserved as records and only two entries relate to the storage of photographic materials: British Standards Institution *Storage of microfilm,*[10] and Kodak Ltd 'The storage of photographic materials and photographic records' in *Data book of applied photography.*[11]

—Kula, Sam 'The storage of archive film'.[12]

—Howgego, James L 'Archivist and art historian'.[13]

—Roads, Christopher H 'Film as historical evidence'.[14]

—Wall, John 'The case for a central photographic archive in colour'.[15]

—'Cellulose nitrate film'.[16]

—'Notice of revised version of BS 1153 (1955)'. Recommendations for the processing and storage of silver-gelatin type microfilm.[17]

—Gray, Madeleine 'Photographic storage in Gwynedd: an *ad hoc* solution'.[18]

A PARTICULAR ARCHIVE CONTAINING VISUAL MATERIALS — THE CASE OF ST ANDREWS UNIVERSITY

The historical accident which placed some of the earliest developments in the calotype process in the small east-coast town of St Andrews, from which came one half of the best-known partnership in photographic history, is the reason why one of the largest and oldest archival collections exists in the university today.

Sir David Brewster, Principal of United College in the university, through his friendship with William Henry Fox Talbot, his position in the scientific world, and his own particular interest in the physics of optics is the key figure, with Dr John Adamson, student, graduate, local physician, and teacher of chemistry in the university, the man who through Brewster's inspiration was to take the first calotype portrait, the first stereoscopic calotype, and who having become the skilled practitioner was to pass this skill onto his younger brother, Robert. This was the Robert Adamson who in January 1843 went off to Edinburgh to set up as a professional photographer and later on that year entered into fruitful partnership with David Octavius Hill. From the earliest attempts of 1839/40 a continuous photographic tradition has been maintained in St Andrews.

Amongst the university's official records file copies of student groups exist from the 1860s (the earliest is 1851). Occasional photographs occur in officials' papers. Planning committee papers and papers of a series of major public planning enquiries to which the university was a party contain significant quantities of photographs, all post-1950. Certain student records contain individual photographs from 1940 and all student records contain individual photographs from 1960. 'A chronological file of photographs of ceremonial occasions and publicity photographs dates from the 1890s. Five student societies have maintained files of photographs of members, activities, and social occasions which have been deposited in the archives since the 1920s.

The bulk of the university's visual material, however, is contained in deposited collections. Apart from 200 miscellaneous volumes or portfolios of topographical drawings and photograph albums, some 14 deposits of family and personal papers contain significant quantities, of which the more important are:

—the Sir D'Arcy Wentworth Thompson papers: zoological drawings of W G Tilesius (8), P J Smit (92), Thomas Scott (475), and others (600); lecture illustrations (747 4 × 4 inch slides); scientific experiment records relating to his two chief interests, growth and form, and the International Commission for the exploration of the sea (1,714 4 × 4 inch slides); fur seal investigations in the Behring Sea and Pribyloff Islands, 1892-6 (1,282 photographs);

—the J H Baxter papers: Walker Trust excavations at the Imperial Palace, Istanbul, 1935 (369 photographs and 350 4 × 4 inch slides);

—the Sir James Donaldson papers: architecture of Italy, 1885-95 (550 photographs);

—the W C M'Intosh papers: zoological and topographical photographs, 1860-1900 (1,800) and 400 coloured zoological lecture demonstration drawings;
—the I C G Campbell papers: archeology and architecture of Turkey, 1935-45 (1,100 prints with negatives).

A general portrait and topographical collection consisting of 49 19th-century albums (4,000 photographs with negatives), an individual portrait collection arranged alphabetically (4,400 items), a group portrait series arranged chronologically (500 items), and a topographical series (1,500 items) arranged alphabetically is largely local in content and files original drawings, paintings, engravings, and photographs in a single sequence but consists mainly of photographs which date from 1839.

The Records of Valentines Ltd, Dundee

These are essentially the records of the topographical views dating from the firm's reorganization in 1878. The registers of views, with the exception of those relating to the overseas branches which were disposed of 1914-16, survive entire until 1967 when the firm ceased to publish postcards (postcards had been the main, but not the only form of photographic publication from 1898). The registers record details of over 500,000 views but the reference prints and negatives of little over 100,000 survive. In addition there is a considerable quantity, but insignificant in relation to total output, of survivals of the firm's commission postcard publishing (15,437) and their fancy postcard publishing (3,849).

Other Photographic Archives

—Sir Robert Rollo: Canada and Fife, 1880s, 500 glass negatives.
—J E A Steggall: British Isles and Continental scenery 1887-1925, 2,624 photographs.
—Lady Henrietta Gilmour: farm animals, family and servants, Glencoe area scenery, 1890-1914, 1,500 glass negatives.
—David Jack: Scottish scenery, architectural survey of St Andrews, 1937, art photography, 1914-60, 1,200 negatives.

References

Separate slip indexes in spring-back binders are maintained of the Valentine photographs. For the others, there is a portrait index, a topographical index, and an index to photographs in the numbered album sequence. A subject index has not been attempted.

REFERENCES

1 Wall, J (compiler) *Directory of British photographic collections.* London, Heinemann, 1977.
2 Barley, M W *A guide to British topographical collections.* London, Council for British Archaeology, 1974.
3 Evans, Hilary & Mary, *Picture researcher's handbook.* London, Saturday Ventures, 1979.
4 Jenkinson, Sir H *Manual of archive administration.* London, 1937.
5 Hobson, J H *The administration of archives.* London, Pergamon Press, 1972.
6 Schellenberg, T R *The management of archives.* New York, Columbia University Press, 1965.
7 Kathpalia, Yash Pal *Conservation and restoration of archive materials.* Paris, UNESCO, 1973.
8 Clavet, A *Guide to Canadian photographic archives.* Ottawa, 1979.
9 'Bibliography of archival literature' in *Journal of the Society of Archivists* 2 1960. 72-3.
10 British Standards Institution *Storage of microfilm* BS 1153. London, BSI, 1955.
11 Kodak Ltd 'The storage of photographic materials and photographic records' in *Data book of applied photography* Vol.1. Data sheet RF-6. London, (no date).
12 Kula, S 'The storage of archive film' in *J. of the Society of Archivists* 2 1962. 270-2.
13 Howgego, J L 'Archivist and art historian' in *J. of the Society of Archivists* 2 1963. 369-72.
14 Roads, C H 'Film as historical evidence' in *J. of the Society of Archivists* 3 1966. 183-91.
15 Wall, J 'The case for a central photographic archive in colour' in *J. of the Society of Archivists* 3 1969. 566-70.
16 'Cellulose nitrate film' in *J. of the Society of Archivists* 4 1970. 67.
17 'Notice of revised version of BS 1153 (1955)' in *J. of the Society of Archivists* 5 1970. 268.
18 Gray, M 'Photographic storage at Gwynedd: an *ad hoc* solution' in *J. of the Society of Archivists* 5 1977. 437-40.

Art Galleries in the UK

Elspeth J Hector

The National Gallery Photographic Library in London described and compared with the photographic collections of the Tate Gallery, the National Gallery of Scotland, and the National Portrait Gallery.

THE NATIONAL GALLERY PHOTOGRAPHIC LIBRARY

Scope

The primary function of the National Gallery Photographic Library, like that of the picture libraries of most galleries, is to provide readily accessible visual records of works of art. The scope of the photographic collection depends upon the scope of the primary collection, so the National Gallery Photographic Library is concerned with illustrations of European painting from the 13th to the 20th century. Although dependent on the scope of the main collection, it is wider in coverage, including photographs of paintings by artists not represented in the gallery, in addition to photographs of works by those artists who are. Particular emphasis is placed on those artists whose works are hanging in the gallery, but the general aim of the photographic librarian is to provide illustrations of a representative sample of the paintings by major and minor artists who fall within the temporal and geographical limits of the primary collection.

Size

The Photographic Library contains approximately 100,000 illustrations: the majority of these are black and white photographs, but the collection also contains a number of black and white and colour reproductions taken from periodicals, sale catalogues, and similar material. The number of illustrations in the library is not related to the importance of the various artists, but to their original output and number of extant works. Thus a major artist may be represented by only a few photographs, and a minor one by many.

Users

The library is for staff use only. Occasionally bona fide students may be allowed to look at the photographic collection, but because of confidential information on some of the mounts it cannot be made more public. The photographs are used by the keeper staff and the Education Department of the gallery as research aids. The visual information of the photographs, combined with the factual details added to the mounts, make the library invaluable in the cataloguing and identification of works of art. It is used also in answering public enquiries. Although the collection cannot cater for subject enquiries, it can be helpful in tracing the location of a particular painting or in suggesting provenance for pictures which may not be well documented. Because the library is used by such a small number of people it functions on a self-service basis. When the staff wish to borrow photographs they fill in loan cards and put these in the appropriate file boxes in the library. When the mounts are returned the borrower may refile them and remove the loan cards or leave them to be dealt with by the library assistant.

Organization

The illustrations are mounted on thin manilla card 14½ × 11½ inches (36.8 × 29.2 cm.) in size and filed in solander-type boxes. Originally the photographs were glued to the mounts but for several years now dry mounting has been used. Ideally each mount contains the following categories of information:

1 Artist's name — surname (or filing element) in capitals
2 Whether signed and/or dated
3 Title
4 Size in inches and centimetres
5 Medium/support
6 Collection/sale/exhibition details
7 Photograph source, negative number, and date.

Often not all the information is available at the time of mounting (for example, the price a painting fetched at auction) but it may be added later. The initial information is typed onto the mounts, but later additions have to be handwritten. In general only minimal provenance details are given provided a reference is made to the source where more detailed information can be found: for instance, the catalogue/inventory number of a collection is always quoted on the mount; and the lot number, date, and name of a sale or exhibition are given so that reference may be made to the appropriate catalogue. This involves using the Book Library in conjunction with the Photographic Library but is the only practical way of dealing with what, at times, amounts to large quantities of provenance information. Although it would be useful to have all available information on the mounts, the addition of it would be too time-consuming.

The photographs are filed alphabetically by artist in a straight A to Z sequence. The number of illustrations of a given artist's work dictates whether or not he has a box to himself or is filed in with other artists. Ideally each artist should have a paper folder containing all relevant illustrations, but in practice only those who are represented by two dozen or more photographs, and who do not merit a box to themselves, are distinguished by having separate folders.

Within the group of photographs relating to one artist, subdivisions are made according to the size of the file. When there are only a few illustrations no specific filing order exists, but when the file of photographs is large subject subdivisions are made according to what seems most appropriate to the particular artist. Broad subject divisions, such as portraits, landscapes, still lives, biblical scenes, mythological scenes, and saints are used throughout the collection, but when narrower subject divisions are required it is impractical to aim at consistency.

The exact nature of these narrower subdivisions depends entirely on the nature of the artist's original work. Sometimes it is adequate to arrange portraits alphabetically by sitter, but sometimes it is necessary to divide them further into male sitters, female sitters, and groups. Similarly, saints are either arranged alphabetically or divided first by sex; the acts of the saints may be interfiled with their 'portraits' or, if the number of representations is large, they are filed separately. Landscape can be subdivided in many ways: broadly into categories like seascape, riverscape, townscape; and narrowly into groups, such as wooded land-scape, river scene with shipping, calm/rough seascape, landscape with cattle, etc. Still lives are usually grouped according to the elements contained in the original paintings — flower piece, fruit piece, dead game, and so on. Biblical scenes can be subdivided consistently into Old and New Testament groups and then ordered chronologically if necessary.

The extent to which it is necessary to subdivide the photographs is a purely practical consideration. Subject division is helpful when it facilitates retrieval and refiling of photographs, but when the number of illustrations is small enough that examination of the entire file creates no problems it is unlikely that the Librarian will attempt any subject arrangement.

Apart from the A to Z sequence of artists there is an anonymous section for unidentified paintings. This is arranged by school, then by century. Where necessary and where appropriate, further subdivisions by town and subject are made.

Acquisition Policy

It is the policy of the Photographic Library to acquire by purchase or exchange a representative collection of photographs of paintings and, very occasionally, drawings by artists active in Europe between the 13th and 20th centuries. Black and white photographs are acquired in preference to colour photographs and other illustrative material: cuttings from periodicals and sale catalogues are included in the library if photographs are not available. There is no attempt to make the collection comprehensive. Selection is based on the relative importance of a particular painting within an artist's *oeuvre*. Only photographs of signed and dated works by artists not represented in the gallery are actively acquired. Photographs of paintings by artists represented in the main collection are acquired in greater numbers, although more importance is still placed on signed and dated works.

The library aims to have photographs of relevant paintings in other public and private collections. Photographs from smaller galleries and private collections, where it is probable that no illustrated catalogue exists, are particularly important. Equally important is the acquisition of photographs of paintings passing through the sale rooms.

Sources

Photographs are purchased or received on exchange from other museums and galleries. All National Gallery paintings have been photographed so it is possible to arrange large-scale exchanges with foreign institutions. The acquisition of photographs from private collections is less easy. The Library subscribes to the Courtauld Institute and the Scottish National Portrait Gallery Surveys which cover private collections in this country, but there is no equivalent source for private collections abroad and one is dependent on the owners or on firms of commercial photographers. Since few countries have centralized or localized photographic records of works of art, commercial art photographers are often a useful source for photographs of paintings in churches and other public buildings.

If the gallery's Photographic Department photographs any non-gallery paintings, such as items on loan or brought in for an opinion, the library receives a print. Outside photography is rarely undertaken by gallery photographers, and if the library requires a photograph of an unillustrated lot in a sale a commercial firm is commissioned to do the work. The National Gallery shares the cost of such saleroom photography with a number of other institutions. Photographs of illustrated items in sales are obtained direct from the appropriate saleroom.

The remaining major source of photographs for this collection is through the export trade. A large number of paintings are exported every year and if the Director of the National Gallery is requested by the

Department of Trade to approve the export of a picture he automatically receives a photograph of the item. The Photographic Library ultimately receives these photographs which provide a very useful visual record of works which might go into private collections and not be photographed again.

A few illustrations are donated to the Library and a number of photographs have been bequeathed to the collection.

Finally, the Librarian takes advantage of any photography which is carried out in the UK and abroad in conjunction with exhibitions, to obtain relevant photographs.

Maintenance

The day-to-day running of the Photographic Library is carried out by one graduate and a clerical assistant who divides her time between the picture library and the book library. Besides checking holdings, ordering, mounting, and filing new photographs, the staff are responsible for maintaining the existing collection. This involves replacing old photographs with new ones, removing and disposing of duplicates, refiling borrowed photographs, subdividing groups of illustrations which have become unwieldy, adding new information to existing mounts, and maintaining indexes. Until fairly recently no indexes relating to the photographic collection existed, but over the last couple of years two indexes have been started: one is an index under artist of the photographs of exported pictures; the other is a collections index indicating the library's holdings of photographs from other public and private collections. It is hoped that a check-list of the artists represented in the library will be started in the near future, and as an offshoot of this it may be possible to have a very broad subject index to the collection. Because the gallery staff have little need for a subject approach to paintings this aspect of the picture collection has not been exploited.

COMPARISON WITH OTHER PHOTOGRAPHIC COLLECTIONS

Having described the National Gallery Photographic Library in some detail it seems appropriate to consider how it compares with other national gallery photographic collections. Both the National Gallery of

Scotland and the Tate Gallery have picture libraries which are broadly similar to that of the National Gallery. The National Gallery of Scotland has some 30,000 items, the Tate around 20,000, both collections, as in the National Gallery, reflecting the scope of the primary collections. Both libraries are primarily for use by the curatorial staff for research and enquiries: the Tate and the National Gallery are similar in restricting public access because of confidential information on the mounts, but the National Gallery of Scotland does allow students and members of the public, at its discretion, to use the collection.

As might be expected, both the Tate and the National Gallery of Scotland arrange their illustrations (mounted on thin manilla card and filed in boxes) alphabetically by artist, with a separate sequence for unidentified works. As in the National Gallery large numbers of illustrations of works by one artist are subdivided by subject according to the nature of the artist's own subject matter. The type of information typed or written on the mount is identical to that in the National Gallery, except that the National Gallery of Scotland does not quote the medium/support.

The Tate Gallery and the National Gallery are similar in acquiring black and white photographs rather than using material gutted from other sources. About half the Scottish National Gallery's collection, however, consists of cuttings from periodicals, catalogues, etc. This may be because of a difference in available funds. Photographs are obtained from the same sources as used by the National Gallery although the latter, probably because it is acquiring larger numbers of photographs, makes more use of commercial sources.

The Tate Gallery Photographic Collection is run by one member of staff working in the afternoons only. The National Gallery of Scotland Picture Archive is run by two museum assistants who are also responsible for the Book Library. Volunteer help is used for mounting photographs and labelling boxes but the curatorial staff decide on subject subdivisions and indicate to the museum assistants which illustrations to order and gut. The National Gallery Photographic Library staff, although advised by the curatorial staff, have more independence and responsibility in the organization and maintenance of their collection. Neither the Tate nor the National Gallery of Scotland indexes its picture library in any way.

These three photographic libraries are basically similar, but if we now look at the National Portrait Gallery's Photographic Library it is possible to see how a different emphasis in the primary collection affects the nature and organization of the secondary illustrative material. In the Tate and the London and Edinburgh National Galleries the value of the primary collection lies in the works themselves. The artist and the aesthetic quality of the painting are of more importance than the subject matter. In the National Portrait Gallery this emphasis is reversed; the subject matter of the painting is of greater importance than the artist, and aesthetic quality is not a determining factor in the acquisition of a painting for the collection. It follows that the scope of the photographic archive is biased towards portraiture, and that sitters are more important than artists.

Before discussing the arrangement of the National Portrait Gallery's Photographic Library, it is worth pointing out a few similarities with the other collections discussed. As before, the illustrations are mounted (dry mounted as in the National Gallery) on manilla card and filed in boxes. The categories of information typed on the card are similar, but the layout is different because the main filing element is the subject instead of the artist. The collection, which is as large as the National Gallery's, consists of black and white photographs and cuttings acquired from the sources already indicated. As in the other galleries, the National Portrait Gallery's photographic collection exists primarily as a research aid for the curatorial staff, but, as confidential information is not added to the mounts, many more outsiders are allowed access to it than in the other institutions discussed. Visitors are restricted mainly because of shortage of staff and lack of space.

The Portrait Gallery's illustrations are arranged in four sequences. The main sequence is arranged alphabetically by name of sitter and includes photographs of portraits of British sitters. A second similarly arranged sequence is concerned with foreign sitters. There also exists a slip index arranged alphabetically by sitter which includes foreign and British subjects and which refers not only to the illustrations in the boxes but also to illustrations published in sale and exhibition catalogues, books, and periodicals. The slips, which number close to a million, contain additional information to the mounts and include provenance and references to exhibitions, etc.

The third sequence of photographs in the archive is arranged chronologically in groups of 25 to 30 years. Within these date spans the illustrations are filed under the name of the artist. An index of artists exists indicating the relevant chronological groupings for each. Thus, one can find all the portraits painted by a given artist or look at all the portraits executed in a period of, say, five years. The existence of a sitter file and an artist file means that the Portrait Gallery orders two copies of each photograph. Sometimes it orders three, since a fourth sequence of photographs exists. This consists of a series of 'type' boxes in which the arrangement is again chronological. The 'type' boxes provide a further subject approach to portraits and include categories such as Lord Chancellors, Judges, Priests, Bishops, Lawyers, Doctors, and so on.

The National Portrait Gallery Photographic Library, although restricted to a particular type of subject matter, is the most complex of the organizations under discussion. It is run by two graduates and a clerical assistant, who also answer numerous written and telephone enquiries.

The scope, content, and arrangement of a photographic library in an art gallery, as illustrated in the examples above, depend on the nature of the main collection, the users and the available funding. The ideal for a photographic library will vary from gallery to gallery and will seldom be accomplished due to lack of staff and funds. It is the photographic librarian's function to achieve the best practical solution within these constraints.

19

The Science Museum, London

Wendy Sheridan

GROWTH OF THE SCIENCE MUSEUM COLLECTIONS

The Science Museum is the national museum for science and industry. Its collections have their origin in the Great Exhibition of 1851 and the establishment of the South Kensington Museum in 1857. Administered by the Department of Science and Art, the museum's purpose was educational. Displays of arts, crafts, industrial products, structures, materials, and manufacturing processes were intended to encourage industrial activity and so stimulate the growth and prosperity of Victorian Britain.

In 1876 the Special Loan Collection of Scientific Apparatus was exhibited, including instruments of historic importance as well as those for teaching and investigation. Exhibits were grouped according to their subject, rather than classified by country of origin as was usual in international trade fairs. The development of the Science Museum reflects this change of approach.

The collections of the Patent Museum were transferred in 1884 to the Department of Science and Art. Due to the energies of its first curator, Bennet Woodcroft (1803-79), the models, plans of inventions, and machines included a significant proportion of historical material, and relics such as 'Puffing Billy'. By 1903 much of Woodcroft's personal collection had come to the museum by gift and bequest. This included a large number of portraits of scientists and engineers which Woodcroft had accumulated as part of a grandiose scheme to produce a 'Gallery of portraits of inventors, discoverers, and introducers of useful arts'.

Towards the modern museum

In 1909 the science and art collections of the South Kensington Museum were administratively separated into the Science Museum and the Victoria and Albert Museum, with one department as the National Art Library. In the following year the Bell Committee began its investigations into the science collections, the museum accommodation, its organization and activities. The now familiar Science Museum East Block facing onto Exhibition Road was opened in 1928. The Science Museum Library, founded in 1883, continued to grow as a department of the Science Museum.

Between the two World Wars the size and scope of the museum collections were amply demonstrated by a series of published catalogues. Detailed and well referenced, these indicate the multimedia nature of the collections; prints, drawings, paintings, plans, and photographs are included, though three-dimensional artifacts predominate. Although out of print, these works remain of immense value for their content. In contrast, the majority of recent museum publications are concerned largely with objects and a new emphasis has been on general presentations directed to a lay public.

THE SCIENCE MUSEUM TODAY

The Science Museum is divided into eight broadly based curatorial departments: Physics, Chemistry, Medicine, Electrical Engineering and Communications, Transport, Civil and Mechanical Engineering, Earth and Space Sciences, and the Library. Within these departments are over 70 subject collections, ranging from aerodynamics through astronomy, domestic appliances, glass, hand tools, illumination, locks, mathematics, microscopes, navigation, optics, photography, printing, railways, ships, talking machines, and time measurement to weighing and X-rays. Each curator has specified subject collections in his charge.

There are over 60 galleries and it has been estimated that an informed visitor would take two years to examine every object on display. The visitor in search of general information, or a specific exhibit, will have to cover an area of some 31,000 square metres of exhibition space, on five floors. About a third of the exhibits reflect current activity; less than a third of the collections are on display at any time. In some galleries a proportion of pictorial material is integrated in the display, but in recent years it has become more usual to use photographic reproductions rather than the original image.

PICTORIAL AND ARCHIVE COLLECTIONS

The Science Museum is a collection of collections. Historically, the various subject collections have included all kinds of material. However, in 1976 the Pictorial Collection was established as a section of the library, charged with centralizing, cataloguing, storing, conserving, and exploiting pictorial material and acquiring additional items. The section is housed at present in the library. Pictures are regarded both as complementary to artifacts and as important in themselves. Furthermore, they require specialized expertise in conservation, storage, cataloguing with emphasis on the subject content, and subsequent exploitation.

More recently a related Archives Collection has been established, with similar terms of reference for manuscript and archival material likewise dispersed throughout the museum. Within many of the archival collections are items of high visual interest and the distinction between 'pictorial' and 'archive' material is at times purely administrative. The collections are available as a service to museum staff, researchers, students, and the public. Archival material is notified to the National Register of Archives. No such facility is yet in existence for pictorial material.

The Pictorial Collection functions as a pictorial archive, not as an art archive. Its philosophy is concentrated upon exploitation of the technical or subject content of an image. That the image is of value, rare, of intrinsic beauty, or by a particular artist, may be of secondary importance. Equally, an artistically poor image by an amateur may contain information of considerable technical interest. There are works by artists who have discovered in science and industry a source of creativity. The oil painting *Coalbrookdale by night* by Loutherbourg is perhaps the most significant example of the genre. In contrast, archives of industrial designers and crafts movements, for example, are represented in the collections within the National Art Library.

TYPES AND SCOPE OF MATERIAL

This summary of the museum's history can only hint at the immense range and rich heritage of its visual materials, their quality and their quantity. Only now is the true importance of the collection beginning to be appreciated.

Recent surveys indicate a 'guesstimate' of about a million items, ranging in size from 2 cm. to 5 metres square. Many collections are unlisted or hide the full extent of their content. Excluded from the surveys and potential transfer were the many dioramas incorporated into exhibits. A deliberate exception to the policy of centralization is that certain items in the Photography Collection, mainly historic photographs, are retained in order to illustrate the development of photographic processes, including cinematography. Also excluded are the photographs of museum objects, held in the Information Office of the museum (*see below*). The emphasis of the collection is on contributions to all aspects of science and industry. The chronological interest is from antiquity to the future. Historically, its weight concentrates on the Industrial Revolution period, with national contributions predominating.

Material is arranged into five broad divisions: portraits, subjects, technical drawings, ephemera, and archives.

Portraits

There are several hundred portraits in the museum, a substantial proportion acquired through the efforts of Bennet Woodcroft. The majority are prints but there are also oil paintings and busts. The sitters are scientists and engineers, with a growing coverage of medical personalities. Carte-de-visite photographs and photographic studio portraits are included. In addition, there is a hologram portrait of Professor Dennis Gabor, inventor of the technique.

The library maintains an index of likenesses reproduced in its holdings of literature and periodicals. Arranged by sitter, this finding list currently totals nearly 25,000 entries.

Subjects

It is as yet impossible to calculate the exact number of items. These include such diverse material as 60,000 stamps; over 300,000 photographs and glass negatives; about 100 oil paintings; prints, drawings and watercolours. Maps are divided between the library's thematic collection, the Pictorial Collection when of visual interest, and as associated material in the Archives Collection. One type of material, the prints, includes about 800 images of ships, 700 railway and locomotive scenes, over 200 balloon pictures, many caricatures, and a wealth of other subject matter, in a variety of processes.

Technical drawings

A great number of drawings, many in line and coloured wash, are collected and arranged generally by the manufacturing firm. They include about 10,000 designs for carriages and car bodies by the firm of Hooper, manufacturers of coachwork, who held a Royal Warrant to Queen Victoria. Locomotive workshop drawings produced by George Stephenson and Co. cover the earliest years of manufacture and are among a number of large holdings of drawings from locomotive builders. There are engine drawings from the firm of Maudslay Sons and Field, and many thousands of sets of ships' plans. The Goodrich Collection contains over 300 original drawings of Admiralty engineering work, including mills, engines, and dockyards. There are some 2,000 notations, drawings, and notebooks by Charles Babbage of his pioneering computer engines. More wide-ranging in subject matter are collections of designs and drawings assembled by practising engineers. For example, an album belonging to the Shropshire ironmaster William Reynolds includes 18th-century studies of pumps and manuscript designs by the civil engineer Thomas Telford.

Ephemera

Ephemera, by definition, are not intended to last. The museum has an incalculable amount, possibly weighing as much as a ton. Trade cards and advertisements of scientific instrument makers, medical certificates, invitation cards, newspaper cuttings, and over 10,000 transport tickets are examples in this category. Printed and archival in nature, a high proportion of this material is graphic in content — pictorial or typographical.

Archives

The Archives Collection has care of holograph letters, business papers of firms, papers of scientists and engineers, and many paper materials, samples, and photographic records. Where visual media are contained in integral archival collections these are cross-referenced into the Pictorial Collection.

FINDING AIDS

Much of this material is still dispersed in the various curatorial departments and is still uncatalogued, but the best approach to the Science Museum's visual sources is via the Pictorial Collection, which then acts as a centralizing or referral agency. Both staff and enquirers are to a great extent dependent on the virtues of patience, ingenuity, and serendipity. Those seeking pictures of museum objects should search the photographs in the museum Information Office (*see below*). Enquiries of a general nature are referred to the resources of the library.

Some material is accessible within each defined group. A catalogue of portraits, arranged primarily by sitter, indexes artists and, where background indicates, subject content. Oil paintings are catalogued. Railway prints are stored by company and the majority listed. There is a hand-list to ships' plans, and the Stephenson drawings are catalogued. Contents of the Reynolds Album and the Goodrich Collection are cited in journal articles, as are several other finite collections. A catalogue summarizing the Babbage holdings is in progress. Trade cards of instrument makers have been listed and an illustrated catalogue published. Many collections have a basic hand-list. There is also a list of about 300 named collections of source material, briefly indicating their general nature.

Cataloguing

Newly acquired material is now catalogued using AACR2. Rules have been extended to suit the requirements of each item. These records are for both the Pictorial and Archives Collections. Library of Congress headings are used as a basis for subject indexing.

Some entries for single items are detailed, some are basic entries for collections of material, indicating availability of lists which are arranged individually according to need, for example sketches of a marine artist, or a calendar of company documents. Basic sorting, physical cataloguing and numbering of material is undertaken before more formalized entries can be made. Records are capable of minimal use as a manual catalogue, and ready for absorption into a computer databank with an on-line retrieval system. Content of entries for pictorial items reflects that conventionally recorded by curators, picture researchers, librarians, archivists, and historians of art and science, with special emphasis on the technical or subject content. Visual indexing systems are planned to assist enquirers in initial selection and to reduce handling of original material.

In 1977 the Pictorial Collection assisted the Museum Documentation Association in a project to program a system of fine art data recording by computer, within a multidisciplinary documentation standard. Multiple indexes were produced and the project identified many useful data fields in information about the image, conservation, and administration. A structured form of data recording in use for the Pictorial Collection is based on this standard. Development of a national museum data record, especially in art, is international in interest. However, the activities in the Science Museum are at present necessarily confined to recording its own holdings. Ultimately, union catalogues may be possible, stemming from the intention to integrate information about holdings of railway prints in the Pictorial Collection, at the National Railway Museum York, part of the Science Museum, and prints loaned to the Great Western Railway Museum, Swindon.

BOOK STOCK

(a) As a Potential Pictorial Source in the Library

Surprisingly, national museums and their libraries are listed in library

Polaroid of print supplied. *Museums Documentation Association.*

THE MENAI SUSPENSION AND BRITANNIA TUBULAR
BRIDGES. / AYS del; T. Picken lith; Day & Son,
Lithrs. to The Queen. - Bangor: G. Humphreys,
[185-]

    Print: lithograph, handcol.; 29 x 38 cm., image
19.6 x 28.3 cm.

    Shipping in the Menai Strait includes sailing
vessels and a paddlesteamer.   Details and
dimensions of each bridge tabulated under image
each side of title

                      Pictorial: 1943-169

Phillimore Collection

AYS, artist
DAY AND SON, lithographers
PICKEN, Thomas, lithographer
STEPHENSON, Robert, 1803-1859
TELFORD, Thomas, 1757-1834

BRIDGES, SUSPENSION
BRIDGES, TUBULAR
BRITANNIA TUBULAR BRIDGE
MENAI   SUSPENSION BRIDGE
RAILWAY BRIDGES - Wales
ROAD BRIDGES - Wales
WALES - Menai Strait
PHILLIMORE COLLECTION

Draft catalogue entry by AACR2 with subject headings. *The Science Museum,*
London.

					Institution : identity number		Part
File PC 543					5cM : 1943 – 169		D

IDENTIFICA-TION & PRODUCTION	Simple name print	D	Method lithograph	D	Title Menai Suspension Bridge & Britannia Tubular Bridge		D

	Person's role	Name		D Production date	Identifier : date	
	artist	'A.Y.S.'		1850 (c)		
	lithographer	Picken, T.				
	printer	Day and Son				
	publisher	Humphreys, G.				

	Production place (printed) 17 Gate Street & Lincoln's Inn Fields & London; (published) Bangor & Wales	Production detail handcoloured	D

C	Full name or classified identification lithograph, coloured & 19 century (mid)	System	Identifier : date	D

DESCRIPTION	Medium	Materials keyword/detail ink & wash (coloured)	Support	Materials keyword/detail paper

	Dimension measured	value & units/accuracy	Dimension measured	value & units/accuracy
	height	19.5 cm	width (support)	38 cm
	width	28.4 cm		
	height (support)	28.5 cm		

	Inscription	Method printed		Position beneath image
	Mark			
	Transcription	Detail imprint, title, and details of bridges		
	Description			

C	Part : content keyword/detail transport, land & railways & bridge, tubular & bridge, suspension & L, M and S region & Chester and Holyhead Railway & ships, sailing & paddlesteamer & Stephanson, Robert & Telford, Thomas & Wales & Britannia Tubular Bridge & Anglesey & Menai Straits & bridge, iron & locomotive & 1850 & Menai Suspension Bridge & bridge, railway	Cross reference	D

	STORE	Store : date PC : 19 April 1977	Recorder : date WS : 6 July 1977

FINE ART   © IRGMA 1975   1/12/75

DESCRIPTION	Condition keyword/detail good (dirty, corner pinholes)	Completeness keyword/detail			

C	Frame	Detail		Max. height	Max. width	Max. depth
	Mount					

ACQUISITION	Acquisition method purchase	Acquired from : date Sinelnikoff, M. : 21 June 1943			
C			D Price	Conditions D Yes/No	Copyright D Yes/No	Valuation : date	D

TRANSFERS	Previous transfers Phillimore Collection.	D

LOANS	Loans & exhibitions	D

PROCESS	Conservation	Other process	Method/detail : operator : date : detail	Cross-reference	D
C	Reproduction				
	Conservation				
	Reproduction				

DOCUMENTA-TION	L	Class	Author : date : title : journal or publisher : volume : detail	Drawing or photo
			ScM : : file : : : 3661/8/22	
			Phillimore, J. : 1850 : catalogue :: one : page 7.	

NOTES	Notes Printed border round picture. Phillimore identifies A.Y.S. as "Pickering".

Published by the Museums Association, 87 Charlotte Street, London W1P 2BX

Catalogue entry using MDA record with specified data fields. *The Science Museum, London.*

ScM PC/543   museum number: 1943-169.

"Menai Suspension Bridge", "Britannia Tubular Bridge"

print.
lithograph, coloured - 19 century (mid).

production: lithograph, artist: "A.Y.S.", lithographer: Picken.
(printed)17 Gate Street - publisher: Humphrys, G.- 1850 (c).
(published) Bangor - Wales.
handcoloured.

condition: 2 (dirty, corner pinholes).

medium: ink - wash (coloured)
support: paper.

```
         height           19.5 cm
         width            28.4 cm
         height (support)  28.5 cm
         width (support)   38 cm
```

inscription: printed, beneath image. (imprint, title, and details
of bridges).

content: transport, land - railways - bridge, tubular - bridge,
suspension - L, M and S region - Chester and Holyhead Railway
- ships, sailing - paddlesteamer - Stephenson, Robert -
Telford, Thomas - Wales - Britannia Tubular Bridge - Anglesey
- Menai Straits - bridge, iron - locomotive - 1850 - Menai
Suspension Bridge - bridge, railway.

notes: Printed border round picture. Phillimore identifies A.Y.S.
as "Pickering"

acquisition: from Snelnikoff, M., 21 June 1943.
transfer Phillimore Collection.

references:
ScM, "file", (3661/8/22)

Phillimore, J., 1850, "catalogue", one, (page 7).

Computer print-out of main entry from MDA record. 'X' denotes some of the
fields selected for indexation. *The Science Museum, London.*

directories as quite discrete organizations. The Science Museum Library is a valuable research source for information relating to museum displays and collections. A complete set of publications, including all catalogues of collections, is available for reference: illustrated trade catalogues of the Great Exhibition of 1851 and subsequent exhibitions are held. The library has sets of published patent specifications dating from 1617. By 1800 it was usual to include drawings in specifications and these are an invaluable source for the designer. The printed book stock is richly endowed with illustrated folios and bound sets of plates. There is some overlap of 19th-century material with the National Art Library. The emphasis of the library is on the history of science and technology, and the large holding of encyclopedias of science, industry, and useful arts since the 18th century contains many contemporary illustrations.

(b) Pictorial Collection Book Stock

A working book stock is maintained for use as quick reference and as a tool for cataloguing and enquiry work. Arrangement is practical, by function and accessibility. An information index is maintained with analytical references, in dictionary sequence, to articles and illustrations in periodicals, book-stock subjects, exhibition scripts and reviews, miscellaneous leaflets and reproductions, and holdings of comparable source material elsewhere. Bibliographic control of literature relating art to industry, science, and medicine has evolved, partly as a response to the many enquiries for 'pictures of the Industrial Revolution', and a series of information sheets has begun with a hand-list of sources for industrial themes in art, including books suitable for use with children.

PHOTOGRAPHY FACILITIES

Library Photocopying Service

The library has facilities for electrostatic copying, photostats, prints from microform, and Beta radiographs of watermarks. Polaroid archival quality photographs in black and white are available to order; these are probably the best form of visual record, with minor loss of tonal contrast in coloured originals and the ability to enlarge details. Information on sizes and costs is available from the service.

Museum Photograph Service

Photographs in black and white of museum objects are on display in the museum Information Office and copies made to order by the photographic studio. There are more than 50,000 photographs, arranged in order of subject collection lists. These include many plans, drawings, book plates, portraits, prints, and oil paintings. Copies of the subject lists are held in the library and in the Pictorial Collection. They are obtainable from the museum Publications Department, with details of the service, reproduction fees, and copyright acknowledgements.

Orders for photographs are placed in the Information Office, or with the Library Photocopying Service, or they may be sent by post to the Science Museum. Colour slides are not currently a public service but half-plate colour transparencies can be supplied. A small selection of prints, posters, and postcards, mostly of three-dimensional objects, is displayed in the museum shop.

Facilities for personal photography, for which there is a fee, are available by written application to the Director of the Science Museum.

20

Art Galleries and Museums in North America

Stanley W Hess

PHOTOGRAPH COLLECTIONS AND LIBRARIES

What is a museum or gallery photograph collection and what purposes does it serve? The answers to these questions are probably as numerous as are the number of institutions involved. Information derived from a recent directory of art libraries and visual resource centres in North America, compiled under the auspices of ARLIS/NA, has indicated that approximately 63% of the art museums and galleries have organized photograph collections.[1] These vary in size and complexity with the degree of dedication to the pursuit of scholarly research and library support provided by the parent institution, and range in size from a few hundred prints to over one and one-half million.

Professional art organizations, such as the Art Libraries Society of North America (ARLIS/NA) and the College Art Association of America (CAA) have only begun to develop standards for art libraries and art librarianship. Thus far published standards have been prepared for staffing art libraries and collection development but do not include standards relating to non-book materials.[2] Much work remains to formulate and refine standards for collection development, art librarianship curriculum development, and staff educational standards, as well as other aspects of physical planning, collections, staffing, etc. The area of non-print librarianship in the arts is only just beginning to come to grips with the problems of developing professional standards. Preliminary work is currently being conducted by the Visual Resources group of CAA.

The success of applying art library standards to institutions on a national scale will depend upon the acceptance of ARLIS/NA standards as well as those which might be developed by other professional groups, by their sister organizations and governmental agencies and foundations which provide services and funding to the arts.

In answer to the leading question of this article, an art gallery or museum should examine its role and function in the community as it seeks to define the role in which its library and research facilities will function. The writer recommends that any medium, and most certainly all large institutions, must have photograph research collections and other appropriate non-print reference materials included in their library services. Appropriate scholarly research is greatly enhanced with access to good quality black and white photographs, colour slides, and microfiches and other micrographic publications which are increasingly available nowadays.

The advent of micrographic publication in the field of art has greatly expanded the ability of libraries to provide illustrative materials of huge collections of unpublished as well as published works of art and architecture, whereas the cost of reproduction by conventional publishing methods was prohibitive. Non-book picture and photograph librarians must be constantly aware of new developments in the publishing and information field which can expand the scope of their collections and services.[3]

AIMS AND OBJECTIVES

Photograph and slide collections in a museum or gallery setting serve many purposes, not all of them directly connected to library services. Museums exist in order to collect, preserve, conserve, and display art, and to disseminate information (education) about that art.[4] Photograph collections in library settings may serve many functions, such as curatorial research, educational visual aids in the classroom or gallery, exhibition displays, publication sources for illustrative material, etc. In addition, photography serves a major role in documenting a collection, providing condition records, and serving as a conservation tool, in addition to providing technical information concerning authentication and verification of works of art.

While many of these services and products may not fall under the direct jurisdiction of the photograph librarian or archivist, that officer should, nevertheless, remain knowledgeable about the subcollections within the institution and provide supporting expertise and assistance in the management and care of these collections, when called for. Photographic records may be found among the files of curators and keepers of collections, registrars, conservators, publications officers, public relations officers, educational staff, designers, photographic studios, as well as the library and archives, as illustrated by the holdings of the Cleveland Museum of Art. Of course photographs are also collected as works of art and will be found in the permanent collections and exhibitions of galleries and museums.

In general, most museum and gallery photograph collections exist primarily for purposes of study and research by staff and patrons, rather than as archives of one-of-a-kind prints. The form of the individual photograph in hard copy provides greater flexibility and convenience to the user not available with slides, books, or many other media formats. In addition, a carefully developed collection can provide access to material often unavailable and unpublished in other media.

Photograph collection development receives its primary direction from the content of the permanent collections of the gallery or museum. As a major tool used in the study and research of objects in the permanent collections, the photograph collection must seek to support research in the areas in which the institution collects. In addition, the librarian must be able to anticipate the need to introduce new areas into a permanent collection and acquire photographs in those areas, on a gradual and continual basis.

ACQUISITION

There are several sources which can be of assistance in the acquisition of photographs, the main one being the museums and galleries themselves. In addition, there are numerous commercial dealers, subscription services, institutions, governmental agencies, and private photographers, all of whom provide photographs and services. A constant review of the subject periodical literature for information on collections, exhibitions, sources of slides, photographs, micrographics, etc. is a must, especially for the large collection. Some material is available only in limited quantities and by special application. The bibliography listed at the end of this article may be of assistance in locating sources.[5] It must be added, however, that existing source directories are far from complete and many have surprising omissions. Whenever possible one should urge authors and publishers to include photograph sources for all illustrations published. Illustration acknowledgements provide an invaluable source for the picture researcher and librarian.

Acquisition is a difficult problem made more so by restraints on budgets and rising costs. The purposes for which the photograph collection is designed dictate to a large extent how the collection should be developed. An art history teaching collection may place emphasis upon carefully selected photographs of key monuments of world art designed to illustrate a specific course of instruction. A research collection, on the other hand, while exercising equal selectivity, is greatly enhanced by the depth of its collecting policy as well as its breadth. Museum collections often combine both elements of research and teaching in their collection development policies, bearing in mind the scope and content of the institution's exhibitions and collections.

In some museums and galleries, the photograph collection may serve as the depository for all photographs documenting that particular institution's activities; in others these photo documents are included in the archives or registrar's files. Whatever the case, such materials should be handled carefully, with attention given to preservation and conservation.

Whenever possible, the photograph librarian should implement a policy whereby photographs of objects taken by the institution's Photography Department are automatically passed to the photograph library. For a number of reasons this policy has not been universally adhered to by institutions in the past, thus exerting a considerable burden on the present administration in rectifying past omissions.

CONSERVATION

There are a number of ways in which photographs are processed for use in research and educational collections. The most common is dry mounting the print on acid-free mount board using an acid-free dry mount tissue. New materials come on the market periodically and old ones are sometimes removed from the market even though they may be of proven quality. If your institution does not have the services of a conservation staff dealing in paper preservation, one can receive assistance from other specialists in paper and photograph preservation and archival materials.[6] Given the investment made in creating and maintaining a photograph collection, it is important that as many steps as possible be taken to prolong the life of the photographs for as long as possible, through temperature and humidity controls and a full range of archival processes, materials and facilities, to and including the instruction of users in the care and handling of the photographs and mounts.

The photograph librarian needs to be constantly aware of new developments and materials being introduced into the market place. The recent development of RC (resin-coated) photographic papers has created a controversy among photograph librarians and archivists as to its longevity and durability. Some conservationists have not yet given it a clean bill of health even though it has been widely publicized by various manufacturers. RC papers have received frequent and ready acceptance by photographers and unless one specifically requests otherwise, a purchaser will more than likely receive prints on RC paper. Some sellers of photographs will offer the buyer a choice between regular archivally washed photographic papers or RC papers. Until RC paper or any other new development in the field has been given clearance by the conservation community of the museum and library world, the librarian is advised to request archivally washed Kodak photographic papers, or their equivalent.

STORAGE

The design of photograph collection libraries is a subject not covered in library literature to any extent. As with any library collection, photographs require a carefully monitored humidity and temperature environment as well as a high level of air filtration. Any material subject to handling is also subject to accelerated deterioration and damage. If the collections are thought of as being somewhat expendable then freer public access might be considered with a possible open-stack access policy. On the other hand, one may wish to have more restricted stack policies as well as archivally approved storage facilities. Some librarians might wish to cut down on handling photographs through the use of small contact prints on catalogue cards. Examples of such techniques have been used by several American institutions and might be considered by others.[9]

Photographs are generally stored in one of two ways: either they are loosely filed in steel filing cabinets, or they are boxed in acid-free *hollenger* boxes and stored either flat or upright on shelves. Both systems have their proponents. One must take into account user needs as well as cost and space factors. The most efficient use of space may require the use of several differing systems according to size of prints, their intended use, rarity, and whether or not they compose a collective entity, such as the *Decimal index of the art of the Low Countries,* (DIAL), the *Berenson archives,* the *Princeton index of Christian iconography,* and others. Many special collections are most useful when they retain their original organization and associated indexes, catalogues, etc.

CATALOGUING AND CLASSIFICATION

While expensive to maintain, catalogues of the photograph collections are invaluable as research tools. Whether catalogues and indexes are computerized, or manual in card or book form, librarians should give serious consideration to their creation, preservation, and maintenance as major research tools. Recent conferences have given major emphasis to those automated catalogue and indexing systems currently in operation in the field of art history.[7] While having great differences, these systems will have a major impact on future developments in art historical research and also on the development and access to information about museum collections hitherto unavailable.

The most common manual systems of cataloguing photographs and slides in the field of art and art history are the Fogg Art Museum Photograph and Slide Library (Harvard University) system, and the Metropolitan Museum of Art Photograph and Slide Library (New York City) system, and the variations thereon. The Santa Cruz automated system developed in California has received considerable acceptance in the USA but may not be the best developed system for art historical research and documentation. Much work remains to be done in this area.

The advent of computer applications to the cataloguing and indexing of photograph collections offers the greatest challenge to art and photograph librarians in many decades. Its expanded use will permit the user greater access to multiple collections as well as increased subject access and a variety of other indexing fields. Together with the application of the computer and expanded micrographic publications of photograph archives, out-of-print publications, and new works, art and photograph librarians have at their disposal vastly expanded opportunities for building first-class reference and study facilities (refer to Sections 1.8 and 1.9 for details). Here, it should be noted that the micrographic communications industries are growing at a rate of from 10 to 15% annually against 1⅓ to 3% in the printing industry.[8]

Standard arrangements of photograph collections in the arts are usually classified by country or culture and media, are subdivided by artist and site, and further subdivided by period, century, decade, or reign. In addition, some photograph collections are subdivided by subject categories, e.g., the Fogg Art Museum Photograph Library, the DIAL index, the Cleveland Museum of Art Photograph Reference Library, etc. Some type of subject access is highly desirable whether this is achieved by a classification system or by subject headings in a catalogue system. In-depth cataloguing and indexing is expensive but can be achieved with the use of original information from museums and commercial institutions, and dealers and distributors. The inclusion of negative numbers in the bibliographic citation is invaluable when conducting research for publication or replacing deteriorating prints. The bibliographic documentation of photographs and illustrations used in publications has rarely been given adequate emphasis, nor has it been fully exploited by writers of all persuasions.

DISCARD POLICY

One of the most difficult problems the photograph librarian has to face concerns whether or not to have a policy of discard. As with book collections, there is a variation of opinion as to whether the economics of library operations warrant the expenditure of time and money on a continuing programme of discard. It has been my practice over the years to restrict discard primarily to situations in which a print is replaced by another superior print. In many instances, particularly in cases of older collections, one is apt to find prints of historical interest, which are perhaps worthy of being treated as works of art, in the permanent collections of curatorial departments. It is not unknown for photograph research and archival collections to have examples of photographs by such artists as Felice A Beato, Frederick Henry Evans, Francis Frith, Nadar, or Henry Fox Talbot, to suggest a few. These should be noted and consideration should be given to transferring them to curatorial departments. At the very least, one should probably remove them from general circulating collections and provide a secure storage facility under lock and key, with due conservation and preservation attention. Such photographs are highly vulnerable to library thieves, amateur and professional alike.

RECOGNITION

Photograph collections have generally not been given the administrative support which they deserve, either from their parent institutions or from the public at large. It is necessary for professionals in the field to exert greater pressure and influence within library and related societies and associations, as well as within their own institutions, to gain greater understanding and support of non-print collections.

Art library societies and related associations are now tackling the problems of standards for art library collections, staffing, education, etc. As these documents are completed and given wide distribution and support, one will hopefully see a change in the conditions and management of photograph and other non-print collections. Within the art library field, the double masters degree is being stressed ever more strongly in job descriptions and hiring practices. More and more candidates are required to have both a professional library degree and a graduate level art history degree. These same standards are also being applied to photograph librarians.

Library school education for the non-book picture librarian in the art field is sadly inadequate throughout most of the USA and Canada. A few programmes and seminars in art librarianship do exist but none devotes much space or time to the special problems, bibliography, etc. of picture librarianship. Thus, it is found that most professionals in the field are largely self-taught and gain their experience on the job. Job opportunities are limited and are found primarily in academia, museums, and some public libraries.

REFERENCES

1 Hoffberg, Judith A and others *Directory of art libraries and visual resource collections in North America.* New York, Neal-Schuman Publishers Inc., 1978.

2 Art Libraries Society of North America *Standards for staffing art libraries.* Washington, DC, Art Libraries Society of North America, 1977.

3 Hess, Stanley W 'Microfiche in the fine arts — source list' (unpublished typescript).

4 Newsom, Barbara Y and others *The art museum as educator.* Berkeley, California, University of California Press, 1978.

5 Suggested sources:
   (a) The American Association of Museums *The official museum directory 1980.* Washington, DC, The American Association of Museums, 1979.
   (b) Brink, Adrian and others (editors) *The libraries, museums and art galleries year book 1976.* Cambridge, James Clarke & Co. Ltd, 1976.
   (c) DeLaurier, Nancy (compiler) *Slide buyer's guide 1976.* New York, College Art Association of America, 1976.
   (d) Evans, Hilary and others *Picture researcher's handbook.* London, David & Charles, 1975.
   (e) Green, Shirley L and others *Pictorial resources in the Washington, DC area.* Washington, DC, Library of Congress, 1976.
   (f) *International directory of arts,* 14th ed. 1979/80. Frankfurt, Müller, 1979.
   (g) Hess, Stanley W *An annotated bibliography of slide library literature.* Bibliographic Studies 3. Syracuse, New York, School of Information Studies, Syracuse University, 1978. 20-4.
   (h) Hess, Stanley W 'Microfiche in the fine arts — source list' (unpublished typescript).
   (i) McDarrah, Fred H (editor) *Stock photo and assignment source book.* New York, R R Bowker Company, 1977.
   (j) Novotny, Ann (editor) and others *Picture sources 3.* New York, Special Libraries Association, 1975.
   (k) Schuller, Nancy S and others *Guide for photograph collections.* Mid America College Art Association, 1978.
   (l) Wall, John *Directory of British photograph collections.* London, Royal Photographic Society, 1977.

6 Suggested sources for information:
   — Consultant on Conservation, International Museum of Photography, George Eastman House, 900 East Avenue, Rochester, NY 14607, USA.
   — TALAS, 104 Fifth Avenue, New York, NY 10011, USA.

— Preservation Office, Library of Congress, Washington, DC 20540, USA.

7   *International conference on automatic processing of art history data and documents, First, Pisa, 1978.* Conference transactions in 3 vols. Pisa, Scuola Normale Superiore, September 1978.

8   *Archival stability of microfilm – a technical review.* Technical Report No. 18, 4 August, 1978. Washington, DC, United States Government Printing Office, 1978.

9   Evans, Grace E and others 'Image-bearing catalog cards for photo-libraries: an overview and a proposal' in *Special Libraries* 70:11, November 1979. 462-70.

21

United States Government Picture Libraries

William H Leary

Photography in the United States government is big business, very big business. Comprehensive and reliable figures are not available, but a few statistics will suggest the volume of government photography. Of some 900 separate federal agencies, at least 400 create or acquire photographs for official purposes. Over 100 of them generate so much photography that they have established picture libraries in Washington to maintain and distribute their current holdings of nearly 10 million images. It is hardly an exaggeration to claim that the United States government has, somewhere, a pictorial record of all major (and some trivial) aspects of political, social, agricultural, industrial, scientific, recreational, and cultural life in America and the rest of the world. Given such diverse subject matter, it is extremely difficult to discern common themes or governing principles of government photography. Thus, no generalizations are completely valid, or, to put it another way, any generalization can be argued with some success. A brief look at its impressive history may aid in defining this significant but not unique field of photography.

Historically, official governmental photography has served two broad purposes: to inform and to promote. In the 19th and early 20th centuries federal agencies used photographs primarily to provide information about little-known places and events or official activities. They documented particularly well the government's responsibilities in military defence, exploration, and construction.

Military agencies have long employed some of the most resourceful and talented photographers: Alexander Gardner, Timothy O'Sullivan, Andrew J Russel, Samuel A Cooley, George Barnard, and Selmar Rush Siebert are a few of the better-known photographers hired by the Union Army to record its activities. The most famous Civil War photographer, Mathew Brady, had no official status. Fortunately, however, his collection was later purchased by the federal government. From those auspicious origins, military photography has expanded enormously while maintaining the highest technical standards. Currently, the Defense Department and related military agencies create as much as half of all still photography generated by the government of the United States.

Prior to the 'New Deal', perhaps the major responsibility of the federal government was to sponsor 'internal improvements' — the construction of federal facilities and other large undertakings, such as dams and canals. One could hardly imagine a more mundane activity but, as a 'builder' the federal government has sponsored some of its most spectacular photography. Often, construction progress photographs are required as evidence that a federal contractor has earned his money. One of the earliest and most impressive examples of this genre are some 100 collodion glass plates made by Lewis E Walker of the Treasury Building Extension between 1857 and 1867. Similarly, the Panama Canal Company has preserved a detailed pictorial record of its monumental undertaking. Early in the 20th century the Bureau of Reclamation created a magnificent set of photographs documenting life in long-forgotten western communities before they were obliterated or transformed by the dams constructed by that agency. These agencies and many others continue to maintain pictorial evidence of their progress in building structures paid for by the American taxpayer.

The most exciting enterprise of the United States government in the 19th century was the exploration of the West and, increasingly thereafter, the rest of the world. Photography's potential for assisting in this task was recognized very early. Indeed, photography was first used by the government as an aid in surveying. E R Smith made daguerreotypes for the US naval astronomical expedition to the southern hemisphere, 1849-52, while Eliphalet M Brown Jr made over 400 daguerreotypes on Commodore Perry's expedition to Japan in 1852. Unfortunately, none is known to have survived. Later, some of the best photographers on the American scene were hired to record the unknown western landscape. The photographs of Timothy O'Sullivan, William

Henry Jackson, John K Hillers and many others did more than simply educate or inform a population eager to know what lay beyond the Mississippi River. They also promoted a new federal responsibility — the conservation of public lands. Jackson's photographs of Yellowstone, for example, played a crucial role in its eventual designation as a national park. The photography of exploration remains an important function of the national government. In the last twenty years NASA has produced millions of photographs recording American exploration of outer space (see also Section 2.22).

As the federal government expanded during the 'New Deal' and later, so too did government's use of photography to advocate or promote. The most celebrated government use of promotion photography (ironically labelled 'documentary') was by the Farm Security Administration during the 1930s. Roy Stryker at the FSA hired Walker Evans, Dorothea Lange, Russell Lee, Arthur Rothstein, and many others to 'document' the effect of the Depression on ordinary Americans; but they documented reality with the clear intention of creating more than an objective record: they also sought to dramatize the plight of the suffering, to promote an active governmental policy to alleviate distress. They succeeded brilliantly, so well that the FSA was abolished shortly after World War II by conservative Congressmen who thought government employees should report, not advocate. A similar fate befell a very recent effort to emulate the work of the FSA. The Office of Economic Opportunity used photographs to advocate federal measures to assist the poor in the 1960s and 1970s. It was abolished by the Nixon administration for the same reasons that led to the earlier demise of the FSA.

A growing percentage of official photography, then, is used to promote as well as to inform or record government activity. Whatever the intended purpose or original source, however, all photographs created or acquired by an agency of the federal government are defined as official records. As a result they may not be disposed of without the prior approval of staff of the National Archives, an agency established in 1934 to preserve forever official records determined to have enduring historical value. Moreover, each federal agency which maintains photographs must submit to the National Archives for approval a schedule of instructions for disposing of the photographs in its possession. Such scheduling greatly increases the likelihood that historically valuable pictorial records will be preserved. It also gives each agency the authority

Lewis Emory Walker. 'Construction of the Department of the Treasury, Washington DC, June 7, 1862'. Public Service Buildings photograph no. 121-BC-9L in the National Archives.

to destroy the mundane photographs that inevitably accumulate — the annual office party pictures or the identification photos of each employee, for example. Partly as a result of this policy of records management, the National Archives now preserves over 5 million historic photographs from the files of some 145 federal agencies.

What other common themes, if any, emerge from this brief historical review of government photography? One general characteristic is that informational value is more important than aesthetic considerations in determining official value. To put it too simply, some have argued that government photography is 'artless'. As we have seen, government departments create photography for two very practical reasons: to inform or to publicize. Government is not in the business of sponsoring art. Frequently, of course, informational or documentary photography achieves the level of high art, but in most cases the achievements of, for instance, a Timothy O'Sullivan or a Russell Lee are fortuitous. Art is neither intended nor expected. It is not surprising, therefore, that most government photographs do not even identify the photographer. It is the information in a picture that is important, not its creator. Consequently, virtually no government library catalogues by name of photographer.

This functional approach to photography has another important practical effect. It contributes, regrettably, to the relatively low status of photographers and picture librarians within the federal bureaucracy. Photographers and lab personnel are usually low-level technicians. After all, it is argued, in this era of 35 mm. technology anyone can be a competent photographer. Similarly, the editing, cataloguing, and servicing of photographs has little priority in most agencies. Once a photograph has fulfilled its immediate purpose, it is argued, why spend good money maintaining it? Thus, it is not surprising that some of the 100 major government picture libraries do not even employ a picture librarian. That work is left to the photographer or a clerk-typist.

A survey suggests another characteristic of government photography: it is available to the public. Indeed, as we noted, government agencies have increasingly used photography to promote and publicize their activities. Thus, they must encourage public access in order to accomplish the agency's objectives. The main incentive to public use is the provision of photographic reproductions for a nominal fee. Indeed, many agencies provide a small number of reproductions at no charge. Most agencies also perform limited research in response to mail or phone enquiries and make available study facilities. Many agencies provide additional special assistance to publishers, including free reproductions or loans. With rare exceptions, government agencies do not charge use fees for publication of their photographs.

With three exceptions, all photographs created or acquired by a government agency are in the public domain and, therefore, may be reproduced by anyone for any purpose. A very small number of photographs is restricted to public access because of security classification. This rare exception is largely confined to the Defense Department, the Central Intelligence Agency, and the Secret Service. The Federal Bureau of Investigation and a few similar agencies restrict public access to investigative photographs which might violate an individual's privacy. Finally, and most commonly, photographs acquired from private sources may be restricted by claims of copyright. No public employee may copyright a work produced on government time. Only about 1,000 photographs are registered for copyright annually in the

John K Hillers. 'Cathedral Spires in Yosemite Valley, California, ca. 1876'. Geological Survey photograph number 57-PS-28 in the National Archives.

United States. However, the Copyright Act of 1976 automatically grants protection until the year 2002 to most photographs created privately since 1906. Thus, government librarians must be particularly careful about reproducing privately created photographs.

While a look at the historical tradition of government photograph collections may reveal a few common characteristics, closer examination exposes many more dissimilarities. In addition to an endless variety of subject matter, the size of government collections varies enormously. Several government agencies maintain photo libraries of more than 250,000 images. Many more, by contrast, maintain only a few thousand images documenting ceremonial and recreational activities at the agency headquarters. Similarly, government collections include all types of current photographic techniques. Everything from standard black and white and colour photography to aerial and satellite photographs, micro-photographs, infrared photographs, and much more can be found in official files.

As a final example of dissimilarity, there is no pattern to the cataloguing of government photography. Some agencies do no more than file photographs in the order in which they arrived in the picture library — if there is one. A few collections, on the other hand, are controlled by an elaborate computerized index. At the Environmental Protection Agency, for example, a researcher can have almost immediate access to photographs documenting all types of pollution. At the touch of a button the computer flashes on the screen every picture in the file showing whatever subject may be of interest. More typically, government libraries file photographs according to some system which provides the access most needed by the agency — perhaps chronologically, or alphabetically by subject, place, or surname. Negatives are generally filed separately, by number, for easy retrieval.

Three recent trends, by no means universal or unique, may help to define government photography more precisely in the future. These developments are disturbing, however, to the archivist charged with preserving forever historically valuable government photography. An increasing percentage of government photography is 35 mm., colour, and produced on contract by non-government personnel. The archival challenge of colour photography is well-known. Given currently available technology, colour photographs cannot be preserved for an extended period of time without enormous expense. Hopefully, government agencies will use their influence to encourage the photo-

NO. PIO 75-123c

General Topic: Landforms

Caption Material:

Double Arch, considered one of the most beautiful of the more than 124 arches in Arches National Park, Utah, has grown to be the second largest arch in the park and typlifies the slow processes of erosion that continue to form, enlarge and topple these natural rock features, according to USGS scientists.

Examples of image-bearing catalogue cards used by the International Communication Agency to index its collection of 60,000 photographs. The cards are produced by a standard microfilm camera. *National Archives and Records Service, Washington DC.*

graphic industry to devote more attention to the solution of this problem.

The archival challenge of 35 mm. photography is equally serious, if less well-known. As noted earlier, the 35 mm. camera is so relatively cheap and easy to use that it fosters the regrettable notion that every man is a born photographer. As a result, the number of images in government files is likely to expand geometrically at the same time as the quality diminishes. As the volume becomes more unmanageable the necessary job of editing will receive less and less attention. Finally, 35 mm. photographs simply do not reproduce as well as those in a larger format. For the archivist, it will be increasingly difficult, but even more essential, to separate the wheat from the chaff.

The growing practice of purchasing photographs or contracting out that responsibility may have contradictory effects. Some believe that it may improve the general quality of government photography. However, the historical evidence does not suggest that outside contractors produce better photographs than government employees. One can predict with greater certainty that contracting will confuse the question of rights. Archivists will no longer be able to assume that a photograph paid for by the government is in the public domain. Moreover, photographs produced on contract outside the agency, and paid for by taxpayers, may never get to the National Archives as intended.

The future of government photography is ambiguous. The uses and appeal of photography for official purposes have expanded dramatically. Immense financial resources and space-age technology are available. On the other hand, there are signs that efforts to maintain the quality of government photography may face serious challenges. Those who appreciate the rich historical tradition of government photography should insist that current exciting possibilities be fully exploited. They should also warn of hazards ahead.

22

The Space Imagery Center: A Prototype Planetary Data Facility

---

Gail S Georgenson

INTRODUCTION

Before the 17th century it was impossible to study the other planets in the solar system. They were mere specks of light in the sky. With the invention of the telescope by Galileo, astronomers began to discuss such phenomena as craters on the moon, rings around Saturn, and a great red spot on Jupiter. The telescope was only a beginning although other planets remained a mystery to us until this century. Then, two decades ago the Soviet Union launched a spacecraft called Sputnik which turned the tide for planetary astronomy. Following Sputnik, President John Kennedy announced that the US would focus its technology toward the exploration of the moon and planets. Soon we had a view of our own planet from space; as spacecraft carried men to the moon and landed instruments on other planetary surfaces. Such views were never before possible through earth-based telescopes.

Since the advent of interplanetary probes the quantity of imagery representing the other planets fills volumes. In fact, in two decades we have amassed more pictures of our solar system than all which had been collected before in human experience. This enormous database is used by planetologists who are interested in determining the nature and history of our solar system. In so doing they further our understanding of the earth's origin and possible future.

The problem of rendering these images retrievable for users surfaced in the early 1970s. The major portion of Apollo lunar photography existed by this time and several unmanned spacecraft to Mars had provided a large quantity of imagery of the 'red' planet. At the University of Arizona's Lunar and Planetary Laboratory (LPL) the material began to accumulate in offices and cupboards throughout the building, as is the case in many fledgling library collections.

NASA'S FIRST PLANETARY DATA FACILITY

To solve this information management problem the National Aeronautics and Space Administration awarded a government grant to the LPL in 1976 with the idea of developing a prototype data collection and retrieval facility. Matching funds for the project were provided by the University of Arizona. Today, this facility is called the Space Imagery Center and constitutes an organized and catalogued working collection of lunar and planetary imagery for use as a research tool in the planetary sciences. As a result of the centre's success, NASA funded six similar facilities which are now open in various regions throughout the US. The centres form a natural network, communicating regularly in order to meet common storage and retrieval challenges.

Members of the Regional Planetary Image Facilities (RPIF) Consortium appear in Table 1. In particular, this paper deals with the development of the Space Imagery Center though the other facilities are nearly identical in collection scope, storage treatment of the photographs and film, and data retrieval methods.

EARLY PLANNING PHASE

Today, the centre occupies about 1,150 square feet of floor space adjacent to the reference library. Together they form the information complex for the LPL. Selecting a location for the centre during the early planning stages involved the following considerations:
1   convenience to the reference library
2   safety and security of the collection
3   amount of space necessary to house the existing collection plus approximately ten years' growth

Table 1

NASA's Regional Planetary Image Facilities

SPACE IMAGERY CENTER
Lunar and Planetary Laboratory
University of Arizona
Tucson, Arizona 85721

PLANETARY IMAGE FACILITY
3303 NASA Road 1
Lunar and Planetary Institute
Houston, Texas 77058

PLANETARY DATA FACILITY
Astrogeological Branch
US Geological Survey
2255 N Gemini Drive
Flagstaff, Arizona 86001

PLANETARY IMAGE FACILITY
Jet Propulsion Laboratory/
   MS 264-111A
California Institute of Technology
Pasadena, California 91103

BROWN REGIONAL PLANETARY
   DATA CENTER
Brown University/Sciences
   Library
Providence, Rhode Island 02912

SPACECRAFT PLANETARY
   IMAGING FACILITY
Center for Radiophysics and
   Space Research
Cornell University,
Ithaca, New York 14853

PLANETARY IMAGE FACILITY
McDonnell Center for Space
   Sciences
Washington University
St Louis, Missouri 63130

4   amount of space available in the building proper.
Unfortunately, the last consideration was at the top of the list. Office
and lab space is a precious commodity at the University of Arizona, a
problem common to most institutions today.

The next task was to determine the exact space necessary for storing
the collection and to prepare recommendations for equipment purchase.
The library staff, consisting of one professionally trained librarian and
several part-time students, conducted an inventory of the collection
scattered throughout offices.

Inventories can be very tedious and may even cause you to wonder
how you *ever* accepted such a creative challenge as planning a library.
Sorting through a collection to determine its contents and scope is a
necessary task. The key to a relatively painless inventory is to be
organized. Devise a floor plan of the areas where material is stored.
Number the cabinets, drawers, and boxes containing the material and
mark them on the floor plan. Use a work sheet to list the contents of

these various storage devices. We allowed four columns on the work sheets to record the following information:

1   location where stored
2   equipment where stored
3   description of contents, including type and format of film/print products
4   cubic footage measured on the inside.

This type of inventory survey is fairly time-consuming, but necessary for planning purposes. Fortunately, many of our images are of similar format, thus allowing us the convenience of spot checking. For example, it was relatively easy to determine that we had 20 boxes of Mariner 9 Mars images, all of 8 × 10 inch format. Had the boxes contained a miscellany of formats and subjects the inventory would have involved many times the staff and hours that it took us. A report issued at the conclusion of the survey pointed out the existence of nearly a half-million images — almost 500 cubic feet of imagery.

COLLECTION DESCRIPTION

The collection includes photography from every NASA imaging experiment flown to the moon and planets, as well as the cartographic products (maps, atlases, and globes) produced from this imagery. Television cameras have been used almost exclusively as the imaging device on all unmanned missions. These systems are entirely electronic. Instead of using photographic film as in a conventional camera, the image tube or vidicon records scenes on a photoconductive target by opening and closing a shutter. Vidicon signals, which indicate variations in light intensity, are converted to digital form and telemetered back to Earth. The images in the centre are hard-copy versions of these data. The Lunar Orbiter and the manned Apollo missions are exceptions, the camera systems being of the conventional film variety. Most of the mission-oriented images are printed on resin-coated paper.

The other major portion of the collection is the earth-based telescopic imagery taken through telescopes in Arizona by the Lunar and Planetary Laboratory. These images are originals and are considered very valuable by the astronomy community that uses them.

The primary data sets for each planet are summarized by planet name in Table 2. The format varies slightly from mission to mission depending

Table 2

MISSION—ORIENTED PLANETARY DATA	Mercury	Mariner 10
		    8 × 10 inch prints
		    70 mm. strip contact prints
		    oversize photomosaics

	Venus	Mariner 10
		    8 × 10 inch prints
		    70 mm. strip contact prints

	Mars	Mariner 6 and 7
		    8 × 10 inch prints
		Mariner 9
		    8 × 10 inch prints
		Viking Orbiter 1,2
		    5 inch strip contact prints
		    5 inch duplicate negatives
		    oversize mosaics
		Viking Lander 1,2
		    5 inch strip contact prints
		    8 × 10 inch stereo pairs

	Jupiter	Voyager 1,2
		    10 × 10 inch prints
		    5 inch strip contact prints
		    5 inch negatives
		    20 × 24 inch photomosaics
		Pioneer 10,11
		    8 × 10 inch prints

	Saturn	Voyager 1,2
		    10 × 10 inch prints
		    5 inch strip contact prints
		Pioneer 10,11

MISSION-ORIENTED LUNAR DATA	Moon	Ranger 7-9
		    8 × 10 inch prints
		Surveyor 1,3,5-7
		    8 × 10 inch prints
		Orbiter 1-5
		    20 × 24 inch prints
		    20 × 24 inch transparencies
		Apollo 8,10-17
		    70 mm. transparencies
		    5 inch prints
		    5 × 48 inch prints

SPECIAL COLLECTIONS	All planets	Earth-based telescopic photos
		    35 mm. film strips
		Slide Collection
		    35 mm. mounted slides

332

on the anticipated user group for each product. As noted in Table 2, product sizes vary from 5 × 5 inch prints to 5 × 48 inch prints. Larger sizes are also common. The format for the 250,000 earth-based telescopic film images is the same for all planets: 35 mm. film strips. Also, the centre has a circulating 35 mm. slide collection which is tailor-made to meet the lecture needs of the faculty and technical staff. The slides represent a wide variety of subjects, such as selected examples of geological features, eclipses, comets, meteorites — virtually any topic relating to solar system studies.

Numerous maps and atlases are contained within the centre. Examples of the former include index maps, United States geological survey maps, tectonic and topophoto maps. Atlases in the centre include some which were produced by individuals at LPL. Storage and access to these data products will not be dealt with in this chapter.

STORAGE CONSIDERATIONS

Environmental Conditions

Initially, the Space Imagery Center was considered a working collection and not an archive. Today, though still considered a working collection, its value has risen such that conservation now assumes a higher priority. The deterioration of photos and film cannot be reversed once it begins, hence a chemically inert environment is the ideal. Such an environment is difficult and expensive to create. Many experts have offered advice on the optimum conditions for archival photographic storage. Some of the information available on the subject is still conjecture. A notable exception is the publication by Weinstein and Booth (1977),[1] a standard reference for photographic collections. This text covers all aspects of photographic collections management, including the major preservation problems.

At the centre a thermostat allows the librarian control over the temperature, an absolute necessity in an archive. The temperature is maintained at 20°C in an effort to prevent the separation of film layers caused by fluctuations in temperature. The base layer and emulsion layer react differently to changes in temperature, both chemically and physically. Emulsion may dry, crack, and flake off whereas the base will shrink, become brittle and break. Temperatures of between 15°C and 20°C should be maintained to prevent such problems.

In many geographic locations, high humidity is a problem for photo archives. Our Arizona desert location provides a different challenge — not enough humidity. The centre's relative humidity (RH) usually falls between 10 and 25%. The RH has been known to fall as low as 5% and remain there for several days. At low RH the photo/film products tend to curl, due to the shrinkage of the emulsion layer when moisture is drawn out. Curled prints and film are difficult to study and hard to refile. Nearly all of the collection now resides in protective sleeves which curtail curling to a degree. Installation of a humidifier to keep the RH at a steady 40% is under consideration.

In addition to maintaining a constant environment, we planned early on to select an area *apart* from other laboratories at LPL as we wanted to be remote from possible contamination by fumes and gases. The centre is located on a floor with offices, the reference library, and the computer room.

Protective Sleeves

Equally as important as the above are the storage media themselves. Envelopes, sleeves, folders, or other forms of enclosures are necessary when storing photos and film. They protect the images from dirt and damage, hence prolonging the life of the products. Some enclosures are better than others. Some are even harmful for the photographic material and should be avoided. It is known that certain paper enclosures contain acids and other chemicals which make them unsuitable for archival storage. Also, glassine envelopes are now considered unsuitable for archival purposes because they too contain chemicals.

Obtaining definitive information on the desirability of one sleeving enclosure over another (particularly concerning newer products) proved difficult during the centre's early planning and development stage. Conflicting information was received from manufacturers. Unfortunately, some decisions regarding sleeving enclosures were made based on incomplete information. Luckily, most of the enclosures we selected are considered fairly safe today. However, information concerning the permanence of various sleeving materials changes rather rapidly from year to year, so what is considered archival today may not be tomorrow.

Mylar (polyester), polyethylene, and triacetate sleeving materials are all used at the centre. We are using mylar for film transparencies, primarily because they are more vulnerable than prints. Mylar is more expensive than most sleeving products and has been shown to have a very long life-expectancy. Our mylar sleeves are seamless, folded envelopes which accommodate 5 inch and 35 mm. film. We would prefer to use only mylar in the centre; however, like most non-profit organizations we are hampered by budgetary constraints. The only problem detected so far with mylar is that it tends to pick up dust because of its static build-up.

The primary sleeving material used for protecting prints in the centre is virgin polyethylene, which is believed to be free of harmful chemicals. This material is purchased on rolls in widths, ranging from 70 mm. to 10 inches. The most commonly used size, the 5 inch format, is precut by the manufacturer and heat sealed on one end. These precut sleeves save many hours of staff time, as well as turn-around time for patron use.

Triacetate is also used for storing prints at the centre. Three-hole sheet protectors for use with ring binders are purchased to protect our standard 8 × 10 inch prints. These sleeves are considered permanent in terms of their chemical stability; however, they tend to dry out and crack in Arizona. Again, we attribute this problem to unusually low relative humidity. As with mylar, triacetate tends to pick up dust. We are attempting to find a more suitable sleeving product for protecting our 8 × 10 prints.

Storage Furniture

The wide range of photo formats produced by the mission imaging teams presents certain equipment design challenges. One major advantage is that all photo products of a given format and mission are stored together. In a sense, each mission represents one subject area. Were it necessary to interfile formats, the task of equipment selection would be far more complex.

We dealt with the question of storage furniture individually for each photographic format. An informal survey of principal users disclosed their preference for the three-ring binder approach to storage. Binders allow users a quick look at a range of photos. Also, from the library staff's point of view, binders have the advantage of being easy to add to, hence interfiling new material is convenient. Our 8 × 10 inch prints and 10 × 10 inch prints lend themselves to being filed in binders. As with sleeves, it is important to select binders made of chemically inert materials. We use a product made of virgin polyethylene with built-in

Flat-file storage of 20 × 24 inch lunar prints. *The Space Imagery Center, University of Arizona.*

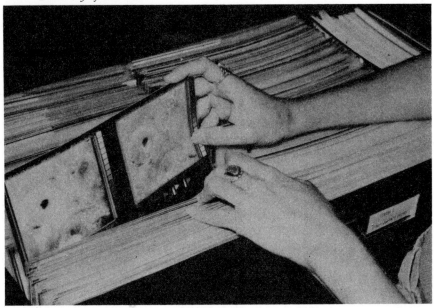

Lateral-file storage of 5 × 5 inch prints of Mars. *The Space Imagery Center, University of Arizona.*

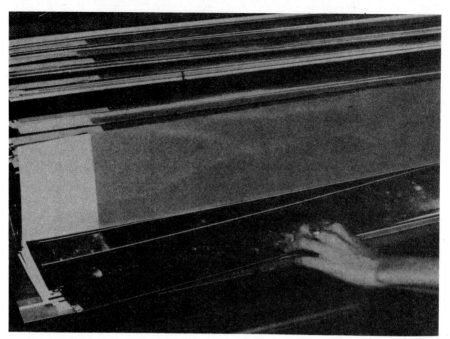

Custom cabinets for storing 5 × 48 inch panoramic camera prints. *The Space Imagery Center, University of Arizona.*

spine labels, thus avoiding scratched table tops which often result from metal spine labels.

The oversized materials need a different storage approach. Large 20 × 24 inch prints and mosaics are very heavy and can only be filed horizontally in flat file drawers (also called plan files or map files). This method is not ideal for browsing and filing purposes; however, the sheer weight of these data presents a storage problem.

Before purchasing the enamelled metal flat files we investigated a new system: a hanging vertical file which allows the photographs to be filed on edge, a method preferable to filing in stacks. The system includes large heavy envelopes which hang from horizontal rods. Unfortunately, the envelopes were not made of material heavy enough to hold our large prints. The weight of the envelopes with the photos was unmanageable for patrons and staff. It is an acceptable system, however, for smaller, lighter items.

Our 5 × 5 inch prints and negatives are stored in enamelled metal file cabinets called lateral files. The 6 inch high drawers with dividers are easy to use for filing and retrieval purposes. These files are wider but not as deep as the traditional filing cabinet, thus eliminating the inherent problem of difficult access. The lateral files are also available with hanging file folders suspended on rods inside the drawers. Our 35 mm. and 70 mm. films are also stored in lateral file cabinets but with smaller drawers. Several drawer heights are available ranging from 3 to 12 inches. The only problem that we have noted with the lateral files is that the photos tend to slip in the drawers. It is possible to line the drawer bottom with a material that has enough tread to stop the photos from slipping.

Custom-made cabinets were designed for the odd-sized 48 inch long prints. Metal shelves were constructed approximately 50 inches long to hold the prints lying down. Each shelf is only 1 inch high due to weight

Space Imagery Center floor plan. *The Space Imagery Center, University of Arizona.*

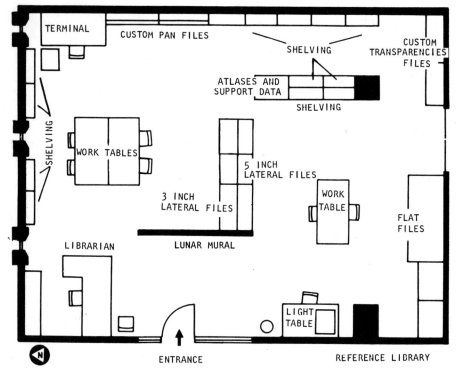

limitations with a shelf of this length. These shelves are then enclosed in a cabinet.

Longer format photos will become popular in the future as radar imaging becomes more sophisticated. A mission to Venus is planned in the late 1980s which will return radar images of the cloudy planet. Aerial photo libraries are often faced with similar odd-sized products. Custom-made cabinets offer the best solution for storing odd-sized prints and film, bearing in mind the preservation philosophy of a chemically inert environment.

Another example of custom-made furniture is a transparencies file for storing the very high quality 20 × 24 inch lunar transparencies. It is a bare wood cabinet with shelves spaced two inches apart. There is a certain degree of sagging in the shelves due to the weight of the transparencies, A preferable design would include more shelves spaced one inch apart rather than two, thereby eliminating the sagging problem.

The centre's floor plan is shown opposite. The shelving along the walls can eventually be turned 90° to allow for additional shelving. The large work tables are needed because our users like to compare a number of photos at one time. In terms of growth it appears that an adequate amount of space exists. It is difficult to project exactly how much space will be needed in future, for such a prediction is dependent upon the future of the space programme itself. Our acquisitions depend entirely on the existence of the space programme.

CATALOGUING AND RETRIEVAL PROCEDURES

Mission Data

All NASA mission-oriented data are assigned an acquisition number during the mission. When this imagery arrives at the centre, it is simply filed sequentially. The mission imaging teams assign numbers according to time taken; therefore, images of a particular area are typically filed together. However, a spacecraft often flies over a given area several times, so in order to conduct a complete search of an area it is often necessary to look in several of the centre's files. Early on in the centre's development, the principal users requested that all images of a given area be filed together for convenient access. Such an approach to filing involves many problems, the most pressing one being overlap between areas. Cross-indexes would be a necessity. Labour involved in refiling nearly a half a million images would be expensive due to the need for extra help. Thus, the idea of filing by area (rather than acquisition number) was abandoned, to the delight of the library staff.

When a collection is filed by acquisition or accession number, external means of retrieval are necessary. The collection is not accessible without an index and several are available at the centre. Both the Jet Propulsion Laboratory (a NASA facility) and the National Space Science Data Center (a NASA contractor) produce indexes of various types. A common one is the 'footprint map', a map of a planetary surface with photo coverage marked up on relevant areas. These index maps are very handy to use, particularly when one develops a familiarity with the planetary surfaces. Supplementary reference information can be obtained when using the footprint maps, such as latitude and longitude of the area being searched or proximity of the area to other surface features.

The Jet Propulsion Laboratory produces another type of index — a computer generated list of image numbers sorted by area. These listings indicate complete coverage of a region for a specific mission. The only drawback to the lists is their lack of editing; all images regardless of quality are included. The listings are useful in that they are comprehensive; however, they are often extremely long, thus involving a tedious search through the files.

In order to expedite selection one must be permitted rapid viewing by way of an automatic system to avoid manually picking through the files. In an automatic system, the pictures that are found to be visually unacceptable for one reason or another can be quickly deleted from the list of possibilities. Since a picture is indeed worth a thousand words a visual display system of retrieval is mandatory in terms of efficiency. In an early effort to install a visual display retrieval system, the centre purchased a microfiche retrieval system. Contained on Cosati-formatted microfiches were all the NASA mission-oriented images, complete with binary coded clips, and stored in a cartridge carousel for automatic retrieval. The computer-interfaced microfiche reader received its instructions from a program stored on the university's DEC-10 computer. The program was complex and included many parameter possibilities for image selection, such as latitude, longitude, sun angle, image resolution, spacecraft angle at time of exposure, and many others. Theoretically, it was possible to conduct an interactive search, tailor-made to a user's needs. Unfortunately, the system was fraught with problems, both hardware and software-oriented. In particular, our microfiche database was too large for the cartridge carousel, hence interactive searching was inconvenient due to the constant need to change cartridges. Today the system is used only rarely.

Our current efforts at putting together a visual display interactive retrieval system involve a videodisc and a more adaptable computer program. Since most of the original digital data are housed at the Jet Propulsion Laboratory, staff there are working closely with a videodisc manufacturer to convert the imagery onto videodisc. At the last meeting of the Regional Planetary Image Facilities Consortium a prototype disc was viewed on a 500 line television monitor by the members. Many of the images contain a data block which was totally unreadable on the 500 line system. The final version of this retrieval system will be recorded and displayed on an 800 line system, the higher resolution allowing the data block to be read. The projected time for this system to come on-line is late 1981.

Updated computer software, which will eventually command the videodisc, has been written by programmers at the Washington University data facility. This interactive program, called BIRP (Better Image Retrieval Program), is already on-line today at most of the data facilities. It is highly user-oriented, continually reminding the searcher of his/her search options. There are 20 engineering parameters (similar in nature to keywords) by which to search. Parameter values are different for each image, just as the information found in books on the same subject varies. In order to narrow a search down continually to a manageable number of quality images, a searcher presents the computer with additional parameters and value ranges, while the list of images fitting the selected parameter values dwindles from 50,000 (in the case of the Mars Viking Orbiter) down to a manageable 9. Clearly, tailor-made computerized searches are more efficient than manual methods of retrieval, and with the addition of a visual display system the retrieval will be even more effective.

Earth-based Telescopic Collection

The other major portion of the centre's collection is the 35 mm. telescopic imagery, utilized primarily by astronomers rather than geologists. Collection of these data began over ten years ago and continues today. Data for each planet are filed by date and time taken, the same way they are referenced by principal users. Imagery is logged into an inventory file just as it has been since this collection began.

Other user groups, such as publishers and students, require access to this valuable collection, usually with a particular subject in mind rather than time taken. Since subject access is unavailable, certain common reference questions and answers are kept by the library staff so that eventually a subject access file can be compiled. This effort is long-term and is dependent upon patron requests.

Slide Collection

The 35 mm. slides are used extensively by faculty and technical staff. This collection of 1,000 slides is currently arranged by subject and filed in binders. As the number of slides grows the present arrangement may need revising, for instance, the subject categories will need expansion and further subdivision to facilitate retrieval will be necessary. In addition, it will be preferable to store a large collection in a slide cabinet rather than binders. Such cabinets utilize space more effectively and are better for slide preservation.

At present, the slide sheets can be viewed on the light table. This method of selection and retrieval is most popular with the scientific users. In addition, a card file is maintained which includes 35 mm. colour photocopies of each slide arranged by subject. This file is necessary to determine exactly which slides are out on loan and which ones need replacing. Prior to the existence of this file the library staff was forever being called upon to describe which slides were out on loan in case they might be useful to the interested patron. The slide file has proved to be extremely useful for collection control. The cards contain several key words including the source for each slide, in addition to the photocopy. Further cataloguing is unnecessary for our purposes. Again, we ascribe to the philosophy: 'a picture is worth a thousand words'. Eventually, we hope to place this growing collection on videodisc for inventory and retrieval functions.

CIRCULATION AND PHOTO REPRODUCTION

The mission-oriented imagery does not leave the centre except for reproduction in our own darkroom. Photographs and film are simply too vulnerable to circulate. Though these data are not originals they are expensive to replace. The earth-based collection is treated in the same way, the only difference being that this collection *is* composed of originals. The library staff is very security conscious, locking the facility whenever it is unattended. No problems relating to theft have occurred at the centre to date.

The 35 mm. slide collection may be borrowed for the duration of the lecture for which the slides are needed. Records of these circulating slides are kept for control purposes. On several occasions slides have been lost; however, this is to be expected, and duplicates are available.

Since the centre provides ample work space for patrons, we receive very few requests to remove imagery from the room other than the slides. As for copying of images, our in-house darkroom serves the photo reproduction needs of the scientific community. Non-scientific users, on the other hand, are referred to NASA photo contractors where pictures can be obtained for a nominal fee. All our imagery belongs to the public sector, so we do not have copyright considerations to contend with at the centre. Our darkroom personnel would be overwhelmed by the added stress on their resources resulting from outside user requests.

CONCLUSION

Use of the collection by segments other than the scientific community continues to grow. School teachers, students, publishers, and amateur astronomers are frequent visitors. The RPIF Consortium is expanding also with the addition of two facilities which will open in the next several years. The inclusion of videodiscs at the facilities will certainly enhance our service capacity and the continued success of this pioneering effort depends on our ability to serve the public. The Space Imagery Center has come a long way from its early beginning in cardboard boxes.

REFERENCE

1   Weinstein, R A and others *Collection, use and care of historical photographs.* Nashville, Tennessee, American Association for State and Local History, 1977.

23

Professional Institutions: Architecture

Robert Elwall

INTRODUCTION

Professional institutions are normally obliged by the terms of their charters to provide for the continuing education of their members. This means the provision of library facilities, and many institutional libraries have become the major collections in their subject field and key links in the library and information network — the Royal Institution of Chartered Surveyors (RICS), the Institution of Civil Engineers (ICE), and the British Architectural Library (BAL) of the Royal Institute of British Architects (RIBA) all fall into this category. Most restrict services to their members; a few like the BAL make their services freely available to all.

Most of these institutional libraries choose to ignore visual documentation altogether — the RICS, the Institution of Mechanical Engineers, and the Royal Town Planning Institute are but three examples. Why is this? Firstly, many are 19th-century creations housed in buildings not designed to accommodate the new media. Secondly, the attitude still persists that the library's sole obligation is to the printed word. Thirdly, these institutions are today in a period of crisis, especially where membership is voluntary and not statutory. The library is inevitably the first to suffer and, within the library, it is the so-called 'fringe' area of picture provision that is hardest hit. Even in a field such as architecture and its allied arts — construction, engineering, planning — where the whole basis of communication is preeminently visual, the picture that will emerge is one of piece-meal achievement and *ad hoc* solutions rather than any coherent policy.

PHOTOGRAPHS AND SLIDES

Writing of the debt of architects to photography in 1867, E W Godwin said:

> As it is impossible that they should visit a tithe of the places where the best examples of ancient art are to be seen, they must be, for the most part, dependent upon the copies which are brought to them, and if these are not accurate — embodying the spirit as well as the form — it will be small wonder if their work, whilst pretending to be founded on the past, is utterly lifeless, and at fault in nearly every particular.[1]

Photographs are an indispensable aid to the study of architecture. Besides their didactic value, expressed in the quotation above, they often represent the only record of buildings subsequently destroyed or altered beyond all recognition. The evidence of a large photograph, too, can often reveal much information hidden in book or periodical illustrations. As Picton has said, 'Architecture is mediated by the photographer.'[2]

Despite the upsurge in interest in photographs as documentary sources, the concomitant rise in their value, and the close historical ties between architecture and photography, it is remarkable how few established collections there are. Why is this? Lack of staff and funds are the two reasons normally proffered. A third reason seems to be that photographs have become the poor relations of slides — a sign, perhaps, of the age of shared experience in which we live. The Architectural Association has a fine slide library, and both the Landscape Institute and the ICE have small collections. Photographs do, however, have the advantage that they are easy to refer to and allow comparative studies to be made on the spot.

The BAL possesses an immensely valuable archive of 60,000 photographs which has never been systematically organized or made fully accessible, despite the proven demand for such a collection. There is very little duplication of material held by the National Monuments Record (NMR) which is the key architectural photographic archive. The bulk of the BAL's collection is post-1945 and the NMR does not collect material after this date. It is difficult to see how the BAL can call itself the national architectural repository without an organized photographic collection to stand alongside its unique archive of books, manuscripts, and drawings. If corrective measures are not taken soon it will become just another historic collection as lack of organization deters would-be donors. Of course, donation is not the best way to build up a collection, especially as many architects regard the camera primarily as an advertising instrument. An established collection would, however, become the natural focus for donations which are increasingly multimedia in form, and the principal repository for the large number of photographs which other institute departments acquire during the course of their work.

A tentative start has been made to fulfil these aims. For the first time the collection has been housed altogether in one place although space prevents this being in close proximity to other library materials and renders closed access inevitable. The latter point is especially unfortunate with commodities like photographs which lend themselves to browsing, but it does allow them to be filed by a simple running number, thus permitting donated collections to retain their integrity — often a condition of deposit.

Retrieval is possible by means of a card catalogue by architect, location, subject, and photographer. The rise of architectural photography as a discipline in its own right has rendered this last imperative. The subject approach is provided by verbal subject headings akin to those used by the BAL's Architectural Periodicals Index. This has the advantage of familiarity for both users and staff and would facilitate any later transference of the photographic index to the Architectural Periodicals Index's computer base.

The NMR has the considerable advantage of being financed by the Department of the Environment. This enables it to employ its own photographic staff to record extant buildings of interest to scholars, and those threatened by destruction. Its collection of 1,000,000 photographs is open access and arranged topographically. There is, however, virtually no cross-referencing by architect or by subject — the sheer size of the collection prevents this. Prints are mounted with linen hinges on 12 × 10 inch cards cut to fit the NMR's box files. These cards have subject and location noted at the foot and, on the verso of the print, the subject, photographer, copyright holder, date photographed, date received, and negative number are all recorded.

Unlike the BAL, the NMR holds a high proportion of negatives which, for safety reasons, are stored separately from the prints. They are stored in four main sequences according to size. Within these sequences the arrangement is further broken down into years. Accession numbers are recorded on the margins of the negatives which are housed in glassine bags within outer manilla pockets. The projecting flap of each pocket is used to note number and subject and these are then housed in steel cabinets. Temperature is maintained at around 15°C.[3]

The case of the BAL is typical. Lack of staff, funds, and space are all factors inhibiting the development of institutional photographic collections. How can this situation be ameliorated and the burgeoning public interest be satisfied? There are two hopeful signs. The first is the willingness of the British Library to provide funds; both the Royal Commonwealth Society and the Royal Anthropological Institute have received substantial grants. The second is the establishment of the National Photographic Centre at Bath which, hopefully, will act as a spur to further advancement.

ARCHITECTURAL DRAWINGS

Architectural drawings may permit unique insights into the gestation of buildings, or, alternatively, they may illustrate visionary or unexecuted schemes. In either case there can be no denying their crucial role as source material for the study of architecture. The British Architectural Library Drawings Collection (BALDC) is the largest and most comprehensive of its kind in existence, with over 250,000 drawings ranging from the 16th century to the present day. The emphasis is mainly on British architects but there are important collections of continental drawings, such as the Burlington-Devonshire collection of drawings by Andrea Palladio, and the Drummond-Stewart collection of Italian baroque stage designs. The collection is housed in Portman Square but remains an essential part of the BAL.

Acquisitions policy is governed by three main factors: first, the collection is the national archive in its subject field; second, finance; third, user demands.

No other archive collects architectural drawings at a national level. The Victoria and Albert Museum collects selected decorative drawings, and the NMR measured drawings. The BALDC does not seek to compete with these, nor with the National Monuments Record for

Scotland which has over 100,000 Scottish drawings. The fact remains that, almost by default, the BALDC has had to assume national responsibilities and this largely accounts for the underlying philosophy of collecting first and worrying about storage and organization later. This is surely the only policy a national archive can pursue, especially if, by this action, drawings are saved from destruction or dispersal.

Lack of adequate finance for the purchase of drawings means that acquisition by purchase must be extremely selective. It is likely that forays into the salerooms will be further curtailed in future as the market value of drawings escalates. Thus, a great deal of reliance is placed upon gifts and, indeed, the bulk of the collection has been amassed in this way. There remains a heavy dependence upon the generosity of donors, especially as firms are now actively being asked to donate drawings.

It has always been a sound library dictum that acquisitions policy should be related to user demands. Yet these remain difficult to assess and even harder to anticipate. Since drawings were first collected with the inception of the institute in 1834, bewildering changes in taste, and in the way in which architectural drawings have been used, have made it extremely dangerous to sail too close to the prevailing wind.[4] In the 19th century drawings were used primarily as exemplars; the rise of the Modern Movement which eschewed 'styles', and sought to make architecture, in some way, an autonomous expression of the *Zeitgeist,* saw practising architects neglect the collection; the rise of architectural history,[5] strongly allied to the growing conservation movement, turned the collection into an internationally recognized centre for the study of architectural history.

There are signs now, with the demise of the Modern Movement, that the wheel has turned full circle. Students are once again turning to the study of the old masters, and practising architects appreciate the importance of the collection when they are involved in restoration work, since the existence of plans and drawings obviates the need for fresh surveys to be undertaken. Perhaps the change in taste is best illustrated by the whittling down of the Lutyens office collection of drawings in the 1950s from 80,000 to a mere 3,000, with the discarding of many working drawings, little valued then but highly prized today. This has left a mark on acquisitions policy to this very day. While quality and usefulness remain factors in deciding what to accept, gifts are now seldom refused and drawings seldom discarded. Quantity can, after all, be a very potent weapon in the battle for extra staff and funds.

The bewildering variety in the size and format of architectural drawings makes storage a major problem. Some drawings are framed; most are filed in solander boxes, horizontal or vertical plan chests, bound into volumes, or mounted in albums. In addition there are numerous sketchbooks. Lack of funds prohibits the adequate housing of many drawings, and there is no air-conditioning or humidity control. There is a desperate need to store less heavily used material elsewhere. The justifiably cautious approach to discarding means storage problems are intensified. Late 19th and 20th-century drawings were often produced in great bulk — successful dynastic operations like that of Alfred Waterhouse could produce as many as 100,000 drawings. Unpredictability of intake is a major problem affecting not just storage but the whole range of the collection's work.

The main problem with storage, however, is the physical location of the collection itself. The growth of the collection and the lack of space at the RIBA headquarters made the move to Portman Square inevitable. While this has enabled the collection to forge its own identity, it has the disadvantage that drawings have to be studied in isolation from other library materials. This is a severe handicap for both readers and staff.

Retrieval of drawings is by means of a printed catalogue, most of which has now been published.[6] There is also a card catalogue which includes both those drawings in the published catalogue (but in less detail) and those acquired since the volumes went to press. The main entry is under the name of the architect but there are additional entries under place and broad subject.

The cataloguing of drawings is both lengthy and arduous. Often dates, attributions, and locations have to be established — perhaps from careful study of the nature of the design; perhaps from the draughtsman's style; perhaps from the nature of the paper itself. Frequent recourse is necessary to external documentary sources. Since the collection is virtually unique, staff have pioneered techniques in this field.[7]

The importance of detailed cataloguing cannot be overstressed. Since the drawings are effectively housed in closed-access conditions retrieval is possible only through the catalogues. The aim should thus be to provide as much detail as possible to prevent unnecessary handling of fragile and irreplaceable material. The printed catalogue is excellent in this respect, but shortage of staff and funds, and the huge backlog of accessions, mean that it has become increasingly necessary to resort to what can only be euphemistically described as 'economical cataloguing'. The drawings are not treated as individual items but as blocks, with the result that both readers and staff are obliged to have more recourse to the drawings themselves than would otherwise be necessary. A good catalogue is a key conservation tool.

Again with conservation, lack of funds and space prove to be inhibitive factors. There are no facilities for an in-house conservationist and it is expensive to use the services of a body like the India Office. What is really needed is an organization in this country akin to the Committee for the Preservation of Architectural Records in the United States which acts as a clearing house and coordinating body, encouraging the proper storage, cataloguing, and conservation of architectural drawings. The Americans seem to be more kindly disposed towards their architectural patrimony.[8]

In 1978 the NMR and the BALDC launched a joint appeal to discover the whereabouts of architectural drawings and to save from destruction the vast number decaying in a plethora of places, ranging from developers' offices to local magistrates' courts. The aim was to establish a central index to the location of all significant pre-1940s drawings in Great Britain. Those in danger would then be saved by the BALDC for the nation. The results were disappointing, but the need for some kind of union catalogue still remains.

The BALDC does all it can to make its unique archive accessible to the nation and to bring architectural drawings to the attention of the public. It has its own exhibition gallery — the Heinz — one of the few galleries in the country devoted solely to architecture. Material is also lent for outside exhibitions and there is an active publishing and micro-filming programme based on the collection's holdings.

With the RIBA supporting to the best of its ability the less glamorous but more essential tasks on which collections like the BALDC depend, the BALDC has shown how much more can be done through the imaginative pursuit of sponsorship — viz. the Heinz Gallery — and through the generosity of donors. Without these the collection could not survive, yet both are insecure foundations on which to build. Will the generosity of donors, for example, continue in the harsh economic climate, or will more drawings find their way into the salerooms? Already the fragility of indefinite loan arrangements has been exposed by the recall of valuable material. If this were to happen on a large scale, key collections would be split up and, perhaps, rendered inaccessible to the general public. The BALDC clearly shows the paradox of an archive trying to fulfil a national role by preserving Britain's heritage of architectural drawings, while relying upon the exiguous resources of a private institute. The case for a large injection of public funds would appear to be incontrovertible.

FILMS AND SLIDES/TAPES

> Architecture's immobility makes it the natural complement of the movie-camera. The basic architectural experiences — standing in a space, looking around, walking along a corridor — find their equivalents in the screen frame, in the panning shot (the camera turns its head) and the tracking shot (the camera walks forward or backward).[9]

Architecture and the film are closely linked. They both use and misuse one another. The film has used architecture as a visual metaphor from the tortured expressionism of Caligari to the cold austerity of neorealism. In turn, architecture and the construction industry have realized the crucial role of film, whether it be exploitative — to promote certain building products and services, as an aid to marketing — or educational and an aid to training.

The vital role film has to play is underlined by the growing number of finding aids. Chief among these is the BISFA *Film guide for the construction industry*[10] which details over 800 films as well as slide packages and slide/tape programmes. The editors have drawn heavily on the *British national film catalogue*[11] to produce an invaluable guide arranged in basic UDC order, with an alphabetical title index and list of distributors. Other aids include the British Universities Film Council's *Audio-visual materials for higher education*[12] and the British Library's *British catalogue of audiovisual materials.*[13] Additionally there are, of course, many catalogues produced by government departments, research associations, commercial bureaus, etc. to help librarians keep abreast of what is available. Chief among the producing bodies in architecture and construction are the Cement and Concrete Association, the Commonwealth Association of Architects, the National Building Agency, Diana Wyllie Ltd, and Pidgeon Audio Visual.

The ICE holds monthly meetings to show the latest films on building services and materials, and its library has a collection of fifty 16 mm. films available for hire to its own members and to organizations and lecturers interested in the work of professional engineers. The collection has been acquired entirely by donation and this is now slowing down. No funds are available for purchase or repair. Donation means that the films are more of a commercial than an educational standard but, despite this, educational institutions are the chief borrowers.

It is important to remember that although institutional libraries do not have the means to collect film material, they are only part of the total information network that exists in such institutions, and often other departments, especially press offices, have much closer links with developments in this field.

CONCLUSION

We have seen that as far as professional institutions are concerned, even in an area where 'seeing is believing' is an established maxim, the printed word still holds sway. It is difficult to see, given the limited resources at their disposal, how their record on visual documentation will improve without either outside help or increased cooperation.

REFERENCES

1 Godwin, E W 'On the photographs taken for the Architectural Photographs Society for the year 1866' in *RIBA Transactions* 17 1866-7. 91.
2 Picton, Tom 'The craven image or the apotheosis of the architectural photograph' in *Architects' Journal* 25 July 1979. 176.
3 For further details see Cooper, Nicholas 'The national monuments record' in *Journal of the Society of Archivists* 3 (6) October 1967. 296-8.
4 For an analysis of the historical development of the collection see Richardson, Margaret 'The RIBA Drawings Collection 1834-1978' in *Architectural Design* 48 (5/6) 1978. 384-6.
5 *c.f.* Watkin, David *The rise of architectural history.* London, Architectural Press, 1980.
6 Under the general editorship of Jill Lever and published by Gregg Press the following volumes have so far appeared: *A, B, C-F, G-K, L-N, O-R, S, Colen Campbell, Jacques Gentilhâtre, Inigo Jones and John Webb, Edwin Lutyens, Alfred Stevens, Antonio Visentini, C F A Voysey, Wyatt family, Pugin family, J B Papworth.* Forthcoming: *Scott family, T-Z, and Palladio.*
7 See Lever, Jill 'Cataloguing the RIBA Drawings Collection' in *Architectural Design* 48 (5/6) 1978. 395-9.

8   See Lever, Jill 'If it's Friday it must be Calgary: report on the storage, cataloguing, and conservation of architectural drawings in North America' in *RIBA Journal* December 1978 499.

9   Durgnat, Raymond 'Movie eye' in *Architectural Review* March 1965. 186-93.

10 British Industrial and Scientific Film Association *Film guide for the construction industry, including information on slide packages and slide/tape programmes.* Lancaster, Construction Press, 1979.

11 Published quarterly by the British Film Institute with annual cumulations.

12 British Universities Film Council *Audio-visual materials for higher education 1979-80.* 4th ed. London, British Universities Film Council, 1979.

13 British Library, Bibliographic Services Division *British catalogue of audiovisual materials.* London, British Library Bibliographic Services Division, 1979.

24

Learned Societies: The Architectural Association

Elizabeth Dixon

The Architectural Association Library is the library of a learned society and is open only to members.

HISTORY

The Architectural Association was founded in 1847 mainly by architectural students who were dissatisfied with the existing office pupillage system of 'picking it up', and wanted to club together to form a school of design which they might attend after office hours: 'By union, we might possess a spacious school, a good library, casts, drawings and in fact everything necessary for study.'

Although the formation of a library was included in the earliest proposals for the new school of design, it was not until April 1862 that the Architectural Association Library was established as the first architectural lending library. Students had insisted that they should be allowed to take books home — 'which cannot be done at the libraries of the British Museum, the Royal Academy or the Royal Institute of British Architects.'

MEMBERS

The AA is an international organization with members and students from more than 90 different countries. At least 90% of the users of the library are students of the AA School of Architecture but, unlike other academic libraries, it also serves the 3,000 members of the association who include distinguished architects and architectural historians and writers. In addition it supplements, with its more extensive bibliographical resources, the service provided to AA members by their own office libraries.

The Architectural Association School of Architecture now has over 470 students and 175 academic, administrative, and technical staff. The school has a first year, an intermediate school (years two and three), and a diploma school (years four and five). The Graduate School — Planning Department, Building Conservation and Graduate Design courses — is open to students with first degrees from all parts of the world. There are also General Studies, Communications, and Technical Studies service units, a workshop, an Extension Studies Department and a summer session.

ARCHITECTS' USE OF ILLUSTRATIONS

Illustrations are a form of communication: they include paintings, photographs, slides, microfiches, films, videotapes, drawings, diagrams, charts and histograms, critical path networks, and graphical presentations in and from computers. They are important to the architect because they provide rapid communication of complex information directly and concisely. Architects use drawings to communicate technical information to builders and other technical colleagues. They use photographs to illustrate designs to clients and to record information for legal, technical, or public relations purposes.

Increasingly, architects use computers for the accumulation, storage, transmission, and dissemination of information. The computer cannot only store and give out information in words, figures, or 'drawings', but can be fed with words and figures which are then manipulated by the computer to be returned as plans, sections, or elevations of buildings, or parts 'designed' within the parameters contained in the words and figures.

Architects refer to illustrations for a variety of purposes: for information about a design which can be conveyed most clearly and succinctly in the form of plans, sections, and elevations; for spiritual regeneration and inspiration — buildings have an emotional effect and may trigger off an architect's creative process or influence the mood and feeling of his own design; to find the best graphic technique for the effective presentation of design proposals and to check a technical detail of design data.

Architects rely to a large extent on visual stimulation. Much of an architect's knowledge of architecture comes from illustrations since he can visit only a small proportion of the world's buildings. One of the ways in which architects use illustrations is by flicking through books and journals to build up a memory store of images. As much as 98% of an architect's 'reading' time may be spent in looking at illustrations and he may recall images which he has seen, perhaps years earlier and, regardless of the scale or function of the originals, relate them to work he is currently doing or use them to handle design problems. The library collection may be used as a source for the book or journal in which he originally saw the illustration.

Many architects build up a picture collection of their own photographs. Usually they are not just beautiful views of buildings but examples of architectural details, the way buildings are set in the landscape, and examples of good (or bad) handling of design problems in which they are interested or which they find difficult.

Architectural students have not had time to acquire memory banks of images or their own picture collections and tackle a design project in various ways. An untalented student may spend days in the library looking at examples of the particular building type in books and journals and then weeks cobbling together the parts which impress him from several schemes into a whole. A talented student will start by looking at examples of the building type specified in the project but will go on to look at other building types which, irrespective of their scale and purpose in relation to his own project, may stimulate his creative abilities.

An architectural teacher will often refer his students to the library to study a design in which the architect has found a satisfactory solution to one of their design problems, rather than seem to take over the design himself.

A practising architect may use illustrations to present his proposals to a client. Examples of the style, finishes, and architectural details that he proposes to use will be selected from any source — photographs, trade literature, professional journals, advertisements, colour supplements — and mounted on boards or made into slides for the presentation.

An architectural writer uses books and journals as a source of illustrations for his own publications. The illustration credits will lead him or the librarian to the sources of the pictures he has selected which may include publishers, journals, organizations, architectural firms, architectural photographers, and slide collections.

Architects are concerned with the manipulation of three-dimensional space. Because they understand more about a design from its plans than from pages of descriptive text, illustrations must be an integral part of information provided for them. Plans, sections, and elevations are so essential to the understanding of architecture that most architectural books and journals are illustrated and in the AA Library it is the book stock and periodicals files themselves which form the illustration (and information) collection. The classification, catalogue, information files, and indexes are all employed to exploit the collection in its dual role.

BOOK STOCK

Since 1862, the association library collection has grown from 10 books and a few journals to over 23,000 volumes. The library's subject specializations are Architecture, Planning, Landscape Design, Building Construction, and Structures but the subject range is wide and includes art, interior design, furniture design, typography, management, sociology, economics, surveying, ergonomics, and climatology.

Until the 1960s the library's book fund was very small and many volumes were acquired through the generosity of AA members and of authors and publishers. Most of the library's small collection of rare and early works were presentations or bequests from members; they include some beautiful volumes of Scamozzi, Palladio, Serlio, Rossini, Piranesi, Repton, and Chambers. The library's growing Modern Movement collection has several of the original *Bauhausbücher* and works by Le Corbusier, Gropius, Berlage, Mendelsohn, and Bruno Taut. There is also a special collection of material concerned with the association and its members.

ORGANIZING INFORMATION

Catalogue

Books and pamphlets are classified by the Universal Decimal Classification System which provides access through the catalogue to information from various aspects and starting points.

In addition to the author and classified catalogues and alphabetical subject index, there are two sections of the classified catalogue in which information may be traced through the architect or place concerned. In the 92: BIOGRAPHY section added entries are filed alphabetically by architects' names for material on the lives and works of architects which is housed with books on the architectural history of the period. There are extensive files of added entries under the UDC common auxiliaries of place (1/9) for material shelved at the main subject, so that material on the statistics, economics, planning, architecture, topography, and history of a particular village, town, county, or country is brought together in the catalogue. There is an alphabetical place index to this section.

CI/SfB

The material in the Technical Library is divided into what is essentially a loan collection of books on building construction and structures classified by UDC, and a reference collection of some 5,000 trade catalogues, pamphlets, and periodical articles arranged by CI/SfB.

The second revised UK edition of *Samarbetskommittén för Byggnadsfrågor,* the Swedish classification scheme authorized by the International Council for Building Research Studies and Documentation (CIB) for the filing of construction industry information, issued by the Royal Institute of British Architects in 1968, is used with an alphabetical strip index to subjects.

The CI/SfB filing system has four tables with subdivisions:

Table 0 — built environment, e.g., planning, landscape, building types
Table I — functional elements, e.g., walls, roofs, services
Table 2/3 — construction forms and materials, e.g., bricks, tiles
Table 4 — abstract concepts, administration, and requirements, e.g., insulation, maintenance.

In addition to the subject index to the CI/SfB, alphabetical card indexes to products, manufacturers, and trade names are maintained.

Information Files

The AA Library has a growing collection of over 38,000 periodical articles, mainly on building types, architectural history, planning, and the work of individual architects. The material is divided into two sequences of articles, published before and after 1970, and is classified by subject with an alphabetical strip index. These files provide an invaluable source of illustrated information which is easily accessible. Members of the library in search of instant information on, for example, the design of a particular building type, can sit down with the books and pamphlets on the subject and a box file of recent periodical articles collected conveniently together. For further information the various periodical indexes and files of journals can be checked.

Perodical Indexes

The most up-to-date index to current literature is the library's own card index in which the 250 journals currently received are indexed selectively by subject. Cards are filed for three years until superseded by printed indexes. This index has the advantage of referring to information which is immediately available in the library.

The AA Library also has a cumulative index to the *AA Quarterly* which so far covers the period from 1915 to 1975, although it is hoped eventually to back-index to the first issue of 1887. The index has an author/name index, a subject/title index, and entries under Book Reviews, Exhibitions, Letters, and Obituaries.

The most comprehensive index to periodicals is the *Avery index to architectural periodicals.*[1] The second revised edition of 15 volumes indexing 460 journals was published in 1973 and supplements covering two-year periods are issued. The first two supplements added 63 titles to the index. The Avery Library of Columbia University has indexed all major architectural periodicals systematically from 1934. Several important American journals and the British *Architectural Review* have been indexed back to their first issues.

The immense importance of the *Avery index to architectural periodicals* as an information tool lies in the fact that it is a world survey (excluding non-western alphabets) from 1934 or earlier, arranged in one alphabetical sequence of subject headings and authors, with a name entry wherever an architect is recorded in an article, thus reducing the search time involved. It covers architecture, archeology, the decorative arts, interior design, and the architectural aspects of city planning and housing. The type of illustration in each article is included in the entry. It cannot, however, be used for tracing current information.

The *Avery index* and the *Avery obituary index* provide access to the principal, and frequently the only, printed source of information about the many architects not included in architectural histories, encyclopedias, and biographical dictionaries and not the subject of a monograph.

The *Avery obituary index of architects and artists* (1963) indexes the obituaries in newspapers and architectural periodicals from 1934. Four important American journals — *American Architect, Architectural Forum, Architectural Record,* and *Progressive Architecture* — have been indexed back to their first issues and the *Journal of the Royal Institute of British Architects* and its preceding *Transactions* back to 1865. Architects' dates of birth and death and the inclusion of a portrait in the obituaries are noted in the index which is one of the quickest ways in which to trace either. The obituaries are often excellent summaries of an architect's life, works, and publications.

The *Architectural periodicals index*[2] of the British Architectural Library is issued quarterly with annual cumulations and is most useful for tracing recently published material, as annual volumes are not cumulated at present. About 300 periodicals on architecture, planning, building, and landscape design are indexed selectively under subject headings with a names index. Entries note the types of illustrations in the articles. This index also has the advantage of referring to material with a known location in Great Britain.

The *Architectural index* (Colorado) is issued annually and indexes 12 American journals. Entries are arranged alphabetically under subject headings with additional entries for names (grouped under 'Architect or Designer') and for locations, states, and foreign countries.

Construction references (The Property Services Agency of the Department of the Environment) is issued twice a year. Details of books, pamphlets, and periodical articles on the construction industry are arranged by the Universal Decimal Classification Scheme. Entries include useful summaries of the contents and note the inclusion of illustrations.

Housing and planning references (US Department of Housing and

Urban Development) is issued six times a year. A selection of books, pamphlets and periodical articles are listed under subject headings with an author index.

General indices to the first forty-two volumes of 'The Studio' 1893-1908[3] covers the early issues of this illustrated record of fine and applied art and is an important source of illustrations. The index of artists lists Josef Hoffmann, R S Lorimer, E L Lutyens, C R Mackintosh, and other architects of the period and the classified index includes headings for architecture, ceilings, chimneypieces, exhibition interiors, and stained glass.

Catalogues of Drawings

The *Catalogue of the Drawings Collection* of the Royal Institute of British Architects 1969[4] is arranged alphabetically by architects' names, with indexes of people, collections, and places, and is profusely illustrated. The collection is principally of British drawings from the late Gothic period to the 20th century but includes the work of many foreign architects. This scholarly work is much more than a location index to the drawings: it is a valuable source of information because entries include dates of birth and death, biographical details, buildings designed, books published, and bibliographies, in addition to details of drawings. Some volumes provide additional material, e.g., the volume on the Wyatt family lists drawings in other collections and has a pedigree of the family with some portraits.

A catalogue of architectural drawings of the 18th and 19th centuries in the library of Worcester College, Oxford compiled by H M Colvin[5] describes a collection mainly of British architects, with more drawings by Hawksmoor than by any other architect. There are indexes of buildings and persons. An appendix of additions and corrections to this work was published in *A catalogue of the drawings by Inigo Jones, John Webb and Isaac de Cas at Worcester College, Oxford* by John Harris.[6]

John Harris's *A catalogue of British drawings for architecture, decoration, sculpture and landscape gardening 1550-1900 in American collections*[7] contains an index of names, places, building types, and details. The eight charming books in the RIBA drawings series[8] profusely illustrated with drawings from the RIBA Collection, edited by John Harris, are now out of print. The titles are *Garden buildings, Georgian country houses, The Greek revival, Indian architecture and the*

British, Monuments of commerce, Royal buildings, Stage designs, and *Victorian churches.*

ENQUIRIES

In the AA Library the need for illustrations, particularly plans, elevations, and sections, is implicit in most requests for information. There is no separate collection of illustrations in the library apart from a small file of portraits of architects, as the book stock, journals, and information files are used as combined information and illustration sources. There is a separate AA slide collection.

Enquiries cover a wide range: Decimus Burton's design for the tent room of the villa in Regent's Park; plans and interiors of San Giorgio Maggiore; the development of shopping arcades; the design of Centre Point and the Post Office Tower; plans, elevations, and sections of the Court Theatre, Vienna; a plan of the design for the gardens at Stowe; recent developments in hospital design; a recent housing development at Bristol Road, Edgbaston; the design for the Italian Pavilion at the Paris Exhibition of 1925; uses of space under motorway arches; Dudok's Hilversum Town Hall; the design of nursery schools; the construction of circular stairs; the design of cylindrical space frames; trade literature and technical information on applications of timber cladding; the development of leisure centres; and illustrations of prefabricated joints.

The sequence of search through the AA Library's resources for the design of a marble doorway by Grinling Gibbons for Blenheim Palace would be:

1 The information files of 40,000 classified periodical articles to look for Blenheim Palace in the large collection of articles on country houses arranged alphabetically by name.
2 The alphabetical place index of the catalogue to find the place number for Blenheim.
3 The Topographical section of the classified catalogue to find the reference to David Green's book, *Blenheim Palace,* classified at 72.034.7(425.72B):728.82.
4 The index and list of illustrations in this book.
5 The alphabetical Biography section of the catalogue to note the titles,

class numbers, and locations of books about Grinling Gibbons and Vanbrugh (the architect of Blenheim).

6 The indexes etc. of these books.

7 *Catalogue of the Drawings Collection* of the Royal Institute of British Architects.

8 The *Avery index of architectural periodicals* to trace entries listed under GIBBONS, G and BLENHEIM Palace.

9 Scan these articles in the periodical files.

10 The subject index of the catalogue to trace the class numbers for country houses, doorways, and domestic architecture.

11 The classified catalogue to note authors, titles, and locations, and also the main class numbers of material on country houses and domestic architecture shelved at the architectural history period number.

12 The place index and Topography section of the catalogue and shelves for material on the architecture and topography of Oxfordshire.

(The doorway is illustrated in David Green's *Blenheim Palace* and there is a more detailed illustration in an article on Grinling Gibbons at Blenheim published in *Country Life,* May 1949.)

Portraits

Portraits of architects can be traced in the AA Library's small file of portraits; in the information files which contain thousands of articles about individual architects; in books by or about the architect (including the dust jackets of books by current architectural writers); through the *Avery index to architectural periodicals* or the *Avery Obituary Index*; in Ware's *Short dictionary of British architects* which is illustrated; in histories of architecture and, for 20th-century architects, Dennis Sharp's *Sources of modern architecture: a bibliography* which has many useful photographs and drawings of architects. Enquiries may also be referred to the Royal Institute of British Architects, the National Portrait Gallery, London, and the Scottish National Portrait Gallery.

EXHIBITION CATALOGUES, TRADE LITERATURE, ADVERTISEMENTS

Catalogues of architects' work and of international exhibitions are obviously valuable, and the importance of also filing catalogues issued by stores and manufacturers, brochures, and a selection of older trade literature can hardly be overemphasized. Advertisements in older journals can be as useful as the articles and as many advertisements as possible should be retained in bound volumes. Old Ideal Home Exhibition catalogues and stores' and manufacturers' catalogues provide more interesting pictures of interiors and furniture of their period than books and journals. The early catalogues issued by Crittall Windows Ltd showing examples of the use of their windows in building may at the same time provide illustrations of buildings which were not written up in the journals of the period.

ILLUSTRATED MATERIAL

Modern

The Courtauld Institute illustration archives 1977[9] are issued in two formats: a paperback edition of 80 pages of illustrations and a looseleaf edition of 160 single sheets of illustrations. The illustrations are taken from the collection of over a million photographs in the Witt and Conway Libraries of the Courtauld Institute. The four archives are: Cathedrals and monastic buildings in the British Isles; 15th and 16th-century sculpture in Italy; Medieval architecture and sculpture in Europe; and Late 18th and 19th-century sculpture in the British Isles. The archives will be published in parts over several years.

A very small selection from the great number of modern illustrated volumes might include: the 'History of world architecture' series, edited by Nervi;[10] 'The Pelican history of art' series;[11] Pevsner's *A dictionary of architecture;*[12] *Who's who in architecture from 1400 to the present day,* edited by Richards;[13] Harris's *Illustrated glossary of architecture 850-1830;*[14] Fletcher's *A history of architecture;*[15] *Key monuments of the history of architecture,* edited by Millon;[16] Sharp's *A visual history of twentieth-century architecture;*[17] and *Contemporary architects,* edited by Emanuel,[18] which provides a biography, a list of works, a bibliography, a critical essay, and an illustration of the work of each of the 600 architects mentioned.

Nineteenth Century

The Architectural Association issued the first volume of a massive collection of sketches and measured drawings in 1867. The drawings in the three series of *AA Sketch Books* include the work of C L Eastlake, G E Street, Detmar Blow, William Burges, and W R Lethaby. The decorated title pages themselves provide a pictorial survey of changing fashion in design from 1867 to 1923. Topographical and subject indexes were compiled but the volumes, although interesting, are heavy and unwieldy to use as an instant source of illustration of a building or architectural detail.

The Architectural Publication Society's *Dictionary of architecture...*[19] has eight illustrated volumes and three volumes of plates. Its long articles are still useful and include architectural terms, details, architectural descriptions of places, biographies, and bibliographies.

Gwilt's *An encyclopaedia of architecture, historical, theoretical and practical...*[20] is illustrated with wood engravings. Later editions were edited by Wyatt Papworth and covered the history, theory, and practice of architecture with sections on material, construction, joinery, perspective, proportion, building types, a list of architects and their works, a list of publications, and a glossary of terms. The illustrations are mainly small.

Loudon's *An encyclopaedia of cottage, farm and villa architecture and furniture...*[21] is a first edition with over 2,000 illustrations, mainly wood engravings, with nearly 100 lithographs. It includes designs for cottages for labourers, gardeners, and bailiffs; for farmhouses, country inns, and parochial schools; and for villas and their lodges, stables, kennels, dairies, garden structures, and furniture.

Parker's *A glossary of terms used in Grecian, Roman, Italian and Gothic architecture*[22] has one volume of text and two volumes of woodcuts giving examples of arcades, arches, buttresses, capitals, corbels, fonts, ironwork, mouldings, tiles, vaults, and some 132 varieties of window.

Stuart's *A dictionary of architecture*[23] — 'adapted to the comprehension of workmen'. This dictionary also ranges widely and the illustrations include the Acropolis, the Amphitheatre of Verona, Balbec, carpentry, Nubian architecture, and Saxon mouldings.

Viollet-le-Duc's *Dictionnaire raisonné de l'architecture française du*

*XIe au XVIe siècle*²⁴ is a very important dictionary with long, illustrated articles. Its coverage includes sculpture and the applied arts.

Surveys of Buildings

The Greater London Council's *Survey of London,* 1900-²⁵ is an architectural and historical record of buildings, copiously illustrated from photographs, prints and measured drawings. A card index has been compiled in the A A Library to provide quick access to the information and illustrations in the survey. The 39 volumes issued so far have been indexed by buildings, streets, and districts.

The Royal Commission on Historical Monuments (England) *Inventories*²⁶ contains detailed descriptions of monuments arranged by parish, lavishly illustrated with plates, plans, and maps. There are similar volumes for Scotland and Wales.

Colvin's *The history of the king's works*²⁷ is an illustrated history of public works from the Middle Ages to 1851, while 'The buildings of England' series edited by Pevsner²⁸ describes almost every worthwhile building in each county, is also illustrated, and includes indexes of architects and places. 'The buildings of Ireland' series, 'The buildings of Scotland' series, and 'The buildings of Wales' series follow the same pattern.

REFERENCES

1 Avery Memorial Architectural Library, Columbia University *Avery index to architectural periodicals.* Boston, Masssachusetts, G K Hall, 1973. 15 vols. and supplements.

2 British Architectural Library *Architectural Periodicals Index.* London, Royal Institute of British Architects. Quarterly with annual cumulations.

3 *General indices to the first forty-two volumes of 'The Studio' 1893-1908.* London, Sims and Reed, 1979 (reprint of 1902 and 1909 editions).

4 Royal Institute of British Architects *Catalogue of the Drawings Collection.* London, RIBA, 1969. 20 vols. and general index vol.

5 Colvin, H M (compiler) *A catalogue of architectural drawings of the 18th and 19th centuries in the library of Worcester College, Oxford.* Oxford, Clarendon Press, 1964.

6 Harris, J (compiler) *Catalogue of drawings by Inigo Jones, John Webb and Isaac de Caus at Worcester College, Oxford.* Oxford, Clarendon Press, 1979.

7   Harris, J *A catalogue of British drawings for architecture, decoration, sculpture and landscape gardening 1550-1900 in American collections.* New Jersey, Gregg Press, 1971.

8   Harris, J (editor) Harvey Miller, 1976-. 'The RIBA drawings' series. London, Country Life, 1968.

9   The Courtauld Institute of Art *Courtauld Institute Illustration Archives.* London, Harvey Miller, 1977-. Four archives published in parts.

10 Nervi, P L (editor) 'History of world architecture' series. London, Academy Editions, 1979-80. 14 vols.

11 'The Pelican history of art' series. Harmondsworth, Penguin Books, 1953-. 44 titles.

12 Pevsner, N et al. *A dictionary of architecture.* 3rd rev. ed. London, Allen Lane, 1980.

13 Richards, J M (editor) *Who's who in architecture from 1400 to the present day.* London, Weidenfeld and Nicolson, 1977.

14 Harris, J et al. *Illustrated glossary of architecture 850-1830.* London, Faber, 1966.

15 Fletcher, B *A history of architecture.* 18th ed. revised by J C Palmes. London, Athlone Press, 1975.

16 Millon, H A (editor) *Key monuments of the history of architecture.* Englewood-Cliffs, New Jersey, Prentice-Hall; New York, Abrams (no date).

17 Sharp, D *A visual history of twentieth-century architecture.* London, Heinemann, Secker and Warburg, 1972.

18 Emanuel, M (editor) *Contemporary architects.* London, Macmillan, 1980.

19 The Architectural Publication Society *Dictionary of architecture...* London, Richards, 18[52]53-92. 8 vols. of text, 3 vols. of plates.

20 Gwilt, J *An encyclopaedia of architecture, historical, theoretical and practical...* London, 1842.

21 Loudon, J C *An encyclopaedia of cottage, farm and villa architecture and furniture...* London, Longman Rees etc., 1833.

22 Parker, J H *A glossary of terms used in Grecian, Roman, Italian and Gothic architecture.* 5th ed. Oxford, Parker, 1850. 3 vols.

23 Stuart, R *A dictionary of architecture.* London, Jones, 1830? 3 vols.

24 Viollet-le-Duc, E E *Dictionnaire raisonné de l'architecture française du XIe au XVIe siècle.* Paris, Bance, 1854-68.

25 Greater London Council *Survey of London 1900-.* London, GLC.

26 The Royal Commission on Historical Monuments *Inventories.* London, HMSO, 1910-.

27 Colvin, H M *The history of the king's works.* London, HMSO, 1963-.

28 Pevsner, N (editor) 'The buildings of England' series. Harmondsworth, Penguin Books.

Universities

Helen P Harrison

I n the field of education picture libraries are to be found at all levels, from schools to universities, with a wide diversity reflecting the needs of the particular users concerned. This section on education libraries deals in some detail with the situation in schools, colleges of art, colleges of education, and polytechnics. The character of picture libraries in universities is more varied than in many other educational institutions, ranging from the national collection of a deposit library such as the Bodleian Library, Oxford, or an archival collection as detailed in Smart *Archival libraries in the UK* (Section 2.17). Further variations can be found in the departmental collections serving particular faculties or subjects and some university collections are similar to the publishing house library described by Amosu (Section 2.37). The Open University. for example, represents a collection built up to aid the design department and the university publishing area.

Even within this one type of academic institution the range of picture collections is notable for its diversity. It would therefore be difficult to provide a representative description of a university library picture collection or even to survey the area adequately. This note is included to indicate the range of collections available without attempting to describe any one collection in detail. The reader is referred to those other sections of the handbook which provide samples of related collections for information on how to organize a picture collection.

University collections can range from the huge collections, such as those in the University of Texas, to the relatively small but significant collections devoted to one aspect or interest of the university, for example the Brunel material in Brunel University, UK. Further, the picture libraries may spread from the national deposit collections where a full photographic service is available of material held in the collections or departmental libraries, for example the Cambridge University Library, the Bodleian, and the Cambridge University Museum of Archaeology and Anthropology, to the consciously collected material maintained for research purposes only. The larger collections are often akin to national museums and established on a semi-commercial basis, supplying prints of material in the library from existing negatives or producing negatives on request. The British Museum and British Library act on this basis. The supply period is usually more leisurely than the commercial organization and hence the semi-commercial aspect of management.

The list of university collections would be considerably expanded if slides were taken into account, especially in art, architecture, and many science departments, notably geology and the life sciences. Also, departments of medicine have large collections of illustrations.

ACQUISITION

University libraries acquire picture material from many sources.

Photography of collections of special materials, manuscripts, and books in the deposit libraries is responsible for many of the largest collections of picture materials housed in university libraries. This usually means that a negative is made and retained by the institution for further printing on demand. Prints may well not be retained in the collection which becomes in effect a negative collection referred to by shelf number order as are the books; for example, the British Library uses this system.

Some large collections like the British Museum library may have their own photographic department and also allow certain agents to photograph the collections; for example, the firm of J F Freeman in London has a selective collection of negatives from the British Museum from which prints can be supplied to users. The British Museum retains copyright but Freeman acts as agent. Other large libraries do not find the same demand and have special arrangements with a local photographer to produce prints and negatives of material as requests are received.

Copyright remains with the library and the photographer in these cases is reimbursed by the user for materials and any facilities, fees or travel expenses.

Donation is another means by which university libraries acquire material. Special collections of material of particular relevance to the university, or of local interest, or where the owner of the material may have a special connection with the university, can all be donated. Sometimes special conditions are attached to these collections: they may have to be kept intact rather than spread through the other collections; an embargo may be placed on the use of the material for a period of time; or certain defined copyright conditions may apply. The university will then decide if the conditions are acceptable and receive or refuse the collection accordingly. In some instances a local firm may close down and the university acquire the material by donation; for example, the University of St Andrews in Scotland acquired the postcard archives of a local firm, Valentines. Brunel University has material relating to Isambard Kingdom Brunel and Nottingham University houses a collection of D H Lawrence material.

Purchase of whole collections or individual items is another form of acquisition. The items may have particular relevance to the local area or to the courses run by the university. Individual items may be purchased to supplement an existing collection or for a particular purpose.

Collections of illustrations may be created for use by particular departments, especially the art and design departments. In the case of the Open University, the activities of the publishing division have resulted in the library becoming a deposit and back-up service for material to be used in the course units produced by the University. The Open University library has a reference collection of photographs used in the course units and acquired by the activities of one group of the library staff who combine a picture research function with other library work. There is also a large collection of illustrative material acquired specifically to be used as a back-up service for the design department. This part of the collection is composed of non-photographic prints, such as book jackets, postcards, colour magazine material, and anything that might provide ideas for a designer. The collection provides a reference tool for in-house production rather than for outside users.

Acquisition

The organization and management of university collections is closely related to the type of user and the recognized function of the collection. The picture librarian in a university will first decide what the collection is trying to achieve and organize it according to the type of material and usage involved. No hard and fast rules can be given, but there are several examples scattered throughout this handbook which will provide guidelines for the university picture librarian.

26

Polytechnic Libraries

Valerie J Bradfield

'Books, duplicated and audio-visual materials complement each other in their contribution to teaching and research, and should be regarded as part of a unified collection.'[1]

W hilst not all librarians in polytechnics would agree with this policy statement, the view is gaining ground in many polytechnic libraries. Many librarians encounter difficulties when they approach the various picture collections with an eye to integration. The concept of an integrated 'learning resource centre' has been adopted at a number of polytechnics, notably Plymouth, Portsmouth, and Brighton, and full integration of materials is being actively pursued at a number of others. However, the picture collection, whatever form it takes, often has to remain apart from this integrated collection owing to its incompatibility, not only in form but in use, user requirements, and permanency.

To understand the status of picture collections in polytechnic libraries it is necessary to understand polytechnic development in recent years. Many criteria govern the choice of a policy and these must be considered. It is then possible to look at specific aspects of the management of picture collections with reference to the information gained from experience and from replies to a recent circular letter.

There is little literature to which the reader may refer. Most descriptions of specific polytechnic collections refer to the whole audio-visual unit or centre, or to a particular medium. None refers only to pictures but slides are well covered and many of Philip Pacey's remarks on 'Handling slides single-handed'[2] are relevant to the picture collection and indicate some of the problems involved. Tim Giles' description of non-book media in Leicester Polytechnic Library does not dwell on any one medium but indicates how the general approach is likely to be conceived.[3] This is all that refers specifically to polytechnic collections. A most useful guide for anyone in a polytechnic picture collection, however, is the relevant chapter by Anthony Coulson in the recent *Art library manual.*[4]

BACKGROUND

Some polytechnics have always existed under a similar name, such as the Regent Street Polytechnic which became the Polytechnic of Central London, incorporating several smaller colleges. The majority of polytechnics were formed by a process of amalgamation and/or absorption. In understanding the organization, problems, and future of picture collections this should be borne in mind. The component colleges had, and sometimes maintained, separate types of resource. The most prominent of these were the audio-visual or non-book materials. Sites are still diverse in some cases and collection development has remained localized. In other polytechnics all policies are centralized and unified.

Pictures tend to be essential tools in only a few subject areas. The art student requires, among other things, 'the widest possible range of visual references to the visible world, in a variety of forms'.[5] The art section tends to be that which has developed picture collections in polytechnic libraries. Some slide collections have been centralized and while they serve humanities, social sciences, science, etc., they tend to be predominantly art-oriented. Illustrations and photographs are often entirely aimed at the art and design student. The education student is the other primary user of picture material. This is often for classroom preparation and display. A wider variety of formats may be involved than in the field of art but the user's needs are similar.

Art colleges, colleges of education, and technical colleges have tended to be among the main ingredients in the creation of polytechnics. Few polytechnics have achieved complete centralization on one campus as the universities have done. This has been due to the many colleges involved and, hence, very dispersed sites. Sometimes 5, 10, or 15 miles may separate a polytechnic's campuses. In these situations the picture collections remain oriented to their own local users and are very often excluded from the new centralized systems. At Brighton all media and cataloguing are fully integrated, both in terms of shelving and on BLCMP, but the Art and Design Faculty picture collection is a separate entity on that site, as is that at the Education Faculty site. The reasons for such arrangements will become clear.

Many schools or faculties of education have maintained their collections, at least as far as pictures are concerned, as in the college of education days. Such collections are 'polytechnic' in name only and their features are described more properly in the section on colleges of education libraries (2.27). Their organization tends to reflect the teaching use and be quite dissimilar from art picture collections. This section will relate mainly to art and related picture collections except where there has been complete integration of library stock.

DEFINITION

Picture collections in polytechnics can cover all forms of audio-visual media but the ones which deserve attention are mainly those not on videotape or on microfilm, but which are maintained in hard copy as illustrations or print collections. Slides are pictures, and are well used, but they have been exhaustively treated elsewhere.[6] Few slide collections relate directly to the illustrations collections although some have supplanted the more cumbersome illustrations. It is feasible, for example, to photograph posters, etc. and to maintain the slides for display and selection, as at Leeds, thus reducing the wear and tear resulting from browsing through hard copy. But this demands viewing or projection equipment, time to do the filming, and many librarians also feel that slides are inadequate for browsing purposes.

Illustrations may be prints, postcards, or illustrations torn from journals and magazines. In fact, any picture which can be integrated into the collection — type specimens, even references to pictures in bound journals — may form part of such a collection. Illustrated encyclopedias and handbooks are essential back-up tools. Picture collections may include some 'special' materials, such as a fashion file including all types of fashion pictures and photographs. Type specimens and page-settings are maintained at Brighton Polytechnic. Teesside keeps overhead projection transparencies as part of its media collection — mainly for the lecturers. This was the only mention of such a collection in the replies received.

Some polytechnics admit to having no picture collections,[7] or only weak ones.[8] Art departments and education departments still maintain their own collections, especially of slides, as at Manchester or Coventry (Lanchester). Others have thankfully 'dumped' them onto the library. Few departments actually maintain picture reference files.

USERS

Who uses such collections and why? Unless well used, any labour-intensive function is likely to be axed in the climate of the early eighties. Alternatively, as we shall see below, more economical maintenance procedures must be sought. Staff often have a louder voice than students, although students may gain the greater benefit from such picture collections. Slides tend to be most heavily used by lecturing staff — as illustrations both central to and auxiliary to their lecture and seminar themes. Pictures tend to be resources for student project work.

Students flip through the illustrations collection for examples of a certain object or for examples of a particular artist's work. The latter, if currently in vogue, may not appear in books or even journal articles for a considerable time after the Sunday paper featured his work in a colour supplement (one of the prime sources of materials for illustrations collections). Some suitable illustrations can be difficult to find in books; for instance, a psychology student may look for a picture reflecting 'the human experience of aggression'; a graphic student may want a picture of a bulldozer or some other unlikely object. The picture collection should be organized to provide them quickly and easily. Its acquisitions should reflect its known users.

Some collections allow students to take illustrations away with them. This is the only option where they are to be subjected to certain destructive reproduction techniques. A constant supply is required and picture collections can sometimes provide this service.

Why not use a book or one of the picture encyclopedias? This is often the librarian's solution to locating pictures as he or she would locate information. Invariably, however, the pictures are not as current or as large as in many magazines or prints and enlargement is not always feasible. In using such tools one also has to be more specific — browsing is less productive and there is more extraneous material to be looked through.

Graphic design students are often heavy users of collections as a source of ideas as well as for illustrative material. The collection of advertisements at Preston is also used by the industrial design and business students studying marketing. The number of possible uses are myriad. In most instances pictures are auxiliary to their studies — a useful back-up resource if available, but not considered essential by all libraries.

COLLECTION POLICY

It may now be fairly clear that in most collections there is a definite issue policy which is fundamentally linked with the philosophy behind the collection. 'We let the students take what they want', is an unusual library policy but a valuable one in a self-renewing collection. It reduces the stock-editing required, built-in obsolescence is minimized, and turnover develops. Students may even contribute journals to be used. Why not let them take the pictures? The effort involved in implementing issue and recall systems is only justifiable where valuable material is concerned.

More than one collection is based on the philosophy that students can return pictures but may keep them if necessary. In these cases, naturally, no attempt is made to make the collection permanent — no mounting or cataloguing is done, the collection is self-indexing. Finance for staffing is often lacking and this is actually quite an economical method of maintaining a picture source file. Its drawbacks might include a dearth in certain fields owing to unforeseen demands from student projects. But in most courses work tends to be highly individualized.

Where an issue system exists, be it Brown, a book in which to sign for pictures, or even a computer issue system akin to that for books, then it is usual for this to reflect a collection which is well preserved, in which pictures are mounted, indexed if not catalogued, and of a high quality. Many may have been purchased and therefore be worth preserving. Only recently have a few libraries managed to maintain such a system.

Amalgamation has often had an adverse effect on the service provided. A few libraries maintain collections of prints but mainly in book or folio form.

The Brown issue system is used at Brighton for the collection of type specimens. These are expensive and need to be controlled but even so they suffer severe losses. Restricting use to the library would hinder the students trying to use them in design projects. The way in which material is likely to be used influences policy, not only in issues but also in acquisition and preservation techniques.

ACQUISITIONS

Before moving into the vexed question of storage and retrieval, a word must be said to indicate the sources from which pictures are acquired, since these are many and varied. As is so often the case they are governed by economics. Finance not only influences what may be acquired but also the staff available to select suitable pictures for retention, or for the student's needs. Selection is time-consuming if it is to be done well, especially if commercial sources are scanned and evaluated. These sources exist but are usually expensive since they usually necessitate a strict preservation and use policy. Posters and charts may often be purchased for the general picture collection but tend to be concentrated in education libraries. The commercial resources have been well described recently by A J Coulson in the *Art library manual*[9] as well as in Section 1.3 of this book.

Many picture collections acquire their resources 'gratis' as a matter of necessity. Purchased items may fill gaps but the majority of illustrations are culled from the many free sources. The Sunday newspaper colour supplements are invaluable, as are the many weekly magazines which are not stored for lengthy periods. In one library, staff bring in their old supplements for tearing up while the library copy is kept intact. Many magazines are unwanted after a couple of years and they provide a source of supply, hence the willingness to permit borrowing of the illustrations. Plates from discarded books may be removed for the picture collection — others, in more valuable books may be indexed to the source. Exhibition catalogues which are not to be permanently retained may be added to the collection, as well as the wealth of posters received, and sought, from exhibitions, manufacturers, and other free sources. The format of these presents special storage problems. Advertisements of all forms, but especially those from magazines and technical literature, are sources of original picture material.

Few librarians with responsibility for a picture collection could say that they have a systematic acquisitions policy. The number of acquisitions may fluctuate from month to month according to time available and suitability of material offered. One librarian-in-charge of a collection pointed out, 'I'll take anything that is offered to me (within reason).'

Where pictures are in the form of slides or photographs the story is rather different. Slides are acquired more frequently from commercial firms, usually in packages based on a theme. These can be located from audio-visual or subject-oriented journals and from publishers' lists which are regularly circulated. Staff often request sets. More frequently, the main source of these types of pictures is on-site duplication from staff slides, photographs, or books. Such collections mushroom quickly. Many art, art history, graphic design, and architecture departments have, for simplicity, lodged their overgrown collections in the library and continue to demand production of new materials 'in-house'. The North-East London Polytechnic has a photograph collection entirely produced at the polytechnic. As budgets for external spending are reduced this seems to be essential if collections are to be maintained.

Maintenance forms a part of the acquisitions policy. If a collection is to maintain its relevance, 'weeding' is essential. Pictures become dated and the point at which the out-dated becomes desirable from a historical point of view is a subject for debate. More usually, currency is maintained and the size of files regulated to balance, not only the picture collection, but the storage space it occupies. This, however, usually applies only to pictures in the form of illustrations. Slides and photographs have a greater tendency to accumulate, even though deterioration may render them useless.

STORAGE

Integrated collections have already been mentioned. Where they exist, storage is in a format compatible with other stock. For example, slide sets are housed in book-like wallets. More frequently slides are found housed in the transparent hanging Rogers holders in a traditional filing cabinet, as are many picture collections. Most pictures, purchased or torn from magazines, will fit into a foolscap manilla folder in a four-drawer filing cabinet. They are then easy to extract singly and are preserved in fairly good condition and also accommodate many users at once since only one or two files need to be removed by each user.

If pictures are mounted the options for storage increase. However, this implies a greater degree of permanency than many collections possess. Leicester Polytechnic's pictures are mounted on stiff card before filing and Preston is at present 'up-grading' its collection by mounting most of the pictures. On the other hand, Brighton is ceasing to do this as the merger with the Polytechnic has reduced the time available for maintaining what is regarded more as a collection of ephemera. A mounted collection of pictures is convenient to use and browse through. It still suffers from heavy usage and is time-consuming without necessarily securing an adequate return.

ORGANIZATION FOR RETRIEVAL

Within any storage medium organization needs to be as simple as possible for the users. Return on effort involved has to be borne in mind when deciding on the organization in a picture collection. Not one polytechnic catalogues individual pictures. In some, however, posters, charts, and sets of slides or pictures of a permanent nature are catalogued — all those seen recently have been added to the computer-produced book catalogue, e.g., using BLCMP. However, the present concern is with general picture collections rather than such special items.

There are two basic methods of organization which will be encountered: those using classificationi and those using subject headings, with or without individual indexes. At Leicester, the UDC classified sequence of illustrations is not separately indexed, rather the subject index to the main library stock serves this purpose. The slides reflect the same organization by UDC but have their own highly specific subject index which can be used for the illustrations also. A similar scheme is found at Preston where Dewey is used.

However, the use of subject headings to organize the illustrations files is more usual. Few collections use a recognized set of headings — most have their own in-house authority file, developed from a standard such as Sears, but also reflecting the courses in the polytechnic. They are usually self-guiding and almost always very easy to follow. Some of the variants worth mentioning are the name files by illustrator, painter, photographer, etc. In these, at least some work representative of the artist is gathered together, although other examples may be scattered through the collection by topic. The same is done with fashion, organized primarily by period and country. Advertisements are likely to be kept apart and filed by the product or service which they represent, e.g., banks, domestic appliances, etc. The typeface collection already mentioned is alphabetically organized under names of typefaces. All these are reflections of user requirements.

Great detail in subject heading lists or indexes is not usually required, although some are more developed than others. Many reflect those used in related slide collections which have been written about elsewhere.[10] The subdivisions under a heading such as 'Painting' will logically be by country, period, and artist, for example. Headings, such as 'Animals', 'Cinema', 'Computer', and 'Entertainments', are common. Most such systems, if not self-indexing, have a subject-heading list with cross-references available nearby. However, an exception to this is the ingenious, if more time-consuming, looseleaf index to Brighton's picture collection. The subject headings refer to the illustrations but the Dewey number is also given, so that books in stock which are well illustrated may also be located. They also reference any pictures in certain of the illustrated journals which are bound and located adjacent to the pictures. The illustrated encyclopedias are also close by. At present the scheme includes *The Studio, Illustrated London News,* etc. and there are plans to extend it to *National Geographic* and *Fortune.* This has been chosen in preference to tearing up copies of these since they are required for their content in other ways, and some are historically important. The access to pictures which is achieved is very wide in its scope and an indication of its value is the intensive use made by students of both the collection and the index.

Ingenious methods of retrieval, especially using micro-images, have been put forward by commercial picture collections. They are rarely to be found in the polytechnics where time and money are at a premium in a different way. The recommendations for college of education resource centres put such suggestions forward but those collections which are now part of polytechnic libraries have not adopted them.[11]

CONCLUSION

The librarian wanting to start a picture collection needs first to be aware of the market — it will almost always lie in the visual arts sections of the polytechnic. Use will develop among students — slides are used more by staff. The simple and easy-to-use collection is not only the most advantageous to the user but also to the librarian. Some filing cabinets, with suspension files and manila folders, are the sum total of essentials. Mounting is an extra, a luxury, or 'up-grading' as one librarian put it. Simple subject headings are always the easiest; a note on the front of the cabinet can explain any internal subdivisions. Alternatively, automatic preselection can be used: subject heading files; fashion files, by period; artist and sculptor files, by name; advertisements, by product; type, by typeface name; architecture, by country then date and architect. The thought must be done at the inception to achieve simplicity of use — the greater the initial effort in planning, the less there is to do at the input stage.

Looking at other collections can be helpful but polytechnics must tailor their own to suit the courses at that institution. Criticism from users is rare but usually centred on complex systems which the user finds hard to understand, even though he may praise its capabilities when light finally dawns. But it is impossible to generalize since, not only are all users different, but not all polytechnics have a collection of pictures. The information used here has centred on those with known collections or problems, especially Brighton, Bristol, Coventry (Lanchester), Leeds, Leicester, North London, North-East London, Central London, South Bank, Thames, Portsmouth, and Teesside.

It may be politic to let ARLIS have the last word as it is the association most concerned with art libraries in polytechnics. Its statement on art libraries in polytechnics dealing with resources states, '...exploitation of [the] stock by art students and lecturers has been and is being hindered and frustrated by: the loss of physical convenience; the destruction of a helpful order; the replacement of an intimate, comprehensible "learning environment" with a vast, impersonal maze.'[12] The picture collection and its maintenance is very much part of the environment and may well suffer at the hands of administrators. Many polytechnic picture collections may founder, or their prospects of development be limited, as a result of current trends towards centralization and uniformity.

REFERENCES

1 Library Association *Library resource centres in schools, colleges and institutions of higher education: a general policy statement.* London, Library Association, 1973. Quoted in Fothergill, R and Butchart, I *Non-book materials in libraries: a practical guide.* London, Bingley, 1978. 1/.
2 Pacey, P 'Handling slides single-handed' in *Art Libraries Journal* 2 (3) Autumn 1977. 22-30.
3 Giles, T 'Non-book media in Leicester Polytechnic Library' in *The Audiovisual Librarian* 4 (4) 1978. 10-15.
4 Pacey, P (editor) *Art library manual.* Epping, Bowker, 1977.
5 'Art libraries in Polytechnics: an ARLIS statement on the provision and exploitation of library resources for art and design courses in polytechnics' in *Art Libraries Journal* 4 (1) Spring 1979. 38.
6 Books and articles are too numerous to mention but there are useful bibliographies in:
— Bradfield, V J *Slide collections: a user requirement survey.* British Library, 1976. (R&D Report 2609.)
— Croghan, A *A bibliographic system for non-book media.* 2nd ed. London, Coburgh Publications, 1979.
— Fothergill. op. cit.
7 The Polytechnic of Central London has only a few slides of photographers' work and a small collection of architectural slides.
8 The Polytechnic of North London admits to little other than a few general slides.
9 Pacey. op. cit. Chapter 24.
10 Bradfield. op. cit.
11 Fothergill, R *Resource centres in colleges of education.* London, Council for Educational Technology, 1973. (Working paper no. 10.)
12 Art libraries in polytechnics. op. cit. p. 45.

27

Colleges of Education

Pamela Shenton

Colleges of education exist to perform two functions: firstly, to instruct students in the skills and techniques of teaching, enabling them to practise these in classroom situations; secondly, to offer students the opportunity to study subjects of their own choice to an advanced level. Most colleges of education offer a wide range of full-time courses, in-service courses, and post-graduate courses leading to diplomas and degrees. In Britain today few colleges of education exist alone. Most have become faculties of education within polytechnics or turned into colleges of higher education offering degrees and diplomas in fields other than teaching, e.g., hospital administration, social work, counselling.

AIMS OF COLLEGE OF EDUCATION PICTURE LIBRARIES

To equip the student for teaching practice as well as his/her own studies, library materials within a college must cater for the needs of 5 to 18-year-olds as well as for those of advanced scholars and their tutors. Visual aids in the library should augment the resources of the main book collection, making material available for:

1 the use of students on teaching practice outside college;
2 the use of students in the course of their own studies within the library;

3   the use of lecturing staff within college for demonstrations and lectures.

CENTRALIZATION AND COOPERATION

It is important that the collection of visual aids in a college library represents all that is available within the college. If materials are centralized students need go to one place only to seek resources. Where small departmental collections exist these are often casually supervised, poorly administered, and not kept up to date or 'weeded' consistently, nor are they available at certain key times, such as evenings.

The establishment of links between teaching staff and librarians is important. It is from them that librarians can obtain advice and help when selecting new materials. Teaching staff know what is needed and how best it can be used in schools. It is a good idea if the librarian responsible for non-book materials is able to visit some schools to see how visual aids are used and become aware of any practical problems involved in their application. Where space allows, classes of children could be invited to visit the library and examine its resources, working closely with the librarian and student teacher on a particular project.

It is useful if the librarian has some idea of the equipment available in local schools in the way of slide projectors or film viewers. It would be pointless to assemble a vast collection of cassette loop-films for loan if it is found that no local schools possess equipment to view them. Before building up a collection of non-book materials, therefore, a brief survey of users' needs could be conducted by means of a duplicated sheet on which students indicate the types of hardware found in their schools and any preferences regarding practice materials. This helps the librarian to provide not only what is most wanted but also that which can best be exploited.

MATERIALS AND THEIR LAYOUT

Materials most likely to be encountered in college library pictorial collections are wallcharts, posters, pictures, cuttings, postcards, portfolios, photographs, folders of archival material, slides, film strips, cassette loop-films, and overhead transparencies. It is important that careful consideration be given to the design of an area of the library to house such materials. They will probably be stored together with audio aids and equipment, which are not being considered here.

Integrating visual materials and books on the same shelves is not as helpful as many advocates claim. Although it can be argued that such an arrangement shows all that the library has on a particular subject, there are many practical problems involved, including:

1   material not housed in a separate area is difficult to supervise;
2   expansion and growth in subject fields and introduction of new subjects cannot be predicted and can be more easily accommodated in a purpose-made area;
3   consultation can be difficult — book shelves can stand close together without hindering the extraction and consultation of a book, but it is not as easy to unroll and examine a large chart in a confined space;
4   examination of some materials requires access to hardware which needs to be close at hand — not practically possible among rows of shelves;
5   consulting and finding material other than books seems to generate considerable noise and excitement amongst students!
6   it is slower and more difficult to refile material if it is spread all over the library;
7   there is a greater risk of theft.

Where space makes integration imperative, problems can be eased by making use of book-shaped storage packs designed to house multimedia, such as those produced by AVLS,[1] although it can be expensive to acquire them in large numbers.

Ideally, pictorial material should be stored in a good-sized, well-lit room which has black-out facilities or viewing booths. There should be a good display area and the whole appear inviting and bright. There could be a few tables and chairs, or carrels, for study, but maximum floor space is needed to avoid congestion. Any blank walls can be used to display wallcharts and posters or for projecting film strips. In addition, a collection of catalogues and leaflets relating to non-book materials should be at hand, both to assist the librarian in selection and to demonstrate to library users the wide range of educational materials on the market.

Charts, pictures, slides, and other illustrations vary in format and therefore need to be filed in a variety of storage units. These could be arranged back to back in the centre of the room, to help spread out the collection and relieve the congestion which inevitably occurs at teaching practice time. The greater the floor space to accommodate stock and students, the easier it is at peak periods. An ideal size for an audio-visual room is no less than 50 × 25 feet. (The Didsbury College of Education Library was built in 1973 on a 24-foot module, and the Audio Visual Room covers two modules which have proved adequate for the storage, preview, and display of materials.)

Cabinets, vertical files, and plan chests are needed to house pictures and charts. Large waist-high tables placed near them are useful, facilitating easy consultation of wallcharts, large pictures, and folders of material which can be spread out and studied with ease. The perimeter of the room could be used for listening and viewing booths. Electrical equipment fixed here will eliminate danger from wires and flex which can cause problems if projectors, etc. have to be pulled into the centre of the room.

Storage of material needs to be convenient and flexible to permit easy interfiling of new topics. To ensure safety, both from fire and theft, and to help keep items dust-free, units should be metal and one should be able to cover, or close and lock them.

SOURCES AND ACQUISITIONS

As there is no bibliographical control on pictures one has a hard task finding what is available and must be on the look out at all times for new items, such as sets of postcards, slides and pictures seen on visits to galleries, or posters in gift shops. In order that direct purchases can be made it is desirable that a portion of the financial allocation be available as petty cash. (This point is also taken up in Section 1.12).

A collection of catalogues listing non-book materials for purchase needs to be maintained for stock selection purposes, such as those produced by:

1   non-profit-making organizations with educational aims, e.g. EFVA;[2]
2   commercial organizations with educational and recreational aims, e.g. Athena Reproductions Ltd, Ladybird Filmstrips;
3   societies, e.g. Railway Preservation Society;

4   galleries and museums, e.g. National Gallery 'Colour Prints Catalogue';
5   book publishers, e.g. for posters of literary characters, portraits of authors and illustrators.

Further publications to consult regularly for reviews of new items include:

1   curriculum journals, e.g. *Education in Chemistry;*
2   newspapers publishing occasional materials, e.g. *The Sunday Times;*
3   journals which are entirely visual, e.g. *Pictorial Education;*
4   newspapers and journals reviewing educational books and materials, e.g. the 'Resources' section of *The Times Educational Supplement.*

A number of books written by specialists and aimed at teachers list materials in defined subject fields:

Handbook for geography teachers[3]
Handbook for history teachers[4]
The teacher's handbook for social studies[5]
Audio-visual materials for American studies[6]
The geographer's vadecum of sources and materials[7]
World religions: a handbook for teachers[8]
Where to find photos of the developing countries.[9]

It is possible to acquire a number of excellent charts and posters free of charge from organizations such as the Post Office. Colourful advertising posters can be had from firms, galleries and museums; foreign materials from embassies and tourist offices; local materials from libraries, record and publicity offices. Further sources of free materials are to be found in *Treasure chest for teachers.*[10]

It can be costly to prepare pictures for use. They may need edge-binding, laminating, or mounting and allowance needs to be made for the cost of stationery involved.

CRITERIA FOR EVALUATION

Some criteria need to be laid down for evaluating material. There are poor and bad visual aids just as there are books, so how does one select?

1 Avoid artists' impressions when photographs can be used. This is particularly important in film strips — it is hardly worth the time and trouble to set up a projector in order to see a drawing of an erupting volcano: it could as easily be drawn on a blackboard.
2 If an object is drawn, the scale should be stated clearly.
3 Accurate use of colour is important especially in pictures of natural objects.
4 Pictures for children should be bright and colourful and not too busy. The centre of interest should be obvious without too many distracting details.
5 We live in a multiracial society and must avoid materials which can cause offence. We also live in an age of equality and need to avoid pictures which demonstrate games, jobs, activities solely for boys or for girls.
6 All pictures should be prominently and clearly titled.
7 Maps should be printed on stout paper and show a date, title, scale, projection, and a key to symbols used.
8 All materials should be visually attractive and stimulating, technically accurate and up to date, and should aid the learning process.

Although it is not always possible to preview materials before ordering, many organizations will accept orders on a sale-or-return basis or supply items on approval. The EFVA[2] catalogues are helpful here as they are well annotated and critical.

It is important to have some long-term plan for the collection and once a workable maximum has been achieved materials should be consistently weeded out and repaired. It is just as important to have a discard policy for visual aids as it is for books. For example, an outdated film strip on African towns, though physically perfect, needs to be checked. Certain shots, such as close-ups of buildings, could be cut out and mounted as slides, the rest thrown away.

When attempting to satisfy a subject request it is useful to know for what purpose a student requires a picture, so that material of the appropriate level can be sought. A teacher of infants will require brightly coloured material showing familiar objects to attract the attention of his pupils. He will also require pictures to encourage speech or movement, such as story-telling wallcharts, without captions. Charts can help to encourage the development of standards, like personal hygiene, road safety, or care of pets, amongst older children. Secondary-school children can benefit from charts which help to illustrate principles, for example, a lever mechanism, or those which summarize and consolidate: how a bank works, events of the reign of a monarch, for instance.

CONSERVATION OF MATERIAL

Because of the ephemeral nature of pictorial material and the fact that most of the collection is available for loan, special consideration must be given to processing. To preserve large pictures from wear the edges can be reinforced by edge-binding. Don Gresswell[11] manufacture machines plus tapes in various colours for this purpose. Colleges could adopt a colour code and separate pictures into groups, for infant, junior, and secondary levels. Laminating entire charts with plastic film is expensive but may be worth while for flimsy items, especially cuttings which are irreplaceable. Reinforced holes can be punched on all corners to avoid pin damage.

Postcards can be effectively used when mounted on 8 × 5 inch cards for ease of handling. Information from the back of a postcard should be neatly transferred to the mount. A dry-mounting press can be used to mount postcards, photographs, and flimsy newspaper cuttings (see Section 1.5). Machines are now available which laminate as well as dry-mount and manufacturers include Ademco Ltd.[12]

MAKING RESOURCES

The value of internally generated materials and packs should not be overlooked. Materials made and used for teaching purposes within a college could be added to the library stock for the benefit of students and staff and, in such cases, it is important that concise guidelines on the use of the material and the level at which it is aimed accompany all items.

Within a college, the ideal is a resource centre where materials can be made, housed, and borrowed. Failing this, the audio-visual area of the library could have a corner for the making of materials. A typewriter can be made available to students for use in the preparation of work sheets, handouts, titling on work cards, etc. A collection of mapograph rolls enables them to produce multiple copies. In this process a rubber roller with a map outline in relief on the surface is attached to a special holder. The roller is inked and applied to paper or pages of exercise books. The Mapograph Company[13] offers a wide range of map outlines, biological and botanical diagrams, historical characters, clock faces, as well as ink pads in various colours. Boxes of templates help students prepare their own charts and work cards. Popular topics include domestic and wild animals and geometric shapes and they can be purchased from most suppliers of educational materials.

CLASSIFICATION, CATALOGUING AND STORAGE

Unlike books, non-book materials do not lend themselves to side-by-side storage on shelves. The librarian must seek alternatives for their arrangement and a variety of storage units will need to be purchased. Within these distinctions a systematic arrangement is needed and a decision must be made whether to use a flexible classified order, such as Dewey, subject headings, or a numerical arrangement in a fixed location.

Pictures may have to be filed in different sized units according to their format. Within each unit arrangement will be determined by the classification chosen. Pictures, being ephemeral, are adequately catered for by subject headings, needing one simple card index for users and a looseleaf flexible system of authoritative subject headings for the cataloguer. All items should carry a class number or subject heading and an accession number, prefixed by a letter or symbol to denote the unit into which they are to be filed. This information is best placed on the back of the picture so that it does not interfere with the pictorial content. Pictures can be assigned prefixes and filed in the following manner:

— PF: folio-sized pictures and pamphlets, stored in pockets suspended in metal drawers.
— PL: large pictures, stored in suspended pockets in lateral filing units;
— PR: rolled charts, stored in 'Planstore' honey-combed filing units.[14]

All the files should be frequently and clearly guided. Where limitations of space necessitate closed access, an index on cards with an accompanying slide or photograph of each chart is helpful to users.

A collection of pictures adequate for a college of education could easily add up to 20,000 items. In such cases cataloguing every item is neither practical nor necessary. Obviously some stock record needs to be kept and for this purpose an accession register could be maintained. A single-line entry including details of accession number, prefix, class number or subject heading, date of acquisition, title, price, and source will serve to identify any lost item which has to be charged for and replaced.

Other types of material of more substance and permanence, like slides, may be best if filed in a fixed location in numerical order. Slides are best stored in plastic pockets suspended from rods in metal drawers; by holding the sheet up to the light or placing it over a light box 24 slides can be viewed at one time. Film strips can be conveniently stored in metal filing units of 15 drawers, each 2 inches deep, with metal dividers to facilitate easy retrieval. Accompanying teaching notes can be filed separately in pamphlet boxes stored on top of the file or on nearby shelves. Film, or cassette loop-film can be stored on edge on shelves, in numerical order. Overhead transparencies should be put in cardboard mounts and filed on shelves in box files.

Materials on the same subject separated by fixed location arrangements can be brought together by a card catalogue, or by a COM (Computer Output on Microform) catalogue which has the advantage of being cheap and can be placed in many locations within a library. Also useful are the print-outs, in subject order, which can be made solely of audio-visual items. In the case of card catalogues, materials of sufficient interest in academic studies should be included in name and subject files with the books, as well as in a catalogue of purely non-book material. Both these arrangements imply that the same scheme of classification is used for visual material as for books.

Where it is not practical to catalogue every pictorial item, certain important charts, folders of archival material, large kits, and all projected materials warrant it. The Anglo-American rules for cataloguing non-book materials can be used for this purpose, and will ensure some standardization for cataloguing the entire library stock.

LIBRARY INSTRUCTION

Prior to their first teaching practice, students should be given a course of library instruction. They need to be guided on the layout of the pictorial section and shown examples of all types of material. Printed guides can be issued detailing the arrangement of files and catalogues, the classification system used, symbols and their meanings, issue methods, and loan arrangements. Further lectures could explain how to select and evaluate materials, and copyright restrictions. A demonstration of materials of different types on particular themes could be given, with the materials varying according to the age group of the children which the students will teach. It is also useful to work with the tutors who are planning curriculum work with groups using library materials.

ISSUE AND RETRIEVAL

A loans policy needs to be formulated before any materials leave the library. Most non-book material should be available for loan, subject to certain precautions being taken, such as the issue of protective roll-cases for charts and portfolios for pictures if students do not have them. Security of material is important if items are to sustain several issues and the journeys to and from college and school. Certain items, like expensive film strips and reproductions of art works, connected with students' study, could be made available for reference in the library or for short loan to tutors, for use within the college.

Issue methods used in colleges vary. Issue of non-book material may be by the same system as the books, but this will present problems in systems where a charging card is attached to an item on issue. A separate system can be evolved for the pictorial material. Books usually have slips or date labels to indicate the return date to the reader. It is not easy to attach pockets or date labels to non-books and in colleges it may not be necessary, as materials are normally issued for the duration of a teaching practice. Material issued for short loan could be placed in boxes or envelopes to which date labels have been attached. Most colleges favour the double or triple 5 × 3 inch slip for non-book material issue, filled in by the reader. One slip could be filed in reader order and the other in class order if desired.

It is advisable to issue non-book material away from the crowded book issue desk, especially at peak periods. This inevitably means a separate file for non-book materials. If it is felt that details of all loans should be in one sequence, and the system chosen makes this possible, coloured cards or slips for non-book material can help to speed retrieval.

References

Some restriction on the amount of material borrowed at one time will have to be made. Students should be encouraged to keep returning materials and borrowing new ones to ensure a healthy circulation of stock. This will also increase issue statistics — vital evidence when an increase in funds is requested and has to be justified!

REFERENCES

1 Audio Visual Library Services, 11/12 Powdrake Road, Grangemouth, Stirlingshire FK3 9UT.
2 Educational Foundation for Visual Aids, 33 Queen Anne Street, London W1M 0AL.
3 Long, Molly *Handbook for geography teachers.* 6th ed. Methuen, 1974.
4 Burston, W H and Green, C W *Handbook for history teachers.* 2nd ed. Methuen, 1972.
5 Mathias, Paul *The teacher's handbook for social studies.* Blandford Press, 1973.
6 Gidley, M and Goldman, D *Audio-visual materials for American studies: a guide to sources of information and materials.* University of Sussex, Centre for Educational Technology, 1970.
7 Hancock, J C and Whitely, P T *The geographer's vadecum of sources and materials.* 2nd ed. G Philip, 1978.
8 Cole, W D *World religions: a handbook for teachers.* The Community Relations Commission, 1977.
9 Harvey, Adam *Where to find photos of the developing countries.* Centre for World Development Education, 1978.
10 *Treasure chest for teachers: services available to teachers and schools.* Schoolmaster Publishing Company, 1978.
11 Don Gresswell Ltd, Bridge House, Grange Park, London N21.
12 Ademco Ltd, Lincoln Road, High Wycombe, Bucks.
13 The Mapograph Company Ltd, 440 High Road, Chiswick, London W4 5TT.
14 'Planstore' manufactured by J H Randall & Son Ltd, Paddington Green Works, London W2.

28

Colleges of Art

Rodney Burke

Art education at college level in the United Kingdom takes place not only at colleges or schools of art and design but also at universities, polytechnics, and colleges of further and higher education. Qualifications range from vocational certificates and diplomas to degrees and higher degrees. The standard qualification is a BA degree, normally preceded by a one-year 'foundation' course.

Libraries for art students take many forms including sections of general college libraries, polytechnic 'learning resources centres', departments of university libraries, and specialized art college libraries. Often, resources are split between main libraries and separate sections catering for the specialized needs of the art school. The following remarks apply to the art sections of all these kinds of library, for their aims are similar despite differences in size, emphasis, and funding.

Picture collections cannot be treated in isolation for visual imagery is the subject and raison d'être of art libraries and their collections as a whole are concerned with images. The majority of the pictures in an art library are to be found in books and periodicals and any search for images must include these media, as well as those usually thought of when picture collections are mentioned. A distinction might be made between two main classes of use and the various media listed in approximate order of usefulness under each heading:

Art historical reference	*Source-image reference*
Books	Books
Periodicals	Periodicals
Exhibition catalogues	Cuttings
Slides	Postcards (of all kinds)
Photographs	Published reproductions
Microfilm	Printed ephemera
Microfiche	Microfiche
Cuttings	Microfilm
Published reproductions	Exhibition catalogues
(including postcards)	

In each case, the images in the library are substitutes for original sources. In the case of art history the original sources are paintings, drawings, original prints, works of sculpture, works of architecture and such like. For design studies they are designed artifacts generally. Basic to both art and design are natural objects and creatures of all kinds. A picture of virtually anything may be required for source-image reference. Certain classes of original material are often included, for instance original prints, drawings, and printed ephemera, but these form a minor part of the collections. The librarian attempts to create not a museum, but something akin to Malraux's 'Museum without walls'.

ART HISTORICAL REFERENCE

The difference between approaching books and periodicals from a picture librarian's point of view and that of an ordinary librarian is that the picture librarian is concerned with individual pictures. This entails classification of the individual picture, whereas librarians normally classify books by subject at *summarization level* without analysis of the contents below that level. Although theoretically essential, in practice it is too time-consuming to index the individual illustrations in books and periodicals. The only practical method is to use published indexes to illustrations. (In the case of illustrations of works of art these are usually designated 'reproductions'.) Unfortunately, there are as yet few indexes of reproductions and they are far from exhaustive. The *Art Index* 1930-[1]

includes references to individual reproductions and is the most widely used aid to retrieval. Some other useful periodicals indexes are: *ARTbibliographies MODERN*,[2] *Art Design Photo*,[3] *Index to art periodicals* (Art Institute of Chicago),[4] *Art in 'Life'*, by Jane Clapp,[5] the *Periodical index* from Avery Memorial Architectural Library,[6] *Design Abstracts International*, for which English and American editions exist,[7-8] *Art in 'Time'*,[9] by Patricia Havlice, *Répertoire d'Art et d'Archéologie*,[10-11] and *Répertoire International de la Littérature de l'Art (RILA)*.[12]

Books devoted to one artist or to a very specific kind of art are of course classified accordingly and, if in turn the book's own index is consulted, a particular reproduction may be found quite quickly. Unfortunately, many pictures may be found only in more general works. The main indexes to reproductions in books are: *Index to art reproductions in books*,[13] *Contemporary art and artists: an index to reproductions*,[14] *Photography index*,[15] *Index to reproductions of American paintings appearing in over 400 books...*,[16] and the ALA *Portrait index*.[17]

When the required reproduction has been found a copy is often required. This may be a photocopy, photographic print, or colour slide. These are usually made within the college by a photographic service department or a media resources or educational technology officer. Of course, suitable reproductions might exist already in the picture files or slide collection of the college. These collections are built up partly by the addition of copies made from books for staff, partly from photographic material originating from commercial and other sources, and sometimes from donations.

Users other than lecturers seldom require slides, which are difficult to handle and view, but to the lecturer they are so important that slide collections are often run by the art history teaching department rather than the library. Art historians require from 10 to 40 slides for each lecture or seminar. It takes some time to assemble each lecture set from individual items and teaching staff may wish to keep them in arrangements which suit their personal requirements. Some lecturers go to considerable trouble to provide slides themselves and require them to be available when needed. Widespread lending is not desirable when slides may be needed for lectures at short notice. Such a departmental collection may not adequately meet the needs of the college as a whole, but college librarians are naturally reluctant to provide parallel resources for a relatively small demand, which is usually met by the department allowing access for reference purposes.

Whether the slide collections are part of the Art History Department, the library, or form a separate service department, it is important that they are managed by well-trained specialist slide librarians; few colleges have satisfactorily graded posts as yet, although some universities and polytechnics have shown the way. Slides need careful storage and regular replacement as their dyes are impermanent and they are easily damaged. Mounting and labelling are major tasks, as are keeping records of the numerous loans and refiling. Nationally there is a shortage of loan facilities for slides so it is more important for each college to have a comprehensive collection than is the case with books, for which adequate interlibrary loan facilities exist.

Slides are usually kept in classified order, either with a separate index/catalogue or with the file of slides itself forming the index/catalogue by means of the slide labels and companion cards carrying the same details as the slide labels which are interfiled with the slides and left in position when the slides are borrowed. Further details may be found in the *Art library manual*[18] where the few special classification schemes are mentioned.

When photographic prints are needed they may be produced from book illustrations, slides or cuttings, bought from other picture collections, from firms such as Alinari, or from museums and art galleries.

A much more economical medium for loose reproductions is printed matter, usually in the form of clippings from magazines or commercial reproductions, including those on postcards. Clippings are also obtained from auction sale catalogues, advertising pamphlets, and discarded or duplicated books or exhibition catalogues. Advertisements in art magazines or auction catalogues are an excellent source of reproductions which are available nowhere else. These clippings are filed in filing cabinets or some kind of solander or pamphlet box. For use in the study of art history they are normally arranged by medium, period, style, artist, or a combination of these. They may of course also be used for their subject matter, when arrangement or indexing by subject is needed. This aspect is dealt with below under 'Source-image reference'.

Each cutting should be fully identified. If each one is mounted on a thin card somewhat larger than the cutting, the details can be typed on the card. Conservation is assisted by the use of good quality paste (wallpaper paste is suitable) and acid-free card. Regrettably, few art college libraries have sufficient staff time to practise such conservation methods and more often than not clippings are unmounted and labelling is informal.

It is now possible to reproduce many hitherto inaccessible picture collections economically in microform. Microfilm and microfiche make possible access to images which have previously been available only at major research libraries, for instance those in manuscripts, incunabula, and other rare books, as well as the contents of the great art and design image collections of the world. Among those already available or in preparation are: the *Marburger index,*[19] a listing of the 500,000 photographs from the Bildarchiv Foto Marburg and the Rheinisches Bildarchiv, Cologne, arranged topographically and indexed by H van de Waal's iconographic classification system Iconclass;[20] *Microfiche set: photographic archive ancient Roman topography and architecture,*[21] some 16,000 photographs comprising the photographic archive of Ancient Roman architecture and topography housed at the American Academy in Rome; *The Victoria and Albert Museum collection: a photographic record of the principal items in the collection of the Victoria and Albert Museum, London;*[22] and the *Index of American design,*[23] listing some 15,000 painted renderings of American artifacts, from settlement to 1900, with a 600-page printed catalogue including indexes of craftsmen, designers, manufacturers, owners, and artists of the renderings. The renderings were originally produced as part of the Works Progress Administration Federal Art Project in the 1930s. The entire collection (1,250,000 pictures) of the Witt Library of the Courtauld Institute of Art is being recorded on microfiche but cannot be published because of the difficulties in establishing copyright ownership. *Guide to microforms in print*[24] and *Subject guide to microforms in print*[25] may be consulted for other available material.

The increasing availability of enormous archives of pictorial material has the potential to revolutionize image availability in art colleges and other small libraries. However, users are not accustomed to micromedia, and few have their own microform readers. Hard copies may be required. It seems essential to provide a reader-printer rather than a simple reading machine. A reader-printer is expensive but enables the original fiche or film to be kept in the library and a copy of the required image of a useful size to be provided for the user to take away. Unfortunately, the image quality is not good and although the microform may be coloured, no colour printers exist as yet. Photographs or slides may of course be made from individual microform frames, and there is now a projector available which projects microfiche in much the same way a slide projector projects slides. The exploitation of microforms is in its infancy and the range of hardware and software available is rapidly improving. As yet there is certainly user resistance, and art librarians are exercising their educative skills to overcome this. Most art libraries now have some kind of microform reading equipment but stocks of material to read vary greatly. (See Section 1.9).

SOURCE-IMAGE REFERENCE

The second main class of use could be called 'Source-image reference'. Here, pictures in books are also extremely important but less accessible, unless the book is devoted to a particular subject or arranged by subject, as in the case of encyclopedias and illustrated dictionaries.

Images of almost anything may be required by artists and designers but natural objects including the human body, animals, plants, and geological structures are the primary sources of the visual arts and design. Less basic, but often used are artifacts of all kinds, including architecture, and topographical views. For this kind of reference the artistic quality of the representation may be irrelevant, as the artist will transform the basic visual data according to his own interpretation. Information, not interpretation, is sought. In most cases a clear photograph, preferably in colour, is ideal.

Basic natural forms are of great importance to the student designer and basic design is usually a component of foundation courses, which train fine artists as well as designers. Often it is possible to use original matter and pictorial reference is only a substitute for this. Many artists scorn the use of pictures as sources and work only from nature or from the imagination. Others find pictures satisfactory as sources, or utilize the particular qualities of pictures to aid their own further interpretations. Picture collections are of most use to graphic designers and illustrators who may be required to depict an object at short notice. Fine artists tend to work in a more thematic way from a narrower range of source material which they may collect themselves, although of course there are many exceptions to this general observation.

Many of the remarks on art historical reference above apply equally to source-image reference. The media are similar, with the exception that slides are seldom used because of the difficulty of handling and viewing. They are sometimes used by artists and graphic designers who project them and draw around the outlines of the enlarged image, but this is a special technique and slides may be prepared from other illustrations especially for this purpose if required. Other kinds of projector are sometimes used which project images from non-transparent originals. More commonly, a photocopy is made from a book or a clipping and is traced or copied. Photocopies can also be cut up or otherwise altered. Colour photocopying is popular with students but available at very few colleges, so source pictures may be required for loan in order that bureau facilities may be used for colour copying. Sometimes the artist may want to use the picture directly as part of a composition (usually in collage). Here cuttings come into their own and, in addition to classified files of cuttings, many libraries keep boxes of discarded magazines for cutting up by students. Restrictions on use depend of course on the value and rarity of the material.

There are two main problems in the provision of source images — selecting the most useful images and indexing them. It is often difficult to decide on the best form, books, periodicals, and cuttings all overlapping to a large extent. Choice of the most useful images depends on the individual college, its courses and the nature of its teaching. A large stock of representations of natural objects and creatures and a section of textual detail are basic. Art colleges teach a wider range of special subjects than is generally realized and subjects such as interior, landscape, and environmental design must be provided for where such courses are taught. Product design students need pictures of all kinds of artifacts. Historical costume reference is important to illustrators as well as to stage, fashion, and textile designers.

If the pictures are in books, normal library classification procedures apply, but if they are in clipping form an alphabetical sequence by name of subject is often used. This has the advantage of forming its own alphabetical subject index and works quite well for a very small collection. For a larger collection it makes sense to use an existing classification, such as Dewey or UDC, preferably the same scheme as is used for the books. Some art libraries use classification schemes which do not extend beyond art subjects, but this does not prevent the use of Dewey or UDC for their picture collections.

The most useful periodicals for source-image reference are not art periodicals but pictorial publications such as *Life* and *National Geographic.* Design magazines and *Which?* are useful for manufactured articles, as are trade and mail-order catalogues. The wealth of illustrations in periodicals may be inaccessible unless they are cut out and filed by subject. Double subscriptions for the best sources are useful where space and funding allow.

Books used for source-image references are often acquired especially for the purpose. Indexing is easier if monographs on subjects which fall neatly into sought classes are chosen, rather than more general books. This does not apply to truly encyclopaedic works, which have the advantage of containing their own full indexes. The multipart illustrated encyclopaedias published serially by Purnell and others are useful when preserved intact as well as for cutting up purposes as they are well indexed and inexpensive. Books of images suitable for reuse by graphic designers and already cleared of copyright restrictions. are available, notably the 'Dover Pictorial Archives'[26] series. Printed ephemera, including advertisements, postcards, and comics, as well as science-fiction and other kinds of popular illustration, are sought after.

College libraries are not well equipped to deal with commercial picture research enquiries and this is a pity, for there is an overall shortage of pictorial libraries. In general, art college picture collections cannot be recommended to professional picture researchers as their aims are educational rather than archival. Much time can be wasted by the lack of indexes for the college user does not normally require the range of sought terms needed by the researcher. Charging for staff time used in assisting a commercial activity is not normally practicable and can place a burden on a small, primarily educational library, as well as creating competition with commercial picture libraries which could be considered unfair. Copyright clearance for publication is also a problem for college librarians. Yet we do try to be helpful, in so far as our limited resources allow, and to play our part in the overall network of provision, aided by staff who are notable for their interest in and knowledge of their subject.

This short essay has attempted to outline the average kind of provision of pictorial material in art college libraries. Certainly much more pictorial matter could be provided, and it could be much better indexed. Art libraries are perhaps oriented too much towards the word and too little towards the visual image. The most promising area of development seems to be in microforms and, if moving pictures are included, in videotapes.

REFERENCES

1 *Art Index.* New York, H W Wilson, 1930-.
2 *ARTbibliographies MODERN* (formerly *LOMA*). Oxford, Clio Press, 1969-.
3 *Art Design Photo.* Hemel Hempstead, Alexander Davis Publications Ltd, 1973-.
4 Art Institute of Chicago, Ryerson Library *Index to art periodicals.* Boston, Mass., G K Hall, 1962.
5 Clapp, Jane *Art in 'Life'.* New York, Scarecrow Press, 1970.
6 Columbia University, Avery Memorial Architectural Library *Periodical index.* 2nd ed. Boston, G K Hall, 1973.
7 *Design Abstracts International* (formerly *ICSID Information Bulletin*). Oxford, Pergamon, 1967-.
8 *Design Abstracts International* (US edition). Elmsford, New York, Pergamon, 1976-.
9 Havlice, Patricia P *Art in 'Time'.* Metuchen, New Jersey, Scarecrow Press, 1970.
10 *Répertoire d'Art et d'Archéologie.* Paris, Morancé, 1910-58.
11 *Répertoire d'Art et d'Archéologie.* New series. Paris, Centre National de la Recherche Scientifique, 1965-.
12 *Répertoire International de la Littérature de l'Art* (RILA). New York, College Art Association of America, 1973-. (Subscriptions c/o Sterling and Francine Clark Art Institute, Williamstown MA 01267, USA.)
13 Hewlett-Woodmere Public Library *Index to art reproductions in books.* Metuchen, Scarecrow Press, 1974.
14 Parry, Pamela Jeffcott *Contemporary art and artists: an index to reproductions.* Westport, Connecticut, Greenwood Press, 1978.
15 Parry, Pamela Jeffcott *Photography index: a guide to reproductions.* Westport, Greenwood Press, 1978.
16 Smith, Lyn Wall and others *Index to reproductions of American paintings appearing in over 400 works mostly published since 1960.* Metuchen, Scarecrow Press, 1977.
17 American Library Association *Portrait index.* Washington DC, US Government Printing Office, 1906.
18 Pacey, Philip (editor) *Art library manual.* London and New York, Bowker, in association with the Art Libraries Society, 1977.
19 Bildarchiv Foto Marburg *Marburger index: photographic documentation of art in Germany.* (Microfiche) Munich, Verlag Dokumentation, 1976-.
20 Waal, Henri van de *Iconclass: an iconographic classification system.* Amsterdam, North Holland, 1973- (in progress).
21 Fototeca Unione *Microfiche set: photographic archive ancient Roman topography and architecture.* Rome, International Union of Institutes of Archaeology, History and History of Art in Rome, 1977.

22 London, Victoria and Albert Museum *The Victoria and Albert Museum collection: a photographic record of the principal items in the collection of the Victoria and Albert Museum, London, on microfiche.* London, Mindata Ltd, 1976.

23 Washington DC, National Gallery of Art *Index of American design.* Cambridge, England, Chadwyck-Healey; Teaneck, New Jersey, Somerset House, 1979.

24 *Guide to microforms in print.* Westport, Microform Review; London, Mansell.

25 *Subject guide to microforms in print.* Westport, Microform Review; London, Mansell.

26 'Dover Pictorial Archives' (series). Dover Publications. (British distributors: Constable and Co.)

29

School Libraries

Sylvia Stagg

The nature of a school's picture collection and the use made of it vary from school to school; it is governed by various factors, such as physical facilities, staff attitudes, and, most importantly, the curriculum. Any attempt to define the current teaching and learning ethos in all schools is clearly impossible but it may be helpful to indicate some of the educational trends of particular significance when considering visual resources and their organization.

PRE-SCHOOL EDUCATION

Young children show an interest in pictures and illustrations long before they can read. They will point to and name familiar objects and if adults respond and encourage them, their speech and sight vocabularies will grow. Play groups and nursery schools aim to reinforce this process of identifying and naming, extending it with the provision of well-illustrated picture books. When reading aloud, teachers show the children pictures, explaining and elaborating where necessary. Children can browse in book corners; activity and play areas are visually bright and attractive, teachers often using the children's early attempts at painting and drawing for their wall displays.

404

THE PRIMARY SCHOOL

There is a similar environment in the primary school but here teachers concentrate on the basic skills of numeracy and literacy. Visual training is an essential prerequisite to mastering the mechanics of reading and visual displays and illustrative material should be designed and selected to encourage both observation and visual discrimination. Many reading schemes currently in use have supplementary material in the form of pictures of poster size or smaller pictures mounted on card, featuring characters and situations in the scheme. This material may carry a short, simple phrase or sentence appropriate to the content of the picture and the vocabulary of the child. The typeface used should be similar to that used in early reading material. Of economic necessity, most primary school teachers make such material themselves, aiming to capitalize on items of local and topical interest as well as the child's natural curiosity.

As the child's reading skill develops, exploration of the environment leads to the need for visually identifying what he or she has found or for finding out in more depth about a discovery. Pictures may actually be a stimulus to this. Gradually the child learns to collect, collate and arrange this information. He or she should be encouraged to present this attractively, often making a scrapbook or folder, and to take pride and satisfaction in the arrangement of the illustration, decoration, and the simple text he or she will write to accompany these. The folders are often displayed with artifacts made by the children.

With the development of the child's conceptual skill and ability, wider cultural studies and interests are introduced and fostered. Children are now taught to consider the way people live in other countries, to think about how the world began and developed, of man's history and progress through the ages, and to explore the physical sciences. The importance of visual stimuli and information as a means of extending this experience and heightening this perception cannot be overemphasized. Much of this information can come from well-illustrated books and magazines, supplemented by pictures around the school, by wallcharts and posters, and by films and television. So unpredictable and diverse are the children's needs at this stage that teachers aim to build up their own collection of visual material, of 'pictures' for use in the classroom: picture postcards, illustrations taken from magazines and newspapers (especially those with colour supplements), calendars, greetings cards, family mementoes, photographs, slides, as well as museum publicity, trade literature, travel brochures — anything that is suitably informative and colourful.

Some of the material is ephemeral, to be cut up by children for use in their folders or mounted in a one-off wall display. Some may have more lasting value and may well be stored in a central location together with sets of pictures and other more expensive illustrative material, where it can be made known and available to everyone. In the primary school this is not a problem as the number of staff is generally small enough for ease of communication. The central collection is usually supervised by one member of staff and kept in the staff room, the school library, a convenient corridor, foyer, or store depending on whether the policy of the school allows children access or not. If children are to have access then items must be easily available (at the right height), easily accessible (small children cannot manipulate heavy plan chests), and protected from damage. Individual suspension allows for browsing and ensures that they are not creased by handling. Smaller items can be stored in pamphlet boxes, box files, cut down cereal packets, or in envelopes often made by the teachers themselves. Cecilia Gordon gives most practical and ingenious suggestions for the storage of visual resources in her book *Resource organisation in primary schools.*[1]

THE SECONDARY SCHOOL

In the secondary school teachers convey more complex and sophisticated skills and there is greater emphasis on the mastery of information. The things a child must know are beyond the teaching capabilities of one person, so he or she moves from one teacher to another, often from one building to another, in distinct contrast to the primary school where throughout the 'integrated day' one teacher looks after a class of children, helping them to learn as interests and needs dictate.

Many secondary teachers have recognized the benefits to the child (especially the slower child) of the teaching and learning methods of his primary school experience, and various attempts have been made to reorganize the more traditional secondary curriculum so as to incorporate the more successful aspects. These include the breakdown of some traditional subject barriers, with the formation of interdisciplinary groupings, often known as 'integrated studies'. A particular example is in Geography and History where, it is argued, the understanding of a nation's history is equally dependent on the understanding of the geography of that country or region. The geographical features determine the life experience of a people; this in turn may lead to a study of their religion and beliefs which may then be contrasted with experiences and beliefs in society today. Such courses allow teachers a greater degree of flexibility, enabling them to choose and tailor the methods and materials most appropriate to the needs and capabilities of individual children. In the design of such courses and materials teachers can build in guides to independent learning to help pupils find and organize information, much of which is visual. Then, using skills first learnt in the primary school, pupils are often required to produce 'projects', a more sophisticated version of the folder.

The syllabus demands of leaving examinations eventually determine a return to a more traditional curriculum but even within these constraints, teachers of some subjects are now able to devise their own courses which take into account pupils' experience, interest, and aptitude. These courses are validated by an outside body but the course work, including written project material with appropriate illustrations (often the result of considerable picture research), is assessed by the teachers themselves.

The secondary school is not only larger in terms of numbers of staff and children but the buildings may often occupy more than one site. The natural communication groups are usually those teachers with similar interests: the members of a subject department, a year group team, heads of departments. There may also be various sub-groups: interdisciplinary teams each working on an integrated studies project, groups concerned with remedial children or those with special handicaps. Each of these cooperative groups is equivalent to the entire staff of a primary school. This presents problems for resource organization which each school must solve according to its individual circumstances. Many consider the centralization of resources to be the most efficient answer, thus making sure that everything is available to everyone, but this assumes that the staff can and do respond to a central stimulus. In practice, there is evidence that large, centrally controlled collections have been underused and, bit by bit, items have drifted away. Where the school has the services of a librarian there is a much greater chance of these collections being well organized and exploited. Some local authorities provide peripatetic professional help to schools but this is only seen as a short-term solution and most schools must manage with the occasional services of a teacher who is given time from teaching to manage the resources collection.

The somewhat disappointing results of centralization have created a reverse trend to decentralization. Such fragmentation can, in ideal circumstances, provide resources immediately where they are wanted but the duplication of expensive stock and equipment has deterred many schools. Decentralization also means that each collection requires maintenance and there is less chance that one department is aware of the holdings of another. The situation is exacerbated the more the schools buildings are dispersed.[2] The solution often suggested is that the most commonly used and expensive materials are kept in a central pool and that local collections are established as groupings require. These user-group collections are then recorded and fed into a central information bank. In practice, such a system is difficult to establish unless specific time and expertise are allocated to it.

STAFF

It is the larger, more diversified collections which make the biggest demands on staff time and expertise. As there is no uniform policy for local authorities to provide staff to manage libraries or resource centres in schools, the quality of management that such collections receive varies enormously. A few authorities appoint professional librarians to their secondary schools as a matter of policy.[3] Most others enlist the services of a teacher on the staff who may or may not have additional qualifications in librarianship. They usually also have a substantial teaching commitment and although they receive financial acknow-ledgement for the additional responsibility, they must spend many hours of their own time if the collection is not to suffer. More significantly, such part-time management means that the collection is professionally unsupervised and its potential is not exploited for much of the school day.

If a school is truly committed to a large-scale programme of resource-based learning, this is clearly unsatisfactory. Clerical staff can assist in the day-to-day routine work, such as the filing of material, and act as custodians. They cannot, however, interpret the visual information needs of the staff and of the pupils and match them to the whole range of visual resources held by the school. Such a person must understand the school's educational philosophy, curriculum and teaching methods, and be able to relate professionally to the staff; he or she must be able to deal sympathetically with pupils who have difficulty in articulating their needs and know how to deduce pupils' capabilities, directing them to or helping them to select suitably appropriate resources. From the experience gained of these needs the 'librarian' must be able to establish and maintain a collection of visual resources.

ESTABLISHING A PICTURE COLLECTION

The pictures and other visual materials that teachers and pupils use in schools may come from various sources.

1 The Picture Loan Collection

This is usually a selection of works of art chosen for their aesthetic value which may include original paintings, drawings, or prints which are purchased centrally by the local education authority and loaned to the school for an extended period, after which time they are exchanged for another collection. Similar arrangements may be made with picture galleries, libraries, museums, and local art societies, as well as with local artists.

2 Commercial Sources

Schools also purchase material in the form of inexpensive reproductions through the normal trade channels. Collections of prints, photographs, posters, wallcharts, friezes, slides, postcards, and suchlike are available from numerous sources, including publishers specializing in the educational market, library suppliers, galleries and museums, industrial and commercial concerns, voluntary agencies, state-controlled industries, radio and TV companies, etc.

3 Regional and Local Sources

Specially staffed resource production centres, such as the Avon Resources for Learning Unit, have produced materials to support the work in local schools. This may also be on a comparatively large scale, such as in the Inner London Education Authority where the material is now marketed nationwide and overseas. Smaller-scale activities at local teacher centres produce the work of teachers, offering printing and reprographic facilities to curriculum groups or the individual.

4   Sources Within the School

Many schools have facilities for teachers to produce their own illustrative materials. Some have separate reprographic departments with equipment for duplicating, photocopying, and photography. Larger schools employ a technical helper, a post called variously an Audio-visual Aids Officer or Media Resources Officer (MRO), whose job is to liaise with teachers, interpreting their requirements and assist them in the production of learning materials. With this help many teachers have been able to produce materials with excellent graphics and artwork. Smaller schools often cannot afford such investment in time and skills so in both primary and secondary schools the visual material is collected and made from various sources by the teachers themselves. Magazines, newspapers, and discarded books are carefully scanned and cuttings taken. Journals such as *Child Education* and *Pictorial Education* are a regular source of visual material with easily detachable pictures and display material bound in with the journal. *The treasure chest for teachers: services available for teachers,* which is published by The Schoolmaster Publishing Company and revised periodically, is a useful source of information on material and services offered by embassies and legations, commercial, industrial, and nationalized concerns, museums and art galleries, as well as the various subject teaching associations.

STORING AND ORGANIZING THE COLLECTION

Most schools experience problems in storing the picture collection because items are of such disparate sizes. In addition, not all storage units give ready access to items, an important factor if busy teachers are not to be deterred from using the collection. Furthermore, unless there is someone permanently available to supervise the collection, it has to be clear not only where an item can be found but where it should be replaced if the collection is not to become untidy and ill-sorted. To offset the variation in picture sizes, some uniformity needs to be imposed. Larger items, such as wallcharts and posters, can be extracted and hung vertically in specialized storage units where they can be readily inspected. Smaller items of different sizes can be mounted if necessary on card (either singly or grouped by subject or interest) of A4, A3, or A2 size. Clear plastic envelopes or wallet-type folders, usually of A4 size, or the less expensive manila envelopes, can take a number of small items or pictures and these can be interfiled with the material if required. Postcards are most satisfactorily stored in standard card cabinets (10 × 15 cm.). The fewer the number of places and sequences a teacher has to look for material, the easier and more convenient it is for teachers to use and to return things. The mounts, cards, or envelopes are usually arranged in classified order.

In smaller schools or in departmental collections the arrangement may be alphabetical by broad subject headings, often reflecting the way the collection has been built up and the teachers' recurring interests and needs. When schools use a classification scheme it is usually the Decimal Classification, either using the abridged version or 'The introduction to Dewey Decimal Classification for British schools' published by the School Library Association. Some schools find that shortening the notation, a practice often recommended, results in difficulty when locating a particular subject which has been filed at random with others under a more general heading, but many school librarians are prepared to accept this. There is, after all, an element of serendipity in any picture searching and an item which can be easily classified can be quickly added to the collection. The number assigned is little more than a location indicator, but in the case of the more ephemeral items this does not matter and for the more significant items the subject content can be indexed as specifically as the librarian thinks necessary.

The most successful index in schools is one which is visually accessible (such as a visible strip index) but there are space limitations in this system for expanding a subject heading. Some schools now have micro-processors and already research is under consideration and there is experimentation to see whether it is feasible to enlist their help in generating an index to the school's resources.

In conclusion, it should be said that many teachers now struggling to manage learning resources without the benefit of training, time, or adequate money would regard any discussion of microprocessors and even picture librarianship as somewhat unrealistic, not to say grandiose!

However, it is difficult to see how the considerable investment made in learning resources is ever to be fully realized unless their management *is* put on a truly professional footing and teachers as well as librarians should not be deterred.

REFERENCES

1   Gordon, Cecilia *Resource organisation in primary schools.* London, Council for Educational Technology with The School Library Association, 1978. 134p.
2   For a more detailed analysis of the implications for schools of using resources *see* Davies, W J K *Learning resources?: an argument for schools.* London, Council for Educational Technology, 1975. 108p.
3   'At present the best figures on the employment of Chartered Librarians are those given to us by the Society of Children's Librarians for 1978. There were 558 members working full time in schools in 47 LEA's.' National Book League *Books for Schools.* London, National Book League, 1979. 70p.

30

Public Libraries in the UK

Jeannette Fauvel and Colin MacDonald

INTRODUCTION

Picture collections in public libraries[1] may include any or all of the forms of pictorial illustration covered by this book, for the collections have developed to meet the needs of a population which could include users of any of the other picture libraries. Naturally, however, public libraries have not tried to compete with the more specialized sources; conversely there has been no clear general direction of development and very few examples of comprehensive planning. Development has tended to be in a piecemeal fashion tied to individual subject departments and often the result of the initial donation of a collection, or the individual enterprise of a librarian. Collections therefore vary greatly in size, scope, organization, and in use. Often, even where collections exist, publicity has been poor and as a result public access is limited. (This lack of publicity extends even into the professional sphere as there are very few articles in periodicals or books covering this area and little emphasis in the library schools.)

Is it then really important to have picture collections in public libraries, or are they just a luxury which many libraries have judged unnecessary? The answer to this would seem to lie squarely with the library user. If there is a demand for pictorial material in addition to that found in books (and this can only be adequately ascertained by initiating such a service), then it should be supplied if at all possible. Those libraries which do not as yet have collections are effectively depriving their borrowers of an important dimension in the provision of information, education, and recreation. One can think of few such services which have failed to meet a demand once started unless unnecessary restrictions have been imposed on use. In addition, the initiation of such services is often relatively inexpensive compared to, for example, the insidious computerization of as many systems as possible for which many borrowers would not thank you.

PICTURE LOAN COLLECTIONS

Although there has not been an organized approach to picture librarianship there are many examples of interesting collections. One service which is relatively well developed in the public library system, albeit with a great deal of variety, is the loan of pictures. (There would probably be even more of these collections were it not for the fact that in a number of towns the local art gallery was the first to develop a collection and has retained this function.) These may be either original works of art or reproductions. Reproductions are clearly much cheaper than originals but then they are often pale imitations of the original work.

A decision as to which a library should buy will depend on what it sees as its role vis-à-vis pictorial art, and on the expertise of the staff involved in selection. If the library merely wants a representative collection of western art with an emphasis on those areas which have proved to be most popular, e.g., the Impressionists, the Pre-Raphaelites, etc. then clearly little artistic knowledge is required and an adequate collection of reproductions can be acquired. If, however, the library feels that it should actively support art, it may wish, in addition, to purchase original prints from both local artists and others of good quality; it is then necessary to have at least one member of staff who is aware and knowledgeable about the modern art world. In practice relatively few libraries have built up collections of original works, but those which have, have included prints by local artists (a print being the cheapest form of original work to purchase). Development in this area seems unlikely given the present economic climate and that of the foreseeable future.

Acquisition of original prints is relatively easy as many towns now have local galleries and a number of London-based dealers tour the provinces on a regular basis, but selection, as already stated, requires some artistic expertise. Reproductions can also be easily purchased, with many large towns having dealers who can acquire the prints produced by galleries and publishers across the world. The only major selection problem is the quality of some of the reproductions which, especially those from some of the larger commercial suppliers, can be somewhat variable.

After acquiring the work the most important consideration is framing. This is of major importance as the aesthetic appeal of even the greatest work of art can be severely diminished by an inappropriate frame. Fortunately, the same dealers who supply reproductions often have a selection of frames. This is not true of some of the bigger commercial dealers, e.g., Athena, who tend to specialize in block mounting and a few rather uninspiring frames. Even the dealers who have good supplies of frames, however, should not be allowed to choose frames without direction, as they vary in their ability to frame well. Also, many have a service which includes sending a number of samples of short pieces (3 or 4 inches long) of suitable frames from which the librarian must select. While, for a librarian in a remote location this may be the only practical method of selection, ideally this should be carried out with longer strips and a selection of mounts. The decision as to whether to heat seal, block mount, perspex mount, frame with glass, etc. will depend on the quality and the type of picture; for example, original prints should always be protected by glass, and modern art is usually better framed with modern-looking materials.

Once the pictures are actually being loaned there is the problem of maintaining the stock in good condition. Ideally, borrowers should be issued with specially designed semi-rigid waterproof bags to transport pictures, but these are expensive and pictures vary in size so much that this may not be practicable. In practice too, as long as they are covered against rain, relatively little damage is done to the pictures. The frames, however, are more vulnerable, but can be replaced. This is another important consideration when purchasing frames, as perspex and some of the metallic-effect frames tend to scratch much more easily than others.

Lending routines, organization of stock and catalogues illustrate the lack of any clearly established procedure for dealing with these collections for they vary widely from one authority to another. Manchester, for instance, has its collection spread throughout the city in a number of libraries including a large collection in the Central Arts Library. Issues are controlled by a Browne system; the loan is for three months; there is a 50p. charge, and fines for overdue pictures are 25p.

for the first month and 50p. for subsequent months. The pictures are permanently displayed on the walls of the libraries (not an entirely satisfactory arrangement) and each library has both a card catalogue, filed alphabetically by artist, and a catalogue of slide copies from which the borrower can select if nothing suitable is instantly available. Loans are made almost exclusively to individuals who can borrow two pictures at a time. Camden libraries, on the other hand, although having the same loan period of three months, have an exhibition of all the pictures in each library's collection at the end of each loan period and the borrowers select from this. There is no charge for the service but there are quite heavy fines (5p. per day), for overdue items. Camden also encourages local artists by giving them an opportunity for public exhibition; their works can be either borrowed or bought and the council pays them a small fee. As well as loans to individuals there are large-scale loans to local institutions. There is no publicly available catalogue but for each exhibition a leaflet is prepared with brief details.

Again, Birmingham libraries at their Sutton Coldfield branch loan pictures for three months, but they charge an annual subscription of £4 + VAT and fine 10p. per week for overdues. A reference catalogue containing reproductions of the pictures in stock is available for consultation and a printed catalogue listing artists and titles is also available. Oldham libraries loan pictures, using a Browne system, for 12 weeks, from their central library and one small branch. They have no charges but impose fines, and feel that the resources spent on producing a catalogue would be better used on more pictures — therefore have no catalogue. Their borrowers are both individuals and local organizations. These examples by no means exhaust all the possibilities, but they do indicate the variety. (More detailed information about the variety can be gained from a survey of UK picture loan schemes carried out by the Library Association in 1971 and published in their *Library and Information Bulletin*.)[2]

How then should a new public library picture loan collection be organized if there is such variety? It would seem to depend largely on where the collection is to be housed. If it is to be an extra service in a library already possessing audiovisual material, then the obvious solution is to control and issue the picture collection in the same way as the rest of the material. If, however, the collection is to be kept separately, then it may be more convenient to have some arrangement similar to that of Camden where the material is only issued during set periods every few months. Often, the decision as to where the pictures are to be housed revolves around whether they are seen to be part of an arts library function or an audiovisual library function; unfortunately there is no conclusive argument either way but a 'rule of thumb' would be to place them in the section which has the largest commitment to the loan of its material.

PHOTOGRAPHIC COLLECTIONS

Some sort of photographic collection is to be found in almost every public library authority in Britain but, as with the picture loan collections, many different practices have developed to make them available to the public. 'Photograph', of course, is a generic term and can include prints and negatives in both black and white and colour as well as more esoteric media, such as lantern slides.[3] All of these come in a variety of sizes and few libraries will have been able to standardize, in fact it is probable that examples of virtually every combination of dimensions exist somewhere within the public library system.

From the earliest days of photography photographers recognized how important the medium could be as a record, not only of topographical features, but also of social history (including customs, costume, transport, industry, and archaeology). Public libraries, however, have often been less perceptive and as a result many of the present collections have developed from the bequest of a pioneer's work or from a number of items from the work of such major photographers as Roger Fenton or James Mudd. Collections of this kind, of course, reflect the bias of the photographers, whose original purpose was usually not to stock a library with a systematic survey but to produce works of aesthetic value. To fill these gaps in the collections a number of libraries decided to acquire similar photographs and eventually became involved in photography themselves, either directly or through agents.

It can be seen, therefore, that there are three main methods of acquiring material for a photographic collection. The first is by donation, either from the work of an individual or from a collection built up by an individual (e.g., a local historian) or from an organization. A good example of the former is the Benjamin Stone collection at Birmingham. Stone travelled extensively at home and abroad and it was because of his popularity as a lecturer that he began his collection of photographs. The collection consists of over 22,000 prints as well as lantern slides, glass negatives, albums, and scrapbooks and was presented to Birmingham in 1921. An example of the latter type is the News Chronicle photographic collection which was acquired by Manchester Public Libraries when the newspaper ceased publication in 1960.

The second acquisition method demands a more active approach by the librarian (and indeed more money) to seek out appropriate material and purchase it. For this the librarian can draw on shops, markets, sales, auctions, etc.; commercial firms for aerial photographs; national organizations, e.g., the National Monuments Record, now part of the Royal Commission on Historical Monuments (England); and professional bodies, e.g., the Royal Institute of British Architects; in fact any source which might conceivably have acquired useful photographs. Local material should be the easiest to obtain and any librarian can quickly build up a list of commercial contacts who will bring any suitable material to his or her notice. More general material may be more difficult to find but as most public library collections are primarily of local material this is not usually a great problem.

In addition to the commercial sources local material can be gained through contacts made with non-commercial sources. The Borough Surveyor will probably be willing to allow the library to copy photographs of redevelopment sites and buildings due for demolition. (This is an important aspect in an age when most of the towns and cities in the country are continually being altered.) Local newspapers may also cooperate, if approached, passing on photographs (which would otherwise be destroyed) of carnivals, processions, royal visits, or other local events. In a similar way local firms and photographers may be willing to pass prints on to the library or make them available for copying. Another approach is to encourage the cooperation of the local residents by organizing competitions or exhibitions. In addition to the entries themselves, this often prompts people to donate family albums or allow the library to make copies of interesting material.

The last method of acquisition brings public libraries completely out of the relatively passive custodial realm into active production of a photographic record. In a number of areas a systematic survey of the local environment has successfully been attempted (e.g., Manchester and Nottinghamshire) but unfortunately in some areas large-scale enterprises such as these have begun with great enthusiasm and waned with the passing of time. The usual survey procedure is to enlist the cooperation of local photographic societies or individual photographers (including, hopefully, the librarian) but they should not be given a free hand as the result may be a series of attractive pictures of little practical use. Instead, they should be instructed to show clearly first of all what the subject is and its location, while accompanying photographs should depict a recognizable part of the main object and some topographical detail. Some details, like advertisements or people in contemporary dress, should also be included if at all possible, so that the item can be dated without recourse to any headings etc. which may in the future be lost or destroyed.

Access to and storage of photographs are the most difficult problems. The public librarian has to balance his desire to obtain maximum usage with his desire to maintain the collection in good condition. With the older items, especially those by famous photographers, security is a major problem and closed access is the only solution. Any fragile material should also obviously be kept on closed access and negatives should not be accessible to the public at all but stored in transparent containers to avoid handling and only brought out for the production of prints or for their condition to be checked. Open access has advantages in that it relieves staff time, allows borrowers to browse, and eliminates the need for detailed cataloguing, but most public libraries have found that they can only risk a small proportion of their collections in this way and so closed access is usually preferred.

Whichever method of access is used, loan services of material to the public are rarely found and given that copying of photographs is relatively easy it would seem unnecessary to institute such a service. The most common method of storage with closed-access systems has been to mount the photographs on standard-sized card and store them in files in filing cabinets, as in Nottinghamshire and Manchester, or in filing boxes, as in Birmingham. The choice of mount will be governed by financial provision and degree of use, though dry mounting, which needs a special press and bonds the photograph to the card, is commonly used.

As already mentioned, the bulk of most public library collections consists of local material and consequently many authorities have devised their own local classification scheme, e.g., Nottinghamshire. Alternatively, it is possible to classify the strictly topographical prints by area and by road, and to arrange subjects into basic Dewey classes. Either way it is essential to index the collection in detail with headings for individual buildings, events, occupations, in fact everything of interest that the photograph reveals, not forgetting the photographer. Unfortunately, not all libraries have managed to do this, generally because of lack of staff but also because of the acquisition of uncatalogued collections as a result of local government reorganization.

Lack of staff and finance are in fact often the major factors which dictate the development of photographic collections as the scope and demand is present in almost every area. There is an upsurge in interest in local history, and users of the collections include not only private individuals but the staff and students of local educational establishments, social historians, advertising agencies, television companies, publishers, and newspapers.

PRINT COLLECTIONS

A number of the photographic collections of local interest have actually developed from an original collection of prints (i.e., drawings, watercolours, etchings and engravings) depicting landscapes, buildings, people, and events. Other libraries have acquired by donation or purchase a print collection alongside the photographic collection. Security is again of major importance as many items may be of considerable value and therefore closed access is the only solution. The smaller items can be stored similarly to photographs but larger items demand the sort of vertical filing cabinets designed for maps.

In many public libraries which possess such collections, whether large or small, prints can usually be divided into three main categories. The first, general topographical, is often the most neglected in terms of cataloguing and indexing for it is usually considered as low priority for staff time. Consequently, researchers can be totally unaware of the existence of unique collections, though M W Barley's *Guide to British topographical collections*[4] and John Wall's *Directory of British photographic collections*[5] are attempts to ease this situation. The second category, local topographical, is usually kept with a photographic collection and benefits from the use of the photographs. The last category, portraits, is not so commonly found but where it has been developed, e.g., Nottinghamshire or Birmingham, the collections are well used and have the benefit for the librarian of being virtually self-indexing.

ILLUSTRATIONS COLLECTIONS

Illustrations collections typify picture provision in public libraries because they vary so widely. There is little standardization and even the term 'illustrations' can include anything from posters to plates, from discarded books or dust jackets to brochures, in fact any pictorial information the library can obtain which does not fit into the other classes. Fortunately, these sources are usually extremely cheap and mounting on card or stiff paper costs more than the illustrations themselves. Storage methods are similar to those used for photographs but often collections exist solely for loan purposes, so that where there is enough space open access is desirable. Subject coverage is normally comprehensive although some authorities have collections in only one or two subject areas. Organization is relatively easy because searching comes under general subject headings, such as animals, birds, transport, architecture, biography, flags, etc. An important consideration is whether it is worth duplicating subjects adequately covered by a book stock, but in many instances a mounted illustration will prove invaluable to designers, artists, lecturers, historians, teachers, and students.

Perhaps the largest and best-known collection is that of Birmingham Central Library's Visual Aids Department which has 390,000 mounted illustrations. The loan period is four weeks with a limit of 100 illustrations on loan to any borrower at one time. Other notable collections exist at Southwark and Hammersmith and both Westminster and Manchester have large collections in their arts departments. Loan periods, issue systems, etc. depend very much on local circumstances and amount of use but most authorities issue protective folders with the illustrations and happily most do not charge for the service.

Slides and Sales

Although slides as a medium in themselves are found in many collections in public libraries they also have a function as a secondary information source, i.e., they can be used either as a guide to primary material (as mentioned above in the section on picture loans), or as a copy so that the original is protected from damage. This second function is very important because slides are easier to handle and store, copies ensure the originals last much longer and they allow the introduction of open access with consequent savings in staff time.

Another function which slides can perform is as a medium for sale. Slide copies of original material are easily made and they can be attractively sold in packs with booklets. Many public libraries have now developed such programmes and also include sales of booklets, prints, photographic prints, posters, maps, postcards, and Christmas cards. Shropshire County is a good example of this trend as it has an active publishing role which at present includes over 20 volumes covering places, industries, railways, and personalities, as well as unframed prints, greetings cards of local views from old prints, and postcards from old illustrations.

This policy brings us back to the comments at the beginning about lack of publicity, for sales programmes are exactly the kind of activity in which public libraries should get involved in order to exploit their collections. It is, however, not only better communication with the public that is needed, but also better communication and cooperation between libraries, and as a result some determination of standards of provision. Meanwhile, hopefully, the material in this book may stimulate development in those authorities which have as yet ignored or under-valued the possibilities of picture collections.

REFERENCES

1   The term 'public libraries' in this chapter only includes services to the general public and not those to schools and other educational establishments which public libraries often organize but are covered elsewhere in this book.

2   'Picture loan schemes in the United Kingdom: report' in *Library and Information Bulletin* No.18. 1972. 2-29.

3   The term also includes ordinary (35 mm.) slides which are found in many public libraries often in large numbers but it is not intended that the more general aspects of their provision should be discussed here.

4   Barley, M W *Guide to British topographical collections*. London, Council for British Archaeology, 1974.

5   Wall, John *Directory of British photographic collections*. London, Heinemann, 1977.

31

A Public Library in Westport, Connecticut

Thelma S Gordon

The story of the Westport Picture Collection began early in the 20th century with librarian Edith Very Sherwood. A writer, art instructor, and lecturer on the history of art, Mrs Sherwood presided at the Westport Library from 1916 to 1945 and was influential especially during those early years when Westport was becoming an artists' colony. Illustrators by the dozens had settled in the town to enjoy the pleasures of country living while working at home within easy reach of the New York advertising and publishing industries.

When the artists began coming to the library for help with their pictorial problems, Mrs Sherwood determined to build a reference collection that would meet their special demands. From then on Westport Library developed along lines different from the small community library. No problem the illustrator gave Mrs Sherwood was too difficult and because she knew how impractical it was for an artist to accumulate enough pictures for every need, she started a research picture file at the library with a gift of her own reproductions. To enhance this basic core, the children's librarian directed a group of volunteers from the Friends of the Westport Library. They clipped hundreds of books and magazines which were fed into the picture files, then heavily used by the children of the town as a teaching device.

Later, the schools acquired their own libraries and school use decreased, but just at that time the designers, advertising and communications people started moving into the area in great numbers, heavily increasing the business demand for picture research. By the 1950s the major use of the collection was business oriented. When a new addition increased the space of the original Westport Library, the entire picture file was moved downstairs and became a permanent part of the adult collection.

Many artists contributed their personal files, adding immeasurably to the size and scope of the picture file. By far the largest and most significant came from the late Albert Dorne, the well-known artist and illustrator who was president and founder of the Famous Artists Schools Inc. When the library received Dorne's gift in 1957, it represented 30 years of compilation — mostly clippings covering a multitude of subjects with emphasis on the 1930s and 1940s as well as World War II and its aftermath. Another important personal file came from Robert Lawson, author and illustrator of award-winning children's books. Rabbit Hill, Lawson's home in Westport, was the locale of his enduring animal story of that name which won the Newbery Medal.

Other files include those of illustrators Gordon Sloan, Hugh Donnell, Clark Agnew, Al Muncheun, and Tom Lovell. Each collection brought its own special emphasis. A few years ago when Tom Lovell retired and moved west to paint, he insisted that his files become a part of the Westport Library. He had received so much help from the pictorial material that he hoped his accumulations would benefit artists in the future. Indeed, they have. With Lovell's collection came a whole new element — hundreds upon hundreds of Hollywood movie set stills in 8 × 10 inch glossies which are used with continuing frequency. Many of them depict interiors of old sailing vessels and turn-of-the-century home interiors. There are several photos of the Wells Fargo Pony Express.

In recent years, the make-up of the collection — mostly clippings — underwent a dramatic change. The library was offered a gift of a large portion of the stock of a bankrupt commercial picture agency in New York. This fantastic collection of approximately 200,000 glossy photographs came into the possession of a local artist who was a constant user of the Westport art collection. The entire 200,000 pieces, which were disorganized and stored in hundreds of dirty boxes, were transported from his barn to a warehouse storage area where they remained for several years while we tried to finance their preparation. Making sense out of the mess was a staggering project and many hours were spent trying to determine how best to go about it. After we had applied for and received a grant from the State, some decisions had to be made and the project began.

As a first step, 60 to 70 large cartons were purchased and labelled with broad subject categories, such as Countries, Children, Warfare, Animals, and two young people were hired to open the boxes and drop the pictures into the carton that was most appropriate. New categories were added as subjects arose.

Among the pictures were many negatives and contact prints that were collected and turned over to two agencies in New York — the International Center of Photography and the ASMP (the society of photographers in communications which is an international guild of magazine photographers). Any questions relating to the whereabouts of negatives have been referred to them. An immediate problem was the condition of some of the pictures which had travelled from a damp barn to a warm, dry basement, causing many to curl and crack. Hundreds were beyond repair and had to be discarded.

After the initial sorting, which under professional supervision took two part-time people about nine or ten months, phase two began and we worked through one box at a time. For instance, in the aforementioned carton labelled 'Countries', all pictures were removed and broken down into subjects, placed in large envelopes, labelled as to what they contained and put back in the carton. In the box that once said 'Countries', there were now some 50 envelopes reading, for example:

1   Paris — France, scenes of left bank
2   Switzerland — mountains, alpine villages
3   Hungary — people rioting in the streets
4   Africa — visit of Queen Elizabeth.

This laborious task took over a year with many different people participating in the work. By this time, our funds had run out and we had approximately 125 to 130 cartons containing 40 to 50 envelopes each. We decided to apply for an additional grant to finish the work. The grant was accepted and in the third year we started phase three which meant opening every envelope and assigning each photograph to a category which would fit into the indexing systems. Every envelope of every box had to be opened, judgements made as to subject assignments, and each illustration had to be stamped, trimmed, labelled, and eventually filed. Fortunately, the grant not only paid for help but also for additional filing cabinets and fiberboard folders to hold the pictures more upright.

Several philosophical issues surfaced as work went on with these fascinating photographs. The main concern was whether to try to preserve them by encasing the pictures in plastic materials and filing them in acid-free folders or acid-free boxes, while trying to control the humidity of the premises in which they would be stored. Agonizing once again over how to handle this situation, the library decided to pursue its existing course of serving as a resource to be used by Connecticut residents, rather than as an archive to preserve for posterity. Cataloguing all those pictures over the three-year period was a long and arduous task, but one that was not without rewards.

The photographs themselves are marvellous and varied, recording world events for the last 50 years or more. Many of the photographers represented are European and this is reflected in their work. There are scenes of political unrest in Europe and Asia during the 30s, 40s, and 50s, hundreds of war photographs, historic scenes of Palestine before it became Israel, China in the 1920s, Middle East war skirmishes, celebrities from the United States and Europe, and travel scenes and fashion photographs by such famous personages as Cecil Beaton and Alfred Eisenstadt.

History becomes alive when one views the recording of past events in visual form. The Shah of Iran crowns himself emperor, Hitler's mountain home near Berchtesgaden is destroyed by the Allies, men wait in the bread lines during the Depression, children of ten work in the sweat shops, crowds throng Times Square on VE Day, and crowds again demonstrate for clemency for the condemned Rosenbergs. Finally, closer to home, there is a picture of the Saugatuck Congregational church of Westport being moved across the Post Road to a new location with the whole town turned out to watch. This picture made the cover of *Life* magazine.

One disadvantage is that in most cases the pictures are not dated. Often the year can be traced to the event but that requires additional work. Dating is important in picture research. Recently, an artist was illustrating a book set in 1937. The fashions, including hair style and shoes, had to be correct for that date; also the furniture, the model radio the characters listened to, the car they drove, all had to reflect the 1930s with accuracy if the paintings were to be accepted. Artists need examples of how the cities and towns looked at the time, so a date is a major priority. Each clipping that goes into the collection is dated and identified as to source whenever possible.

Another important detail is that, since January 1978, the copyright laws state that all artists and photographers hold copyright on their original work, and rights and permissions must be obtained before the work can be reproduced commercially. This is a fact patrons must be made aware of. Ordinarily these problems do not arise since most of our borrowers are illustrators who use the pictures for historical accuracy, likeness, or model position rather than reproduction.

Where do the results of the picture research at the Westport Library lead? Final products are book jackets, record covers, advertisements, magazine illustrations, film strips, TV commercials, as well as slide shows.

What are the current problems facing the picture collection? Mainly, it is not being kept up to date. The historical coverage is fine, but times change and new subject headings and materials should be added. For instance, jogging becomes popular and suddenly we face a barrage of requests for pictures of joggers, and a folder has to be produced in a hurry. Patrons need up-to-date models of heavy equipment, such as machinery and farm tractors. Current television stars are often requested. There is always a demand for material on science fiction and women in business situations — not as secretaries but as executives. Disco scenes are also frequently requested. To be a top-notch picture librarian one must be aware of current trends, current events, people in the news, fads and fashions. One should have a sense of anticipation about what will catch on. Time must be spent seeking out pictorial information on those subjects so that they can be in a file by the time people ask for them. Having a good memory is a major prerequisite. It is important to remember where the pictures are because it is not possible to index everything. One picture may have 20 subjects in it, but it can only go in one place — an all too familiar pattern for the picture librarian.

Who can use the picture collection? Anyone with a Connecticut card can use the picture collection and pictures borrowed from the library circulate for a month. They are packaged in a special envelope designed for the picture collection by a local artist and designer. If a borrower needs an extension of time on the pictures, renewal is possible.

The Westport Library takes pride in being the caretaker of this major resource, one of the largest and most varied in the country, and a wealth of information and opportunity awaits the users in this picture file.

32

Commercial Libraries: Historical Material

Terence Pepper

INTRODUCTION

The three main general historical commercial picture libraries in Britain are the BBC Hulton Picture Library (known as the Radio Times Hulton Picture Library until 1 October 1980), the Mansell Collection, and the Mary Evans Picture Library. These three collections are primarily business undertakings charging prospective users for the loan of prints or illustrative material for reproduction in books, periodicals, newspapers, or in television programmes, advertising, or for other commercial purposes. Thus, they are not open to the general browser or research student.

Some extent of the type of use and profitability of such collections can be given by the April 1979 report of the BBC Advisory Committee on Archives.[1] This records that the Hulton Picture Library receives about 4,800 requests per year, some of which involve up to 200 prints per request. Income earned for the BBC during 1976/7 by the library amounted to £55,581 which gives an idea of the general usage of a busy library. The Hulton Picture Library is the largest of its kind and has a stock of over six million prints. The library was acquired by the BBC in 1958 as the Hulton Picture Post Library, having as its basis the library of *Picture Post* magazine which was published between 1938 and 1957 and thus contains records of all the picture stories covered by the magazine, with photographs by many of the leading photo-journalists of the time. Already by then it had acquired a number of other collections, including an important collection of over a million historical prints, maps, and photographs assembled by Augustin Rischgitz who had operated the first truly comprehensive pre-20th-century historical picture collection. Other collections also in the library are the W & D Downey collection of portraits of royalty and celebrities from 1860 to 1920, the Gordon Anthony and Derrick De Marney theatre collection (*c*.1935-55), and the Baron ballet and theatre collection among many others.

The creation of the Mansell Collection was due to its present director, Miss Louie Boutroy. She is the niece of Augustin Rischgitz and after his death managed his collection for a time with the help of her sister. However, after the latter's death the collection was sold to Hulton and Miss Boutroy worked for a time there helping to integrate the collection, adopting the specially devised Gibbs-Smith classification scheme.[2] In the late 1950s, though, when the collection of topographical photographs and photographs of works of art taken by W A Mansell from the 1870s onwards came on to the market, Miss Boutroy purchased this and, combining it with the subsequent purchase of the Dorien Leigh Agency (which included portrait, topographical, and subject photographs by E O Hoppé taken between 1910 and 1935), and other large collections of illustrated books, periodicals, and prints, created an illustrations library which now contains over three million items.[3,5]

The Mary Evans Picture Library is the newest of the three main picture libraries and was started by the husband-and-wife team of Hilary and Mary Evans in 1964, evolving out of their shared enthusiasm for book and print collecting. What began as a folder of prints in a cupboard is now an extremely well-organized collection of over a million and a half images.[7]

CLASSIFICATION

The classification system used by the Hulton Picture Library and the Mansell Collection is the one devised in the late 1940s by Charles Gibbs-Smith, who had experience of dealing with six picture libraries used by the Ministry of Information during the war. The guiding principle behind his system was that a picture library must produce the largest number of pictures on a given topic in the shortest possible time. He therefore devised a classification that was as simple as possible and that was related to the way in which press enquiries arose. For the most part, research is done by, or at least under the guidance of, the picture library staff, so that their knowledge is all important. Gibbs-Smith maintained that librarians should constantly be in contact with the material itself and that the system should as far as possible be self-indexing and able to be practised at the picture files rather than at separate indexes which in turn lead one to a particular file.

He first divided material into people, places, and things. In the *Picture Post* library subjects were further divided into separate but parallel sequences of historical and modern prints, the modern section containing the constantly growing *Picture Post* material. This division is still maintained in the BBC Hulton Library with 'modern' being defined as post-1920. (This division is not maintained by the Mansell Collection, nor is the colour code indicating the main divisions with which the Hulton Library is also marked.) The 'things' subject pictures are arranged in classified order in separate manila folders in filing cabinets. The main subject heading is indicated by the first three letters of its name, e.g., BIB — Bible illustrations, ZOO — Zoology. These subject words were carefully chosen to avoid repetition. The first subdivision is then indicated by a four-letter notation, with further subdivisions normally written in full, e.g., BIB:OLD-T:ABRAHAM, ZOO:ANIM:ANTEATER.

Gibbs-Smith specified that the classification should not be too detailed because users often prefer to select one of many alternative prints rather than have to ask for a single exact item. Although logical subject order is sacrificed to the demands of the alphabet, the system is simple, easily memorized, and categories can easily be expanded or adapted when required. 'Places', the topographical section, is arranged by continent but can be broken down into subdivisions of particular streets or buildings if there is a bulk of material, such as for European capital cities. The portrait sections at both the Mansell and Hulton Picture Library also contain, where appropriate, illustrations of homes, relics, graves, and scenes from the character's life, as in the case of Napoleon. For a few categories, such as Dance, Theatre, Cinema, some of the lesser known personalities are filed alphabetically under their subject headings rather than bulking out the main portrait sequence.[4,6]

The Mary Evans Picture Library has devised its own classification system based on the type of requests it receives. It consists of 1,000 categories, many of which overlap to some extent with the Gibbs-Smith headings.

Cross-references are of course crucial as there may be any number of subsidiary subjects in a picture as well as the main filed subject. Gibbs-Smith devised an elaborate gridded card on which cross-references could be clearly noted and Mary Evans has cross-references clearly marked under nearly all their subject headings. Nevertheless, despite the most complex cross-references, the visual memory of each member of staff is possibly the most valuable key to the less predictable requests, such as a recent one from a sociology magazine seeking an illustration of 'someone being unkind to an old person'.

In practice, the systems used at Mary Evans and Mansell seem to work well as a large number of the users seek and obtain same-day service. The situation with the BBC library however seems, from the user's point of view, less than satisfactory with a minimum of a two-week delay before any material is available for loan, though this is of course the minimum length of time taken by museums to process material. The BBC April 1979 report[1] recommends a different classification system, finding the present system 'unsuitable for speedy, efficient, and accurate access'. One advantage the two other collections possess is the fact that they do allow far greater access to their collections by prospective users than is currently possible in the case of the BBC.

TYPES OF MATERIAL AND METHODS OF STORAGE

Already some indication has been given of the types of material that form the stock of a picture library but at this stage it is worth examining these in greater detail and discussing the possibility of starting a similar collection. First though, it is important to categorize the stock of a picture library into primary and secondary material. The latter will form the basis of the issue stock and will consist of copy photographs, the reference negatives from which prints are made, Ektachromes of coloured material, and photostats which are now increasingly used by the Mary Evans Picture Library. The primary material will consist of original photographs, such as Francis Frith's views of Egypt or Roger Fenton's Crimean War photographs in both the Mansell Collection and the Hulton Picture Library; original negatives, such as those of the London Stereoscopic Company with Hulton or by the photographers

Speaight and E O Hoppé in the Mansell; lithographs, woodcuts, engravings, broad sheets, maps, and all other kinds of printed ephemera much of which is common to each collection, e.g., *Vanity Fair* chromolithographs. In fact, a great many of the images available from the three collections can be found in non-commercial sources, but it is the system of arrangement and the speed of availability that make it economic for the collections to exist.

One of the most useful items consists of two complete runs of the *Illustrated London News,* which Mary Evans and Mansell each possess and which provide an excellent source of out-of-copyright social history and portraiture. Each collection has cut up one set of volumes and classified the illustrations by subject, while the other set is kept intact for reference. Here, one might mention the usefulness of the ALA *Portrait index,* which is an invaluable and unique guide to retrieving engraved portraits from the *Illustrated London News, The Magazine of Art, Harpers,* etc. The high cost of photographic copying has generally meant that the physical cutting up of all but the most valuable books and periodicals has been an economic necessity for commercial libraries, but now the rapidly improving technology for copying being pioneered by firms such as Polaroid is gradually changing this. There is also a growing interest in colour copying onto transparencies and Ektachromes.

For storage purposes it is generally found most convenient to keep original material and photographic copies of it in the same steel-drawer filing cabinets, which are a common feature of each collection. Occasionally, where space permits, particularly valuable material which should not be handled regularly, such as frail photographs or rare prints, is kept separately. Larger material is kept in a separate but parallel sequence, as are Ektachromes and colour transparencies. Where a black and white photograph is kept of a subject that also exists as an Ektachrome this should be clearly noted on the caption of the print.

Reference negatives are best filed in a numerical sequence based on the chronological order in which they are added, so ensuring their expansion in one direction only, while a card index of negatives is obviously arranged alphabetically by subject.

MAINTENANCE AND PROCESSING

Prints that can be easily damaged should be mounted on acid-free paper or card. Mary Evans Picture Library uses a standard blue card as backing for its prints. It affords them good protection and its distinctive colour makes them instantly recognizable. A further advantage of mounting old prints on a dark card is that, if for any reason there are marks or writing on the back which tend to show through, a dark mount will disguise this. A dry-mounting machine is essential and extremely useful for mounting old engravings and prints, although one would never recommend this for museum objects; as prints in a commercial picture library have an entirely different use, this approach is justifiable. The only disadvantage of card over paper is that it adds considerably to postal costs, as well as taking up more space in the filing cabinets. For this reason, it is not used by the Mansell Collection which prefers a stout paper mount, or no mount at all where multiple copies exist.

Damage to irreplaceable material is always a problem. Mary Evans Library and the Hulton Picture Library make it a general rule never to allow original material to leave the collection. The former will make quick polaroid copies or send photostats if urgency is required. The cost is easily calculated and is largely borne by the client. The Mansell Collection uses an outside photographer to copy its prints. However, it also often sends out original engravings and sepia photographs, believing that the risk involved has to be balanced against the high cost of photography, the delay in fulfilling the order, and the time spent in processing new negatives and prints. Generally, it is possible to copy only the most valuable items, or material likely to be in high demand; otherwise transactions would often result in a financial loss to the library.

Captions

Correct and useful captions are essential and the librarian must decide how much information should be specified. In some cases, commercial agencies are reluctant to reveal the full source of a print on the grounds that an unscrupulous client may then attempt to procure the same illustration from a non-commercial source, but generally captions published to pictures are tantalizingly sparse and brief, even where more information is available. For example, it is not the practice of Mary Evans to caption with the name of the artist or photographer a woodcut engraving from the *Illustrated London News* though the date it appeared is usually given. The guiding principle would appear to be that a user is interested in the subject of a picture but not necessarily in who created it, although obviously this information could be discovered if required. Sometimes prints are extremely difficult to caption because the original caption is inadequate or entirely missing; in such cases the onus is on the user to check whether or not the print is suited to his purposes, and the most the librarian can do is ensure that none of the information provided is misleading or incorrect.

Copyright

All commercial picture libraries try to ensure that the material they send out for reproduction is not in copyright elsewhere. The question of copyright is extremely complex, but generally speaking copyright on material sent out by historical picture libraries has usually lapsed under the 50-year rule. The charge made to clients, although sometimes referred to as a copyright fee, is in fact only a service or reproduction fee. On the rare occasions where prints which are in copyright are sent out to another source it should be clearly specified and then permission for use has to be sought from the actual owner.

Both the Mansell Collection and the Mary Evans Picture Library operate as agents for other collections. Mansell holds the British reproduction rights for the Italian firm Alinari which has photographed practically every painting, building, and work of art in Italy and when any of these photographs are used (Michelangelo's *David* in the Accademia is one of the most frequently requested) a surcharge per print is made. Mary Evans holds the reproduction rights to the important Sigmund Freud photographs and the fascinating collection of the Society for Psychical Research and, in each case, charges 33⅓% over its standard rates in order to pay a royalty to the owners.

Issue System

It is difficult for commercial picture libraries to establish a time limit for loans because the length of time that different users need to retain material varies so widely. Newspaper or advertising agencies tend to return material after only a week or two, while book publishers consider that a year or even longer should be regarded as a reasonable loan period. Mary Evans sends out reminders to users after one month, while the Mansell Collection does so after three months. For valuable Ektachromes, a monthly hiring fee acts as an encouragement to expedite a quick return if the subject is not to be used. It is obviously important to keep checks on loan material, and the holding fee imposed by Mary Evans after a month is an efficient method of helping to ensure that material which is not to be used should quickly be returned for possible recirculation.

Clearly, it is crucial that the issuing library should have full details of what has been lent to whom and for how long, so a follow-up and charging system can be properly operated, and that if material is lost it can be replaced by recourse to the reference negative numbers. Mansell date-stamps all prints sent out on loan and issues a consecutive number for each loan to a particular user. Mary Evans allots a separate job number to each request and then numbers from one the number of items in the job.

CONCLUSION

The growth of public and academic libraries has occurred over a long period, affording time for them to develop long-term policies for the optimum use and exploitation of their material. However, in the private sector the constraints of running a commercial enterprise, where time to plan and organize must often be sacrificed to expediency, must to some extent inhibit methods and practice that might be adopted in the public sector. On the other hand, the genuine enthusiasm of the owners of the two privately run libraries adds a quality and efficiency hard to engender in a publicly funded library. It seems likely that these libraries will continue to survive as long as there is no comparable library in the public sector which is able to compete in a similar fashion.

ACKNOWLEDGEMENTS

I should like to record my thanks to David Lee, librarian of the BBC Hulton Picture Library, Ursula McMullan of the Mansell Collection and Hilary and Mary Evans, for their help in the preparation of this article.

REFERENCES

1   British Broadcasting Corporation 'Report of the Advisory Committee on Archives' in *BBC Report.* April 1979.

2   Gibbs-Smith, Charles 'The Hulton Picture Post Library' in *Journal of Documentation* 6 (1) March 1950. 12-24.
3   Jenkins, Valerie 'The sepia legacy of Uncle Gus' (A history of the Mansell Collection) in *Evening Standard*. 16 February 1979. 19.
4   Moss, Daphne 'Pictures: Radio Times Hulton Library' in *ASLIB Audio Visual Workshop 7-8 May 1970*. ASLIB, 1971.
5   Pepper, Terence 'The Mansell Collection: an illustrations library' in *ARLIS Newsletter* 25. December 1975. 13-14.
6   Smith, Gaye 'Radio Times Hulton Picture Library' in *ARLIS Newsletter* 14. March 1973. 28-9.
7   Turner, Jill 'Love and knowledge builds huge collection' (The Mary Evans Picture Library) in *Library Association Record* 78 (8). August 1976. 361-4.

33

Specialist Commercial: The Cooper-Bridgeman Library

Harriet Bridgeman

INTRODUCTION

Commercial libraries range from the large general collections to smaller collections started in response to a given need or situation. There are many such specialist collections catering for particular subjects or acquiring material by type or format. One library may specialize in colour material, another in art subjects, indeed some of the largest of the type deal with art materials: agencies such as Alinari or Scala. Other smaller libraries, such as the Cooper-Bridgeman Library detailed here, grew out of a need to centralize material on a particular theme and take over the material used by those specialized publishers who do not maintain libraries of their own material.

Scientific subjects are often collected on a similar basis and contain the work of one or more specialist photographers — libraries, such as Bruce Coleman Inc., which acts as an agency for several photographers in the biological sciences, or Biofotos, based on the prolific work of one specialist photographer, Heather Angel.

Material may be collected by type or format, for example those libraries which specialize in aerial photographs. Aerial photograph libraries in themselves can range from the large commercial organizations, such as Aerofilms, to the important Committee for Aerial Photography, in the University of Cambridge or, further, to a government department, as in the case of the Directorate for Overseas Surveys. Not all such libraries can be described as commercial although usually the material is available for reuse against payment of fees or for research purposes. The dividing lines are not strictly drawn.

Helen Harrison

The Cooper-Bridgeman Library was formed in 1971 as a specialist art library since the irony existed that, although London was a great art centre, there was no comprehensive photographic library in London specializing exclusively in art subjects.

The main advantages of the library seemed twofold. First, there was the obvious advantage to picture researchers, authors, and editors in having a large selection of art material from a very diverse number of sources located in a central 'bank'. Second, it provided a depository for publishers who had spent a substantial amount of money on a highly illustrated project but had no further use for the material after the book's publication. The reuse potential, and the income to be drawn from this, was able to provide substantial motivation for an art publisher to sustain his production of highly illustrated art books at a time when colour separations and printing were becoming increasingly expensive. We received material then, as we do now, from publishers and similar organizations on a 50/50 agency basis.

Another aspect which provided motivation to the formation of the library was the inconvenience caused to museums, art galleries, private house owners, etc. from the repeated requests by photographers or publishers to photograph the same painting or object. We have an arrangement with a number of organizations whereby we hold a file transparency of all the most important works in their collection and they refer any photographic requests direct to our library.

Since art publishers require a high degree of technical excellence and faithful adherence to the original, the colour transparencies are all large format ranging in size from full plate (8½ × 6½ inches) to, in almost all instances, a minimum size of 4 × 5 inches. If a particular transparency is not in stock, in certain instances there is a 35 mm. reference slide and soon there will also be a microfiche which is usually an adequate guide, allowing a prospective client to make up his mind and ensuring that the master transparency is not recalled from another client unnecessarily.

The material comes from art galleries, museums, and other public collections, dealers, and private owners from all over the world. It consists of subjects either personally photographed by us, ordered through the photographic service of one of the above organizations, photographed by a local photographer, or deposited with us by a publisher or photographer who, in his turn, may have initially acquired the material by any of the methods already stated.

The Cooper-Bridgeman Library is mainly used by publishers,

greetings card companies, calendar companies, advertising agencies, and the like. Occasionally the material is used by students for research purposes.

COPYRIGHT

With regard to copyright in the transparencies, we follow the dictates set out by Charles H Gibbs-Smith in his essay 'Copyright law concerning works of art, photographs and the written and spoken word' in the *Museums Association Information Sheet* No. 7. The reader is also referred to Section 1.11 of this book. The recommendations of both experts can be very briefly summarized as follows:

Copyright in Paintings of all Kinds of Drawings (Excluding Portraits)

The copyright in any painting or drawing — other than a portrait — belongs to the artist, and continues (with heirs and assigns) until 50 years after the end of the calendar year of his death.

The owner of such a painting or drawing, even if he commissioned it, may not reproduce it in any form without the artist's permission.

But such an owner may do what he likes with the work, and may even mutilate or destroy it if he wishes.

It is an infringement of copyright to copy the work in any way, or in any medium, even by making a three-dimensional version of it. It is also an infringement of copyright to publish, or issue to the public, any photographs or other reproductions of the work, except as noted below.

But it is not an infringement:

1   to photograph the work — or have it photographed — for private study or research, either by the owner or by anyone else, so long as it is 'fair dealing';
2   to publish a photograph of the work to accompany a criticism or review of it, or to publish it in direct connection with another work for the purposes of criticism or review, i.e. for comparison;
3   to exhibit the work in any way the owner, or anyone else, pleases;
4   to show (as opposed to making) slides of the work on the screen during a lecture, etc.

In view of the widespread belief that the ownership of a work of art confers rights of reproduction on the owner, it cannot be overemphasized that such ownership only confers the right to deal as one likes with the work as an actual physical object, i.e. to give away, sell, or destroy it, but not to reproduce it.

If the owner (or commissioner) of the work wishes, he can try and persuade the artist to sell him the copyright of the work but there should be an agreement in writing to this effect, and a considerable fee will probably be demanded.

Copyright in Portraits (Painted or Drawn)

The law is completely different when it comes to the copyright in painted or drawn portraits for the copyright here belongs to whoever commissions the work, and the artist has no rights whatsoever in the portrait he has drawn or painted.

The copyright runs until 50 years after the end of the calendar year in which the artist dies.

STORAGE

Each transparency is kept, in the conventional fashion, in a transparency sleeve. The caption, typed on a small white label which is applied to each sleeve, gives such information as the title and date of a painting, the name and dates of an artist, country of origin, medium, and location. The transparencies are stored in a numerical sequence relating to the date on which they were acquired, in Kodachrome boxes. These in turn are kept in fireproof cabinets for insurance purposes.

CATALOGUES

A catalogue which is updated annually, and has recently been put on to a computer, lists the transparencies according to their category and chronologically and geographically within each category. For example, it begins with the artists whose works are represented in the library; the names are listed alphabetically and as far as possible under each artist's name, in the order in which they were executed within the artist's lifetime. The decorative arts, such as furniture, metalwork, and ceramics are listed according to country, each of these following an alphabetical sequence, and the transparencies are listed chronologically within the scope of their country.

Apart from the catalogue, subjects are listed on file cards so that if, for example, a client requests an illustration of bull-fighting or a coronation but has no particular subject or artist in mind, reference can be made quickly to the material available.

LOAN PROCEDURES

When material is loaned out, it is entered on a delivery note in quintuplicate. Two copies are given to the hirer, one of which he or she signs and returns to the library as proof of receipt of the material. Two of the other copies are filed chronologically, so that after one month a reminder can be sent out stating that the return of the material is overdue, unless it is actually going to be used, with a second reminder as a follow-up should no attempt be made by the client to get in touch. The other copy is filed alphabetically so that it is possible to see what material a client holds at any given time. A note is also made on the box from which the transparency has been taken as to who has hired it and on what date. Not only is this a further record but it also facilitates recall of the transparency should the same subject be required by someone else.

The delivery notes, on which the transparencies to be sent out are listed, state the conditions of hire and include an indemnity clause in the event of loss of or damage to a transparency, whereby the hirer is responsible for compensation of up to £200 on each item.

STAFF

The library is run by a part-time manager, a librarian, and an assistant librarian. The manager, apart from having an overall interest in the library, visits trade fairs, book fairs, and generally tries to bring in new business. The librarian and her assistant deal with the day-to-day running, from the enquiries through to the invoicing. A bookkeeper is also involved.

Having been one of the earlier of the commercial picture libraries to start off in London, the Cooper-Bridgeman Library is now well established. The need for such an organization has been proved and business is now conducted with its turnover increasing annually. As a member of the British Association of Picture Libraries and Agencies the Cooper-Bridgeman Library is aware of the direction in which picture libraries are moving and the requirements that a specialist commercial library must now meet.

34

Managing the Photographer's Picture Resources

Roger Bradley

Photographers as they progress accumulate a backwash of negatives, prints, and transparencies which can vary between 2,500 and 250,000. The management of this stock is essential both for the easy retrieval of negatives where reorders are involved and for the exploitation of stock pictures for publication.

This account describes a system evolved for one photographer with alternatives suggested by others. The three main forms of photograph to be considered are:

1 negatives — black and white or colour
2 prints
3 transparencies.

As will be shown, a simple card index can interlink the materials.

NEGATIVES

In the particular case being considered most of the negatives are 24 × 36 mm. or 6 × 6 cm. of 36 and 12 exposures respectively.

After film processing, contact sheets are made on 20.3 × 25.4 cm. (8 × 10 inch) paper providing space for 6 strips of 6 exposures of 35 mm. film, 4 strips of 3 exposures 6 × 6 cm. film, or 4 pieces of 4 × 5 inch sheet film. These are made using glass to flatten the negatives or a contact printing frame, such as the Paterson 35 mm., 6 × 6 cm., or proof printer. The last has plain glass making it suitable for any size negatives; the others have the advantage of plastic retaining strips to keep the negatives locked in place.

The negatives are then placed in sleeves. Various types are available to contain either a single strip of negatives or the entire film. They are available in either translucent or clear material. The latter has the obvious advantage of obviating the need to remove the negatives for the production of contact sheets. The negative sleeves are punched to allow filing in a ring binder. The contact sheet is also punched and placed alongside its negatives.

If contact sheets are constantly consulted it may be preferable to file them separately to avoid damage to the negatives. In either case a numbering sequence is required. A letter prefix can be used to indicate the year, followed by an accession number. After the alphabet is exhausted one can start again, doubling the prefix. A simple b or c after the number indicates black and white or colour film. This letter/number sequence is printed on each contact sheet and its negative file.

This approach works well with the wide range of subjects photographed by the author of this section. Other photographers prefer to establish a file for each client or under a series of topics. One is happy to have three containers marked 'Alive', 'Dying', and 'Dead'!

Where there is a steady demand for reprints it may be advisable to pinpoint each negative. One photographer uses this lengthy sequence:

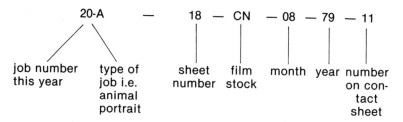

Whatever numbering sequence is used, it should also be applied to any prints.

PRINTS

Few prints can be made for stock because of the high cost of photographic paper, but the contact sheet with a magnifier makes it easy to isolate worthwhile pictures. A photographer will prefer to work with contact prints and supply full size prints only on demand to the client.

Prints which are usually on 20.3 × 25.4 cm. paper are housed in photographic paper boxes and stored on specially designed shelves. They are filed under broad topics which are printed on the front edge of each box. Alternatively they could be placed in manila folders and kept in a standard filing cabinet. If archive permanence is important, special acid-free boxes may be obtained. Whatever the method of storage it is important to remember that each print should bear the letter/number code of its negative.

TRANSPARENCIES

Unlike negatives, these may be conveniently treated individually. After a cull of unwanted pictures, each transparency is captioned and stored in 24-pocket plastic files. These are suspended in a normal filing cabinet.

They are filed under topics because this makes for easier browsing — useful when compiling slide/tape programmes. Each file has two labels affixed to the top edge. They indicate:

1   the topic, and
2   the accession number of the particular file.

An alternative is to number each job and file in order of accession number, depending on the card index to find particular pictures. With the topic system there is still a need for cards to cross-reference the system. This is because a broad topic such as Nigeria may contain slides which merit their own topic files, for example bicycles.

CARD INDEX

This provides for cross-referencing and makes it easier for people, other than the originator, to find pictures.

To recap:
— Each negative film and its contact sheet is assigned a chronological letter and number — so K67b might indicate the 67th film shot in 1972 which happened to be black and white.
— Each slide file has along its top edge the particular topic and an accession number for the file.

Two types of card are made:
— A topic card for all types of photograph.
— An accession card for transparencies (negatives are already in accession order).

TOPIC CARD

TRANSPORT — ROAD — BICYCLES							
6,	12,	14,	21,	48	A14B,	K17C,	P42
	118	,	127		A19, R75		

ACCESSION CARD

NIGERIA

1 Jos Plateau	13 Bicycles outside shop
2 ,, ,,	14 ,, ,, ,,
3 ,, ,,	15 Bicycle repairman
4 ,, ,,	16 Selling food in the street
5 Bus Station, Jos	17 ,, ,, ,, ,, ,,
6 ,, ,, ,,	18 ,, ,, ,, ,, ,,
7 ,, ,, ,,	19 ,, ,, ,, ,, ,,
8 Market traders, Jos	20 ,, ,, ,, ,, ,,
9 ,, ,, ,,	21 ,, ,, ,, ,, ,,
10 ,, ,, ,,	22 ,, ,, ,, ,, ,,
11 ,, ,, ,,	23 Taxi, Jos
12 ,, ,, ,,	24 ,, ,,

Further cross-reference cards may be used to find an entry under the correct heading, i.e., Bicycles — *see* Transport—Road—Bicycles. In the search for pictures of bicycles, the card 'Transport—Road—Bicycles' is found showing that transparencies of this topic exist. Ordinary numbers indicate a slide file containing at least one bicycle picture, while a box around the number reveals that the file contains bicycle pictures exclusively.

The letter/number/letter entries indicate a negative/contact sheet containing pictures of bicycles. The next stage, in the case of a negative, is to find the appropriate file as indicated along the front edge, e.g. K-1-7C.

In the case of a transparency, take the number on the topic card and look it up in the accession file. This will reveal the name of the topic of the file in question. It will also list the contents of that slide file which, if wanted, can be found alphabetically.

This system organizes the material and allows for cross-referencing to be added when necessary but, in the end, the test of any retrieval system lies in whether you find your picture when you need it — quickly.

SUBJECT SPECIALIZATION

As suggested earlier, many photographers accumulate picture categories almost accidentally through assignments, hobbies, skills, holidays, and religious and cultural backgrounds.

Individual photographers often specialize, combining their photographic skill with a personal knowledge of the subject. For instance, intelligent coverage of equestrian events is made much easier by being a rider yourself. Another advantage is having contacts in an area to which other photographers would not have easy access.

An individual photographer would probably be advised to specialize, perhaps combining with others to provide greater coverage. There are no subjects to be avoided but where the market is well provided for, new photographers will have to offer exceptional work.

MARKETS

These include magazines, books, educational resources, television, and exhibitions. Initial contact may be speculative or promotional. Subsequent requests for photographs may depend not only on the photographer's skill but on the impact made with the customer. Successful transactions often lead to a chain of requests for further material and systematic reminders sent to customers help to keep business flowing.

Rates vary but NUJ (National Union of Journalists) minimums should be watched and comparisons made with other photographers in the same field. Fuller information on markets, conditions/fees may be obtained through membership of the NUJ, Bureau of Freelance Photographers and by reading the *Writer's and Artist's Yearbook.*

CONTACTS

— Association of Fashion, Advertising and Editorial Photographers Ltd (AFAEP), 10A Dryden Street, London WC2E 9NA.
— British Association of Picture Libraries and Agencies (BAPLA), PO Box 93, London NW6 5XW.
— Bureau of Freelance Photographers (BFP), Focus House, 497 Green Lanes, London N13 4BP.
— Society of Picture Researchers and Editors (SPREd.), BM Box 259, London WC1N 3XX.

Recent published information concerning picture libraries and fees:
— Camerawork Number 15, HMPW 119 Roman Road, London E2 0QN.

Fees and conditions for freelancers submitting pictures for publication:
— Hotshoe Number 6, 17 South Molton Street, London W1.

Photo libraries listed in:
— *British Journal of Photography,* Issues 26, 27, 28, 29
— Henry Greenwood & Co. Ltd, 28 Great James Street, London WC1N 3HL.
— *International Directory of Photographic Information Services* includes photo libraries and professional bodies.

SUPPLIERS OF PHOTOGRAPHIC STORAGE MATERIALS

Negative and slide storage
            Kenro Photographic Products
            High Street
            Kempsford, Gloucestershire GL7 4EQ

Negative and slide storage
Contact printing frames
>Paterson Products
2-6 Boswell Court
London WC1N 3PS

Slide and negative storage materials
>Photo Science Ltd
Charfleets Road
Canvey Island, Essex SS8 0PH

Slide storage
Slide holders for standard filing cabinets
>Slide Centre
143 Chatham Road
London SW11 6SR

Slides
Plastic-pocketed sheets for suspension filing, albums, etc.
>Nicholas Hunter Filmstrips
Mutton Yard
40 Richmond Road
Oxford

>Macfarlane Robson Ltd   (Rogers Slide Holders)
Hedgefield House
Blaydon-on-Tyne, Co. Durham

>Diana Wyllie Ltd   (DW Viewpacks)
3 Parks Road
London NW1 6XP

Archive print storage materials
>Goldfinger Ltd
329 The Broadway
Muswell Hill
London N10

Print storage
Archival print storage boxes
   G Ryder & Co. Ltd
   Denbigh Road
   Bletchley
   Milton Keynes
   Buckinghamshire

35

An Advertising Library Collection

Patricia Oliver

1 INTRODUCTION

The existence of a formalized picture collection in the world of advertising agencies is limited to one small collection in a large London agency. The development of that collection has been based on the demands and needs of the Creative Department in the agency — that is, art directors, copywriters, TV producers.

It is the result of the management policy within the organization that meeting these needs has been appreciated as essential to the reputation of the agency, as one providing more extensive and sophisticated services for its clients than any other agency. Smaller organizations are unable to invest staff time and cash in a reference source for their creative personnel.

2 THE ORGANIZATION

The organization itself is one of the largest agencies in the UK, with a staff of 540. Of these, 120 form the Creative Department, possibly the most vital to the success of the agency. These are the people directly concerned with the writing and designing of advertisements and making television and radio commercials. The department is divided into groups, each headed by a creative supervisor. Each creative supervisor is a former copywriter or art director who takes overall responsibility for all the accounts in his or her group, and who guides the group in order to produce the best possible work.

Each group has its own accounts — the products or services for which it produces advertising. Within each are a number of copywriters and art directors. TV producers also work with creative people inside the agency although they are not allocated to specific groups. They act in liaison with production companies and artists outside the agency, working with them to turn television scripts into effective commercials.

By the very nature of the business any reference source has to be as varied and diverse as the accounts the agency handles.

3 HISTORY AND DEVELOPMENT OF THE 'CREATIVE REFERENCE LIBRARY'

The library was set up in the 1940s with a staff of one and very limited resources. The basic book collection was very small indeed, but the idea of building up a collection of pictures for use by creative staff, to give them ideas, was already there. There was no real development, however, until 1971, when one of the creative directors on the agency Board saw the possibilities of the collection, and brought in the present librarian, who already had experience in several departments in the agency. It was only then that an investment was made in terms of two people and cash for the expansion of the book stock. The existence of a standard Information Centre and Library to serve the rest of the agency meant that the creative librarians could concentrate on their own very specialized function.

The library has now become an integral part of the Creative Department. Evidence of this lies in the fact that new staff are brought there immediately on arrival and introduced to the stock and the service.

4 THE COLLECTION

The collection today consists of three main types of material:
— books
— files of illustrations
— periodicals.

Books

The book collection is small consisting of some 1,500 volumes. The main subject areas covered are:

— History of art
— Architecture
— Costume and fashion
— Antiques
— Heraldry
— Individual artists (mainly traditional, not modern)
— Art annuals
— Graphics
— Photography
— Posters
— General illustration reference works
— Cartoons and comics
— Children's characters
— Travel books
— Botany
— Natural history
— Cookery
— Biographies
— Dictionaries (illustrated) and books of quotations
— Encyclopaedias (illustrated).

It must be remembered that the existence of a much larger Information Department Library means that this collection can be limited to purely pictorial books, since users can always refer to a larger book stock for statistics or factual information.

Selection

Selection of material is based on the suitability of the book for the needs of the art directors, i.e., it must be pictorial, and ideally in colour. In the same way the development of the subject areas listed above has been based on specific requests, as in the case, for example, of biographies, or on the regular demands of creative staff.

The librarian prefers to rely on personal purchasing of books, not on publishers' lists or the standard bibliographical sources. She must be able to see the book at first hand to judge its suitability for her users. Publishers' lists are used only for purchase of the standard art annuals covering graphics, posters, photographers, or for illustrated dictionaries or collections of quotations for use by the copywriters.

Because of the unique function of this library, second-hand books form an important part of the book stock. The librarian regularly browses through second-hand bookshops in London, visits jumble sales, or has personal contacts for old books. Specific requests are met if possible by borrowing books from other libraries but unless a book is of long-term interest it will not be purchased.

The currency of a book is not important if it has potentially useful illustrations for an art director looking for ideas. Some of the most useful books, for example, are those general publications with illustrations which can be used direct with no copyright problems. Art directors find it invaluable if they can use an illustration directly.

For these reasons no book is ever discarded. It is virtually impossible to say categorically that a book has outlived its usefulness, the more so since selection is made on such tight criteria. With a relatively small collection the problem of storage does not become a major one.

Processing and Arrangement

Staff time is at a premium and for this reason processing is kept to a bare minimum. Each book receives a 'Library' stamp and a date stamp, and is filed immediately. There is no classification or catalogue in existence in the library, partly due to the staffing limitations, and partly due to the users, who have neither the inclination nor the training to use a catalogue.

Arrangement is based on the judgement of the librarian with experience of the users, their requirements, and habits, and on her knowledge of the stock, and permits immediate location of relevant material.

Files of Illustrations

The most unique feature of the Creative Reference Library is its amazing collection of some 2,000 reference files built up over so many years and carefully maintained since the beginning. There are few subject areas not covered by these files, which are arranged in the broad subject categories listed below, in a very simple alphabetical order.

Each category has numbered subdivisions, and colour coding helps the librarian in their filing. A cross-reference system is maintained on the outside of the files, to assist the staff in their searching and retrieval. New categories are created when necessary by subdividing existing divisions of the broad categories. Subject categories include:

Artists
Actors and actresses
Agriculture
Anatomy
Architecture
Animals
Antiques
Aviation
Birds
Celebrities:
  historical
  literary
  miscellaneous
  political
  royalty
  sporting
Children
Cinema
Commerce
Costume (up to Edwardian)
Dancing
Domestic scenes
Education
Entertainments
Fashion (from 1920s)
Fictitious characters
Fire service
Fish
Flags, badges and symbols

Geographical — countries
Geographical — miscellaneous
Geographical — weather conditions
Geographical — British towns
Geographical — English counties
Historical events
Industrial
Insects
Legal
Lettering and design
London
Maps
Medical
Men
Military
Music
Naval
Photography
Postal service
Radio and television
Radio and television celebrities
Religion
Reptiles
Science and chemistry
Ships and shipping
Shops and shopping
Social scenes:
  flowers and plants
  food and drink

fruit	Transport — roads
vegetables	Transport — railways
furniture and furnishings	Travel
gardens and gardening	Trees
Sports and pastimes	Types
Telephones	Vegetables
	Women

Special collections include illustrators' and photographers' works (alphabetical by name).

Selection

The prime source for the files is magazines which are carefully scanned by the assistant librarian and torn up. The range of material is very wide; consumer, trade publications are obviously vital to the needs of the creative staff, but so are scientific and technical journals, geographical and business magazines, and any 'fringe' magazines for minority groups. In fact, there is little that can be ruled out as a possible source for pictures.

As already described, the basic use of the stock is for art directors looking for ideas, or for photographs which they can use as a basis for a slide or chart in client presentations. Colour is obviously an important element and there is little in black and white among the photographs. The development of the collection is heavily influenced by the clients and the company's new business intentions. Obviously, if a pitch for new business is being organized in a particular field, then there will suddenly be heavy emphasis on the collection of illustrations in that subject. It is therefore essential for the librarian to be aware of and to anticipate possible new areas of interest.

Periodicals

The periodicals collection is fairly small and concentrates on art magazines and the consumer press. Only the latest issue is kept on display for staff to browse through, then removed for cutting for the files. The browsing facility is essential for creative staff who need to get a feel for the whole range of advertisements in the press that their clients are using. Obviously, an awareness of competitive advertising is a crucial element in the preparation and planning of a campaign.

In addition, the librarian is a centralizing source for the whole department for periodicals. She controls the circulation of magazines to each creative group.

Loans

All material is lent freely to creative staff, although firm control is needed. A Loans Book is kept for each collection — books and files — and details are kept to a minimum. Staff time means that it is impossible to complete complicated forms, and the users would not consider recording anything other than the briefest of details.

The librarian is nevertheless extremely strict on chasing items which have been on loan for more than three weeks. No-one is allowed to keep material for longer than this period.

5   ADDITIONAL SERVICES

Film Equipment

One of the vital roles fulfilled within the Creative Department by the reference library is the control and coordination of cameras. The TV producers obviously have a heavy demand for equipment to be available at any time and for any purpose. The library coordinates loans very efficiently, and ensures that the necessary equipment and films are always available, no matter how short the notice.

One of the advantages of this role is that photographs are often donated to the library and can be amalgamated into the collection.

Art Supplies

The library is also responsible for the purchase of art supplies for the agency as a whole, not only for the Creative Department. This is a mainly administrative function, ensuring that art buyers and controllers have all the material they require for their work in preparing for client presentations and advertisement copy.

6   STAFFING

The library has always been staffed by just two people. For this reason there has been little opportunity to organize the stock in a very sophisticated way. The background and educational qualifications of staff do not lie in academic librarianship but in other advertising agencies. It is much more vital to have an understanding of the work of an art director or a copywriter and of the clients the agency works for, than it is to understand a library classification scheme. Nothing can replace the years of experience gained in the agency itself and the involvement in the department's work.

The rewards lie in seeing the result of hours spent looking for the right illustration or for a new idea eventually turned into a successful advertisement.

The prime function of the staff is twofold:

1 to answer the enquiries of creative staff and assist in searching and retrieving relevant illustrations from any source, internal or external, and

2 to maintain and develop the collection in order to answer these enquiries as quickly and as comprehensively as possible.

7 ADMINISTRATION

The day-to-day administration of so small a library requires little time. The department's budget is incorporated with the main books and magazines budget for the agency as a whole. Expenditure is left to the discretion of the librarian, and since so many second-hand books are bought, presents little problem. Any regular standing orders or major publications which cannot be obtained from bookshops in London are purchased by the Information Services Department on behalf of the creative librarian, so that involvement with invoicing is kept to a minimum.

36

National and Regional
Tourist Boards

Judith J Harries

M any countries, especially those with a major tourist trade have
some information or tourist organization dealing with a range
of topics — how to get there, what to see, what to do, and
how to get around the country. Material ranges from timetables to
lavishly illustrated brochures and these often, but not always, contain
pictures drawn from a collection.

The offices dealing with tourism range from the information services
based in the country, area, or town concerned, to the tourist boards
described here, through the national tourist organizations based in other
countries detailing the attractions of particular areas, e.g., the Swiss
National Tourist Organisation in London and other major cities, and on
to the embassies which may hold small collections of pictures of their
country, usually in the press or public relations office, e.g., Australia
House or the French Government Tourist Office in London.

The tourist boards, in the context of this discussion, are those of the
United Kingdom. However, many of the principles can be applied to the
systems in other countries, because there is usually a regional network
which is concerned with both national and local policies.

The United Kingdom has four co-equal tourist boards: the British
Tourist Authority (BTA), the English Tourist Board, the Scottish
Tourist Board, and the Wales Tourist Board. Each is financed in large
part by the government and is an independent statutory body. The
BTA's special function is to promote tourism to Britain from overseas,
with a general responsibility for tourism within Britain as a whole. There

is an agreement with Northern Ireland, the Channel Islands, and the Isle of Man to promote their tourist interests abroad also.

The English, Scottish, and Wales tourist boards are responsible for ensuring that our visitors from abroad or within the United Kingdom find in England, Scotland, and Wales the facilities, services, and welcome they expect. The main objectives of the English Tourist Board are to encourage people living in England to take their holidays there and to encourage the provision and improvement of tourist amenities and facilities in England. To do this more efficiently there are 12 English regional tourist boards, sponsored and financially aided by the English Tourist Board, to cover the whole country. These tourist boards are responsible for the planning, development, and marketing of tourism in their particular areas.

This may sound complicated, but it is very important that the person responsible for organizing any tourist board photographic library or collection is aware of the national network, because it affects the overall policies, funds, objectives, and organization of the photographic system. It would be true to say that there is a different set-up within each board but a familiar pattern throughout.

The term 'photographs' in this section on regional tourist boards refers to colour transparencies (slides) and black and white photographs. Tourist boards obtain their photographic stock in a variety of ways:

1 by employing staff photographers
2 by means of in-house photography (amateurs within the tourist board)
3 by commissioning freelance photography
4 by buying the copyright on individual photography
5 by holding photography of various photographers (professional and amateur)
6 by maintaining a list of freelance photographers who cover their region or parts of their region.

1 *Staff photographers* It is usually the national tourist boards who have the funds to employ full-time photographers, and it pays them to do so because their demand for photography is greater. The BTA employs three; the Scottish, Wales, and Northern Ireland Tourist Boards employ one at each board, but the Wales and English Tourist Boards come into a different category (see 3 below).

460

2 *In-house photography* Photography is done by various members of staff within that board. This refers to the regional boards and, historically, it started because it is the cheapest way of supplying photographic material.

3 *Commissioning freelance photography* Both the Wales and the English Tourist Boards fall into this category. Neither employs a staff photographer, nor do they do in-house photography, but both successfully use freelance photographers. That is, they both pay freelance photographers to go out and shoot exactly what they want and then put it into a system (which we will discuss later) for further use or reuse.

4 *Buying the copyright on individual photography* This means that when the tourist board sees photography suitable for its purposes it approaches the person holding the copyright, be it a professional photographer or a keen amateur, and buys it outright. That is, it becomes the copyright owner and can use the photograph again and again, and reproduce it however it wishes, either for editorial or advertising use. In the latter case, the agency must have model release signed by those people clearly visible in all photography.

5 *Holding photography of various photographers* The tourist board files photography that has been sent on approval but that does not belong to it. It uses the material for reference and if it decides to use any the copyright holder is approached to discuss reproduction fees and conditions.

6 *Maintaining a list of freelance photographers who cover their area* This means that the tourist board simply keeps a list of photographers holding suitable photography and they are approached, individually, as the need arises.

SPECIAL CONSIDERATIONS

The type of photographic material used by tourist boards is governed by special considerations which are both national and local. National policies are expressed to the regional tourist boards by the BTA which receives its directives from the government. Local or regional policies are a result of the tourist boards each working together with the English Tourist Board, and then local government and the trade interests in that specific region. By looking at the names of the 12 English regional tourist boards, one can appreciate the wealth of special considerations applying to each area:

> Cumbria Tourist Board
> East Anglia Tourist Board
> East Midlands Tourist Board
> Heart of England Tourist Board
> London Tourist Board
> Northumbria Tourist Board
> North West Tourist Board
> South East England Tourist Board
> Southern Tourist Board
> Thames and Chilterns Tourist Board
> West Country Tourist Board
> Yorkshire and Humberside Tourist Board

Broadly speaking these considerations relate to how each region fits into the national network and general policies on tourism, and then local aspects are taken into account.

Imagine a prospective tourist planning a holiday in England. He will probably have heard of London and even have images such as the Tower of London or 'Big Ben'. He then examines some of the literature published by the BTA and begins to be interested in regional travel. The BTA has used market research and regional research studies to help define those attractions specific to each region. Overlaid, by the government, are directives pertaining to areas which need to be developed and will benefit from an enhanced tourist trade. The main aim is to bring revenue into areas not doing so well by giving every region the chance of attracting its share of the tourist trade. In this way England is considered as a whole.

Now apply this to the photographic material used to attract the tourist. When the BTA publishes a main guide (promoting all regions and also Great Britain as a whole — thus including Scotland, Wales, Northern Ireland, etc.) it has to use photography in two ways: to convey the image and flavour of each region and to illustrate tourist attractions, activities and accommodation around the country. The regional tourist boards with their own publications use photographic material to illustrate their areas in detail, and try to convey the message that there is something to interest everyone.

USER POPULATION

The user population, in the first instance (that is before reuse) is the tourist board itself, in its own print and publications, and in the press for further publicity and advertising. There is also an increasing use of colour transparencies in audio-visual presentations by the tourist boards. These are the main reasons why photographic material is collected in the first place, the object being to sell the product in an appealing way. Because this aim will never change, it is pointless if the work of a staff or freelance photographer, executed for the tourist board, is discarded after use. By filing it efficiently it may be reused, first of all by the tourist board and then by other users. There is also an obvious financial benefit.

REUSE

It should be possible for tourist boards, when they own the copyright of the photography, not only to use the material again and again themselves, but also to let other people use it. This means two things: the tourist board's product is seen more and exposed to a wider market and, if a fee is charged to some of the users, it is an economy whereby some of the expense for originating photography may be recovered.

Reuse can either occur within the tourist trade itself or commercially outside. Most, if not all, tourist boards do not charge a reproduction fee if the material is being used to sell, promote, or advertise their region. They do, however, charge a reproduction fee if the material is used commercially, as on a chocolate box or in a book for editorial purposes. The BTA does not charge any reproduction fee for photographic material when it is being used abroad to promote the United Kingdom, although it does ask the user to pay for any transparencies that may be lost in this process.

Over the last few years the regional tourist boards have become more interested in obtaining and holding their own photographic stock rather than relying on other sources to cover some of their needs and trying to secure the rest through freelance photographers. They do use freelance photographers, but in a planned way to enable them to reuse the material, and, of course, their own in-house people, as mentioned before.

From this, three objectives are now beginning to emerge:
1 Immediate use in the board's own publications
2 Reuse by themselves and other users
3 Revenue from reproduction fees.

Revenue from reproduction fees is a relatively new aspect for regional tourist boards, and has only come about as a consequence of the individual photographic stocks growing. However, it is an extremely important aspect, because it usually leads to better photography both for the boards themselves and for reusers. This 'better photography' is financially possible because commercial reusers are helping to deploy some of the cost by paying reproduction fees.

SUPPLY AND RETRIEVAL

Supply and retrieval actually operates on two levels: within the tourist board and outside it, and each is equally important. When a tourist board accumulates photographic stock through its own use of photographic material, it must be put into order and kept so. This is vital for two reasons: the tourist board must be able to locate the material when it wishes to use it; and if it is to charge reusers in the commercial category it has to be able to supply them with the material on demand. To make this possible there must be a clear, workable system dealing with:

> Storage
> Captioning
> Categorizing (usually district/area and then broken down into sub-jects within that district/area).
> Cross-referencing
> Checking out
> Checking back
> Service fees (including print fees for black and white prints where applicable)
> Payments for lost transparencies
> Reproduction fees for commercial use.

The application of these factors is, in reality, often the responsibility of one person at each of the tourist boards and that person usually fits into one of the following categories: photo librarian, publicity officer, information officer, Press and Public Relations Department, marketing manager. There is one exception. The English Tourist Board (ETB) deals with its photographic stock (obtained by commissioning freelance photographers) by giving it to someone outside the ETB to put into a system. That person runs an agency and the photography is dealt with on a commercial basis. In this way the ETB recovers part of its photographic budget.

A librarian who has never been involved in photographic systems should not be dismayed. There now exists a wide variety of commercial picture agencies and libraries. Over 100 of them belong to the British Association of Picture Libraries and Agencies (BAPLA, PO Box 93, London NW6 5XW, England). They produce a handbook and, after looking at the different types of material held it would be possible to approach suitable ones to visit for the purpose of examining their particular systems. People within this field are professional and, when approached frankly, very helpful to newcomers when they know what is being required of them.

A trained librarian, however, is used to compiling data, using systems, and cross-referencing material. Cross-referencing skills are very useful if one has to apply a method suited to the photographic material within a particular tourist board, relating specifically to the way it is used within that tourist board. The librarian about to embark on a picture collection should try to seek out the pitfalls beforehand. There are problems in keeping a complete and detailed record of photographic materials by numbers, and there are problems with copyright when photographic material is not owned by the collection. The variations on these problems can be sought out by talking to an experienced picture person or, in some cases, an experienced freelance photographer. It is also necessary to gain a basic technical knowledge, to be able to recognize a good print from a bad one, and to know when one is asking for the impossible from a photographer or printer, either in terms of time or quality. Efficient supply and retrieval very much depend on the librarian who should know something about everything relating to holding photographic stock and the ways in which it may be used.

37

A Publishing House Library: Phaidon Press

Margaret Amosu

P haidon Press was founded in Vienna in 1923 by two young men, Ludwig Goldscheider and Bela Horowitz, who had been friends from their schooldays. Goldscheider was a student of art and literature, and Horowitz, a lawyer. The latter managed and directed the new firm and Goldscheider designed and edited. Their first lists contained plays, poetry, literary biographies, translations of Shakespeare, Dickens, and others. In 1937, as German fascism threatened Austria, they came to London as political refugees, re-establishing their liberal humanist press first under the wing of Allen and Unwin and, soon afterwards, independently. Not long before coming to Britain they seem to have begun the specialist art book publishing for which the firm subsequently became famous, with books on Rembrandt, Titian, and on the art of ancient Egypt and Greece. All these appeared later in English translations.

Nothing quite like the first Phaidon books with the London imprint had appeared in Britain before, except in rather costly editions, such as Finberg's beautiful books on Turner. The Phaidon books were cloth-bound in a simple but distinct style and contained a hundred or more large reproductions, mostly in monochrome, with a few colour plates. They cost 10 shillings each. Among the first titles were books on Van Gogh, Cézanne, Botticelli, Rodin, and the Impressionists and their low price made a new and largely unknown world of art accessible to thousands of people, particularly young people whose awareness of pictorial art derived from the reproductions of *Cherry Ripe* and *Sir*

Isumbras at the Ford on their classroom walls. While the Phaidon books were cheap enough to be popular and to sell easily, they were written and edited by scholars, and used by scholars and critics. Many such were and are associated with the Press: Ganz, Berenson, Pope-Hennessy, Gombrich (whose *Story of Art,* first published in 1949, has gone into 13 editions and been translated into as many languages), Blunt, Suida, and many others. In addition, these early editions are still sought after by students because the size of the plates makes them very useful, especially in countries with few or small collections of classical art.

While the popular works have continued to be produced throughout the years, the list shows many *catalogues raisonnés* and major historical and critical studies produced to the highest possible standards. The market for such works is inevitably limited by their very nature and they can only be printed in small editions. This side of the Press's work becomes ever more costly and difficult to continue because of the currently greatly increased competition, particularly in the popular market (due perhaps to the technical advances in colour printing) which formerly to some extent subsidized the scholarly books.

A recent article in *Art Libraries Journal*[1] by an academic publisher discussed the costs of producing such art books. For some reason the writer seemed to overlook one of the aspects of costs that are peculiar to books such as those published by Phaidon Press: this is the cost of obtaining the reproductions of the pictures used. Purchase or rental fees and — in the case of living or recently dead artists and photographers — copyright fees, are all substantial. The staff finding and procuring the photographs are normally graduates with either wide general or highly specialized knowledge and experience; they have to be paid commensurate salaries. The pictures have all to be collected before the designing, editing, and production processes can start and may take many months to get. If they are being purchased this does not matter, but hiring is different: in a recent scholarly work containing over 400 illustrations the rental fees for just three of the colour plates totalled more than £1,000. In another similar book on architecture the author needed special viewpoints for photographs of well-known buildings to illustrate his theme and specialist photographers had to be commissioned to travel to various parts of Britain to make them. This latter book is being published in an edition of less than 3,000. Many more examples could be quoted, but these two are typical and may suffice to show why scholarly art books in particular are very costly and differ in significant ways from many other academic publications.

BACKGROUND OF THE LIBRARY

This necessarily brief sketch of the historical and economic setting of the library at Phaidon Press may help to explain its rather unorthodox character.

Since the Second World War there has been an important development in library provision. The libraries of large industrial firms, such as Glaxo, Pressed Steel, Courtaulds, and many others too numerous to name, have become very important as part of the pattern of special library provision in Britain. Such major libraries all evolved from service departments supporting the companies' research and managerial staffs and were not systematically planned from their beginning. In small firms, such as Phaidon Press, this evolution is in its early stages.

The library grew up round the editors who collected reference material for their day-to-day use — journals, such as the *Burlington,* catalogues of galleries, exhibitions and sales — and who acquired the firm's own and many other books, together with enormous numbers of photographs in various forms. Over the years, so much material had accumulated that it could not be left unorganized any longer and about five or six years ago a librarian was appointed for the first time. The initial task was immense, but good foundations for the library were laid. Succeeding librarians were less effective, possibly because the nature of the library and its role in the firm had never really been defined.

The people employed in the library are called library assistants but in fact carry out an aspect of the editorial process rather than do library work: they are library *users* rather than staff making the library functional for others to use. Their primary duty is picture research and procurement and, as this is intensive and at times complex work, always being done to deadlines, there is not time for what a professional librarian would regard as the normal duties of an assistant. The librarian is responsible for ensuring that all the varied aspects of picture library work are covered and for carrying them out herself. While such work is extremely interesting both for itself and as an organizational challenge, it is not orthodox librarianship.

The writer, the present librarian, came to the post without experience of an art or picture library, nor of the world of private enterprise, but with some administrative experience, and familiarity with the financing procedures normal in higher education where, once the budget has been agreed, departmental autonomy prevails. This pattern did not apply in the commercial setting, yet to turn the existing collection of books and pictures into the sort of functional instrument a working library should be, requires expenditure from which no speedy or clearly visible return can be hoped. A small company in an undercapitalized industry such as publishing, particularly specialized publishing, does not have the resources to make an investment which cannot demonstrate a quick and certain profit.

As a result, every professional decision has to be taken with the knowledge that only the barest financial support can be provided. This has to be accepted and it is challenging to discover how much can be done in an unpromising situation. None of the procedures instituted is of a high professional standard. Their only merit is that they work and have cost very little in terms of equipment and labour to establish and do enable books and information to be controlled and found more quickly than in the past.

THE COLLECTIONS

The collections making up the library are not homogeneous. There are many more pictures than books. The pictures are in several forms: glass negatives, black and white prints, films, colour transparencies. The books too fall into several groups. There is an archive collection, that is, copies of all the books published by the Press in all forms (hardback, paperback, coeditions, reprints, new editions, translations) since its establishment in Britain in 1937. There is an open-shelf collection of some 4,000 volumes, plus large numbers of gallery, saleroom, and exhibition catalogues. A third collection is a kind of index, linking the books and the illustrations in them; it is known as the 'photofile index' and consists of annotated copies showing the picture side of each book's editorial history: sources, ownership, notes of special conditions of use, and so on.

The archive collection has been arranged in chronological order by year of publication. This is rational, simple to understand, and does not require classification. Each title has a unique number made up of two parts. The first part, two digits, indicates the year of publication and is separated by a stroke from the second part, a number taken from a running sequence; thus, for example, Bindman's book on Blake published in 1977 has the number 77/631. At the time the archive was arranged in this way it was possible to shelve all editions and translations with the first original edition and each was given the same number with appropriate suffixes. As it was not physically possible to leave space for the future, this arrangement does raise some problems and introduces some illogicality into the system, but the information so provided, at a time before it had been possible to make any sort of catalogue, is very useful and often needed. Coloured spine labels have been used to distinguish between the various book collections because the same works are frequently found in all three. Red is used for the archive. Many of the titles in this collection are now extremely rare.

The open-shelf working collection has been treated in the normal way; that is, it is classified and catalogued. The choice of a classification scheme was neither easy nor obvious. Dewey, LC, Bliss, the Fogg picture classification, and several other special one-off schemes were examined but none seemed entirely satisfactory for the relatively tiny collection and its purposes. Yet a home-made scheme quickly runs into problems which become ever more pervasive and intractable, creating difficulties for one's successors. It was finally decided to use the 1952 edition of Bliss[2] because it is a very flexible and faceted scheme, with many auxiliary schedules. For example, all the gallery catalogues are kept together in one place by using the geographical schedule. The main problems arise from Bliss's generosity with alternative placings, none of which at times quite fits the library's needs! But if firm decisions are made and recorded in the schedules and index, and the kind of modifications possible in Bliss inserted, it can be made to work well.

Catalogues of sales and exhibitions devoted to one artist or group are treated as monographs but most contain information about illustrations of a great diversity of objects and pictures. So far, no decision has been finally taken about their placing and use but it is probable that they will also be simply incorporated. One reason for the delay is that both contain much unique information about relatively unknown material and it would be useful to index them and relate them to existing *catalogues raisonnés*. Unfortunately there is neither sufficient staff time nor money to do the work.

The 'photofile index' was not so easy to deal with. It is not a collection of books for use as such but a special form of information record. It was started a few years ago in an *ad hoc* way but is now a useful tool, bringing together in one place much information otherwise widely scattered. Beside each picture is recorded details of ownership, costs, copyright fees, reproduction fees and the dates on which these were paid, when the photograph was returned to its owner or whether it belongs to Phaidon Press, special conditions of use, and much other information. These volumes are arranged in yet another sequence, an alphabetical name sequence. Large bright yellow labels distinguish these books from the working and archive collections. No cataloguing or classification knowledge is needed to maintain the photofile; as all work is completed on a title the picture researcher concerned deals with the copy for the file, which is self-indexing.

The actual physical form of the various catalogues was also the subject of considerable thought. One card catalogue already existed for the Ektachromes but ultimately it was felt that for a small library, old-fashioned sheaf catalogues would prove the most suitable. They are simple to produce and maintain; unit entries can be prepared on an ordinary typewriter in five or even six copies (if as many are needed); the sheets are easily interfiled; small post binders occupy less space than card cabinets; users and staff can sit at a table to use them and they can be moved about easily. Different coloured sheets are used, pink for the archive, yellow for the photofile, and white for the open shelves. Blue sheets are used for the subject catalogue, which also includes geographical entries for artists' birthplaces. We find that used sparingly and with immediate significance colour is a useful aid in a library's record system, especially where, as in this library, several different collections occupy shelving in the same area.

The photographic collections also fall into three distinct groups: very large numbers of glass negatives, tens of thousands of black and white prints, and about 7,000 positive colour transparencies, usually called Ektachromes.

The glass negatives are stored in boxes, numbered but otherwise unidentified. A start has been made in producing contact prints and providing some details of title and painter but the costs of this work are high both in materials, staff expertise and time, so that it is in abeyance. Many of these early glass plates have historical interest. Very great care was taken by Goldscheider, the senior Phaidon editor, not only to meet the highest standards of book production and design but also of photographic reproduction, so that only the most skilled and sensitive photographers were commissioned, especially for sculpture. Modern techniques make it unlikely that these glass plates will ever be used again on a large scale but they cannot be discarded. They contain pictures of much material effectively untraceable now in private collections and works of art destroyed or otherwise lost during the Second World War. Among them too are many unpublished photographs as whole collections were bequeathed to Phaidon Press by the families of photographers, such as Schneider-Lengyel who photographed Rodin and Michelangelo sculpture for Phaidon.

The black and white prints occupy more than 20 packed filing cabinets. There is no catalogue to them and when they are needed laborious searches have to be made. At present they are arranged by the country of birth of the artist or, if known, by the place of origin of the artifacts. We use the invaluable *Checklist*[3] published by the Courtauld Institute as authority for country of origin and the spelling and alphabetization of names. Plans are in progress to reorganize these prints but the time needed must be measured in years rather than months.

Because Ektachromes are both costly to make and buy, and at the same time very sensitive to heat and strong light, they have to be carefully stored. Steel cupboards with lateral suspended filing are used, housed in a dark, air-conditioned atmosphere. The Ektachromes of paintings are arranged in one sequence alphabetically by artist and are thus self-indexing and rapidly accessible. The anonymous materials, such as illuminated manuscripts, artifacts, and all other materials are classified by the Bliss system. Subject and geographical catalogues are being added to the original card catalogue made by the first librarian. A current project being carried out in cooperation with the Production Department and University Microforms, a commercial firm, is to put all Ektachromes and all film (that is film made from Ektachromes for use in our books) onto microfiche for reference purposes. These will be available to authors for use when preparing new books and will have numerous other uses.

ENQUIRIES

Enquiries of many kinds about pictures that have appeared in our books are received daily and it is usually the library's responsibility to deal with these. Such enquiries come from all over the world, from other publishers, from universities, television companies, authors, and many members of the public. Many of the latter want to buy copies of pictures seen in Phaidon books. All enquiries are answered even if at times they demand some research. Many people are referred to the galleries owning the pictures, or to public libraries, or to print-selling shops, such as Athena or the Medici Society. One of the most useful sources of this kind of information is the UNESCO *Catalogue of Reproductions of Paintings prior to 1860.*

CONCLUSION

The working library of Phaidon Press is not comparable to an art library in a university, art gallery, or research organization. Its purposes and problems are quite different and its book and journal collections unbalanced and small. But, by being cared for and organized by professional librarians, it serves its internal purposes effectively and has contributed to the national information resources, if only on a minute scale.

REFERENCES

1   Nicholls, J 'The costs of academic publishing' in *Art Libraries Journal* 3, 17-24. 1978.
2   Bliss, H E *The bibliographical classification.* New York, Wilson, 1952.
3   *A checklist of painters c. 1200-1976 represented in the Witt Library, Courtauld Institute of Art, London.* London, Mansell, 1978.
4   UNESCO *Catalogue of Reproductions of Paintings prior to 1860,* 10th edition. Paris, UNESCO, 1977.

38

Picture Collections in Newspaper Libraries

Sandra K Hall

INTRODUCTION

It's 11.30 p.m. in a newspaper photo library — 20 minutes before the paper 'goes to bed' to be printed. The telephone rings. The caller says: 'Pull the file on Freddie Xylophone. Get some of him in prison garb from last year, and some older ones of him with a beard.'

The photo librarian makes a selection from the hundreds on file and hurries them to the photo editor who is preparing the layout of a page. He learns that Freddie, a terrorist, has just broken out of the local high security jail.

How will the file photos be used? If a more up-to-date record of his recapture is unavailable, the photos will be issued to illustrate the story. It's highly unlikely that a photo can be taken of his being apprehended, in time to run in the morning's first edition.

The newsroom is a hive of activity with the staff reconstructing as a team the details of the breakout. There are unconfirmed rumours of prison guards being held hostage. Once again it is the photo librarian who is relied upon, to pull the photos from a collection of one and a half million. One of the guard's names presents a puzzle: it's Eldon Smith. There are four individuals with that name. Fortunately, Eldon the guard has a caption pasted to the back of the photo that identifies him conclusively. To double check, the photo librarian pulls out his clip file and compares. It's back to the newsroom.

The angle of the story will determine which photos are used. If hostages are confirmed, their photos will be run, and also photos of Freddie with and without a beard, in case he disguises his appearance. Every story in the newspaper each day represents a different challenge to the photo librarian. It is easier to select a file photo for a feature on volleyball players' salaries than it is for a story on narcotics, abortion, or rape.

PLACE OF THE LIBRARY IN THE ORGANIZATION

During the past decade, there have been significant changes in newspaper technology that have affected all aspects of the paper. One significant change has been in the speed with which copy is handled. This impact of electronics on the newspaper has meant that editors are better able to handle a last-minute breaking story, such as Freddie's escape.

Editing, correcting, hyphenating and justification, head-line writing, and typesetting are all done on a screen at the desk of a reporter or editor. There is no newsprint, and there are no pots of glue. Besides increasing the speed with which news is handled, the use of computers has also led to a better-looking product.

There has been a graphics revolution. More modern typefaces, such as Bodoni, are being used. Offset photographic printing has meant a cleaner, sharper appearance. More open space has been used in the new-style page layouts. More graphs, charts, cartoons, maps, illustrations, and diagrams are being used. Photographs have multiplied, and colour photographs, which were virtually unknown in newspapers a decade ago, enhance the appearance.

The increased importance of graphics has led to a slow realization of the value of a properly organized and maintained photo library. The photo library is usually a part of the library, rather than a separate department, and the photo librarian, usually equivalent to an assistant librarian, reports to the chief librarian, who in turn usually reports to a key editor, such as the executive editor. Quite often, the photo and graphic resources of the paper are scattered, primarily between the photo library and the Photo Department. The photo editor, in charge of the Photo Department and the staff photographers, frequently acts as a link between the two. Besides supervising the photographers, he or she

475

selects photos for use in the paper and often assists in the selection of photos for permanent retention in the library.

Frequently, the Photo Department organizes and maintains its own negatives collection. The rationale for this is that photographers need access to them for printing. Also, in negative form, they are sensitive to careless handling. Besides, they are not very useful for picture selection until a proof has been made. A 1977 survey of photo library procedures by William D Chase,[1] reported that of 170 libraries responding, only 67 filed negatives. The other 103 reported that the Photo Department had this responsibility.

There can be a further scattering of photo resources between departments. Specialized departments, such as Sports, Lifestyle, and Entertainment often maintain their own collections, although this is changing gradually, while artists and cartoonists quite frequently have their own collections. Since this chapter is concerned with the photo library attached to the editorial arm of the newspaper, this does not take into account the fact that advertising, marketing, research, and promotion also have their own illustrative resources.

If it sounds confusing to have illustrative and graphic materials scattered throughout the newsroom, it is. It would be a sound measure to consolidate more of the resources and the responsibilities in a photo library. Assuming an adequate budget and staff, the graphics centre could serve the needs of a range of departments: photographers, artists, cartoonists, cartographers, illustrators, and layout personnel. In order to be effective, it needs to have more than photographs in its collection, just as an effective newspaper library needs more than newsclippings.

The photo library at the Gannett Rochester (New York) Newspapers is an example of an effective graphics centre. Their collection includes not only photos, but also pictures clipped from magazines, books of illustrations that are no longer copyrighted, store catalogues, and a collection of reference books on insects, aeroplanes, costume, etc. However, a full-scale graphics centre lies in the future for most newspapers.

THE COLLECTION — GENERAL

The typical photo library includes a wide variety of different types of photographs. Most of the following types would be found in the medium-sized library:

— laserphotos, from the wire services
— glossies (prints)
— 35 mm. colour transparencies
— colour separations (colour photos prepared for immediate use)
— metal cuts, if the paper does not have 'cold type' capability
— Veloxes (the cold type equivalent of a cut. This is a screened print which may only be used in the same size and is usually only retained if the subject is used frequently, or if the original is very valuable and should not be handled).

UNIQUE FEATURES OF THE PHOTO LIBRARY COLLECTION

The timeliness of a newspaper photo library collection is of paramount importance, and differentiates it from other collections. A 1972 study by the late Jim Criswell of the *Houston Post*,[2] showed that 50% of photographs that ran in the paper were less than two years old. The thousands of photos of the Vietnam War, for example, are seldom used. Newspapers by their very name, are concerned with the present.

Because of deadline pressures, the photo librarian must each day sort, identify, select, and classify the daily input as expeditiously as possible, for prompt retrieval later by editors rushing to complete a layout. Very often, art needs are not known until deadline time. All photo libraries have common features and some have unique systems designed to serve their own users' needs.

STAFF

In a medium-sized newspaper library, with a daily circulation of about 75,000 to 150,000 and 6 to 10 library employees, one person is usually designated the photo librarian and is allocated some clerical assistance.

There is no concrete data on the career paths of newspaper photo librarians. In general, they have a library background and an interest in their speciality. They have certain traits in common: they must keep abreast of the daily news, have a vital interest in current events, and they need an in-depth knowledge of their local community. In addition to a good news sense, they must have a good grasp of what has graphic impact in a photo, and what makes a picture 'worth a thousand words'. They must be able to differentiate photos that are timeless, from those of transitory interest. They must have an eye for detail, an understanding of graphic layout and perspective, and it is important to have more than a passing familiarity with Photo Department procedures, such as developing, spotting, and cropping.

SOURCES OF PHOTOGRAPHS

The source of the photograph determines to a very large extent the way in which it is handled.

Local photographs of 'spot news' events, such as accidents or fires, are taken by the newspaper's own Photo Department. Staff photographers also shoot assigned events, such as interviews, dedications of new buildings, sports and entertainment events, and the like. Local events may generate hundreds of photos a day, of which only a few ever appear in the paper. Very often, the negative is not even printed. It is usually retained for at least six or nine months for possible use. Many newspapers retain the negative indefinitely.

Photos that are candidates for use are usually printed in standard dimensions of 8 × 10 inches or 5 × 7 inches. Different sizes can be made from these, particularly for head shots of people. Photos are often cropped to highlight details. Those that do appear in print are either discarded or retained after use. They are discarded if there is little likelihood that they will be used again. If they are retained, they are identified, classified, and filed.

Beyond the paper's own circulation area, a news service, such as the Associated Press, is relied upon to provide reporting coverage and photographs from member newspapers. The AP provides photos of regional interest, and on national and international subjects each day. A photo of Freddie Xylophone, following his escape and taking of hostages would be transmitted at least regionally to neighbouring states, if not nationally. They are transmitted very rapidly by laser, in a ready-to-use format, with a descriptive caption attached.

Laserphotos are 8 × 10 inches and printed on dry silver paper. One hundred and twenty five are transmitted each day to each paper and of these about one fifth is filed for possible later use. They are usually interfiled with other photographs, unlike their predecessor, the tissue paper thin flimsy wirephoto, which used to be mounted on card stock and chemically 'fixed'. Laserphotos do not require special handling although sometimes quality may vary due to vagaries in transmission or paper stock used. In the middle 1970s, the Newspaper Division of Special Libraries Association expressed concern about the archival permanence of laserphotos and their susceptibility to discolouration. Experiments are continuing into improving the paper quality at a reasonable price.

A member newspaper may request file photographs from the huge AP Photo Library, for a nominal printing fee. This collection covers a vast range of subjects and numbers over ten million negatives.

Other sources of photos include those that arrive unsolicited at the newspaper from many organizations and businesses. Very often they accompany press releases, for example, on a political announcement, or news of a business promotion or appointment. Free photos may be furnished by tourist agencies, or by the entertainment and sports industries. They can be useful for building up a collection, although sometimes their suitability and quality vary.

SELECTION CRITERIA

What is selected for permanent retention is of great importance. Photos are very bulky and therefore conservation of space is a consideration. Obviously, the most important consideration is the later efficient retrieval of suitable photos for running in the paper, or for use by an artist. Often, a rotating file is set up, in which all photos that appeared in the paper are kept for 6 to 12 months. Although the likelihood of sports photos of routine action being used again is very slim, they are retained in case of litigation.

The experienced photo librarian chooses from the day's input those photos with graphic emotional or mood impact, which might be used again. The photo of the naked child fleeing from the napalm attack in Vietnam that graphically sums up the horror of war would be kept; a photo of soldiers eating a meal might be discarded. However, if it had strong impact it might be kept, for example, wounded soldiers feeding each other; or if it had detail on uniforms or canned rations and the like, it might be kept for reuse by a designer.

Other criteria are photographic quality, timeliness, and subject. If artists and illustrators rely on the photo collection to assist them with their drawings, a blurry photo of Afghan tribesmen, even if unexceptional or inferior, may be kept if it has excellent detail of headgear or weapons. A dramatic but fuzzy photo of a bandit fleeing a bank may be retained, if that is the only photo of the suspect.

PROCESSING

There are as many different systems and techniques as there are libraries. A detailed description of a variety of techniques may be found in *Guidelines for newspaper libraries.*[3] The following steps are typical:

1   The photos are sorted into two categories — those that are returned file photos, and those that are new and require classification.
2   A clerk matches the photos with clips of photos taken from the paper. The cutline or caption is glued to the back. The photo is dated and pages given a page reference. This information is considered essential, and it helps avoid potentially libellous mistakes. It also guides editors in their selection, so that they do not reuse the same photo consistently.
3   If it is a file photo, it is filed.
4   If it is a new photo, it is examined for retention, or discard.
5   Photos that are to be retained are classified.

CLASSIFICATION

Negatives are usually filed separately. Subjects and personalities are also usually separated.

People

People are filed by last name, followed by first names and initials. Titles are added, as is occupation, if known. This saves time when it is not known which Joe Jones is the burglar and which is the investor. A name more local news, perhaps using even more graphics and

REFERENCES

illiam D 'The newspaper photo library'. Newspaper
ecial Libraries Association Conference, 5-9 June 1977, New
. Copies of the paper available from: American Newspaper
Assn Foundation Library, PO Box 17407, Dulles International
ashington DC 20041, USA.
m 'Study of newspaper library pictures' in *Houston Post.* 1973.
is paper also available from ANPA Library.
for newspaper libraries. Written by members of the Newspaper
ecial Libraries Association, published by ANPA, 1974, rev.
e: $15 from ANPA Library.
ary News. Publication of the Newspaper Division/Special
Assn. Free to members of the Division. For non-members
ns are $20 for two years. Published four times per year. Write to:
, Editor, News Library News, Contra Costa Times, PO Box
lnut Creek CA 94596, USA.
Newspaper Division of Special Libraries Association has an audio-
s available for rental. One topic is *Newspaper photo library files.*
ailable from Joy C Hill, Photo Librarian, Gannett Rochester
s, 55 Exchange Street, Rochester NY 14614, USA.

authority file which may include the dates of photos, the negative accession number, and 'see' and 'see also' references to groups and oversize photos can be very useful.

Dates are extremely important when filing photos of people. With frequent changes in hairstyles and fashion, editors wish to avoid using out-of-date ones. An alert photo librarian notes when it is time to reshoot photos of prominent people. For some tips on how to keep a file current, see an article by Vickie Houk in *News Library News,* Winter 1980.[4]

Photos of two or more people represent a problem in classification. Sometimes an extra print can be made for each file. Other systems are discussed in *Guidelines for newspaper libraries.*[3]

Subjects

The rules for the establishment of subject headings for the newspaper clipping files are usually adapted for the subject files in the photo library.

The basic principles are to file under specific plural nouns, followed by geographic and chronological breakdown as needed. For example, the preferred heading is FIRES — TUCSON — 1979, rather than TUCSON FIRE 1979.

There are two important differences between the classification of photos and clips, however. The first is that in the USA and Canada, multiple newspaper clippings are typically cross-filed under many subjects and personalities. For example, a story on Edward Kennedy announcing his candidacy for the US Presidency, would be cross-filed under at least the following headings:

> KENNEDY, EDWARD—ELECTIONS
> ELECTIONS—PRESIDENTIAL—US—1980
> DEMOCRATS.

Depending on the gist of the story, additional clips may be taken for cross-filing. Some subjects might be: KENNEDY, JOHN F; KENNEDY, ROBERT; CHAPPAQUIDDICK; and so on. If all the announced candidates were mentioned, there might be 40 or 50 clips made of the story. The photo librarian, in contrast, has only one copy of the photo that accompanies the story. It is easy enough to decide to file it under KENNEDY, EDWARD if it is of him making the announcement. If he is with his ex-wife, or mother, or at JFK's grave, it becomes more difficult.

The second major difference between clips and photos is that a clip is filed by the story element, whereas a photo is filed by its graphic subject element. This principle is illustrated by the following example:

A story on unusual weather in the Arizona desert that brought light snow, may be filed as a clip under WEATHER, as the general story element, and maybe also under SNOW for the specific element. A photo of snow on cactus, that accompanies the story, would be filed under CACTUS. This is the graphic element that an artist or illustrator would most likely need.

Some photo librarians set up their files using a classified subject heading approach. Subjects are arranged in hierarchical order within large types, such as SPORTS, ENTERTAINMENT, EDUCATION, etc. A subject heading list should be maintained to keep control of headings, and to record 'see' and 'see also' references. It may be kept on 3 × 5 inch cards, on a visible file, or a recent trend is to store it on a computer.

Finally, most photo collections use mood and emotion categories for evergreen photos that are in heavy demand by artists, illustrators, and editors looking for a photo to accompany a feature. The alert photo librarian watches for such photos, that illustrate poverty, despair, happiness, sorrow, alcoholism, loneliness, and boredom.

Negatives

Since negatives cannot be written on, essential data is usually logged into a book, or card file, kept on a Rolodex or on-line. Some newspapers, such as the *Toronto Globe and Mail,* microfilm their negatives. Important information that is logged includes name of photographer, date, accession number, and so on.

Since negatives are vulnerable to dust, fingerprints, and scratches, extra care is required in their handling. Often they are kept in plastic see-through sleeves, from which they can be printed without removal. The sleeves are often filed in legal-size envelopes and placed in pamphlet or other specially designed boxes.

FILING EQUIPMENT

Photos, other than specific exceptions mentioned above, are usually housed in manila folders, or envelopes that are stored in filing cabinets,

or on open book shelving. power files.

CHECK-

A sign-out sheet that record whom, is usually sufficient. ' the missing photographs are enforcing the rule of prompt estimated that of every seven photo library, only one has c Sometimes the photos are us ideas, or for layout of a sectio

WEEDI

Jim Criswell[2] estimated that paper are file photos. Since ph priority and since they are very Weeding also helps preserve fil

The same criteria apply to retention. Timeless, graphic or flag on Iwo Jima in World War donated to an historical library

If the negatives for local iter will not be lost. Also, the Ass mentioned previously.

THE

The future looks bright for the evolve into graphics centres. Sc viewdata-type Teletext systems of staff photographers and new newspapers coexist with this

stressing even photography?

1   Chase, W
    Division/S
    York, NY
    Publishers
    Airport, W
2   Criswell, J
    Copy of th
3   *Guidelines*
    Division/S
    1976. Pric
4   *News Lib*
    Libraries
    subscriptic
    Ellie Woo
    5088, Wa
    Also, the
    visual seri
    Details av
    Newspape

39

Broadcasting Libraries

David Lee

The views expressed in this chapter are those of the author, and not necessarily those of the BBC.

This chapter will try to outline the specific features and problems of illustrations librarianship as seen in libraries which serve broadcasters and are financed by broadcasting organizations, but not collections *on* the subject of broadcasting.[5] The ideal broadcasting library may not exist in totality, and in discussing what it may do it is safest to begin by describing the illustration needs of broadcasters. In the present context we are mainly concerned with the makers of television, for whom pictures are life blood.[2] Broadly speaking, the broadcaster needs pictures for illustration or verification, that is as source material for showing on the programme or as visual information used in the creation of programmes. Each can be dealt with in turn.

Many, perhaps most, of the broadcaster's images are provided currently by programme makers in the course of their work, whether as news sequences shot on location or as studio work on a large or small scale. A broadcasting library, where it exists, and not all concerns have them in name, will not be expected to provide this kinetic material either currently or retrospectively unless the discussion is widened to include television film libraries. We are more concerned with providing stock shots, stills in the broadest sense, as additional material to that obtained by television cameramen. The correspondent or statesman interviewed needs the pictorial background of today's Afghanistan or Zimbabwe, or yesterday's Abadan or Suez. Any programme with a historical perspective will require servicing with perhaps hundreds of still photographs, many of which, for economy's sake if for no other reason, will have to come from within the organization. There are programmes made of stills alone, with a strong commentary, but on the whole stills or non-moving pictures lend a brief historical flash or other dimension to an item.

An enormously wide range of material is needed, covering people, places, and events of all times. Colour is obviously an added advantage, although monochrome sometimes gives historical verisimilitude. An active policy of acquisition is necessary if the library is not to be by-passed or treated as a mere agent for other people's pictures.

The broadcaster's other main need for pictures, apart from transmission, is as pictorial reference. The reference library serving programme makers is called upon very heavily to provide pictures of people, costumes, and every kind of scene for the designers of plays, not merely historical dramas but modern plays and features of all kinds. The fashion for 'non-fiction' dramas can be particularly taxing for the picture provider. The recent (Timothy West) *Churchill,* for instance, needed enormous numbers of pictures to ensure accuracy in the appearance of costume, looks and gestures of many individuals, as well as to help in the faithful reproduction of locale, vehicles, etc. The problem of colour can be particularly acute in cases like this, in that accurate representations in colour may not have been made at the time.

Illustrations for reference are as likely, perhaps more likely, to come from published books and journals as from a library of stills or an illustrations collection, and in an ideal situation the organization should have all these materials close together. The problems of finding just the right illustration at the right moment are considerable, but that is the essence of librarianship.[7]

Broadcasting organizations which do not have a good library of illustrated books and collections of illustrations/stills have heavy recourse to public, national, and special libraries on a casual basis, and to commercial picture libraries more frequently. The large stock of historical photographs, engravings, and other illustrations which a library, such as the BBC Hulton Picture Library possesses, is invaluable and major news agencies are not concerned with the current scene alone. Cooperation between broadcasting libraries is not very common as there is built-in rivalry between organizations as there may be between programmes and programme areas. The broadcasting librarian has at times very delicate problems of precedence and confidentiality. No broadcasting library is the centre of a network of illustration libraries, though advice on further sources will be sought from a knowledgeable staff, and an illustration specialist may well act as a channel through which commercial libraries, for instance, like to put their illustrations, counteracting any unreliability there might be in direct contact with television film makers. Cooperation in obtaining illustrated books is much more common, and regional library cooperation is usually supplemented by *ad hoc* arrangements between librarians.

The librarian providing pictures for transmission works under a number of constraints after finding the material. The first of these is copyright and as the user can be remarkably vague on this subject, the librarian must make the position clear on each picture provided, if his or her organization does not hold the copyright. Section 1.11 in this book makes a useful start on this complex subject. Handling agency pictures is not usually the broadcasting librarian's function and is usually done by the programme maker, but it may come his way. A thorough knowledge of the various agencies and their specialisms can be acquired[4, 10] but with it must go a cast-iron understanding of copyright law and practice.[8, 9]

Quality of picture, particularly for transmission, can be a further problem in broadcasting libraries, though one which recedes historically. Whereas a poor picture of Sydney Opera House would not be acceptable, Rasputin's blurred image might almost be welcome. Pictures can be of the best quality if negatives are held and are able to be used for blow-ups. Control over part of a picture's quality may be required, and the need for in-house technical darkroom facilities near broadcasting libraries is obvious, as speed is often a desperately important factor in television production. Life in a broadcasting library is curious in this mixture of tempi. Some material may be provided on any day for design use in a production which will not be transmitted for months or years, yet other pictures are required the same day or afternoon, and not just one picture. The hunger of some picture users can be so great that a limit may have to be laid down by the harassed librarian. Clients' and departments' idiosyncrasies are soon learned and their thanks are often generously given, but pictorial credit on the screen is still rather rare.

Photocopies of pictures may be supplied rather than prints (usually 8

× 6 or 10 × 8 inch), but really only for the preparation of long-term programmes, such as drama serials, as there is an in-built extra stage with photocopying.

The final constraint to be mentioned is that of research *on* the pictures. The broadcasting library contains in its books, journals, and picture files of various kinds an enormous number of pictures about which little is known. It is distressing to the librarian sometimes not to be able to do further research which will enable a particular picture to be used in a programme. Sometimes it is time which stops such work, but often it is the sheer anonymity of the picture in the file. There is a moral here for the captioning of material, but perfection is hard to achieve in the hurly-burly of broadcasting.

Pictures are usually stored in folders, either in vertical or lateral files. They may be dry mounted but more often are not, with mounting being carried out, preferably on a copy, by the production people. It is advisable to retain the file copy and use the negative to make a print for use, particularly if the file is consulted for reference as well as production purposes. One of the problems a broadcasting librarian finds is that so often there is competition for pictures, notably when they are required for obituary programmes and anniversaries.

Negatives are likely to be kept apart from their prints, causing some problem and delay in tracing them. This is not the place to discuss storage and conservation problems of negatives which are considerable, especially if there are old glass negatives in the stock; rather the reader is referred to Section 1.6.

A copy of the picture, and not the original, should be issued because it could be subjected to severe and even destructive treatment. Even if the picture itself survives, information on the back of it may be lost. Unfortunately the transfer of information from the original to the copy is time-consuming and errors do creep in. People in a hurry do not tend to keep separate items, such as envelopes, with the pictures. It is not, incidentally, the habit of broadcasting libraries to put their prints in transparent envelopes. They are more akin to press libraries than to archival collections. Recopying of images, building up a miniature library for a programme is quite common, though programmes should not be encouraged to make copy negatives of pictures which are the copyright of other organizations. If these are made temporarily, they should later be destroyed and use fees paid to copyright holders. Programmes quite often return new copies they have made to the broadcasting library.

Desperate as they are to obtain images at one point, they can be equally desperate to dispose of them later.

Lamination of pictures may well be unhelpful in the transmission of images, but is useful for illustrations in reference collections. Special equipment is not common in the broadcasting library itself, apart from the ubiquitous lightbox for negatives, partly as use can be made of programme technical facilities. Space is also usually short in broadcasting libraries.

The actual arrangement of pictures varies greatly in the different organizations. Decimal classification and UDC are found but alphabetical subject heading schemes, perhaps based on Library of Congress or Sears, are more common. Catalogues and perhaps any form of bibliographic control may be lacking. The pictures may be 'self-indexing', with cross-references in the picture files and references to negatives placed on the reverse of the file copy. Complex systems of cataloguing are usually avoided, though the claim 'we try to use common sense' may sound a little thin when the collection reaches the million mark or more.

Colour material may be placed with the black and white, and if a self-indexing system is used it should be, or else it should be reproduced in monochrome and inserted. Colour is, however, thanks to its variety of forms, from the hand-tinted engraving or double-crown poster to the tiny slide, often filed separately, and even the librarian who wishes to avoid catalogues may wonder whether indexes are preferable to perpetual reminders to staff to check all possible sequences. Storage of colour material is now a problem of finance rather than availability of systems.

An ideal retrieval system for all pictures *may* be a 35 mm. visual catalogue of images, perhaps on aperture cards which can bear information as well as pictures. Certainly a descriptive card catalogue is of no more than indicative value. A roll microfilm record of pictures held would seem to be of archival interest only, and impractical in everyday terms. The archival side of broadcasting libraries' work has been understandably rather neglected in the hurly-burly of film-making, but size at least may bring responsibilities on the archival front, and the BBC has recognized this.[1] The Annan Report drew attention to the problem also, for both the public and commercial systems.[6] It is a fact that there are no common standards on library service to broadcasters in the independent sphere, despite IBA's own excellent library system.

Selection of pictures in a broadcasting library, if it carries out the two functions of illustration and verification, may be less important than acquisition. The needs are so unknown and wide-ranging that anything may be useful. The link with a first-class book library is important, as it provides heavily illustrated books on the one hand, and reference material to ensure accuracy in captions on the other. So often a programme's visual researcher will begin by scanning a selection of illustrated books on the chosen topic. Pictorial journals, particularly of the past, are also immensely useful, and the longer established broadcasting libraries do have some of these. An illustrations collection, formed by cannibalizing books, journals, and ephemera can add to the store of images for reference. Within the constraints of copyright and quality such material may be usable in programmes, but often may not be. Illustrations collections are notorious for their piecemeal qualities and their rapid deterioration, and only ruthless control by specifically deputed staff will keep them usable. Notes on useful illustrated books may be placed in the illustrations file, but it is doubtful if the practice is particularly valuable in a broadcasting context. Books actually sitting on the shelves are those used and ideal books not obtainable quickly might as well not exist in the case of many urgent projects.

Pictures for transmission use, leaving aside occasional use of book illustrations, are filed separately, and their choice is in some ways more difficult, depending upon what is on the market. Are there old Irish pictures available for purchase just at the time they are wanted? In another way, the librarian may have more control if there are photographers available to the organization. That much-needed picture of Kabul or Fort Victoria could perhaps be taken by a stringer not averse to improving his income. Material acquired in this way incidentally should have its copyright position made clear to all concerned, including the photographer. The broadcasting library is not likely to buy agency material for its own stock, and it is rather more likely that programmes will hire it when needed. Historical pictures, from scrappy postcards upwards, are often offered to broadcasting libraries and may be worth buying if they are out of copyright and of good enough quality for informative or even transmission purposes. Often they are not worth buying, and the days of the cheap photograph have gone. Special collections also come onto the market, and their acquisition is very desirable if it gives the library a mine in which much digging for future programmes can take place.

Picture research in a television context may be carried out by researchers specifically engaged by that programme, or group of programmes, or more general researchers employed by the organization. Freelance work is common in this field.[3] In addition, certain in-house staff in the broadcasting library will have some responsibility for finding pictures. The two types of researcher will probably work together, for often access to the picture library will not be open, on grounds of lack of space, complexity of arrangement, and general security. The programme picture researcher's job is to know not only the nearest libraries but also the whole range of picture resources — public, commercial, industrial, news — each with its own set of rules, practices, and prices. The prospects of this type of researcher are clearly better than those of the in-house people, but both do similar work. Picture research work with publishers of books and journals may well precede or follow work in television, and editing, in either medium, is likely to be the next stage in a career. Training of in-house picture researchers in broadcasting libraries is, frankly, very limited. The work is often very interesting, although the lack of time for research in depth, in the broadcasting context, is frustrating to some.

The loan of pictures, whether for reference or transmission use may be very uncontrolled, as large numbers of pictures may be called for quickly. As mentioned earlier, it is better if file copies are not lent, for they may never be seen again. On the other hand, duplicates are expensive to make and space-consuming if made in advance. Instant darkroom facilities are a help but problems of priorities occur there all the time. The issue of pictures is tedious in view of the bulk, and if there is control it is likely to be by some individualized picture number given upon accession or first use. Computer issue of pictures may be useful, though returns can be so quick that batch processing has its drawbacks. In reality return is more often slow or non-existent, and expensive in staff time used in chasing. Unfortunately, to the user pictures as individual items seem small and unimportant, and are treated even more cavalierly than books. They are also obtained from so many sources, on a large project, that their orderly return goes by the board. A broadcasting library is likely to be strictest in its controls over colour material. The librarian must be tempted to issue copies of his pictures for camera use and not expect them back. He or she will avoid much 'waste' time spent in recording and chasing them, noting totals simply for accounting purposes, but is this financially justified in view of the cost of making prints?

If pictures are lent rather than given, they may be required for a long time by the picture editors, who will be considering them in conjunction with many others borrowed from other organizations. It is the broadcasting librarian's experience that when there are returns he will receive many of other people's as well as his own.

Sometimes pictures borrowed for a programme may also be used in an accompanying publication. It is strongly recommended that a second set of pictures be supplied to the publication's editor, with equally clear details of copyright for this second group of users.

Broadcasting libraries may of course serve radio as well as television, but there is not the need to reproduce pictures. The greatest use is for the provision of illustrations at times when visual topics are being discussed. Photocopies will often be sufficient, and copyright is not usually a problem. Most broadcasting organizations publish some material as books, booklets, and programme journals. A small proportion of a broadcasting library's stock of pictures is used in these publications and acknowledgement may be appropriate.

A further function of the broadcasting library, separate in larger organizations, may be the storing and use of publicity pictures, that is those taken of personalities, programmes, and technical developments. As a highly commercial operation it is probably better separated from the programme servicing library, but the income may look good on the balance sheet. General pictures in a broadcasting library are not on the whole sold to individuals or for use elsewhere. Such libraries have enough work of their own, and commercial picture libraries are better geared to such work.

What has been said in this chapter on the place of illustrations in the broadcasting library reveals an almost confusing variety of roles. In practice, not all of these functions are done by any one library and they may be split up between various parts of the parent organization. In the case of the BBC the size of some of these operations has caused specialization into at least four libraries, with the merit of special treatment of particular materials or services, but with the disadvantage that content, important to the potential user, may give way to form. The client has to master the various resources.

Not all the staff in broadcasting libraries are qualified, particularly in the visual areas. It is felt in some quarters that in illustration work, as opposed to reference and information work, general education and visual ability are sufficient. Whatever your views, broadcasting librarianship is a demanding and stimulating occupation.

REFERENCES

1 British Broadcasting Corporation *Report of the Advisory Committee on Archives.* London, BBC, 1979.

2 Collison, R L 'Libraries for television' in *The Library World.* July 1965. 1-5.

3 Evans, Hilary *The art of picture research: a guide to current practice, procedure, techniques and resources.* Newton Abbot, David & Charles, 1979.

4 Evans, Hilary and Mary (compilers) *Picture researcher's handbook.* 2nd ed. London, Saturday Ventures, 1979.

5 Hewlett, R D 'Broadcasters and libraries' in *EBU Review* 27(2) March 1976. 12-15.

6 Home Office *Report of the Committee on the Future of Broadcasting* (Cmnd 6753) (Chairman: Lord Annan). London, HMSO, 1977. Paragraphs 29.25 to 29.32.

7 Pacey, Philip (editor) *Art library manual: a guide to resources and practice.* London & New York, Bowker, 1977. Chapter 24, 'Illustrations', by Anthony J Coulson.

8 Shepard, Valerie A *Reproduction fees, photography, etc: guidelines for museums.* London, Museums Association, 1975.

9 Gibbs-Smith, C H *Copyright law concerning works of art, photographs and the written and spoken word.* 2nd ed. London, Museums Association, 1974.

10 Wall, John (compiler) *Directory of British photographic collections.* London, Heinemann, 1977.

Bibliography

Abse, Joan *The art galleries of Britain and Ireland. A guide to their collections.* London, Sidgwick and Jackson, 1975.

Ackerman, C W *George Eastman.* London, Constable & Co. Ltd, 1930. 51.

American Library Association *Portrait index.* Washington, US Government Printing Office, 1906.

American library directory edited by Jaques Cattell Press. 31st ed. New York, Bowker, 1978.

American National Standards Institute Inc:

Practice for storage of black and white photographic paper prints. PH1. 48-1974. New York, 1974.

Requirements for photographic filing enclosures for storing processed photographic films, plates and papers. PH4.20-1958 (R1970). New York, 1970.

Viewing conditions for photographic color prints. PH2.41-1976. New York, 1976.

Annual art sales index. Weybridge, Art Sales Index Ltd.

Art bibliographies modern. Oxford, UK; Santa Barbara, Calif., Clio Press, 1970-. (1969, 1970 title: *LOMA*)

Archival stability of microfilm – a technical review. Technical Report No. 18, 4 August, 1978. Washington, DC, United States Government Printing Office, 1978.

Archivum, Revue internationale des archives, 1975. Paris, Archivum, 1975.

Arnold, H J P *William Henry Fox Talbot. London, Hutchinson Benham, 1977.*

Art at auction. The year at Sotheby Parke Bernet. London, Sotheby Parke Bernet.

Art design photo. Hemel Hempstead, Alexander Davis Publications Ltd, 1973-.

Art index. New York, H W Wilson, 1930-.

Art Institute of Chicago, Ryerson Library *Index to art periodicals.* Boston, Mass., G K Hall, 1962.

Art Libraries Society, North America:
ARLIS/NA Newsletter. Washington, DC, 1972-.
Standards for staffing art libraries. Washington, DC, 1977.

Art Libraries Society, UK:
ARLIS Newsletter. London, 1969-.
Art Libraries Journal. (Quarterly). London.
'Art libraries in polytechnics: an ARLIS statement on the provision and exploitation of library resources for art and design courses in polytechnics'. *Art Libraries Journal* 4 (1) Spring 1979.

Arts Review yearbook. London, Eaton House.

Arvidson, R E and others *A user's guide to BIRP-software for interactive search and retrieval of image engineering data.* St Louis, Missouri, Washington University, McDonnell Center for the Space Sciences, 1979.

ASLIB directory. Volume 1: Information sources in science, technology and commerce. Volume 2: Information sources in medicine, the social sciences and the humanities. London, ASLIB, 1977, 1980.

Audiovisual aids: films, filmstrips, transparencies, wall sheets and recorded sound. (8 separate sections.) London, National Committee for Audio Visual Aids in Education, 1971-.

Audiovisual market place: a multimedia guide. (Annual). New York, Bowker.

Baker, Charles (editor) *Bibliography of British book illustrators 1860-1900.* Birmingham, Birmingham Bookshop, 1978.

Banks, Paul 'Preservation of library materials'. *Encyclopedia of Library and Information Science* 23. New York, Marcel Dekker, 1978.

Barley, M W *A guide to British topographical collections.* London, Council for British Archaeology, 1974.

Beall, Karen F (compiler) *American prints in the Library of Congress. A catalog of the collection.* Baltimore, Maryland, Johns Hopkins University Press for the Library of Congress, 1970.

Bénézit, E *Dictionnaire critique et documentaire des peintres, sculpteurs, dessinateurs et graveurs de tous les temps et de tous les pays par un groupe d'écrivains spécialistes français et étrangers.* (10 vols). Paris, Librairie Gründ, 1976.

Berger, P 'Minor repairs in a small research library; the case for an inhouse minor repairs workshop'. *Library Journal* 104, 15 June 1979. 1311-17.

Beswick, N *Organising resources.* London, Heinemann, 1975.

Bettmann, Otto *Bettmann portable archive... a graphic history of almost everything.* New York, Picture House Press Inc., 1966.

'Bibliography of archival literature'. *Journal of the Society of Archivists* 2, 1960. 72-3.

Bibliography of museum and art gallery publications and audiovisual aids in Great Britain and Ireland. Cambridge, UK, Chadwyck-Healey, 1980.

Bland, David:

A *history of book illustration: the illuminated manuscript and the printed book.* London, Faber, 1969. 459p.

The illustration of books. Part 1. History of illustration. Part 2. Processes and their application. London, Faber, 1951.

Bliss, H E *The bibliographical classification.* New York, Wilson, 1952.

'Blueprint for the 70s'. *A seminar on library planning: planning the special library.* New York, SLA, 1972.

Blunt, Anthony and others *The nation's pictures; a guide to the chief national and municipal picture galleries of England, Scotland and Wales.* London, Chatto and Windus, 1950.

Blunt, Wilfrid J W *The art of botanical illustration.* London, Collins, 1950.

Bohem, Hilda:

Disaster prevention and disaster preparedness. Berkeley, California, Task Group on the Preservation of Library Materials, University of California, 1978.

'A Visible File Catalog for Photographic Materials'. *The American Archivist* 39 (2), April 1976. 165-6.

Bradfield, V J *Slide collections: a user requirement survey.* (R&D Report 2609). British Library, 1976.

BRD, Osterreich, Schweiz. (2 vols). New York, Bowker, Pullach bei München Verlag Dokumentation, 1971.

Bridson, Gavin and others *Guide to natural history manuscript resources in the British Isles.* London, Bowker, 1978.

Brink, Adrian and others (editors) *The libraries, museums and art galleries year book 1976.* Cambridge, James Clarke & Co. Ltd, 1976.

British Industrial and Scientific Film Association *Film guide for the construction industry, including information on slide packages and slide/tape programmes.* Lancaster, Construction Press, 1979.

British Library, Bibliographic Services Division *British catalogue of audiovisual materials.* London, 1979.

British Standards Institution:
Recommendations for the processing and storage of silver-gelatin-type microfilm. BS 1153. London, 1975.
Recommendations for the storage and exhibition of archival documents. BS 5454. London, 1977.
Repair and allied processes for the conservation of documents. BS 4971. Part 1:1973.
Storage of microfilm. BS 1153. London, 1955.

British Universities Film Council *Audio-visual materials for higher education 1979-80.* 4th ed. London, 1979.

Brooke, B (editor) *Art in London.* London, Methuen, 1966.

Brothers, A *Photography.* London, Charles Griffin & Co., 1892.

Broxis, P F *Organising the arts.* London, Bingley, 1968.

Brunner, Felix *Handbook of graphic reproduction processes.* London, Academy Editions, 1962.

Burbidge, R Brinsley *A dictionary of British flower, fruit and still life painters.* (2 vols.). Leigh-on-Sea, F Lewis, 1974.

Burgess, Renate *Portraits of doctors and scientists in the Wellcome Institute of the History of Medicine.* London, Wellcome Institute of the History of Medicine, 1973.

Burston, W H and Green, C W *Handbook for history teachers.* 2nd ed. London, Methuen, 1972.

Caring for photographs. New York, Time-Life Books, 1972.

Castle, Peter *Collecting and valuing old photographs.* London, Bell and Hyman, 1979. 176p.

Catalogs of the art exhibition collection of the Arts Library, University of California at Santa Barbara. (Microfiche). Cambridge, UK,

Chadwyck-Healey, 1977.

Catalogue of American portraits in the New York Historical Society. (2 vols). New Haven, Connecticut, Yale University Press, 1974.

Catalogue of colour reproductions of paintings prior to 1860. 10th ed. Paris, UNESCO, 1977.

Catalogue of exhibition catalogues. Boston, Mass., G K Hall, 1972.

Catalogue of reproductions of paintings 1860-1973. Paris, UNESCO, 1974.

Chamberlain, Walter:
Etching and engraving. London, Thames and Hudson, 1973.
Woodcut printmaking and related techniques. London, Thames and Hudson, 1978.

Chase, William D 'The newspaper photo library'. Newspaper Division/ Special Libraries Association Conference, New York, 5-9 June 1977.

A checklist of painters c.1200-1976 represented in the Witt Library, Courtauld Institute of Art, London. London, Mansell, 1978.

Christie's pictorial archive. (Microfiche). London, Mindata, 1979-.

Christie's review of the season. London, Hutchinson/Christie.

The Civil Service yearbook. London, HMSO.

Clapp, Anne F *Curatorial care of works of art on paper.* 3rd rev. ed. Oberlin, Ohio, Intermuseum Conservation Association, 1978.

Clapp, Jane:
Art in life. Metuchen, New Jersey, Scarecrow Press, 1959 (with later supplements).
Sculpture index. (3 vols). Metuchen, New Jersey, Scarecrow Press, 1970.

Clavet, A *Guide to Canadian photographic archives.* Ottawa, 1979.

Cole, W D *World religions: a handbook for teachers.* London, The Community Relations Commission, 1977.

Collison, R L 'Libraries for television'. *The Library World.* July 1965, 1-5.

Columbia University *Avery index to architectural periodicals.* 2nd ed. (15 vols with supplements). Boston, Mass., G K Hall, 1973.

Colvin, H M (compiler) *A catalogue of architectural drawings of the 18th and 19th centuries in the library of Worcester College, Oxford.* Oxford, University Press, 1964.

Colvin, H M *The history of the king's works.* London, HMSO, 1963-.

Conservation sourcebook. London, Crafts Advisory Committee, 1979.

Cooper, Barbara and others *The world museums guide.* London, Threshold/Sotheby Parke Bernet, 1973.

Corbett, E V *The illustrations collection.* London, Grafton, 1941.

The Corning flood: museum under water. New York, Corning Museum of Glass, 1977.

Courtauld illustration archives. London, Harvey Miller, 1976-.

Crawford, William *The keepers of light: a history and working guide to early photographic processes.* New York, Morgan and Morgan, 1979.

Criswell, Jim 'Study of newspaper library pictures'. Houston, Houston Post, 1973. (Copy of this paper also available from ANPA Library.)

Croghan, A *A bibliographic system for non-book media.* 2nd ed. London, Coburgh Publications, 1979.

Cunha, George *Conservation of library materials: a manual and bibliography on the care, repair and restoration of library materials.* 2nd ed. Metuchen, New Jersey, Scarecrow Press, 1971-2.

Dalley, Terence (compiler) *The complete guide to illustration and design techniques and materials.* Oxford, Phaidon, 1980.

Daniel, Howard *Encyclopaedia of themes and subjects in painting.* London, Thames and Hudson, 1971.

Darling, Pamela W 'Microforms in libraries: preservation and storage'. *Microform Review* 5, April 1976. 93-100.

Davies, H 'Storage of audio-visual materials in the library: a survey'. *Assistant Librarian* 69, January 1976. 6-8.

DeLaurier, Nancy (editor) *Slide buyers' guide 1976.* New York, College Art Association of America, 1976.

Derry, T K and Williams, T I *A short history of technology.* Oxford University Press, 1960.

Design Abstracts International (formerly *ICSID Information Bulletin*). Oxford, Pergamon, 1967.

Design Abstracts International (US ed.). Elmsford, NY, Pergamon, 1976-.

Diamond, R M 'A retrieval system for 35 mm. slides utilized in arts and humanities instruction' in Groves, P S and others *Bibliographic control of non-print media.* Chicago, American Library Association, 1972. 346-59.

Dictionary of architecture... London, Richards, 1853-92.

Directory of British associations and associations in Ireland. London, CBD Research.

Directory of European associations. (2 vols). London, CBD Research.

Doloff, Francis W and others *How to care for works of art on paper.* 3rd ed. Boston, Mass., Museum of Fine Arts, 1979.

Dondis, Donis *A primer of visual literacy.* Cambridge, Mass., MIT Press, 1973.

Dover Pictorial Archives. (Series). New York, Dover Publications. (British distributors: Constable and Co.)

Driver, A H *Catalogue of engraved portraits in the Royal College of Physicians of London.* London, Royal College of Physicians, 1952.

Durgnat, Raymond 'Movie eye'. *Architectural Review* March 1965. 186-93.

Eastman Kodak:
Kodak color films. Technical Publication E-77. 7th ed. Rochester, New York, 1977.
Preservation of photographs. Technical Publication F-30. 1979.
Prevention and removal of fungus on prints and films. Technical Publication AE-22. 1971.
Storage and care of Kodak color photographs.
Storage and preservation of microfilms. Publication D-31. 1978. (Also published in *Microforms in libraries.* Microform Review 1975.)

Eaton, George T 'Preservation, deterioration, restoration of photographic images'. *Library Quarterly* 40 (1), January 1970. 85-98.

Eder, J M *History of photography.* English language ed. New York, Columbia University Press, 1945.

Ellison, John W *Storage and care self-evaluation forms.* Amherst, New York, State University of New York at Buffalo, 1979. Available for: films, film strips, film loops, transparencies and slides; microforms; original paintings/prints and non-original prints; photographs and negatives.

Emanuel, M (editor) *Contemporary architects.* London, Macmillan, 1980.

Encyclopedia of art. (5 vols). London, Pall Mall, 1971.

Encyclopedia of associations. (3 vols). Detroit, Gale Research.

Encyclopaedia of photography. (2 vols). London, Focal Press, 1965.

Encyclopedia of world art. (15 vols). New York, McGraw-Hill, 1968.

Engen, Rodney K *Dictionary of Victorian engravers, print publishers and their works.* Cambridge, UK, Chadwyck-Healey, 1979.

Eskind, Andrew H and others 'International Museum of Photography at George Eastman House: conventions for cataloguing photographs'. *Image* 21 (4), December 1978. 1-31.

Evans, Grace E and others 'Image-bearing catalog cards for photolibraries: an overview and a proposal'. *Special Libraries* 70(11), November 1979. 462-70.

Evans, Hilary *The art of picture research. A guide to current practice, procedure, techniques and resources.* Newton Abbot, UK, David and Charles, 1979.

Evans, Hilary and Mary, *Picture researcher's handbook.* London, Saturday Ventures, 1979.

Evans, H, Evans, M and Nelki, A *The picture researcher's handbook.* Newton Abbot, UK, David and Charles, 1975.

Evans, Hilary and Mary *Sources of illustration 1500-1900.* Bath, UK, Adams and Dart, 1971.

Fetros, John G 'Cooperative picture searching and collection development'. *Special Libraries* 62(5/6), May/June 1971. 217-27.

Fisher, George Thomas *Photogenic manipulation part 1.* 2nd ed. London, George Knight and Sons, 1845. 28.

Fisher, Stanley William *A dictionary of watercolour painters 1750-1900.* London, Foulsham, 1972.

Fletcher, B *A history of architecture* rev. by J C Palmes. 18th ed. London, Athlone Press, 1975.

The focal encyclopaedia of photography. (Various eds.). London, Focal Press.

Fothergill, R *Resource centres in colleges of education.* (Working Paper no. 10). London, Council for Educational Technology, 1973.

Fothergill, R and Butchart, I *Non-book materials in libraries: a practical guide.* London, Bingley, 1978.

Fototeca Unione *Microfiche set: photographic archive ancient Roman topography and architecture.* Rome, International Union of Institutes of Archaeology, History and History of Art in Rome, 1977.

Francis G 'Important applications of photogenic drawing'. *The Magazine of Science IV,* 27 April 1839. 28.

Frankenberg, Celestine 'Specialization: pictures: a dialogue about the training of picture librarians'. *Special Libraries* 56(1) January 1965. 17-18.

Fredericksen, Burton B and others *Census of pre-nineteenth century Italian paintings in North American public collections.* Cambridge, Mass., Harvard University Press, 1972.

Garrett, Albert *A history of British wood engraving.* Tunbridge Wells, UK, Midas, 1978.

General indices to the first forty-two volumes of 'The Studio' 1893-1908. (Reprint of 1902 and 1909 eds). London, Sims and Reed, 1979.

Gernsheim, H and A:

The history of photography. Rev. ed. London, Thames and Hudson, 1969.

The recording eye. New York, Putnam, 1960.

Gibbs-Smith, C H *Copyright law concerning works of art, photographs and the written and spoken word.* 3rd ed. London, Museums Association, 1978.

Gibbs-Smith, Charles 'The Hulton Picture Post Library' *Journal of Documentation* 6(1), March 1950. 12-24.

Gidley, M and Goldman, D *Audio-visual materials for American studies: a guide to sources of information and materials.* University of Sussex, Centre for Educational Technology, 1970.

Giles, T 'Non-book media in Leicester Polytechnic Library'. *Audio-visual Librarian* (4), 1978. 10-15.

Godwin, E W 'On the photographs taken for the Architectural Photographs Society for the year 1866'. *RIBA Transactions* 17, 1866-7.

Goodison, J W *Catalogue of Cambridge portraits: the university collection.* Cambridge, UK, Cambridge University Press, 1955.

Gordon, Cecilia *Resource organisation in primary schools.* London, Council for Educational Technology with The School Library Association, 1978.

Gotlop, Philip *Professional photography.* London, Thames and Hudson, 1973.

Grant, Maurice Harold *A dictionary of British landscape painters from the 16th century to the early 20th century.* Leigh-on-Sea, UK, F Lewis, 1952, reprinted 1976.

Gray, M 'Photographic storage at Gwynedd'. *Journal of the Society of Archivists* 5, 1977. 437-40.

Greater London Council *Survey of London 1900.* London, GLC.

Green, Shirley L and others *Pictorial resources in the Washington DC area.* Washington, DC, Library of Congress, 1976.

Gross, Anthony *Etching, engraving and intaglio printing.* Oxford University Press, 1970.

Grove, Pearce (editor) *Nonprint media in academic libraries.* Chicago, American Library Association, 1975.

Guide des musées de France. Fribourg, Switzerland, Office du Livre, 1970.

Guide to key British enterprises. London, Dun and Bradstreet.

Guide to microforms in print. Westport, Connecticut, Microform Review; London, Mansell.

Guidelines for newspaper libraries. Written by members of the Newspaper Division/Special Libraries Association. ANPA, 1974, rev. 1976.

Gwilt, J *An encyclopaedia of architecture, historical, theoretical and practical...* London, 1842.

Hall, James *Dictionary of subjects and symbols in art.* London, Murray, 1974.

Hancock, J C and Whitely, P T *The geographer's vadecum of sources and materials.* 2nd ed. London, G Philip, 1978.

Harris, J *A catalogue of British drawings for architecture, decoration, sculpture and landscape gardening 1550-1900 in American collections.* New Jersey, Gregg Press, 1971.

Harris, J (compiler) *Catalogue of drawings by Inigo Jones, John Webb and Isaac de Caus at Worcester College, Oxford.* Oxford University Press, 1979.

Harris, J et al. *Illustrated glossary of architecture 850-1830.* London, Faber, 1966.

Harris, J (editor) *The RIBA drawings series.* London, Country Life, 1968.

Harvey, Adam *Where to find photos of the developing countries.* London, Centre for World Development Education, 1978.

Havlice, Patricia Pate:
   Art in 'Time'. Metuchen, New Jersey, Scarecrow Press, 1970. 350p. ('An index to all the pictures in the art section of *Time* magazine.')

World painting index. (2 vols.). Metuchen, New Jersey, Scarecrow Press, 1977.

Hendriks, Klaus 'Preserving photographic records: materials, problems and methods of restoration'. *Industrial Photography* 27(8), August 1978. 30-3.

Hess, Stanley *An annotated bibliography of slide library literature* (Bibliographic Studies, No.3). Syracuse, NY, Syracuse University, School of Information Studies, 1978.

Hess, Stanley W 'Microfiche in the fine arts — source list'. (Unpublished typescript).

Hewlett, R D 'Broadcasters and libraries'. *EBU Review* 27(2), March 1976. 12-15.

Hewlett—Woodmere Public Library *Index to art reproductions in books.* Metuchen, New Jersey, Scarecrow Press, 1974.

Hicks, Warren B and others *Developing multi-media libraries.* New York, R R Bowker, 1970.

Hill, Donna *Picture file: a manual and a curriculum-related subject heading list.* Hamden, Connecticut, Shoe String Press, 1975.

Hill, Maureen (editor) *National Portrait Gallery. Concise catalogue 1856-1969.* London, National Portrait Gallery, 1970.

Hobson, J H *The administration of archives.* London, Pergamon Press, 1972.

Hoffberg, Judith A 'Ephemera in the Art Collection'. *Library Trends* 23, 1975. 483-93.

Hoffberg, Judith A and others *Directory of art libraries and visual resource collections in North America.* New York, Neal-Schuman Publishers Inc., 1978.

Houfe, Simon *The dictionary of British book illustrators and caricaturists 1800-1914.* Woodbridge, Antique Collectors Club, 1978.

Howgego, J L 'Archivist and art historian'. *Journal of the Society of Archivists* 2, 1963. 369-72.

Hudson, Kenneth and others *The directory of museums.* London, Macmillan, 1975.

Hunnisett, Basil *Steel-engraved book illustration in England.* London, Scolar Press, 1980.

Hunter, John E 'Emergency preparedness for museums, historical sites, and archives: an annotated bibliography'. *History News* 34, April 1979. Also published as Technical Leaflet 114 by the American Association for State and Local History.

I see all. The world's first picture encyclopaedia. (5 vols). London, Amalgamated Press, 1928.

ICSID Information Bulletin, see *Design Abstracts International.*

International conference on automatic processing of art history data and documents, First, Pisa, 1978. (3 vols). Conference transactions. Pisa, Scuola Normale Superiore, 4-7 September 1978.

International directory of arts. 14th ed. 1979/80. Frankfurt, Art Address Verlag Müller GmbH KG, 1979.

International directory of photographic archives of works of art. Paris, Dunod; London, Crosby Lockwood, 1950, with supplement 1954.

International Federation of Film Archives, Preservation Committee. *Film Preservation.* London, NFA, 1965.

Internationales bibliotheks handbuch. World guide to libraries. (4 vols). Pullach bei München, Verlag Dokumentation, 1970-.

Irvine, B J *Slide libraries.* Colorado, Libraries Unlimited, 1979.

Jenkins, Valerie 'The sepia legacy of Uncle Gus' (A History of the Mansell Collection) *Evening Standard* 16 February 1979. 19.

Jenkinson, Sir H *Manual of archive administration.* London, Lund Humphreys, 1937. 2nd ed., 1965.

Jirgensons, Mary 'Thinking visually about subject headings for picture files'. *Picturescope* 26(4), Autumn 1978. 100-23.

Johnson, J and others *The dictionary of British artists 1880-1940.* Woodbridge, Antique Collectors' Club, 1976.

Kathpalia, Yash Pal *Conservation and restoration of archive materials.* Paris, UNESCO, 1973.

Kellys' manufacturers' and merchants' directory. London, Kellys.

Kerslake, John *National Portrait Gallery.* (2 vols). Early Georgian portraits. London, HMSO, 1977.

Kindlers malerei lexikon. Zürich, Kindler, 1964-.

Kloster, Gudrun B (editor) *Handbuch der museen: Deutschland.* BRD, New York, Bowker, 1971.

Knight, David *Zoological illustration.* London, Dawson, 1977.

Kodak Ltd 'The storage of photographic materials and photographic records. *Data book of applied photography vol.1.* Data sheet RF-6. London.

Kula, S 'The storage of archive film'. *Journal of the Society of Archivists* 2, 1962. 270-2.

Lancefield, R and others *Suppliers' list for archive conservation.* Society of Archivists Conservation Group, 1978.

Lever, Jill:
'Cataloguing the RIBA Drawings Collection'. *Architectural Design* 48(5/6), 1978. 395-9.
'If it's Friday it must be Calgary: report on the storage, cataloguing, and conservation of architectural drawings in North America'. *RIBA Journal* December 1978. 499.

Levis, Howard C *A descriptive bibliography of the most important books in the English language relating to the art and history of engraving and the collecting of prints...* London, Dawson, 1974. 141p. (First pub. 1912, 1913.)

Lewis, Elizabeth M:
'A graphic catalog card index'. *American Documentation* 20(3), July 1969. 238-46.
'Control without cards'. *Art Librarians/North American Newsletter* 1(3/4), Summer 1973. 17.

Lewis, Frank:
A dictionary of British bird painters. Leigh-on-Sea, UK, F Lewis, 1974.
A dictionary of British historical painters. Leigh-on-Sea, F Lewis, 1979.

Lewis, John N L and others *The graphic reproduction and photography of works of art.* London, Faber, 1969.

Lewis, Stanley T 'Experimentation with an image library'. *Special Libraries* 56(1), January 1965. 35-6.

Libraries, museums and art galleries yearbook. Cambridge, James Clarke and Co. Ltd, 1976.

Library Association *Library resource centres in schools, colleges and institutions of higher education: a general policy statement.* London, 1973.

Line, Joyce *Archival collections of non-book materials: a preliminary list indicating policies for preservation and access.* London, British Library, 1977.

LOMA, see *Art bibliographies modern.*

Long, Molly *Handbook for geography teachers.* 6th ed. London, Methuen, 1974.

Loudon, J C *An encyclopaedia of cottage, farm and villa architecture and furniture...* London, Longman Rees etc., 1833.

Lubell, Cecil *Textile collections of the world. Volume 1: An illustrated guide to textile collections in United States and Canadian museums. Volume 2: United Kingdom and Ireland. Volume 3: France. An illustrated guide to textile collections in French museums.* London, Studio Vista, 1976-7.

McCoy, Garnett *Archives of American art. A directory of resources.* New York, Bowker, 1972.

McDarrah, Fred W (editor) *Photography market place. The complete book for still photography.* 2nd ed. New York, Bowker, 1977.

McDarrah, Fred W (editor) *Stock photo and assignment source book.* New York, Bowker, 1977.

McNeil, R J 'The Shell Photographic Library'. *ASLIB Proceedings* 18(5), May 1966. 128-37.

Mallalieu, H L *The dictionary of British watercolour artists up to 1920.* Woodbridge, Antique Collectors' Club, 1976.

Malraux, André *Museum without walls.* London, Secker and Warburg, 1967.

Marburger index. Photographic documentation of art in Germany. (5,000 microfiches). Munich, K G Saur, 1977-81.

Mathias, Paul *The teachers' handbook for social studies.* Poole, Dorset, Blandford Press, 1973.

Metcalf, Keyes D *Planning academic and research library buildings.* New York, McGraw-Hill, 1965.

Metropolitan Museum of Art, New York *Library catalog.* (25 vols with additional supplements). Boston, Mass., G K Hall.

Mid America College Art Association, Visual Resources Committee: *Guide to photograph collections.* New Mexico, MACAA, 1978. *Guide to equipment for slide maintenance and viewing.* 1979. *Guide for management of visual resources collections.* 1979.

Milhollen, H 'Pictures invade the catalog: two examples of illustrated cards'. *Library Journal* 71(11), 1 June 1946. 803-4.

Millon, H A (editor) *Key monuments of the history of architecture.* Englewood-Cliffs, New Jersey, Prentice-Hall; New York, Abrams.

Monro, Isabel Stevenson and others:
  Index to reproductions of American paintings. A guide to pictures occurring in more than eight hundred books. New York, H W Wilson, 1948.
  Index to reproductions of European paintings. A guide to pictures in more than three hundred books. New York, H W Wilson, 1956.
Moss, Daphne 'Pictures: Radio Times Hulton Picture Library'. *ASLIB Audio Visual Workshop 7-8 May 1970,* ASLIB, 1971.
The municipal yearbook. London, Municipal Journal.
Museum of Modern Art, New York City *Catalog of the library.* (14 vols). Boston, Mass., G K Hall, 1976.
Museums and galleries in Great Britain and Ireland. (Annual). Dunstable, ABC Historical Publications.
Museums of the world. A directory of 17,500 museums in 150 countries including a subject index... 2nd ed. Pullach bei München, Verlag Dokumentation, 1975.
Museums yearbook. London, Museums Association.

National Fire Protection Association *Protection of Records,* NFPA No. 232-1967. Boston, Mass., 1967.
National Gallery *Illustrated general catalogue.* London, 1973.
National Gallery of Art, Washington *Index of American design.* Cambridge, Chadwyck-Healey, 1979.
Nervi, P L (editor) *History of world architecture series.* (14 vols). London, Academy Editions, 1971-.
Neumaier, Linda *National Portrait Gallery, Smithsonian Institution permanent collection illustrated checklist.* Washington DC, Smithsonian Press, 1979.
'The new art — photography' *The Mirror* xxxiii (946), 27 April 1839.
Newhall, Beaumont *The history of photography.* 4th rev. ed. London, Secker and Warburg, 1972.
Newsom, Barbara Y and others *The art museum as educator.* Berkeley, University of California Press, 1978.
New York Public Library. Astor, Lenox and Tilden Foundations. The Research Libraries:
  Dictionary catalog of the Prints Division. (5 vols). Boston, Mass., G K Hall, 1975.
  Dictionary catalog of the Art and Architecture Division. (30 vols

with annual supplements entitled *Bibliographic guide to art and architecture*). 1975.

Nicholls, J 'The costs of academic publishing'. *Art Libraries Journal* 3, Winter, 1978.

Novotny, Ann (editor) and others *Picture sources* 3. New York, Special Libraries Association, 1975.

Nunn, George W A *British sources of photographs and pictures.* London, Cassell, 1952.

O'Donoghue, Freeman *Catalogue of engraved British portraits preserved in the Department of Prints and Drawings in the British Museum.* (6 vols). London, British Museum Publications, 1914-25.

Official museum directory. New York, National Register Publishing Company for American Museums Association, 1978.

On view. A guide to museum and gallery acquisitions in Great Britain and America. (Annual). London, Plaistow Publications.

Ormond, Richard and others (editors) *Dictionary of British portraiture. Volume 1: The Middle Ages to the early Georgians: historical figures born before 1700. Volume 2: Later Georgians and early Victorians: historical figures born between 1700 and 1800. Volume 3: Victorians. Volume 4: Twentieth century.* London, Batsford, 1979-.

Orth, Thomas W *A selected bibliography on photographic conservation, January 1975-December 1978.* Bibliography No. B9119. Rochester, NY, Graphic Arts Research Center, Rochester Institute of Technology, 1979.

Ostroff, Eugene:
Conserving and restoring photographic collections. Rev. ed. Washington DC, American Association of Museums, 1976. (Originally published in *Museum News,* 1974).
'The preservation of photographs'. *Journal of Photography* 107, 1974. 309-14.

Pacey, P (editor) *Art library manual.* London, Bowker, 1977.

Pacey, P 'Handling slides single-handed'. *Art Libraries Journal* 2(3), Autumn 1977. 22-30.

Parker, J H *A glossary of terms used in Grecian, Roman, Italian and Gothic architecture.* 5th ed. (3 vols). Oxford, Parker, 1850.

Parry, Pamela Jeffcott:
   Contemporary art and artists. An index to reproductions. New York, Greenwood, 1978.
   Photography index: a guide to reproductions. Westport, Connecticut, Greenwood Press, 1978.
The 'Pelican history of art' series. Harmondsworth, Penguin Books.
Pepper, Terence 'The Mansell Collection: an illustrations library'. *ARLIS Newsletter* 25, December 1975. 13-14.
Petrini, Sharon and others *A hand list of museum sources for slides and photographs.* Santa Barbara, University of California, 1973.
Pevsner, N The 'Buildings of England' series. Harmondsworth, Penguin Books.
Pevsner, N et al. *A dictionary of architecture.* Rev. ed. London, Allen Lane, 1975.
Picton, Tom 'The craven image or the apotheosis of the architectural photograph'. *Architects' Journal,* 25 July 1979. 176.
Piper, David *Catalogue of seventeenth century portraits in the National Portrait Gallery 1625-1714.* Cambridge, Cambridge University Press, 1963.
Plenderleith, H J and others *The conservation of antiquities and works of art. Treatment, repair and conservation.* 2nd ed. Oxford University Press, 1971.
Poitevin, A L *Improved photographic printing.* British Patent No. 2815, 13 December 1855.
Poole, Mrs Reginald Lane *Catalogue of portraits in the possession of the university, colleges, city and county of Oxford.* (3 vols). Oxford, Clarendon Press, 1912-25.
Public Archives of Canada *A researchers' guide to the national photography collection.* Ottawa, Canada, Public Archives of Canada, 1979.

Rahmani, L Y *The museums of Israel.* London, Secker and Warburg, 1976.
Register of British industry and commerce. (Annual). London, IPC Kompass. Similar directories available for other countries.
Répertoire d'art et d'archéologie. Paris, Morancé, 1910-58.
Répertoire d'art et d'archéologie (New series). Paris, Centre National de la Recherche Scientifique, 1965-.
Répertoire international de la littérature de l'art (RILA). New York

College Art Association of America, 1973-. (Subscriptions c/o Sterling and Francine Clark Art Institute, Williamstown MA 01267, USA.)

Report of the Advisory Committee on Archives. London, BBC, 1979.

Report of the Committee on the Future of Broadcasting (Cmnd 6753). Chairman: Lord Annan. London, HMSO, 1977. Paragraphs 29.25 to 29.32.

Richards, J M (editor) *Who's who in architecture from 1400 to the present day.* London, Weidenfeld and Nicolson, 1977.

Richter, Gisela M A *The portraits of the Greeks.* (3 vols). Oxford, Phaidon, 1965.

Roads, C H 'Film as historical evidence'. *Journal of the Society of Archivists* 3, 1966. 183-91.

Roberts, Laurence P *Roberts' guide to Japanese museums.* Tokyo, Kodansha International Ltd, 1978.

Rodwell, S 'Media storage'. *Educational Broadcasting International* 10, March 1977. 16-20.

Royal Commission on Historical Manuscripts. *Record repositories in Great Britain. A geographical directory.* London, HMSO, 1979.

Royal Commission on Historical Monuments. *Inventories.* London, HMSO, 1910.

Royal Institute of British Architects. *Catalogue of the Drawings Collection.* London, RIBA, 1969.

Royal Photographic Society:

The recognition of early photographic processes, their care and conservation. Five papers presented at a symposium held 16 March, 1974. Obtainable from the Society. (Also published in the *Journal of Photographic Science.*)

The conservation of colour photographic records. Monographic (1), 1974. Proceedings of a symposium held 20 September, 1973. (Also published in the *Journal of Photographic Science.*)

Schellenberg, T R *The management of archives.* New York, Columbia University Press, 1965.

Scientific and learned societies of Great Britain. London, Allen and Unwin, 1964.

Scoones, M A 'The Shell Photographic Library'. *Audiovisual Librarian* V1.1 (3), February 1974. 95-105.

Sharp, D *A visual history of twentieth-century architecture.* London,

Heinemann, Secker and Warburg, 1972.

Shaw, Renata:
'Picture organization: practices and procedures. Parts 1 and 2'. *Special Libraries* 63(10), October 1972. 448-56; *Special Libraries* 63(11), November 1972. 502-6.

'Picture professionalism'. *Special Libraries* 65(10/11), October/November 1974. 421-9.

'Picture searching 1. Techniques'. *Special Libraries* 62(12), December 1971. 524-9.

'Picture searching 2. Tools'. *Special Libraries* 63(1), January 1972. 13-24.

Picture searching techniques and tools. New York, Special Libraries Association, 1973. (SLA Bibliography no.6).

Shepard, Valerie A *Reproduction fees, photography, etc: guidelines for museums.* London, Museums Association, 1975.

Shifrin, M *Information in the school library.* London, Bingley, 1973.

Simons, W W and others *A slide classification system for the organization and automatic indexing of interdisciplinary collections of slides and pictures.* Santa Cruz, University of California, 1970.

Singer C et al. *A history of technology* (7 vols). Oxford University Press, 1954-8. 1979.

Slythe, R Margaret *The art of illustration 1750-1900.* London, Library Association, 1970. 144p.

Smith, Gaye 'Radio Times Hulton Picture Library'. *ARLIS Newsletter* 14, March 1973. 28-9.

Smith, Lyn Wall and others *Index to reproductions of American paintings appearing in more than 400 books mostly published since 1960.* Metuchen, New Jersey, Scarecrow Press. 931p.

Spaulding, Carl M 'Kicking the silver habit: confessions of a former addict'. *American Libraries,* December 1978. 563-6, 665-9.

Standing Commission on Museums and Galleries *Guide to museums and galleries.* London, HMSO, 1974.

Stephens, Frederick George *Catalogue of political and personal satires preserved in the Department of Prints and Drawings in the British Museum* (to 1832) (9 vols). London, British Museum Publications.

Stock Exchange official yearbook. London, Stock Exchange.

Stolow, Nathan 'Conservation standards for works of art in transit and on exhibition'. *Museum and Monuments XVII.* Geneva, UNESCO, 1979.

'Standards for the care of works of art in transit'. *Contributions to the London Conference on Museum Climatology.* London, IIC, 1968. 271-84.

Stuart, R *A dictionary of architecture.* (3 vols). London, Jones, 1830?.

The Studio: a bibliography. The first fifty years 1893-1943, with an introduction by Bryan Holme. London, Sims and Reed, 1978.

Strong, Roy *National Portrait Gallery. Tudor and Jacobean portraits.* (2 vols). London, HMSO, 1969.

Subject collections: a guide to special book collections and subject emphases as reported by university, college, public, museum and special libraries in the United States and Canada. 5th ed. New York, Bowker, 1978.

Sykes, Jane and others *Design resources for teachers.* London, Design Council Publications, 1976.

Talbot, W H F:

Engraving pictures obtained by photographic process on steel, etc. British Patent No.565. 28 October 1852.

Improvements in the art of engraving etc. British Patent No.875. 14 October 1858.

'Description of Mr Fox Talbot's new process of photoglyphic engraving'. *Photographic News* 1(7), 22 October 1858. 73. (Examples of photoglyphs published in *Photographic News,* 12 November 1858).

Tansey, Luraine 'Classification of research photographs and slides'. *Library Trends* 20(3), January 1975. 417-26.

Thieme, Ulrich and others *Allgemeines Lexikon der bildenden Künstler von der Antike bis zur Gegenwart.* (37 vols). Leipzig, Seemann, 1907-50.

Thomas, D B:

From today painting is dead (an exhibition catalogue) No.893. The Arts Council of Great Britain, 1972. 59.

The Science Museum photography collection. London, HMSO, 1969.

Thomson, Elizabeth W *Index to art reproductions in books compiled by the professional staff of the Hewlett-Woodmere Public Library.* Metuchen, New Jersey, Scarecrow Press, 1974. 371p.

Tooley, R V *English books with coloured plates 1790 to 1860. A bibliographical account of the most important books illustrated by English artists in colour aquatint and colour lithography.* Rev. ed. London, Dawson, 1978. 452p.

Treasure chest for teachers: services available to teachers and schools. Schoolmaster Publishing Company, 1978.

Tull, A G 'Film transparencies between glass'. *British Journal of Photography,* 125, 1978. 322-3, 349-51, 353.

Turner, Jill 'Love and knowledge builds huge collection' (The Mary Evans Picture Library) *Library Association Record* 78(8), August 1976. 361-4.

Vance, Lucile and others *Illustration index.* Metuchen, New Jersey, Scarecrow Press, 1957 (with later supplements).

Vanderbilt, Paul:
'Filing your photographs: some basic procedures'. *History News* 21, 1966.
Guide to the special collections of prints and photographs in the Library of Congress. Washington DC, Library of Congress, 1955.

Vicary, Richard *Lithography.* London, Thames and Hudson, 1976.

Victoria and Albert Museum departmental collections. (Microfiche). London, Mindata, 1978-.

Victoria and Albert Museum *National art library catalogue. Author catalogue.* (10 vols). Boston, Mass., G K Hall, 1972.

Viollet-le-Duc, E E *Dictionnaire raisonné de l'architecture française du XIe au XVIe siècle.* Paris, Bance, 1854-68.

Vollmer, Hans *Allgemeines Lexikon der bildenden Künstler des XX Jahrhunderts.* (6 vols). Leipzig, Seemann, 1953-62.

Wakeman, G *Victorian book illustration.* Newton Abbot, David and Charles, 1973.

Walker, Charles V *Electrotype manipulation Part II.* 3rd ed. London, George Knight and Sons, 1841. 30.

Wall J (compiler) *Directory of British photographic collections.* London, Heinemann, 1977.

Wall J 'The case for a central photographic archive in colour'. *Journal of the Society of Archivists* 3, 1969. 566-70.

Waters, Peter *Procedures for salvage of water-damaged library materials.* 2nd ed. Washington DC, Library of Congress, 1979.

Watkin, David *The rise of architectural history.* London, Architectural Press, 1980.

Weber, Wilhelm *History of lithography*. London, Thames and Hudson, 1966.

Weinstein, Robert A and Booth, Larry *Collection, use, and care of historical photographs*. Nashville, Tennessee, American Association for State and Local History, 1977.

Wessel, Carl J 'Environmental factors affecting the permanence of library materials'. *Deterioration and preservation of library materials*. London, University of Chicago Press, 1970.

What is where in national museums? London, British Tourist Authority, 1975/6.

Where to find photographs instantly. New York, Bowker, 1977.

Who owns whom. (Annual). London, Roskill. Separate editions for North America, United Kingdom and Republic of Ireland, continental Europe.

Wilhelm, Henry:
   'Colour print instability'. *Modern Photography*, February 1979.
   'Colour print instability: a problem for collectors and photographers'. *Afterimage* 6, October 1978. 11-13.
   Procedures for processing and storing black and white photographs for maximum possible permanence. Grinnell, Iowa, East Street Gallery, 1970.
   'Storing Color Materials'. *Industrial Photography*, Oct 1978. 32-.

Williams, Gwyneth A (compiler) *Guide to illustrative material for use in teaching history*. London, Historical Association, 1962, reprinted 1969. ('Helps for students of history' no.65).

Wilson, Arnold:
   A dictionary of British marine painters. Leigh-on-Sea, UK, F Lewis, 1970.
   A dictionary of British military painters. Leigh-on-Sea, F Lewis, 1972.

Winternitz, E *Musical instruments and their symbolism in western art*. London, Faber, 1967.

Witkin, Lee D and others *The photograph collector's guide*. London, Secker and Warburg, 1979.

Wolstenholme, Gordon and Kerslake, J F (editors) *The Royal College of Physicians of London. Portraits. Catalogue II*. Amsterdam, Elsevier, 1979.

Wood, J C *A dictionary of British animal painters*. Leigh-on-Sea, F Lewis, 1973.

Woodbury, W B *An improved method of producing or obtaining by the aid of photography surfaces in relievo and intaglio etc.* British Patent No, 2338. 23 September 1864. (See also Patent No. 1918, 26 July 1866 and Patent No. 947, 30 March, 1867.)

The world of learning. (Annual. 2 vols). London, Europa.

Wright, Christopher *Old master paintings in Britain. An index of continental old master paintings executed before c.1800 in public collections in the United Kingdom.* London, Sotheby Parke Bernet, 1976.

Wright, John Buckland *Engraving and etching: techniques and the modern trend.* New York, Dover, 1973.

Writer's and artist's yearbook. (Annual). London, Black.

Yale University portrait index 1701-1951. New Haven, Connecticut, Yale University Press, 1951.

Yule, John Arthur Carslake *Principles of color reproduction applied to photomechanical reproduction, color photography and the ink, paper and related industries.* New York, Wiley, 1967.

ADDENDUM

Briggs, James R 'Environmental control of modern records'. *The conservation of library and archive materials and the graphic arts.* Abstracts and reprints of the International Conference on the Conservation of Library and Archive Materials and the Graphic Arts. London, The Society of Archivists and the Institute of Paper Conservation, 1980. 94-103.

Mid America College Art Association *International Bulletin for Photographic Documentation of the Visual Arts.* 1980- (formerly *MACAA Slides and Photographs Newsletter,* 1974-80).

Morrow, Carolyn Clark and Schoenly, Steven B *A conservation bibliography for librarians, archivists, and administrators.* Troy, New York, Whitston Publishing Company, 1979.

Rempel, Siegfried 'The care of black-and-white photographic collections: cleaning and stabilization'. *Technical Bulletin 9.* Ottawa, Canadian Conservation Institute, 1980. 21-3.

Sandner, Fred et al *A bibliography on the storage and care of non-book materials in libraries with selected annotations.* ERIC Report, ED 179 246. Washington, DC, Educational Resources Information Center, 1979.

Swartzburg, Susan G *Preserving library materials: a manual.* Metuchen, New Jersey, Scarecrow Press, 1980.

Walsh, Timothy *Archives and manuscripts: security.* 'Basic Manual' series. Chicago, Society of American Archivists, 1977.

Waters, Peter 'An assessment of lamination and encapsulation'. *The conservation of library and archive materials and the graphic arts.* Abstracts and reprints. London, The Society of Archivists and the Institute of Paper Conservation, 1980. 74-83.

Index